Nero
the man behind the myth

This publication accompanies *Nero: the man behind the myth* at the British Museum from 27 May to 24 October 2021.

This exhibition has been made possible as a result of the Government Indemnity Scheme. The British Museum would like to thank HM Government for providing Government Indemnity and the Department for Digital, Culture, Media and Sport and Arts Council England for arranging the indemnity.

This publication was produced during the uncertainty of the global pandemic. Information about the exhibition is as expected at the time of going to print, but may be subject to change due to reasons beyond our control.

First published in the United Kingdom in 2021 by
The British Museum Press
A division of The British Museum Company Ltd
The British Museum, Great Russell Street, London WC1B 3DG
britishmuseum.org/publishing

ISBN 978 0 7141 2291 5 (PB)
ISBN 978 0 7141 2290 8 (HB)

A catalogue record for this book is available from the British Library

Designed by Will Webb Design
Colour reproduction by Altaimage, London
Printed in Belgium by Graphius

Further information about the British Museum and its collection can be found at britishmuseum.org

The papers in this book are natural, renewable and recyclable products and the manufacturing processes are expected to conform to the environmental regulations of the country of origin.

Nero
the man behind the myth

Thorsten Opper

The British Museum

Contents

Sponsor's foreword

bp is pleased to continue its support for the British Museum amid the unprecedented challenge of a global pandemic and its impact on arts and culture in the United Kingdom.

Nero: the man behind the myth vividly explores the reign of the leader long considered one of Rome's most egotistical, extravagant and evil.

Nero the ruler is well known. The last male descendant of the emperor Augustus, he came to the throne in AD 54 at just sixteen years of age. As ruler, he presided over the Great Fire of Rome – which some even said he started – and is also thought to have murdered members of his own family. It is fair to say that Nero represents none of the qualities we expect in our leaders today.

But accounts of his time as ruler have always been open to interpretation. After becoming leader at such a young age, was Nero destined to fail? Is his legacy misrepresented? Was he a much-maligned young man whose intentions were misunderstood? Or, was he every bit the wretched, ruthless ruler that history has judged him to be?

As a visitor to this exhibition you have the unique opportunity to make up your own mind, aided by the spectacular items on display and the journey expertly curated by the British Museum.

For many years bp has proudly made UK arts and culture accessible to all. Through our partnership with the British Museum, we are pleased that visitors can once again enjoy a world-class offering from this great institution.

I hope you enjoy this exceptional experience, captured beautifully in this publication.

Peter Mather
Senior vice president and UK head of country, bp

Director's foreword

Nero is famed as the emperor who fiddled while Rome burned, a tyrant who was cruel and ruthless towards his family, and a somewhat pathetic megalomaniac prone to excess. Yet is this a reliable portrait? In many ways this image of Nero is one that resonates with our times: a world with deepening social and economic challenges, in which fake news, contested facts and the polarisation of opinion amid political machinations are commonplace.

In the case of Nero, distorted histories emerged in the decades after his death, authored by a small number of Roman politicians and writers, such as Tacitus and Suetonius. These were not objective accounts, rather texts that fell within a rhetorical genre, written by those hostile to him and motivated by concern for the relationship between the elite and the emperor. The themes were then perpetuated through the centuries – even into modern film and scholarship.

The fifth emperor of Rome, and a descendant of Augustus, Nero would rule for nearly fourteen years. It is objects and sources from the period that this publication and the exhibition it accompanies draw on, rather than the later textual traditions, to help evoke a more nuanced understanding of the emperor. These statues, wall-paintings, armour, writing tablets, coinage and jewellery allow new interpretations of Nero, his reforms and political achievements. Information from new archaeological projects further refines our understanding.

We meet Nero's family and his tutor Seneca, as his accession to the throne promised a new golden age. The exhibition follows the campaigns Nero sent to the fringes of the Roman Empire. To the east, Nero's troops confronted the mighty Parthians and achieved a diplomatic settlement. To the west, in Britain, Nero's armies would confront the rebel queen Boudica. Objects from Britain evoke the human reality and suffering of the ensuing battles, but also the creative entanglement of Roman and Celtic artistic traditions.

Back in Rome, the cityscape was transformed. A magnificent new palace, the Domus Aurea, decorated with materials from across the Empire, was the culmination of this activity. Visitors to the exhibition will also get a sense of what it was like to live in Nero's Rome, where theatre, chariot races and gladiatorial combat were important preoccupations. A charred and warped window grille evokes the power and devastation of the fire that ripped through Rome in AD 64: Nero was not in the city at the time. The exhibition culminates with the senatorial conspiracies that prompted Nero to commit suicide at the age of 30.

Special thanks are due to the many UK and international museums who have made this exhibition possible through generous loans.

I would like to express my gratitude to our long-term exhibition partner bp. Without their support, the British Museum would not be able to present such exhibitions, allowing UK and international visitors to explore the complex character of Nero – real and imagined.

Hartwig Fischer
Director, British Museum

The Julio-Claudian family from Augustus to Nero

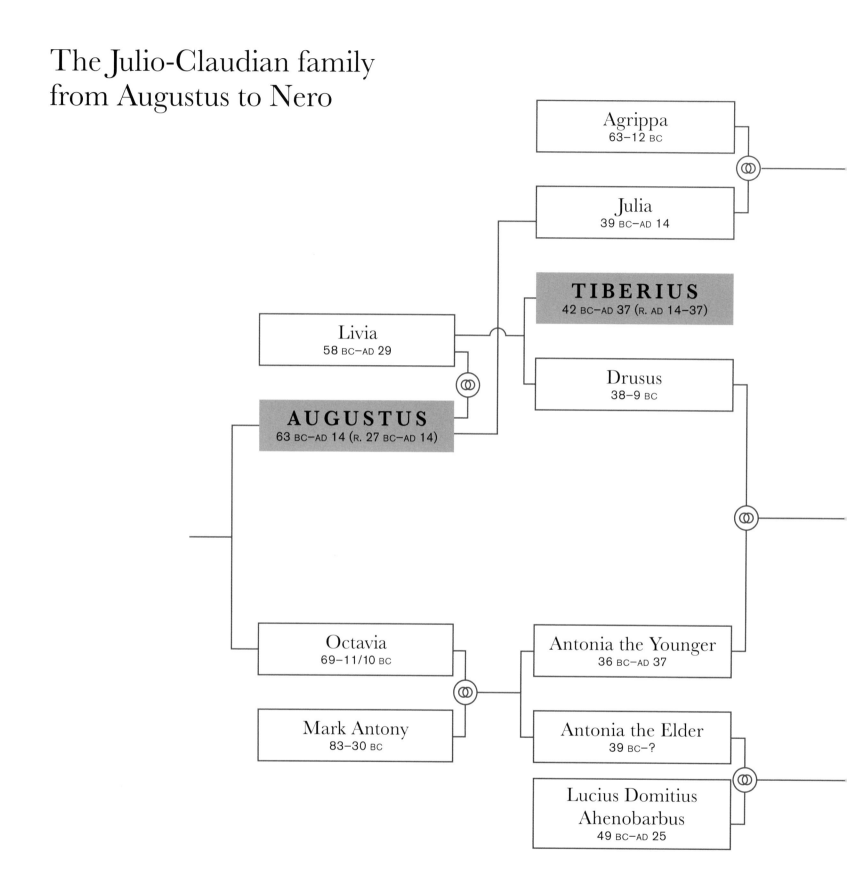

Agrippa
63–12 BC

Julia
39 BC–AD 14

TIBERIUS
42 BC–AD 37 (R. AD 14–37)

Livia
58 BC–AD 29

Drusus
38–9 BC

AUGUSTUS
63 BC–AD 14 (R. 27 BC–AD 14)

Octavia
69–11/10 BC

Antonia the Younger
36 BC–AD 37

Mark Antony
83–30 BC

Antonia the Elder
39 BC–?

Lucius Domitius
Ahenobarbus
49 BC–AD 25

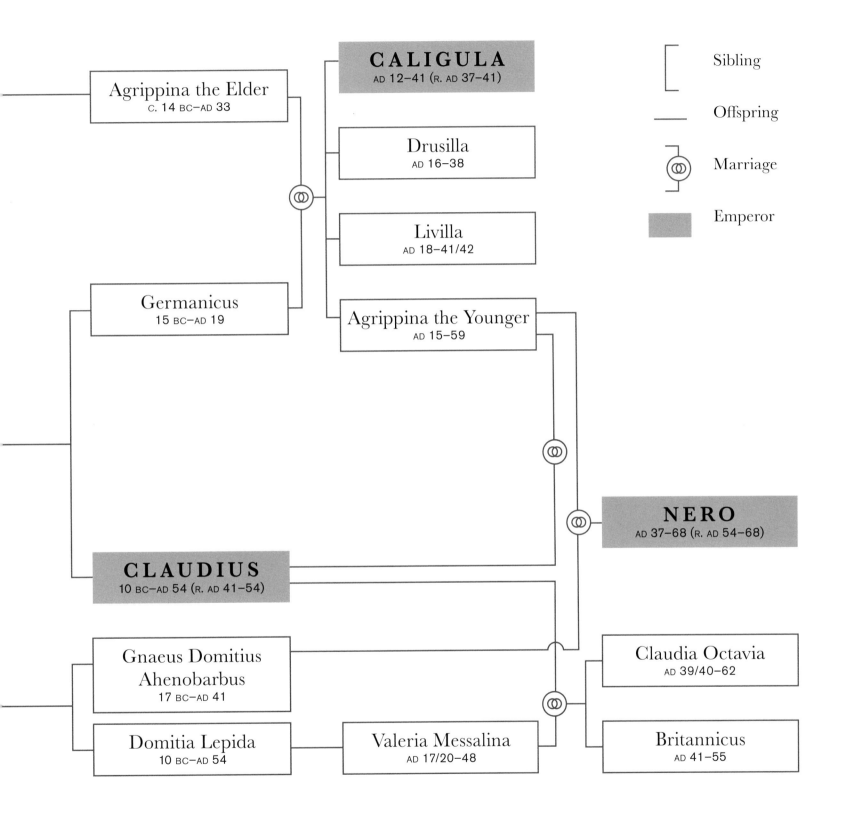

Agrippina the Elder
C. 14 BC–AD 33

Germanicus
15 BC–AD 19

CALIGULA
AD 12–41 (R. AD 37–41)

Drusilla
AD 16–38

Livilla
AD 18–41/42

Agrippina the Younger
AD 15–59

CLAUDIUS
10 BC–AD 54 (R. AD 41–54)

NERO
AD 37–68 (R. AD 54–68)

Gnaeus Domitius
Ahenobarbus
17 BC–AD 41

Domitia Lepida
10 BC–AD 54

Valeria Messalina
AD 17/20–48

Claudia Octavia
AD 39/40–62

Britannicus
AD 41–55

Sibling

Offspring

Marriage

Emperor

INTRODUCTION

THE
LAST
EMPEROR
DESCENDED
FROM THE
JULIAN LINE,
THE LINE
DESCENDED
FROM
AENEAS

CASSIUS DIO, *ROMAN HISTORY*, 62.18.5

Han-era annals from ancient China record several remarkable comets that were traced in the skies during the mid-first century AD. Thousands of miles to the west, in Rome, they were observed, too, and people wondered what marks of divine intent and future destiny they might signify. In hindsight, they came to be interpreted there as ominous portents of impending turmoil and the demise of Rome's young ruler, Nero Caesar Claudius Drusus Germanicus (r. AD 54–68).[1] Of course, no such link really exists, and if events had unfolded only slightly differently, these celestial phenomena might have been read instead as promising harbingers of imminent triumph and eternal glory. And herein lies the real appeal of looking anew at Nero and his times.

Nero was the fifth member of the same extended family to hold sole power since the reign of his famous ancestor Augustus, which had begun some eighty-five years previously, and he would also be the last. These were formative decades for the Roman Empire, a period of rapid social and economic transformation that brought vast opportunities, but also profound inner tensions that were about to burst out into the open. Nero emblematically embodied this change and the inability of a deeply divided Roman society to adjust, which ultimately led to the outbreak of a violent civil war that recalled the worst horrors of the dying days of the Roman Republic. His is a captivating story. It plays out over a vast canvas, but crucially, in many ways it is also much less clear-cut and predetermined than we might have come to assume. For if Nero's name seems vaguely familiar today (probably more so than that of any other Roman emperor, with the exception perhaps of Augustus and Hadrian), it is a familiarity based almost entirely on notoriety. It conjures up dark recesses of the human psyche – a monster, a matricide, a megalomaniac, deluded, incapable, pathetic, a ruler who proverbially 'fiddled while Rome burned' (and initiated the first great persecution of the Christians to deflect the blame).

It is no accident that we should think of Nero mostly in those terms. For the prevailing image of Nero was very deliberately and artfully created by a group of elite Roman writers already in the half century or so after Nero's death through enforced suicide in June AD 68, and it has been accepted almost unchallenged until relatively recently. It is fascinating to unravel how and why this was done so successfully, and this must be at the root of any new investigation. These accounts have shaped Nero's image and legacy for almost two millennia, and while this afterlife is varied and truly fascinating in its own right, it has also become a major obstacle. Lingering doubts and probing questions have been suppressed, and with them perhaps an adequate understanding of Nero's true significance within Roman history. And doubts there should have been from the beginning. The same sources that describe Nero as evil and delusional, an enemy of the state, surprisingly also mention several 'false Neros' – imposters who emerged in the years after his death in the eastern provinces of the Empire and gathered a considerable mass following there. This hints obliquely at Nero's enduring popularity among the common people, a popularity that seems at odds with the official accounts, at least at first.

How much a strong, unquestioned tradition can restrict our ability to see and think for ourselves, and thus become self-perpetuating, is aptly illustrated by a once famous Nero portrait in the Musei Capitolini in Rome (Fig. 1).[2] A fair measure of its undiminished popular appeal is demonstrated by the fact that this marble head is now among the very first results brought up by internet search

Fig. 1
Portrait of Nero
AD 50–98 (with later restorations)
Marble
H. 45 cm
Musei Capitolini, Sala Imperatori,
Rome
MC 427/S

This sculpture is a fascinating
palimpsest that combines multiple
layers of history and reception.

engines under Nero's name, and it still graces the occasional cover of scholarly books on the subject.[3] First documented in the seventeenth century, it is an impressive, finely modulated portrait, its size larger than life. After recent cleaning, it is quite easy even for the untrained eye to distinguish between the ancient and restored elements that make up the sculpture. It quickly becomes apparent that only a small part of the face is ancient, mostly the area of the eyes, forehead and bottom fringe of hair, marked out by its honey-coloured patination from the pure white marble around. Ironically, this small fragment originally belonged to a likeness of the emperor Domitian (although this may have been re-carved from a Nero portrait about two decades after Nero's death). The rest is a Baroque reconstruction, highly accomplished in its carving technique, and extremely well-informed in antiquarian terms: it is partly based on Nero's ancient coin portraits, but importantly it also seems to express elements of Nero's character that can only be gleaned from the written sources. The oddly turned head with its heavy, thick-set features, small eyes and narrow, full-lipped mouth lend the portrait an almost manic intensity, an air of decadence suitable for a cruel tyrant and would-be artist. The resulting portrait is a penetrating character study, brilliant and at the same time deeply flawed, for it is far removed from the images produced during Nero's lifetime and the messages they tried to convey.

Despite all this, recent interpretations of the Capitoline bust have updated the image for the present and given it a new lease of life (Fig. 2). They sit alongside many other such creations. Surely the most iconic evocation of Nero in the modern era remains his portrayal by the actor Peter Ustinov in the 1951 film *Quo Vadis*. Perhaps in the same way that its artistic antecedents in Baroque and later opera did in the past, this cinematic version has shaped the perception of Nero for an entire generation, and is only now slowly beginning to fade from

Fig. 2
Nero
2019
Salva Ruano
Mixed media
H. 36 cm, W. 23 cm
From the series *Césares de Roma*

A hyper-realistic version of the Capitoline portrait.

public consciousness.[4] Yet these representations – alongside a long line of historical paintings, some by renowned artists, which also continue to exert a hold over the imagination – only give compelling physical form to a caricature, a heavily manipulated, distorted image of Nero that was first created in antiquity very soon after his death. The Capitoline portrait, though intended to be true, in its own way is an instructive example of how this process operates: it picks up enough authentic elements to be recognisable (the superficial resemblance to genuine coin portraits, in this case), but then expands, alters and manipulates them to create a very different, yet utterly believable, interpretation. The ancient literary sources operated in a similar manner, as will become clear, so that we deal with multiple layers of alienation. Nero's history, in other words, is threefold: it encompasses first the events of his lifetime, then the way they were reinterpreted and recorded immediately afterwards, and finally the life this partly artificial figure has taken on subsequently. Recovering the real Nero therefore entails turning him back from an object into an active subject of history.

In our modern world, extended narrative accounts require more and more pictures, and it has long been an obvious but also intrinsically lazy option to use paintings and film stills unquestioned, disregarding the presumptions and filters they transport into the present. To conclude this brief glance at imaginary character portraits and the expectations they simultaneously reflect and project forward, we can once more return to the Capitoline Nero. It has its equivalent in a portrait that was for centuries taken as the likeness of Nero's tutor, mentor and minister, the Stoic philosopher Lucius Annaeus Seneca. Forced to take his own life in AD 65, Seneca faced his end with the noble calm befitting his creed (or so the ancient authors tell us). Accordingly, the image of an elderly man, preserved in many ancient versions, rugged, gaunt, yet full of an intense energy, was taken to be his true and faithful portrait (Fig. 3). In the early seventeenth century the artist Rubens used it as inspiration for a famous painting of Seneca's suicide (Fig. 4). Great was the consternation, therefore, when an inscribed ancient portrait herm came to light outside Rome in the early nineteenth century, which revealed a very different Seneca, at odds with any notions formed by the literary tradition (Fig. 5).[5] Undoubtedly the image of the idealised Seneca had also partly shaped early modern notions of a 'Stoic' senatorial opposition to Nero, men who conspired against him and were implicated in his downfall. It is an arduous and sometimes painful task to purge our visual memory of this powerful tradition, but a necessary one if we want to understand Nero on his own terms.

There is of course a wealth of information on Nero and the Neronian period, dating to both Nero's lifetime and the years immediately thereafter – monuments, paintings, sculptures, inscriptions, papyri, writing tablets, coinage and the like – and important discoveries continue to be made, some of which will be included in the following pages. However, it is the literary texts in particular that have shaped our understanding and often predetermined how other evidence is interpreted. They still form the backbone of any narrative history of his reign, and it is vital to understand them within the context in which they were originally produced.[6]

These ancient sources, mostly from the genres of historiography, biography and poetry, fall into several chronological groups that inevitably reflect the contemporary experiences and concerns of their authors. They can, to an extent, also be seen as successive stages of discussion, redaction and elimination

Fig. 3
Portrait of an elderly man
Roman
Villa of the Papyri, Herculaneum, Italy
Bronze
H. 33 cm, W. 24 cm, D. 21 cm
Museo Archeologico Nazionale di Napoli
5616

This likeness of an unidentified, possibly Greek, poet or thinker was long erroneously believed to depict Nero's tutor and advisor, the Stoic philosopher Lucius Annaeus Seneca.

Fig. 4
The Death of Seneca
c. 1612/13
Peter Paul Rubens (1577–1640)
Oil on wood
H. 185 cm, W. 154.7 cm
Alte Pinakothek, Munich
Inv. 315

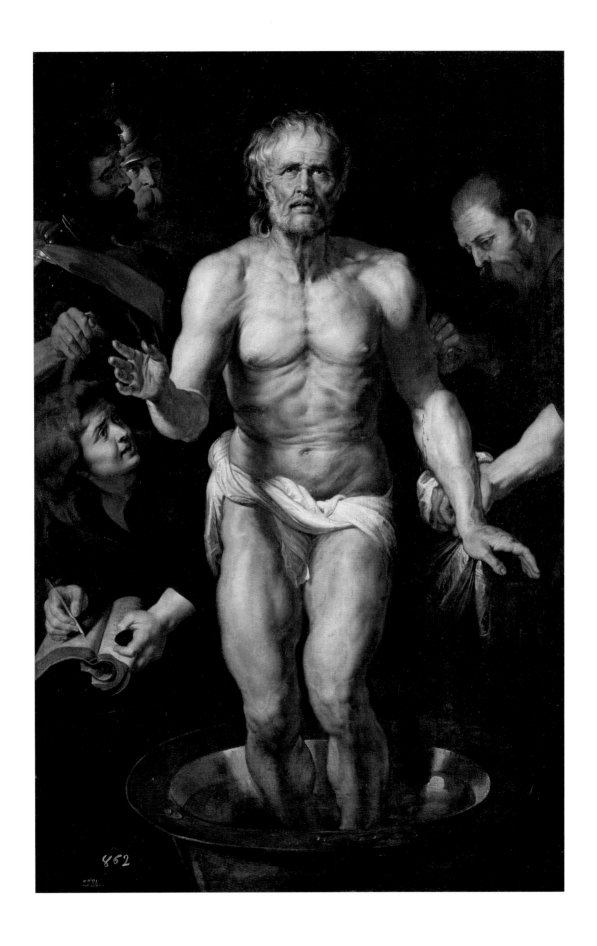

Fig. 5
Inscribed double herm with portrait of Seneca (left) and Socrates (right)
Early 3rd century AD
Rome, Italy
Marble
H. 28 cm
Antikensammlung, Staatliche Museen zu Berlin
SK 391

This double herm, found of the Caelian Hill in Rome, portrays the Stoic philosopher Lucius Annaeus Seneca together with the Classical Athenian philosopher Socrates. Seneca's fate – he was eventually forced to commit suicide – mirrored that of Socrates almost 500 years previously. The latter was compelled to take his own life by drinking hemlock in 399 BC.

that eventually resulted in an elegantly yet forcefully formulated consensus view of the senatorial elite. This was the leading class of Roman society (almost all Roman authors were senators or knights; see p. 33), which operated in a complex, and at times troubled, interaction with the emperor. Under Nero, this relationship came under particular strain, and as a result these accounts are extraordinarily hostile.

The main texts relevant to Nero arguably survived in a centuries-long transmission process precisely because of the way their uncompromising, highly partisan outlook resonated with successive generations of elite readers, who shared the worldview they so clearly expounded. The most significant are Tacitus' *Annals* and *Histories*, and Suetonius' *Lives of the Caesars*. Rediscovered in the Renaissance and widely disseminated from then on, they are readily available in excellent modern translations. They are engaging and full of intrigue and intimate detail that still makes them both deeply entertaining and dangerously persuasive – a great part of their appeal down the centuries. Similarly important is Cassius Dio's *Roman History*. Portions of Tacitus' and Dio's texts are lost, and generally the information provided by these three authors is complementary, with occasional differences that need to be reconciled.

Publius Cornelius Tacitus was born shortly after Nero became emperor, in AD 55 or 56, into a Roman family long settled in one of the Gaulish provinces. Rhetorically talented, he embarked on a successful political career under the Flavians (the short-lived new dynasty established after the year of turmoil that followed Nero's demise), and their successors, the emperors Nerva and Trajan. Tacitus' major historical works were written from the perspective of an experienced elder statesman in the second decade of the second century AD, more than forty years after Nero's death. For the senatorial class, Nerva's accession in AD 96 (after the assassination of Domitian, the last ruler of the Flavian dynasty), followed by Trajan's in AD 98, seemed the happy fulfilment of a struggle that had lasted for more than a century. While they recognised the practical need for a single person to be at the head of the Empire, senators wanted to be respected by the emperor as his peers and to retain exclusive access to a number of offices and privileges. Importantly, they also came to reject any notion of automatic hereditary succession, which had become the norm first under the Julio-Claudian family and then again with the Flavians. Nero's rule, and later Domitian's, was perceived by these men as an aberration and an existential threat, and their writings reflect this with brutal partisanship. The sections of Tacitus' *Annals* and *Histories* that relate to Nero are closely linked by an inner logic: the *Annals* elaborate his perceived moral depravity that led to grave political failings as a leader; the *Histories* the resulting breakdown in discipline and order among the masses he had so wrongfully indulged and the ensuing civil war.

Gaius Suetonius Tranquillus was born shortly after Nero's death, possibly in the Roman province of Africa. After rhetorical training in Rome he practised law, then entered the imperial administration, holding important court positions under Trajan and his successor Hadrian. Suetonius' *Lives of the Caesars* established the genre of imperial biography. While the flavour of his *Life of Nero* differs from Tacitus in tone and choice of detail, it expounds a similar worldview and is often even more direct in its selection of evidence and blunt condemnation of the emperor.

The *Roman History* by Cassius Dio, a senator from the Greek East who wrote in the first third of the third century AD, provides the final major ancient source text. His attitude closely echoes those of his social peers from the previous century. Dio's account of Nero (only preserved in two Byzantine summaries), while cognisant of Tacitus and Suetonius, builds its narrative with recourse to some earlier texts that served as common source material for all three authors.

Together, these works provide the bulk of the familiar Nero story: the intrigues of his cunningly seductive mother Agrippina, which led to Nero's adoption by the reigning emperor Claudius (his great-uncle) and then to preferment over Claudius' own male offspring in the line of succession; his reckless exploits as a youth; the murders of Claudius and Claudius' natural son Britannicus, as well as other potential rivals; the exile and killing of Claudia Octavia, Nero's first wife; the acrimonious rift with his own mother Agrippina and her bungled murder. Other well-known narrative elements are Nero's improper obsession with chariot races, theatrical and musical performances, and his sexual perversions, as well as his promiscuous mingling with the masses and unseemly craving for their approval, coupled with a general disinterest in the real affairs of state. And then of course there were his demeaning stage performances in full public view; the almost complete destruction of Rome by a devastating fire, followed by the construction of an absurdly grand mansion; the brutal oppression of all noble opposition. Finally came the conclusion: a deluded artistic tour of Greece, growing discontent and rebellion at home and, in the end, an ignoble, pathetic suicide.

The focus is on intimacies and crude excesses of a morally depraved court. The fickle masses feature as leering beneficiaries of a corrupted and corrupting regime. This wider link between tyrant and rabble is made explicit in its most cogent, persuasive form by Tacitus – a mark of the deeply conservative, to some modern minds even reactionary, outlook held by men of his background.

Most elements of this basic anti-Neronian narrative, though less socially explicit, can be traced back to an earlier Flavian-period discourse. The uncompromising image of Nero as bloodthirsty tyrant and instigator of horrendous crimes, for example, first appears in the tragic play *Octavia*, written by an anonymous author almost immediately after Nero's demise. *Octavia* starkly sets the tone, and most of the next generation of Roman writers who took Nero as their subject seem to have been intimately familiar with its outlook and sentiment, merely expanding the play's basic plot in a different genre. Pliny the Elder (Gaius Plinius Secundus, *c.* AD 23/4–79), a Roman knight from Cisalpine Gaul, wrote a lost history that covered the period from Tiberius to Nero and the incoming Flavian dynasty. Its tone must have been highly partisan and sharply critical of Nero and his entire family, the Julio-Claudians, judging by occasional references in Pliny's extant work, the *Natural History*. Other important historical accounts were written by Fabius Rusticus and Cluvius Rufus; these, like Pliny, were used as source material by later authors but are essentially completely lost to us.

Much modern research has been taken up with the question of how these lost source texts might have differed from each other in substance and in tone (that is, their attitude to Nero). Fabius Rusticus, for example, had been close to Seneca, while Cluvius Rufus was an insider of Nero's court, with intimate knowledge of its workings, which inevitably implicated him in some of Nero's actions. We may regret the loss of these texts and the wealth of detail they would have contained, but there can be little doubt that they were equally damning of Nero. Too much was at stake for their authors, who had to justify their own actions and ingratiate themselves with a new regime. Histories of this type may, however, have been the origin of the notion of a *quinquennium Neronis*, Nero's 'five good years'. This expression, attributed to no less an authority than the later emperor Trajan, has been the subject of much debate among modern historians, who argue over which five-year period within Nero's reign of almost fourteen years it might define. Perhaps it was always a more fluid notion, allowing anyone who had been active under Nero to claim that they had served during the 'good' years, or had valiantly performed against the odds thereafter. Other texts, too, provide important detail and background context, such as the *Jewish War* and *Jewish Antiquities* by Titus Flavius Josephus, born in AD 37 into an elite family in Jerusalem. Poets of the subsequent Flavian period, such as Statius and Martial, praised the new regime under which they were writing in sharp contrast to its predecessors, a delicate task given that the Flavians had been cautiously loyal to Nero until the end. Martial in particular did much to tarnish Nero's reputation down the millennia, in elegant topical verse that distilled rumours and opinion into a potent new truth of great suggestive force.

For modern readers of these texts, it is important to understand how much they owe to a particular technique taught in the rhetorical schools which provided the Roman elite with a great deal of its discursive vocabulary. The concept of *vituperatio* is crucial here, a brutal verbal assault on an opponent's moral standing, in court or in politics.[7] Deviation from traditional norms, excessive luxury, social and particularly sexual transgression were the topics to be elaborated for this purpose, and an author's skill lay in providing ever new salacious detail to enliven a basic theme. Veracity was not expected, rather a commensurate and believable match between the described outrage and the scale of the subject's perceived wrongdoings in other fields.

This approach was particularly successful when it could latch on to real actions or statements, grotesquely exaggerating or decontextualising them, or sometimes simply taking literally what was stated metaphorically. Panegyric, that is, laudatory court poetry, was particularly vulnerable to this type of literary subversion, as its most extreme claims required a consenting audience at the best of times. In a complex process of analytical deconstruction and reconstruction, these texts can thus be re-examined and re-evaluated. As a result, many of the specific stories told about Nero – among them some of the best-loved and most famous anecdotes – evaporate as fact-based evidence. This may seem a sad loss, but a new appreciation of the inventiveness and dramatic skill of their authors (borrowing, it has been argued, from the techniques of contemporary stage plays) may offer some compensation. It was a tight-knit group of writers that was responsible for many of the texts we have: Tacitus was on close terms with his younger fellow senator Pliny the Younger (Gaius Plinius Caecilius Secundus, nephew and adopted son of the Elder Pliny, from whom he would have derived much of the anti-Neronian outlook that shines through his writings). Pliny the Younger in turn was a patron of Suetonius and benefactor of Martial. Tacitus, Pliny the Younger and Suetonius may have received their rhetorical training from the same famous orator, Quintilian. Senatorial authors were alert to the fact that they ultimately controlled how history would be remembered, and they liked to remind their rulers that this was so. In the *Panegyricus*, a work in praise of Trajan, Pliny the Younger hints at the way this hold on memory could be leveraged.

By contrast, it is much harder to recover an official earlier, Neronian narrative. Themes of Neronian poetry can be traced, for instance, in individual works by Calpurnius Siculus and the so-called Anonymous Einsiedlensis, although their Neronian date (while accepted here and generally) is sometimes disputed, and their identities remain enigmatic. A sense of the self-perception of Nero's court and the wider expectations projected on to it by contemporary Romans is a vital guide to the interpretation of Neronian art and visual culture, adding nuance to what might otherwise appear overly generic material. In this war of words, literary history and analysis feature unusually large.

Petronius' *Satyricon* provides evidence of a different nature. One section, the *Cena Trimalchionis*, describes a banquet of the fabulously wealthy but deeply vulgar freedman Trimalchio and his companions, with their seemingly ridiculous social pretensions (see p. 245). Beyond its ribald humour, the text provides a telling insight into the changing dynamics of first-century AD Roman society and the resulting status anxieties among different social classes, both those on the rise and others fearing for their traditional status and privileges. The author is usually identified with Titus Petronius Niger, nicknamed *arbiter elegantiarum* or arbiter of taste, part of the inner core of Nero's lavish court. Here, too, some scholars have recently argued for a different identification or later date, but the general sentiment that pervades the *Satyricon* is characteristic of an extended period, regardless.

This leaves Seneca, another close insider of Nero's court, and his rich writings. These provide perhaps the closest glimpse of the often shared, but at times also contradictory, elite mindsets of the age. We can perceive the outlines of a psychopathology of first-century AD Rome – a society under prolonged stress, with profound tensions between and within classes and age groups, and traces of a partly suppressed cultural revolution. Nero, member of a new generation, is perhaps best understood as an embodiment of this difficult and contested transformation, both a product and a catalyst of the period. These and other sources underpin much of the following chapters.

The study of ancient Roman history and society is a dynamic field. There have been numerous excellent studies on Nero and the wider first century in recent decades, and many more in the last few years. Anglophone readers are particularly well served here.[8] Miriam T. Griffin's *Nero: The End of a Dynasty* has gone through several editions and remains the standard academic biography, alongside Edward Champlin's more recent *Nero*. Two edited volumes, *The Cambridge Companion to the Age of Nero* and *A Companion to the Neronian Age*, gather up-to-date contributions by eminent experts in their fields on a broad variety of relevant themes and can serve as in-depth introductions and guides to more specialist academic literature. Harder to access for the general reader but worth mentioning because of the many stimuli it has provided to the debate is *Reflections of Nero: Culture, History, and Representation*. The material culture of the period, alongside much else, is covered by two exhibition catalogues in Italian and German: *Nerone*, which accompanied a major show in Rome in 2011, and *Nero: Kaiser, Künstler und Tyrann*, produced in conjunction with a set of exhibitions in Trier in 2016.[9] Our view of Nero has changed considerably as a result of this sustained research and the recent renaissance in Nero studies. Yet big questions remain; this account is intended to provide a wide-ranging and well-illustrated overview that explores Nero in the context of his times and draws on a rich array of different evidence.

The story follows Nero's life, from his birth and family history to becoming Rome's youngest emperor for almost two centuries, his successes and failures, private life and grand politics. It encompasses many famous events and stretches from Britain and its rebellious queen Boudica to the mighty Parthian Empire in greater Iran, from luxury trade with the worlds of the Baltic and the Indian Ocean to expeditions in search of the sources of the Nile, fierce uprisings and forgotten military conquests. The text examines the great fire of Rome in AD 64, Nero's new palace – the glorious Domus Aurea or Golden House – his controversial performances on the race track and on stage, and his relationship with the elite and the plebs. It was a full life – Nero was still only thirty when he died, but had already reigned for over thirteen years. The devastation of Italy during the civil war that followed made many long for his return.

By chance, the natural disaster that befell the cities of Vesuvius (including Pompeii and Herculaneum) some eleven years after Nero's death has preserved much relevant material not available elsewhere, including graffiti that mention Nero and his second wife Poppaea (see Fig. 149, p. 188) – if not quite a 'history from below' then evidence that complements, and at times contradicts, the 'official' histories.

In the end, it is perhaps less surprising that Nero failed, than how close he came to changing the nature of the Roman Empire and the way it was governed.

Map of the Roman Empire

ROMAN EMPIRE

Rome
Naples

Antioch

Alexandria

PARTHIAN EMPIRE

I

NERO AND THE FAMILY OF AUGUSTUS

A new heir

On 25 February AD 50, Rome's reigning emperor Claudius (r. AD 41–54) officially adopted as his son a young relative, a great-nephew named Lucius Domitius Ahenobarbus – the future emperor Nero. The child Domitius had celebrated his twelfth birthday only two months before. Adoption meant that he legally changed family, from the *gens* ('clan') Domitia to the *gens* Claudia, and took on a different name to confirm his new identity. From now on, he would be called Tiberius Claudius Nero Caesar, or more officially Nero Caesar Claudius Drusus Germanicus, names carried by famous past Claudii and redolent of the family's long and proud history.[1]

A small number of portrait statues survive that show how the new member of the imperial family was introduced to the Roman people at about this time (Figs 6 and 7), usually as part of dynastic sculpture displays in public buildings.[2] The boy's features give little away; the small mouth, strong chin and prominent ears would remain a constant in portraits throughout his life. The hair has a simple fringe that reaches halfway down the forehead, with a slight parting above the left eye, something he maintained into early adulthood – a much plainer, almost austere version of hairstyles chosen for previous princes. On some of the statues he still wears a *bulla* around his neck, a gold capsule for amulets that formally marked him out as a child. Sources describe the colour of his hair as *subflavus*, blond with a perhaps reddish tinge, and undoubtedly the marble images were painted to highlight this aspect, so rare among Mediterranean people and easily exploited later on for its association with the imagined physical appearance of certain gods.[3] Most of all, these statues exude an air of childlike innocence, of a character not yet fully formed – a perfect foil for the vast range of expectations soon projected on to the boy by family, competing court factions, members of the upper classes and the masses of the Roman people, the *plebs*. They were the only statues to survive the removal and destruction (*damnatio memoriae*) of Nero's images decades later.

Domitius had become Claudius' stepson about a year earlier, in AD 50, when the emperor, then approaching the age of sixty, took the boy's twice-widowed mother Agrippina (Julia Agrippina, or Agrippina the Younger) as his fourth wife. Over the following months, other measures made clear that he was to be considered the heir designate, even though Claudius already had a natural son of his own, Britannicus, from a previous marriage. A mere four-and-a-half years after his adoption, on 13 October AD 54, the young Nero, two months shy of his seventeenth birthday, became the fifth and last ruler of the Julio-Claudian dynasty.

Nero's ancient biographers ascribed this turn of events to the cunning intrigues of Agrippina, who, consumed with ambition, first seduced and then manipulated the elderly Claudius into acting against his own best interests (see pp. 61–7; p. 177). There are good reasons to question this version of events, for, despite his relatively young age, the boy possessed a unique pedigree that made him in many ways the best possible candidate in the line of succession: he was descended on both his father's and his mother's side from Augustus, Rome's first emperor, who was his great-great-grandfather and his great-great-uncle. His father, Gnaeus Domitius Ahenobarbus, came from an eminent, ancient family, and his maternal grandmother, Octavia, was Augustus' sister. His mother, in her own right, united the bloodlines of the Iulii and the Claudii, the two main family

Fig. 7
Nero as a boy
C. AD 49–51
Basilica at Veleia, Italy
Marble, with traces of red pigment
H. 153 cm
Museo Archeologico Nazionale,
Parma
Inv. 826

This statue of Nero was part of a group representing several generations of the Julio-Claudian family, including Agrippina and the emperor Claudius. It is of the same type as Fig. 6 and demonstrates how the new crown prince's image was disseminated across the Empire. The support by his left foot is carved to look like a *capsula*, a container for book scrolls. This was a common prop for portrait statues and alluded to the sitter's expensive elite education. Within three or four years of this sculpture being made, Nero delivered well-received speeches before the senate in both Latin and Greek, a mark of his careful tuition. The head was carved separately for insertion into the draped body. The hair is rendered in great detail, adding vibrancy to the otherwise simple coiffure.

branches of the ruling dynasty (see family tree, pp. 8–9). Claudius lacked a strong direct blood link to Augustus, one of the Iulii, and in the rigorously patrilineal world of Roman social norms this mattered, particularly because in the decades since Augustus' death in AD 14 the legitimacy of the family's continued claim to supreme power had come under increasing pressure. Seen from this angle, the history of the Julio-Claudian dynasty, particularly of the four men who ruled over the half century after the death of Augustus, can be read as a complex and ultimately doomed struggle to adapt his powerful yet difficult legacy to an increasingly fractured society. The diverse and in many ways contradictory demands of that society would prove impossible to reconcile.

Leading members of the senatorial class formed the main obstacle to any further formal transformation of the political system. Despite the many practical changes in the way the affairs of state were now run, they retained a disproportionate influence. Augustus' greatest propaganda triumph was that he had ended the civil war following Julius Caesar's assassination and nominally restored the Republic – but in the end, this placed an impossible burden on his successors. By definition, this restoration did not allow for the open transition to a quasi-monarchical system that would have fully aligned senatorial upper-class ethos and career structure to the new form of government. Instead, the institutions of the Republic and the gradually emerging and expanding imperial court eventually came to coexist in parallel.[4] There was surprisingly little social overlap between their respective office holders and no incentive for men of a senatorial background to seek court appointments. This led to ongoing friction, dissent and repeated moments of open and at times violent rebellion. Of the three men who had followed Augustus up to Nero's adoption, Tiberius had spent the last part of his reign away from Rome and the senate, Gaius, more commonly known as Caligula, had been assassinated, and Claudius, the third, had faced a conspiracy and military revolt only a year into his reign. The presentation of a viable heir, closely related to Augustus himself and to the man originally chosen by him as his eventual successor, Germanicus, was an astute and urgent move by the elderly Claudius to stabilise his own rule. In order to understand the complexities of this dynamic, and as a consequence the limited choices available to Claudius and then to Nero after him, it is worth dwelling for a moment on the decades following Augustus' decisive victories in the civil war in 31 and 30 BC (see pp. 30–1). The young Nero was born into this world of simmering conflict and shifting mentalities, and many of his actions can only be understood against this background.

The Augustan principate: Restored Republic or new order

Augustus had died aged seventy-six in AD 14, a little over twenty-three years before his great-great-grandson Nero was born. In such remarkable longevity lay Augustus' good fortune, for it allowed him to hold de facto sole power largely unchallenged for more than four decades, a time that came to be remembered as a blessed era of universal peace and prosperity.[5] The previous period of savage civil war, and Augustus' role in it, was almost forgotten as a result, certainly among the masses. Towards the end of his life, a whole generation of Romans

Fig. 8
Statue of Augustus
c. 10–1 BC
Via Labicana, Rome, Italy
Marble with traces of red pigment on the plinth
H. 207 cm
Palazzo Massimo alle Terme, Museo Nazionale Romano, Rome
Inv. 56230

Augustus is shown in the toga, a ceremonial garment only freeborn citizens (*ingenui*) were allowed to wear. He mandated its use on official occasions as a unifying marker of Roman identity against foreigners and the enslaved population. His head is covered, indicating that he is performing a religious sacrifice. The hairstyle follows his main portrait type, introduced after the civil war period, probably around the time of the 'Restored Republic'. He wears the soft leather boots of a senator, another clear marker of status.

had known no leader other than him. His critical achievement over these years was the gradual transition to a carefully framed new system of rule that allowed for formal political reconciliation, and, more importantly, going forward gave the nobility a face-saving way of accommodating what would, in effect, be a monarchy. All the time-honoured political offices and institutions of the state that were crucial for the traditional self-perception and class identity of the senatorial elite nominally remained in place. In reality, however, the results of Augustus' approach would be highly ambiguous in the longer term. The tacit understanding of the real balance of power could be undermined if this notion of a restored Republic was taken literally.

The new system of governing the state came to be known as the principate, derived from the Latin term *princeps* ('leader' or 'first man') that was applied to Augustus. The foremost strongmen of the late Republic had claimed this title, but, crucially, it also carried a more conservative notion of highly constitutional authority. The *princeps senatus*, for example, was the most respected senator, a 'leader of the house' by virtue of his seniority, dignity and experience, and, theoretically, a first among equals whose status ultimately depended on his peers. This contrasted markedly with other appellations Augustus had used during the civil war period such as *Dux Italiae* ('Leader of Italy'), with its clear connotation of extraordinary powers. He retained the title *imperator* (from which the word 'emperor' derives), traditionally awarded to military commanders through acclamation by their troops for battlefield victories, men whose *imperium*, or authority to command, was originally awarded by the senate and people in connection with certain offices. Augustus had very effectively framed the final phase of the civil war as a conflict with foreign powers, a tactic made possible because of the political and personal alliance between his last remaining rival, Mark Antony, and the queen of Egypt, Cleopatra. His epochal naval victory over their combined fleets at Actium off the coast of north-western Greece in 31 BC and the conquest of Egypt a year later (as a result of which Antony and Cleopatra took their own lives) proved decisive.

The basic framework for Augustus' hold on power was set in place over the following years. In 29 BC, the doors of the Temple of Janus in Rome, by tradition left open in times of war, were ritually closed, a potent symbol that peace had returned. Augustus then celebrated a spectacular triple triumph to commemorate his victories at Actium, and the conquests of Egypt and Pannonia (a troublesome region south of the Danube which he had successfully attacked in 35 BC). A highly important symbolic moment followed in January 27 BC, when Augustus laid down the various extraordinary powers he had been voted and formally handed authority back to the senate. This was the point at which the old Republic was officially restored, as expressed in the slogan '*res publica restituta*'. The senators in return asked him to continue to look after the state as consul, one of two who were elected annually to this highest political position of the Republic, which they nominally held for a year. They also awarded him *imperium proconsulare*, a supreme formal authority in key provinces where the bulk of the army was stationed. This essentially put the military in his hands for ten years, although these powers were repeatedly renewed and formed the main basis for Augustus' subsequent rule. In addition, the senate voted him various honours for the salvation of the state. Among them was the title 'Augustus' – his given name was Gaius Octavius – an honorific translatable perhaps as 'the Venerable' (Fig. 8).

As a result, Augustus could claim to exceed all others in reputation and authority, but not to hold higher formal power than his respective colleagues in office. In truth, the combination of different powers he held was unique to him and far exceeded anyone else's, a fact that was, tacitly, widely acknowledged. Suetonius refers to Augustus' system of rule as a 'new order' (*novus status*).[6]

Over the years, there were some modifications to the way the principate was constituted formally. In 23 BC, for example, Augustus ceased to hold the consulate, which by then he had assumed annually for ten years, but was instead awarded tribunician powers for life. The 'tribunes of the people' had originally been introduced to champion the cause of the Roman *plebs*, with important prerogatives including the right to call meetings, initiate legislation and exercise vetoes. This redistribution of Augustus' official authorities was doubly advantageous: it freed up the consulate for other aristocrats who continued to prize it highly for reasons of prestige, and it aligned him notionally more closely with the *plebs*. The people at any rate – probably rightly – regarded Augustus as the main guarantor of peace and a paternalistic guardian of their interests. They were much less concerned with constitutional subtleties and, following a major famine and resultant disturbances, demanded that Augustus should become consul for life or assume the extraordinary powers of a *censor* or even *dictator*, offices normally only awarded irregularly and for limited duration. Augustus declined, because it was clearly unacceptable to the aristocracy – as Caesar's assassination by disaffected senators had shown. He did, however, take personal control of a newly created public grain supply as well as an official police and fire service, populist measures that were of great importance to his successors. To an extent, this put him firmly within the tradition of the *populares*, aristocratic reformers who had traditionally advocated land distribution, tax reforms and debt relief, and whose last prominent exponent had been Julius Caesar. In opposition were the *optimates*, the party of the wealthiest and most reactionary senators. Emperors from then on would attempt to accommodate both the senators and the people, and at times they felt a strong temptation to play off one against the other.

Augustus also carefully controlled the potential for individual aristocrats to create an independent popular support base by limiting over time their expenditure on public spectacles, their right to celebrate a triumph and the opportunity to dedicate in their own name major monuments in the city of Rome. Certain members of the nobility were thus deprived of traditional opportunities for gaining prestige. Their value systems and expectations had not moved in line with the political realities of the new principate.

Julio-Claudian society

The transition to the principate brought with it profound changes to the way Roman society operated on a practical level. Some of these were simply accelerations of developments that had begun under the Republic, others were a direct result of the new status quo, but they manifested themselves gradually, perhaps little noticed at first. The results were felt most keenly in Rome itself, the unrivalled political and economic centre of the Empire. The metropolis in this respect evolved at a faster pace than the rest of the Roman world, leading to a widening gap between the attitudes and value systems among different groups of

the Empire's population. Severe fractures, first obvious during the reigns of Caligula and Claudius, erupted violently at the end of Nero's rule. Several factors contributed to this. One was the trickle-down effect of economic prosperity, stimulated by successive conquests and a long period of peace. The overdue political integration of the Empire, which brought unprecedented numbers of provincials into the senate, was another. Finally, and despite assurances to the contrary, the increasing monopolisation of power in the hands of the *princeps* and his court was fundamental. All these developments combined to threaten the exclusive status of the senatorial class in particular. The 'Restored Republic' brought with it new and parallel hierarchies of wealth and power that competed with existing ones. When emperors attempted to reward social mobility through new marks of formal status, they encountered resistance from the old elites.

Traditional Roman society was deeply hierarchical. Through various privileges and dress codes the differences between groups of the population were consciously and very visibly marked, and this formal social stratification was regularly reinforced further through particular rituals. Members of the higher orders could thus be recognised at first sight. At the pinnacle of the Roman social order stood the senators, men who were required to have a minimum property census of one million sesterces. The number of senators had varied through time, but was capped at 600 by Augustus. They were entitled to wear two wide purple stripes on their tunics, and a special type of soft leather boot. Entry to the senate for wealthy young men of good family came with election to the office of quaestor, the lowest rung on the career ladder of traditional posts, the so-called *cursus honorum*. This was followed by an aedileship, then a praetorship and finally the highest office, that of consul. Each post came with responsibilities over various areas in the military and administration. Former praetors and consuls were given provinces to govern after their term of office, usually a year or two, had ended, and commanders of the main military units, the legions, were drawn exclusively from their ranks. Occasionally 'new men' broke into the senate, but most came from already established families, proud of their ancestors and certain of their privilege, making membership in some ways hereditary (Fig. 9).[7]

The second order was formed by *equites* or knights, for whom a property census of 400,000 sesterces applied. In the first century about fifteen thousand knights were spread throughout the Empire, clustered in cities of wealthy old provinces outside Italy. Entry into the order of knights was not automatic, but had to be granted by the emperor. Various privileges made it a very appealing status, and, as opposed to senators who had to respect certain restrictions when it came to their economic activities (following aristocratic ideals, senators should live off the profits from their lands), knights could engage freely in sectors such as trade and banking. Markers of their rank were the *anulus aureus*, a gold ring, and a tunic with two narrow stripes of purple.[8] New men in the senate came almost exclusively from equestrian families.

Senators and knights were treated differently under Roman law from the rest of the freeborn population; they could expect to receive much milder sentences for any crimes and were normally exempt from corporal punishment and execution. Secret trials and killings, such as those that occurred under Caligula and Claudius, and later Nero, therefore caused particular outrage among them.[9]

At local level, *decuriones* or town councillors formed the most privileged social class. They, too, required a minimum property census; the enslaved population and freedmen were excluded.[10] Below them came the remaining freeborn Roman citizens, *ingenui*, of whom the capital's *plebs urbana* was the most influential group; much of the emperor's attention was therefore focused on them. This, too, was subdivided and structured further, for example through professional organisations and guilds, the *collegia*. Only Roman citizens were entitled to wear the toga.

The next group in the social order were *liberti*, formerly enslaved, who had been freed by their masters and had gained limited citizen rights. By a peculiarity of Roman law and social norms, they continued to owe their masters loyalty and were considered part of their extended family household. Their status was closely linked to that of their patrons – a rich and influential patron's freedman could outrank in perceived dignity a poor freeborn member of the *plebs*. To an extent, this even applied to the enslaved people, or *servitium*, numbering in their millions and who otherwise formed the bottom layer of society.[11] *Peregrini*, freeborn non-citizens, represented the remaining group. They formed the majority population of the provinces.

While the façade of this fairly rigid pyramidal structure of status was maintained, it was increasingly hollowed out by economic and political changes. By modern standards, Rome had always been administered by a surprisingly small government. Senators graduated through various offices in the state administration and military during their career. They were supported by a limited staff of professional clerks, a mix of freeborn citizens and enslaved men owned by the state, who supplied vital expertise and continuity (Figs 10a and b). In addition, there were secretaries, clerks and other helpers from the aristocratic office holders' own private household staff. Among the grandees of the late Republic, these households could run into the hundreds and thousands. With the emergence of the principate and its peculiar outward continuation of Republican practices, this meant that the nascent imperial court, or *aula caesaris*, emerged out of Augustus' private household. Important administrative tasks were therefore taken on by his *servi* and freedmen. With increasing workload and specialisation, the imperial court grew in size and authority. For the emperor, the great advantage was that he could control his staff more directly and rely on their loyalty. Over the decades, imperial freedmen who held key quasi-ministerial functions could become enormously powerful, wielding considerable influence and patronage. This process reached its climax under Claudius, whose freedmen Polybius, Callistus, Pallas and Narcissus became closely associated with his regime. Senators, unsurprisingly, greatly resented this development, for it both offended their dignity and threatened their authority.

Other posts that developed with the principate similarly went to knights rather than senators, because the emperors felt that they could rely on them more. In exercising powers on the *princeps*' behalf, the *equites* depended entirely on his authority. Senators, by contrast, fundamentally considered themselves the emperor's social equals, a claim that was marked symbolically by the convention that the emperor should greet them with a kiss.

These new equestrian posts included the prefectures of major offices established in Rome, such as the command of the Praetorian Guard, the paramilitary fire and police services, and the grain supply. Similarly, the governorship of Egypt (one of the Empire's wealthiest provinces and vital for the grain supply), which had become an imperial crownland after Augustus'

Fig. 10a
The 'Altar of the scribes'
AD 25–50
Necropolis of Via di Porta San Sebastiano, Rome, Italy
Marble
H. 130 cm, W. 67 cm, D. 45 cm
Terme di Diocleziano, Museo Nazionale Romano, Rome
Inv. 475113

Quintus Fulvius Eunus dedicated this funerary altar to his sons Faustus and Priscus. Both were clerks (*apparitores*), who worked on the staff of senatorial magistrates (*curule aediles*) tasked with Rome's urban administration, including the capital's food supply.

Apparitores like Faustus and Priscus were salaried assistants on whose administrative experience officials, including magistrates and priests appointed annually, relied. They formed corporations according to their respective functions. Entry into one of these corporations afforded freedmen and those born outside Rome numerous opportunities to give and receive favours and advance socially in the capital. Faustus and Priscus were *scribae*, who enjoyed the highest prestige among *apparitores*, followed by *lictores* (men who served as bodyguards to magistrates and carried their insignia), *viatores* (runners) and *praecones* (announcers).

The high quality of this marble altar with its fine carving reflects the comparative wealth and elevated status of its dedicatees. The scene at the top shows clerks and officials at work.

conquest, was always given to a knight rather than a senator. Again, the result was that a knight, theoretically below a senator in the social order, could in practice hold far more power and influence. Knights also served the emperor as financial officers (*procuratores*) and governors on his behalf in minor provinces. In addition, they filled most of the command posts in the army, with the exception of the most senior ranks, which were reserved for senators.

On the economic front, too, senatorial status came under increasing threat. There had always been senators who fell on hard times financially and, failing their formal census requirement, lost their seats (unless wealthy friends or the emperor, out of friendship or respect for their family, bailed them out). Now, there could be knights with a fortune much greater than that of a 'poorer' senator, though many knights chose not to seek admission to the senate even if they were entitled to. Even worse, there were phenomenally wealthy freedmen who, through clever business transactions, had made vast fortunes that dwarfed those of many senators.

One of the most important ways in which wealth and status were expressed in the formal protocols of daily life was the *salutatio*. This was the traditional morning ritual in which friends and clients, including freedmen and freeborn, visited the house of their patron, usually a wealthy citizen or influential politician. Patrons measured their social standing by the size of their *clientela*. After the morning reception, clients were expected to accompany their patron to the Forum and generally support him, for example during elections. In return they expected support from their patron in the form of favours and recommendations, and also cash hand-outs, so-called *sportula*. The amount of money involved increased over the decades from the late Republic to the early Empire, and patron–client relationships became ever more transactional.

Fig. 10b
Detail from the 'Altar of the scribes'

A finely observed scene showing a crowd of petitioners pleading their cases to the officials (see Fig. 10a).

In a phenomenon peculiar to Roman culture, the emperor's household functioned very much along the same lines, only on a much larger scale. Ostentatious displays by others were thus carefully monitored as signs of potentially seditious aspiration. If the wealth and size of private residences and thereby their capacity to receive a large clientele had always been an important marker of political influence, they now became increasingly relevant as markers of competitive social posturing – luxury and status compensating for loss of real political influence (see p. 217; p. 243).

Much first-century poetry, usually written by young knights, is preoccupied with the more tedious aspects of these rituals, including various perceived indignities. Social advancement for some inevitably brought status anxiety for others. Seneca, himself a member of the senate, relates the acute discomfort felt if not by individual senators who found themselves attending the morning salutation of former *servi*, among them freedmen in the imperial administration, then certainly by their scandalised peers.[12] To them, this topsy-turvy world of social relations was reminiscent of the festival of Saturnalia, when for a few days in December masters and the enslaved symbolically changed places. By the mid-first century growing numbers of senators and knights expected the emperor to crack down hard on such developments, not to encourage them.

The principate worked chiefly through the immense personal authority and charisma of Augustus. His enormous wealth and control of the military formed the backbone of his rule, but in public, a policy of clemency and reconciliation, coupled with the natural seniority that came with his longevity, defined his legacy. The first serious test of the principate was the question of succession – in the Republic such supreme power was not meant to be transferred on hereditary principles.

The line of succession

Augustus had no son. In the competitive world of the Roman nobility, this lack of an heir left him vulnerable in the long term and needed redress. As soon as he had consolidated his power and there was no prospect of a male child of his own, Augustus therefore ensured that he always had a nominated heir and began to plan his succession far into the future. High overall mortality and the resultant frequent failure of male family lines meant that Roman law offered strong provisions for adoption, including of adult men. Augustus himself had been adopted by his great-uncle Julius Caesar to guarantee leadership of the Caesarian faction and the continuation of the Julian line.[13] Augustus accordingly used adoption for this purpose, as would future emperors. Ultimately, however, his succession over several generations depended entirely on the female line, through his daughter Julia and his sister Octavia, and their daughters and granddaughters. With ruthless determination, and the legal sanction afforded him by his position as *pater familias* (the senior male of his family), he compelled his female relatives into repeated marriages and divorces to suit his political alliances and dynastic plans. The younger males in his family fared little better.[14] The detachment with which he punished relatives who did not comply, through banishment and even death, set a pattern for all of his Julio-Claudian successors.

Fig. 11
Portrait of Livia
25–1 BC
Possibly Italy
Marble
H. 27 cm, W. 21 cm, D. 26 cm
British Museum
1856,1226.1722
Bequeathed by Sir William Temple

Livia Drusilla (Livia for short) became the role model for imperial women. Married to Augustus for fifty-three years, she gained great influence as his private counsel. In public, she was presented as a pious and demure Roman matron, in line with Augustus' professed restitution of traditional Roman values after the civil war period. The hairstyle of this portrait, with the characteristic central *nodus* ('knot') and braided strands that lead to a chignon at the back of the head, projects this conservative message and is typical of the first decades of Augustus' rule. It represents a careful balance between Livia's increasing prominence in public life and her status as a traditional Roman woman.

The assumption of complete female subservience was widespread, particularly among the nobility, and Roman society had developed numerous practices that were at least in part designed to ensure male dominance. Roman women were usually married off as fourteen- or fifteen-year-old girls, generally about half the age of their future husbands, though men could be even older if it was not their first marriage.[15] Divorce was not unusual, and given the perils of childbirth and the age difference between husbands and wives, both men and women were frequently widowed, with the expectation that they should remarry. To protect a family's wealth, marriage between close relatives (such as first cousins) was common, and this was particularly true within the imperial house, where additional political and dynastic considerations came into play.[16]

Women of the Julio-Claudian dynasty, because they ensured the continuation of Augustus' blood line, gradually attained an influence and public

Fig. 12
Portrait of Augustus
Before AD 14
Possibly Italy
Marble
H. 41 cm, W. 27 cm, D. 26 cm
British Museum
1879,0712.9

Images of Augustus continued to
be produced under his successors,
whose legitimacy derived entirely
from their family ties to the first
princeps and founder of the Julio-
Claudian dynasty.

prominence quite unprecedented in Roman history (see. p. 176). This posed a dilemma. Even by the standards of his day, Augustus espoused extremely traditional and conservative social values. He upheld tight restrictions on the role of women in public life and expected them to conform to notions of honour, virtue and modesty that culminated in the ideal of *pudicitia*, female moral and sexual chastity. In his politics he tried to reconcile these social attitudes with his need for an heir, with mixed results.

After an early betrothal and two short-lived marriages contracted for political reasons, Augustus began a relationship with his third wife, Livia (Figs 11 and 12). At the time she was still married to another man, Tiberius Claudius Nero, a member of the powerful patrician *gens* Claudia, by whom she already had one son, Tiberius, and was expecting another, Drusus (the Elder). Augustus, too, was still married to his second wife, Scribonia, but divorced her as soon as their daughter Julia was born in order to wed the pregnant Livia in 38 BC. Despite the unusual beginnings of their union, Augustus determined that Livia should be presented publicly as the exemplary embodiment of a traditional Roman woman, initially perhaps in calculated contrast to his rival Antony's companion Cleopatra (Figs 13 and 14). Livia was only five years younger than Augustus and his close confidante, and this may have helped make their marriage a successful and long-lived one, even though they had no surviving children. In many ways, she became the role model for women of the imperial family.

Augustus' attempts to ensure the continuation of the family line had begun early. Over several decades he arranged marriages between various members of his family and prominent rivals, including his fellow triumvir Mark Antony, raised stepsons (contrary to legal custom, which dictated that children remained with their father following a divorce), and adopted his grandsons as his own children. With the marriage of one such grandson, Gaius Caesar, to Livia Julia, also known as Livilla, who was Livia's granddaughter, Augustus seemed to have succeeded in uniting the Julian and Claudian lines. However, it was not to be. Gaius and his brother, Lucius Caesar, died suddenly within two years of each other. Now in his late sixties, and with his succession arrangements thrown into complete disarray, Augustus made urgent alternative provisions that would ultimately pave the way for Nero's succession some fifty years later.

In AD 4 Augustus adopted his last surviving grandson, the fifteen-year-old Agrippa Postumus, son of Julia and her second husband, Agrippa. He also adopted his stepson Tiberius, perhaps prompted by his mother Livia. She finally saw her eldest son, who had been passed over for so many years, recognised as official heir. Yet for Tiberius, already in his mid-forties, the event may well have been marred by yet more bitterness, as it was clear that he was merely meant to serve as a placeholder for a future successor. Before Tiberius' own adoption, Augustus had obliged him to adopt the eighteen-year-old Germanicus, his nephew. Tiberius' actual son, Drusus, about the same age as Germanicus, would naturally have been his father's successor. After the premature demise of others, Augustus probably intended to identify a number of potential heirs in case there should be further unforeseen deaths. However, it inevitably sowed the seeds of distrust and rivalry between different branches of the imperial family that would haunt the next decades.

Through the complexities of dynastic interrelations, Germanicus was Augustus' great-nephew and Livia's grandson. His marriage to Agrippina the

Fig. 13
Aureus of Mark Antony, with a portrait of his wife Octavia on the reverse
38 BC
Uncertain mint
Gold
Weight 7.9 g
British Museum
1842,0523.1

Augustus' sister Octavia played a major part in his political and dynastic plans. Her short-lived marriage to Mark Antony was contracted solely to foster the fragile alliance between the two triumvirs, but it produced two daughters who became the mothers and (great-)grandmothers of future emperors, including Nero.

Fig. 14
Tetradrachm of Mark Antony with Cleopatra on the reverse
c. 36 BC
Minted in Syria
Silver
Weight 14.4 g
British Museum
TC,p237.1.CleMA

Antony divorced Octavia after he became involved with Cleopatra, the Greek queen of Egypt, in opposition to Augustus. Octavia's public image was similar to Livia's and contrasted strongly with that of Cleopatra (here with a royal 'fillet', or diadem). The latter was maligned as a decadent and promiscuous outsider by Augustus and his supporters.

Elder, Augustus' granddaughter, offered a second attempt at uniting the Julian and Claudian lines, as a result of which Germanicus and his children would occupy a special place among future generations of the ruling family. Germanicus' sister Livilla, after the death of Gaius, was now given to Tiberius' son Drusus, while their brother Claudius, who suffered from various physical impairments, was deliberately kept out of the limelight.

In the years leading up to these arrangements, Augustus' relationship with his daughter Julia had broken down irretrievably. In 2 BC she was charged with adultery (a delicate moment, as Augustus had just introduced new legislation to promote family values) and accused of plotting against him. Julia's third marriage, to Tiberius, was dissolved, she was banished and several of the young men around her were forced to commit suicide or exiled. Her treatment foreshadowed the fate of countless other female family members. Moreover, and for reasons that are not entirely clear, Augustus revoked Agrippa Postumus' adoption in AD 6 and exiled him, thus eliminating his last surviving grandson from the line of succession. Various factions had by now it seems begun to anticipate Augustus' demise and tried to position themselves accordingly.

Augustus passed away on 19 August AD 14 and was deified by senatorial decree. In his testament, he asked that his widow Livia should be awarded the honorific title *Augusta*. Livia's son Tiberius had been the heir designate for ten years, but his transition to power was not smooth. While the senate quickly voted Tiberius the same executive powers as Augustus had enjoyed, thereby confirming him in the role of *princeps*, there was considerable unrest among the military, with some units in Pannonia and Germany in open rebellion (Fig. 15). Although Tiberius had been the leading general of his generation, he was not popular among the troops. They saw in the change of ruler an opportunity to improve their conditions after years of service spent in warfare and hardship.

Germanicus, charismatic and married to Augustus' granddaughter, was regarded with much more affection than Tiberius (Fig. 16). His soldiers even

Fig. 15
Statue of Tiberius
AD 19–23
Sanctuary of Diana Nemorensis,
Nemi, Italy
Marble
H. 212 cm
Ny Carlsberg Glyptotek,
Copenhagen
IN 709

This commanding statue was
found in a room with three niches
for sculptures and may have
formed part of a group with images
of Germanicus and Drusus the
Younger. The raised right arm
probably held a lance, in a Jupiter-
like pose. The simple coiffure
dates the portrait to after Tiberius'
accession in AD 14, when this
new portrait type was created; his
earlier hairstyles were more closely
matched to Augustus' own.

Fig. 16
Statue of Germanicus
AD 1–50
Augusteum of Rusellae, Etruria, Italy
Marble
H. 219 cm, W. 170 cm
Museo Nazionale Archeologico e
d'Arte della Maremma, Grosseto
97735

Germanicus' portrait formed part
of a dynastic group alongside
images of Tiberius and possibly his
son Drusus the Younger. Augustus

had obliged Tiberius to adopt
Germanicus in AD 4, which put him
second in the line of succession
after Tiberius himself. Germanicus'
premature death prevented him
from becoming *princeps*, but his
son Caligula and grandson Nero
continued the family line, and both
acceded to the throne. Rusellae's
Augusteum was the assembly hall
of the local *augustales*, mostly
wealthy freedmen who promoted
the emperor cult in order to further
their own social advancement.

demanded that he should take over the principate instead. This set a dangerous precedent. However, through an offer of money combined with other benefits, Germanicus finally induced his men to recognise Tiberius. Despite this clear demonstration of loyalty, whatever bond of trust that may have existed between Tiberius and Germanicus was now compromised. According to the sources, which perhaps reflected later rumours, Tiberius became envious of Germanicus and suspicious of his future aspirations.

For the next two years, Germanicus campaigned ardently in Germany.[17] Eventually, Tiberius ordered him back, granting Germanicus a triumph that only added to his immense popularity in Rome. In practice, Tiberius' decision marked the end of Roman offensive operations aimed at extending the Empire beyond the Rhine (Figs 17a and b).[18] Thereafter, he dispatched Germanicus on a major diplomatic assignment to the East. After a lengthy inspection tour that took in Greece, Asia Minor and Egypt, Germanicus suddenly fell ill in Syria in AD 19 and died. Rumours immediately spread that the Roman governor there, Piso, had poisoned him on Tiberius' behalf. Germanicus' widow Agrippina had by then borne him nine children, of whom three boys and three girls survived into adulthood.[19] Germanicus' tragic fate and the sad sight of his bereaved family moved the people of Rome when she returned to the city with his ashes.[20]

After Germanicus' death, Tiberius' son Drusus remained a clear candidate to succeed his father. Yet four years later, in AD 23, he too passed away. Drusus' marriage to Livilla had produced twin boys (one of whom died in infancy) and a daughter. The surviving boy, Tiberius' grandson Tiberius Gemellus, became the emperor's obvious heir, but his cousins, Germanicus' three sons and Tiberius' grandsons by adoption, were also contenders. All were much older than Gemellus, which put them at an advantage. A bitter rivalry between these two branches of the imperial family and their supporting factions escalated dangerously over the following years.[21]

It was not just family affairs that were difficult. Tiberius' relationship with the senate had become increasingly strained. While his seniority and military reputation commanded respect, he lacked the immense patience, tact and subtlety that the first *princeps* had shown towards senators in order to maintain the illusion of the 'Restored Republic'. Tiberius, in contrast to Augustus, came to abhor the outrageous sycophancy and occasional obstinacy of the senate. Exchanges which openly acknowledged that real power lay with the *princeps* risked undermining the senators' dignity and made a mockery of the new order.[22] In consequence, Tiberius spent increasing amounts of time away from Rome, and in AD 26 he permanently withdrew to his palatial villa on the island of Capri. The equestrian commander of the Praetorian Guard, Sejanus, now ran affairs in the capital on his behalf. In possession of unprecedented power, Sejanus could manipulate the emperor by controlling the flow of information that reached him. According to rumour, he had already poisoned Drusus in collusion with Livilla, with whom he was said to have had an adulterous affair. Alternatively, he may have pursued the widowed Livilla to enhance his own position and eventually gain paternal control as stepfather over her infant son, Tiberius' grandson and possible heir Gemellus – he repeatedly asked Tiberius for Livilla's hand. This pattern would repeat itself in future decades, with female members of the imperial family and their young children becoming prized trophies of ambitious men with an eye to the throne.

Figs 17a and b
The 'Sword of Tiberius'
About AD 14–16
Mogontiacum (Mainz), Germany
Tin, iron, gold, bronze
L. 58.5 cm, W. 8.7 cm
British Museum
1866,0806.1
Donated by Felix Slade

The 'Sword of Tiberius' was found in the River Rhine, near a major legionary fortress at Mogontiacum. It is typical of the early Julio-Claudian ('Mainz') type. The richly decorated scabbard celebrates concord in the imperial family and a predictable, stable succession. The main scene shows the reigning *princeps* Tiberius, in divine guise, enthroned and flanked by the gods Victory and Mars. He receives a small figure of Victory from Germanicus, his adopted son, who stands in full body armour. This alludes to Germanicus' successful military operations against Germanic tribes between AD 14 and 16 and perhaps his triumph in AD 17. Inscriptions on the shields stress Tiberius' role as guarantor of Roman victories: 'VIC(TORIA) AUG(USTI); FELIC(ITAS) TIBERI(I)'. 'Felicitas' denotes the good luck that comes in battle through divine favour. Below is a portrait medallion of Augustus, the first *princeps*, between double bands of oak leaves; at the bottom a female personification with double axe in front of a sanctuary with military standards, perhaps referencing earlier victories over Alpine tribes. Given the mutinies among the army at the beginning of Tiberius' reign, these scenes were meant to instil trust and loyalty. The sword may have belonged to a centurion or someone of a lower rank – what looks like gold and silver is in fact gilded and tinned brass.

Perhaps at Sejanus' instigation, Germanicus' widow Agrippina and her first-born son were banished to different islands in AD 29.[23] Two years later, the senate declared her second son a *hostis*, or enemy of the state; he was imprisoned on the Palatine and died there in AD 33. This left Germanicus' youngest son, Gaius, whose nickname Caligula, or 'little boot', came from the soldier's footwear he had worn in his father's camp when a small boy. Germanicus and Agrippina's daughters, Drusilla, Livilla and Agrippina (the Younger), also survived. In AD 30, Tiberius summoned Caligula to Capri, where he supervised his upbringing. Gemellus was around ten at the time and so still too young to succeed, but Caligula had just turned eighteen. A year later Sejanus, for many years a regent in all but name (a period many senators experienced as a time of terror), fell from grace and was executed.

Tiberius, Rome's second *princeps*, died in March AD 37, aged seventy-eight. In his will he shared his fortune in equal parts between his great-nephew (and grandson by adoption) Caligula and his grandson Tiberius Gemellus. The troops acclaimed Caligula on the day Tiberius died, and the senate recognised him as *princeps* two days after that through the customary transfer of powers (Fig. 18). Caligula adopted Gemellus and accorded him the usual honours of an heir apparent, a compromise that avoided questions over succession in the short term.[24]

On his accession, Caligula (born Gaius Julius Caesar, like the dictator, and now Gaius Caesar Augustus Germanicus) was only twenty-four, more than half a century younger than his late predecessor had been. The people of Rome greeted their young *princeps* with genuine enthusiasm; for the past decade they had been deprived of the presence of a ruler in the city, and the largesse that usually came with it. As the son of the war hero Germanicus and great-grandson of Augustus, Caligula held great promise for an invigorated principate (Fig. 19).[25]

He took great care of his sisters, whom he honoured by including their names in the mandatory vows and good wishes for the emperor – an extraordinary and unparalleled act of reverence for female members of the imperial family. In addition, they were awarded the right to attend circus games in the imperial box.[26] Coins of the period show the three young women (Fig. 20), close in age and according to literary sources great beauties, and dynastic statue groups honoured them together with their brother.

Yet Caligula's youth and relative inexperience in dealing with the senate also posed difficulties. The patriarchal norms of Roman society prized seniority and maturity, and the long reigns of Augustus and Tiberius had accustomed senators to mature, even elderly men as *principes*, despite Augustus' own youthful beginnings.[27] Caligula reached out to his only senior male relative, his uncle Claudius, who finally entered the senate after years on the sidelines and now became his colleague as consul.[28] More influential advisors were Macro, prefect of the Praetorian Guard, and the senior senator Marcus Iunius Silanus, the father of Caligula's recently deceased wife. Following their counsel, Caligula stated his intentions to work with the senate and put an end to the *maiestas* (treason) trials that had marred the end of Tiberius' reign. Tiberius was interred in the Mausoleum of Augustus, but not deified (the senators would rather have condemned his memory). Caligula instead dedicated the Temple of the Deified Augustus amid a year of splendid festivities accompanied by lavish gifts to the Guards, the army and the people of the capital.

Fig. 18
Portrait of Caligula
AD 37–41
Provenance unknown
Marble, with traces of original
pigment
H. 28 cm
Ny Carlsberg Glyptotek,
Copenhagen
IN 2687

Only one official version of
Caligula's portrait was created
during his short reign. This marble
head is remarkable for the visible
traces of its original polychrome
finish that have been preserved
(for example in the detail of the
eyes with pupils and eyelashes,
and individual strands of hair
extending the carved sideburns).
Scientific research has confirmed
in recent years that all Roman
marble sculpture was originally
painted, including the skin parts.
Most of Caligula's portraits were
removed, re-carved or destroyed
after his assassination, adding
to the significance of this
particular sculpture.

Fig. 19
Miniature bust of Caligula
AD 37–41
Probably from Italy
Bronze
H. 24 cm, W. 7.4 cm
Colchester Museums

Small-scale busts of this type were
linked to private devotion. Images
of emperors were often added to
lararia (shrines of the household
gods). The bust rises from a
globe, which rests on a base with
an ornate, inlaid palmette frieze.
Caligula's images took on ever
more divine attributes, elevating the
princeps beyond the human realm.
They reflected public expectations
rather than centrally prescribed
models and hint at the growing
gulf between the attitudes of the
princeps towards the senatorial
elite and the population at large.

Fig. 20
Sestertius
AD 37–8
Minted in Rome, Italy
Copper alloy
Weight 29.2 g
British Museum
R.6432

Having lost his older brothers, Caligula (obverse) accorded his sisters Agrippina, Drusilla and Julia Livilla unprecedented honours as soon as he became *princeps*. They were included in official oaths, and represented on coins as the allegorical figures of Securitas, Concordia and Fortuna (Security, Harmony and Good Fortune), as seen here on the reverse. At court banquets they shared places of honour next to their brother. Agrippina gave birth to Nero during the first year of Caligula's reign.

Towards the end of AD 37, to the great distress of the people, the emperor became severely ill; he officially named Drusilla, his favourite sister, as main heir to his fortune and throne. In practice this would have made her husband, his brother-in-law and confidant Marcus Aemilius Lepidus, his successor. Macro and Silanus turned to the official designated heir Gemellus, raising once more the spectre of factional strife. Having recovered, Caligula forced Gemellus and later Silanus to commit suicide, while Macro and many others were accused of a range of crimes and killed or driven to take their own lives. Drusilla herself died the following year. Stricken with grief, Caligula honoured her memory in extravagant ways; she was deified by decree of the senate, the first woman of the imperial family to achieve this status.

A major senatorial conspiracy against Caligula came to light at the beginning of AD 39; numerous high-ranking plotters were put to death. The emperor's relationship with the senate deteriorated rapidly and finally collapsed altogether. With retaliatory cruelty, Caligula set out to humiliate individual senators and the senatorial body as a whole, exposing their lack of any real authority despite their exalted status. The threatened appointment to the senate of Caligula's favourite racing horse, Incitatus, was one such calculated, and public, insult. To senators, it was a sign of *insania* or madness. Yet it was so only in a metaphorical sense, as an extreme departure from the tactful political theatre of Augustus' 'Restored Republic'. It came as such a fundamental threat to their very identity, however, that some among the senatorial elite may have genuinely doubted Caligula's mental state.[29] The whole concept of the principate as a carefully balanced compromise that traded dignity for power was now at the point of collapse.

Eager to father an heir, Caligula married several women in quick succession, the fourth and last of whom was Milonia Caesonia, who bore him a daughter. His widowed brother-in-law Aemilius Lepidus found his prospects rapidly diminishing and turned to his late wife's sisters Agrippina and Livilla in an attempt to recover his position. The three of them, together with the two consuls in office and the governor of Upper Germany, Gnaeus Cornelius Lentulus Gaetulicus, who commanded one of the Empire's strongest army groups, conspired against the emperor. Caligula had planned a major offensive in Germany – he was, after all, Germanicus' son – and ordered extensive military preparations. He rushed north, caught Gaetulicus unprepared and had him executed, along with Lepidus. Agrippina and Livilla were exiled on politically motivated charges of adultery.[30]

In Rome, a mood of panic spread among the political elite, amid a flood of denunciations. Caligula returned to the city on his twenty-eighth birthday, in August AD 40, after a year's absence.[31] He refused further honours from the senate, which he only attended surrounded by bodyguards, and he kept former consuls' wives and children with him in the palace. Terrified senators began to approach him with gestures of veneration normally reserved for gods, a feature of Hellenistic kingship that he did not discourage. A temple was dedicated to his *numen*, his divine will, with a golden statue of him inside. At court, he relied almost exclusively on freedmen and knights; ritual humiliations of senators continued. During the last months of his reign the principate became an undisguised monarchy. Multiple plots against the emperor were hatched and, after a reign of not even four years, Caligula was assassinated in January AD 41, together with his wife and infant daughter, his only child.

According to tradition, his uncle Claudius was found by a soldier of the Praetorian Guard hiding in the palace, presented at the camp and hailed emperor almost against his will (Fig. 21). The Guards clearly needed a *princeps* in power, as their own status and income depended on the very institution of the principate. It seems more likely that Claudius, along with Caligula's freedman Callistus and others, played an active part in his nephew's demise.[32]

The rise of the Domitii Ahenobarbi

The Domitii Ahenobarbi (Ahenobarbi means 'Redbeards') were a family of considerable prominence that had been closely allied to the reigning Julio-Claudians for several generations.[33] The Ahenobarbi line had produced notable senators and generals in the days of the Republic and a long line of consuls, beginning in 192 BC. Ancestral military successes meant that the clan could hold its own among the status-conscious Roman nobility. A venerable temple of Neptune close to the Circus Flaminius in the Campus Martius publicly proclaimed their fame; it had been dedicated by an ancestor of Nero, also called Gnaeus Domitius Ahenobarbus (with stubborn regularity, Ahenobarbi males were named Gnaeus or Lucius in alternating generations), for a naval victory in the Aegean in the decade between 130 and 120 BC.[34] Several beautiful reliefs, among the earliest examples of this type preserved in Roman art, have been attributed to the base of its cult statue – they show a procession of marine creatures, and elected officials carrying out a census of Roman citizens, perhaps an allusion to Gnaeus' term as *censor* (Figs 22 and 23). A gold coin minted in 42 BC by a later Gnaeus, Nero's great-grandfather and also a fleet commander, depicted the temple and a portrait of his heroic forebear – the thickset facial features oddly reminiscent of the mature Nero, perhaps a family trait (Fig. 24).

In the first century BC, the family was a major player in the protracted internecine conflicts of the dying Republic. Nero's great-great-grandfather, Lucius Domitius Ahenobarbus, ardently opposed Julius Caesar politically and in the field of battle. Income from his vast estates allowed him to hold lavish public games and build a mass following, and he held out the promise of land distribution from his private holdings to his troops.[35] In 49 BC he was taken prisoner during Caesar's siege of Corfinum in central Italy. Pardoned and released, he took up arms again, furnished a small fleet, but died fighting Caesar

Fig. 21
Statue of Claudius
About AD 50 (the top of the head
and left hand with sword are
restored)
Forum of Gabii, near Rome, Italy
Marble
H. 194 cm
Musée du Louvre, Paris
MA 1231

This statue formed part of a
dynastic group that included a
similar figure of Claudius' older
brother Germanicus. The heroic
body type (nude, except for a
mantle draped around the hips
and left arm) evokes divine images
from ancient Greece. Details of
the coiffure indicate that Claudius'
portrait was re-carved from
a likeness of his nephew and
predecessor Caligula.

in the decisive battle of Pharsalus in Greece a year later.[36] All this turned him into a widely known public figure.

His son Gnaeus, having also been captured and pardoned by the dictator, may have been among the conspirators who planned Caesar's assassination in 44 BC. After Caesar's death he left Rome, like many other nobles, and joined the senatorial party that gathered in the East. He took command of their naval forces in the Adriatic, where a victory gained him the title of *imperator*, which he proudly advertised on coins (Fig. 25). In 40 BC, he reached a political settlement with Mark Antony and joined his side. Just before the decisive naval battle of Actium in September 31 BC, having already voiced concerns about Antony's increasing reliance on Cleopatra, queen of Egypt, he switched allegiance to Octavian (the future Augustus). This was an act of great political symbolism and the beginning of the close link between the two families.

Presumably to strengthen this new alliance, in 29 BC Augustus admitted Gnaeus' son Lucius into the patrician class, a notable advancement as until then the family had belonged to the plebeian nobility. Two years later Lucius married Antonia the Elder, daughter of Augustus' sister Octavia and Mark

Figs 22 and 23
Frieze slabs from the so-called 'Altar of Domitius Ahenobarbus'
Late 2nd century BC
Marble
H. 80 cm, W. 560 cm
Musée du Louvre, Paris
MA 975 (top)

Glyptothek, Munich
Inv. Nr. 239 (bottom)

These reliefs have been attributed to the base of a cult image in the Temple of Neptune on the Campus Martius, Rome (see Fig. 24).

They show a census of Roman citizens, soldiers and accompanying sacrifices (Fig. 22, top), and a procession of marine creatures (Fig. 23, bottom). They were found in the general vicinity of the Temple of Neptune, but their attribution to the building and the link with the Ahenobarbi remains hypothetical.

Antony. The match is a clear indication of Augustus' regard for the Ahenobarbi's power and influence and the support they could lend him in consolidating his new position as *princeps*. Lucius' career progressed accordingly. While governor of Illyricum, he led a Roman army north and reached deep into Germany, erecting altars to Augustus beyond the River Elbe in territory never before reached by a Roman general. In recognition, Augustus awarded him triumphal insignia and he subsequently operated alongside the imperial princes Tiberius and Drusus, Augustus' stepsons (Drusus was also Lucius' brother-in-law) in Germany; another sign of Augustus' trust in his ability and loyalty. Lucius was later appointed one of the executors of Augustus' will.

Lucius' marriage to Antonia produced three children, a son, predictably called Gnaeus, and two daughters, Domitia and Domitia Lepida. The boy was thus a grandson of Mark Antony and a great-nephew of Augustus, as well as a cousin of the imperial princes Germanicus and Claudius. The family's distinction led many archaeologists to believe that they may have been represented among Augustus' relations on the major monument dedicated in his honour by the senate, the Ara Pacis or Altar of Peace (Fig. 26). Even if this is not the case, statues of famous

Fig. 24
Aureus
AD 42
Uncertain mint
Gold
Weight 8.2 g
British Museum
1844,0425.467.A

This aureus was minted in AD 42
by Gnaeus Domitius Ahenobarbus,
Nero's great-grandfather. The
reverse shows the temple of
the sea god Neptune in Rome,
probably dedicated by an earlier
Ahenobarbus, whose portrait
may be on the obverse, for naval
victories in the Aegean. Gnaeus
Domitius Ahenobarbus carried
the title 'imperator' ('IMP' on the
reverse), following a naval victory
under his command in the civil war.

Fig. 25
Denarius
About AD 41
Uncertain mint
Silver
Weight 3.8 g
British Museum
1867,0101.1247

Like the aureus (Fig. 24), this
denarius extols Gnaeus Domitius
Ahenobarbus' naval victories and
illustrious ancestry.

The reverse shows a victory
monument (trophy), made of
captured armour, on a ship's prow.
The obverse depicts a bearded
Ahenobarbus ancestor. According
to family mythology, their forebear
Lucius Domitius Ahenobarbus'
beard had been turned red (literally
'bronze-coloured') by the divine
twins Castor and Pollux, and many
of his descendants later sported
red beards.

Ahenobarbi, particularly those who had attained consulships or celebrated triumphs, must have been prominent in Rome's cityscape.[37]

The family's close links with their Julio-Claudian relatives continued into the next generation. In AD 28, Tiberius arranged the marriage between Gnaeus Domitius Ahenobarbus and Agrippina the Younger, Germanicus' oldest daughter, who was not yet thirteen. Tiberius personally attended the pair's betrothal at Misenum and ordered a lavish wedding ceremony in Rome.[38] Four years later, in AD 32, Gnaeus served as consul for a whole year, by then a particular honour as the period of tenure had long since been shortened to allow more senators access to the coveted office. Towards the end of AD 36, however, something must have soured his relationship with the emperor, for he was accused of an incestuous relationship with his sister Domitia Lepida, in what seems a trumped-up charge. There is little specific detail, but he is said to have escaped trial only because of Tiberius' death in March AD 37.[39]

Gnaeus and Agrippina's only child, Lucius Domitius, the future Nero, was born on 15 December in the same year, ten years into their marriage and nine months after Caligula's accession. Not only was Gnaeus now the brother-in-law of the reigning emperor, but the family was also further rehabilitated in AD 38 through another dynastic union. It was then that Caligula's uncle Claudius married Valeria Messalina, the daughter of Domitia Lepida.

This good fortune, however, was not to last. Gnaeus was soon embroiled in the factional strife at court. In AD 39 his wife Agrippina was exiled (see p. 47) and Gnaeus died the following year on his estates at Pyrgi in Etruria. Two-year-old Lucius Domitius was in effect orphaned and taken in by his paternal aunt, Domitia Lepida, to be brought up in her household. Suetonius records that he was tutored

Fig. 26
Ara Pacis Augustae, 'Altar of Augustan Peace', south frieze
13–9 BC
Rome, Italy
Marble
H. 160 cm, L. 822 cm (approx., south frieze)
Museo dell'Ara Pacis

The Ara Pacis Augustae was commissioned on 4 July 13 BC to commemorate Augustus' return to Rome, following three years on a military and inspection tour of Spain and France. It was located on the Campus Martius and consecrated on 30 January 9 BC. The main frieze depicts Augustus, members of his family, priests and other officials in a religious procession. The figures at the eastern end of the south frieze, including two couples with young children (pictured), have often been identified as members of Nero's family, but their precise identities remain conjectural. Augustus' niece Antonia the Younger, her husband Drusus and their son Germanicus (Nero's maternal grandfather) are thought to be on the left and on the right may be Antonia's older sister Antonia the Elder and her husband Lucius Domitius Ahenobarbus (Nero's paternal grandfather), together with a son and daughter.

there by a barber and a dancer, but this seems little more than a slur; if there is anything to it, it only hints at Domitia Lepida's wealth and extensive household staff.[40] Modern commentators have speculated about the psychological impact Nero's father's death and his mother's exile may have had on the young boy. The early death of a parent was common, however, and children often grew up in a step-family. Emotional warmth in elite Roman households was provided by nurses and nannies rather than parents.[41] Nero's experience therefore would not have been all that different from that of his peers.

In many ways, the Domitii Ahenobarbi were a typical family of the Republican nobility: wealthy, competitive and tied into a complex web of alliances or enmity with other clans. A large family mausoleum on the Hill of the Gardens (the modern Pincio) above the Campus Martius and a grand mansion by the Forum, the Domus Domitiana, were imposing markers of the family's status. What set them apart from other senatorial clans was their close and enduring links to the Julio-Claudian family and concomitant vested interest in the continuation of the principate. Other noble families saw the ultimate rise of the family under Nero as a provocative challenge and constant reminder of their own unrealised ambitions. To them, Nero remained first and foremost a Domitius Ahenobarbus; they felt that their claims to the throne were just as strong as his.

Claudius and his reign: Messalina, Agrippina and the young Nero

Less than three weeks after Claudius' turbulent accession in January AD 41, Messalina gave birth to a son, Tiberius Claudius Caesar Germanicus, later known as Britannicus. The event must have seemed a most fortunate omen for the new principate. Over the following months, Claudius proudly took to holding the little

boy when addressing his soldiers, and at the games he sat him on his lap and presented him to the adoring crowds.[42] Court art and official coinage celebrated the emperor's young family and prospective heir (Figs 27–30).[43] Messalina's position was greatly enhanced, even if Claudius declined the title of *Augusta* for her, which had been offered by the senate. However, he publicly celebrated his own ancestry with monuments in honour of his late father Drusus, and a year into his reign he induced the senate to deify his grandmother Livia, all measures intended to enhance his and his immediate family's prestige.

These public gestures and their reflections in the official imagery were important, for even if Claudius could now cautiously entertain longer-term dynastic aspirations, for the moment his position as *princeps* remained heavily compromised. Caligula's assassination and the subsequent debate in the senate about the future of the principate had demonstrated a fundamental weakness of Claudius' authority. The names of several descendants of late Republican grandees and members of the wider imperial family who were more closely related to Augustus than Claudius had been put forward before the Praetorians' declaration had ended attempts to install a senate-nominated candidate.

Perhaps as a direct consequence of his comparatively weak position and a lack of alternatives, Claudius' response was a determined attempt to conciliate the nobility and reset the relationship between *princeps* and senate. He reached out to potential rivals and their families and offered them prestigious offices and marriage alliances. To achieve these ends, he ruthlessly coerced the women in his wider family to acquiesce, invoking his combined authority as *princeps* and *pater familias*, as his predecessors had done before him. His new noble relations, however, did not abandon their own ambitions as he had hoped.[44] The repercussions of his failure to establish a loyal network affected the rest of his own and much of Nero's reign and are crucial to a proper understanding of many of Nero's (and Agrippina's) later actions.

Claudius' dynastic arrangements began with his own daughters (Fig. 30) and were intended to accommodate some particularly influential families. His older daughter (by a previous wife), Claudia Antonia, was given in marriage to Gnaeus Pompeius Magnus, who had a pedigree of astonishing grandeur. On his father's side he was a descendant of Marcus Licinius Crassus and on his mother's of 'Pompey the Great' (Gnaeus Pompeius Magnus), two of the titans of late Republican politics who had formed the first triumvirate with Julius Caesar. His family must have retained much of their ancestors' combined wealth and powerful client networks. For this very reason Caligula had prohibited the young man's use of the ostentatious cognomen 'Magnus', but Claudius now allowed him to reinstate it (see Fig. 32, p. 60).[45] By chance, the family's tomb in Rome was discovered in the nineteenth century; it contained portraits of various forebears, including the two triumvirs, and gives the best sense of how families of the Roman nobility displayed their distinguished ancestry, something otherwise only described in the literary sources.[46] Magnus' father, Marcus Licinius Crassus Frugi, was given a major military command in Africa and other distinctions.

Claudius' younger daughter, Claudia Octavia, then aged only between one and two, was betrothed to Lucius Iunius Silanus, a great-great-grandson of Augustus through descent from his daughter Julia. His paternal family still carried the resonant cognomen Torquatus, after a torc adopted as an emblem by a famous Republican ancestor following his victories over Celts. This, too, had been temporarily prohibited by Caligula, as a symbol of dangerous pride and aspiration, and Silanus' father, a leading senator, had perished under that emperor.

At the same time, Claudius' widowed mother-in-law Domitia Lepida (who was also his cousin) was made to marry Gaius Appius Iunius Silanus. Older and more experienced than Claudius' new (and prospective) sons-in-law, he may have been intended as a senior placeholder while the others embarked on their careers.[47] This would have provided a potential male guardian until Claudius' own son came of age, modelled perhaps on Augustus' arrangements for his grandsons and adopted heirs.[48]

Claudius also recalled his nieces Agrippina and Livilla from exile (see p. 186). Livilla returned to her husband Marcus Vinicius, who had escaped the earlier purges. Agrippina, widowed by the death of Gnaeus during her banishment, was reunited with her son Lucius Domitius (the future Nero), from whom she had been separated for more than a year (Fig. 31). The boy's paternal inheritance, which Caligula had effectively claimed for himself, was also restored.

Later the same year, Agrippina married the extraordinarily wealthy Gaius Passienus Crispus, a man many years her senior. He first had to divorce his then wife, who happened to be Agrippina's sister-in-law, Domitia (the older sister of Gnaeus Domitius Ahenobarbus and Domitia Lepida), and relations between the two women never recovered.[49] Suetonius claims that Agrippina had actively looked for a powerful new husband and first unsuccessfully pursued the wealthy and influential Servius Sulpicius Galba.[50] With minor reservations, most modern historians have accepted this narrative. It seems, however, quite inconceivable that a young woman of the imperial family would have been allowed this level of independence. As events would show, it is more likely that Claudius himself assigned Agrippina's new husband, perhaps after initially approaching Galba. Together with Livilla's husband Marcus Vinicius, Galba had been one of those named as a potential *princeps* following Caligula's death. An offer of marriage to his niece might seem a plausible attempt by Claudius to accommodate a rival, who was at the time in command of several legions in Upper Germany.[51] However, Galba declined. Twenty-seven years later he rebelled against Nero and usurped the throne for himself (see p. 264). Passienus, on the other hand, was a noted orator and legal mind, and had been consul in AD 27. In addition to his wealth, he may have offered stability and simply forestalled interest from other, more ambitious, men who might view a widowed imperial relative and her young child as a highly desirable prize. Pliny the Elder states that Passienus Crispus became all the more famous for having Nero as his stepson.[52]

Whatever the case, Claudius' new policy of alliances very soon began to show signs of strain, as some of the nobles he had tried to accommodate were involved in conspiracies against him. The sources (although Tacitus' account for the years from AD 41 to 47 is mostly lost) begin to turn to his wife Messalina, and then to Agrippina, who are singled out as driving forces behind many of Claudius' retaliations against some of the senators and knights involved. It has long been recognised that the ensuing tale of female rivalry and intrigue should be treated with extreme caution.[53] There can be little doubt that the influence these women could exert within the court, and the public recognition Claudius extended towards them, provoked strong resentment among the senatorial authors involved (see p. 176). They described the women around Claudius in extremely negative terms; in particular, they characterised them as sexual

Fig. 28
Sardonyx gem with portraits of Messalina and her two children (?)
Around AD 40; 17th century (enamel setting)
Sardonyx, enamel
H. 9.3 cm, W. 7.9 cm
Bibliothèque nationale de France
camée.277

The woman in the centre wears a laurel wreath and has the hairstyle of a Julio-Claudian princess. She bears close resemblance to the portrait in Fig. 27. By her side are two small figures that represent allegorical figures or young children of slightly different ages. Both were altered later in antiquity. If the woman portrayed is Messalina, the other figures may be her children by Claudius: her young son Britannicus in the horn of plenty, and her daughter Claudia Octavia.

Precious cameos of this type were created for the court and circulated among the imperial family and members of the senatorial aristocracy.

Fig. 29
Didrachm
AD 43–8
Minted in Caesarea Mazaca (modern Turkey)
Silver
Weight 6.7 g
British Museum
1893,0804.3

On the obverse is a portrait of Messalina ('MESSALINA AUGUSTI', Messalina, wife of Augustus [Claudius]). On the reverse are Claudius' three children: Britannicus in the centre, flanked by Claudia Octavia and their older half-sister Claudia Antonia (with horn of plenty).

Fig. 30
Glass *phalera*
AD 41–54
Camulodunum (Colchester), England
Glass, in a bronze or iron setting
H. 5.6 cm, W. 5.2 cm
British Museum
1870,0224.2
Bequeathed by Felix Slade

Phalerae were given out to soldiers as marks of distinction, like modern medals. They often showed portraits of members of the imperial family, as the *princeps* was commander-in-chief and wanted to ensure loyalty among his soldiers. The portraits here have been identified as Claudius and his three children (shown behind his shoulders and in front of his chest). The *phalera* is preserved with its original metal setting. It would have been stitched to leather straps and worn over body armour, normally as part of a larger set. More elaborate *phalerae* for higher ranks were made of silver.

Fig. 31
**Miniature portrait of Agrippina
the Younger**
AD 37–9
Chalcedony
H. 9 cm, W. 5.5 cm, D. 5.2 cm
British Museum
1907,0415.1

This exquisitely carved likeness
in semi-precious stone depicts a
young woman with the elaborate
coiffure worn by Julio-Claudian
princesses. Her hair is parted in
the centre and styled in parallel
waves that are drawn to the nape
of the neck, where they were
fastened into a looped queue.
Small ringlets frame her forehead
below the waves.

Several life-sized marble versions
of this portrait-type are known.
They originally belonged to
full-length statues or busts.
The facial features bear a strong
resemblance to other members
of the Claudian family. The woman
probably is Agrippina the Younger,
although her sisters Drusilla and
Livilla, or even Messalina, have
also been proposed.

The earlobes were drilled for the
insertion of earrings, presumably in
gold or silver, or miniature pearls.
The head was originally inserted
into a bust of different material,
perhaps coloured marble.

transgressors, in a very obvious attempt to discredit them on moral grounds.
Claudius, we can be sure, remained firmly in control. Transferring the blame
to the imperial women may have been an attempt by the senate to distract from
its own complicity in passing death sentences on many of the conspirators. For
a critical modern analysis, however, there remains a considerable challenge:
Messalina in particular only emerges through these stories, and it is very hard
to gauge her real role in events (see p. 184).

Before the end of AD 41, Livilla was accused of adultery and exiled again, as
was her alleged paramour, the senator, philosopher and author Lucius Annaeus
Seneca. The true motivation is much more likely to have been political; Seneca
had in the past been accused of involvement in the conspiracy against Caligula,
and Claudius possibly had reason to fear a new plot.[54] Livilla was executed soon
after, but her husband Marcus Vinicius remained in Rome. Perhaps he was
too powerful to be challenged at this point, but Livilla's death served as a stark
warning and weakened his position. Further plots in AD 42 and AD 43 saw
the execution and forced suicide of multiple conspirators. It is likely that the
execution of Appius Silanus, Domitia Lepida's new husband, came about as a
result of his involvement in a failed rebellion, but the sources blame Messalina,
citing the spurious claim that she destroyed him because he had rejected her
advances.[55] Silanus' participation in the early stages of a bigger plot should not
be dismissed entirely. Instigated by Lucius Annius Vincianus, who had also
plotted against Caligula, this conspiracy involved numerous senators, knights
and at least one governor, Scribonianus of Dalmatia. The rebellion collapsed
after five frantic days when the latter's troops, who were only ten days' march
from Rome, chose to remain loyal to Claudius. The protagonists were executed
or took their own lives, and the events are referred to as civil war, *bellum civile*,
hinting at their magnitude.[56] The repercussions were felt for a long time, even if
Claudius immediately made a point of reaching out to the conspirators' relatives,
especially their sons, whom he supported financially and allowed to embark on
senatorial careers.[57]

Another plot led to the execution of Claudius' niece Julia. With her fell
the prefect of the Praetorian Guard, Catonius Iustus. Little is known about
the detail, but the general atmosphere of suspicion and instability at the court
is tangible. The new prefects of the Guard were loyal to Messalina.

It is against this atmosphere that Claudius launched his invasion of Britain
in AD 43. Preparations had been ongoing – in fact, planning may have started
under Caligula – and two new legions had been raised for the purpose. This was
a very costly measure and the first time since Augustus that military capacity had
been increased.[58] The primary motivation may well have been an attempt to
stabilise Claudius' rule through the prestige gained from conquering new lands
'beyond the Ocean', rather than more specific military or economic
considerations. For this purpose, Claudius briefly joined the campaign in person
and witnessed the storming of Camulodunon (Colchester), the capital of one
of the main tribal federations in the south-east of Britain (see p. 98). He was
accompanied by a large entourage of courtiers, friends and relatives, no doubt
partly to keep his eye on them rather than leaving them behind in Rome while
he was absent. Among those with Claudius were Marcus Licinius Crassus Frugi,
his sons-in-law Gnaeus Pompeius Magnus and Lucius Iunius Silanus, Marcus
Vinicius, as well as Servius Sulpicius Galba. The generals included Titus Flavius

Fig. 32
**Inscribed altar of Gnaeus
Pompeius Magnus**
c. AD 47
Licinian Tomb, Rome, Italy
Marble
H. 70 cm, W. 56 cm, D. 120 cm
Museo Nazionale Romano, Rome
78163

The inscription reads: 'CN(AEUS)
POMP[EIUS] CRASSI F(ILIUS)
MEN(ENIA) (TRIBU) MAGNUS
PONTIFEX QUAEST(OR)
TI(BERI) CLAUDI CAESARIS
AUG(USTI) GERMANICI SOCERI
SUI' ('Gnaeus Pompeius Crassi,
son of Magnus of the Menenia
Tribe, Pontifex, Quaestor father-in-
law of Tiberius Claudius Caesar
Augustus Germanicus').

Even though Magnus and his
father Frugi were executed on
Claudius' orders, they were
commemorated on their funerary
altars in normal fashion.

Fig. 33
Portrait of a young man
1 BC–AD 54
Licinian Tomb, Rome, Italy
Marble
H. 28 cm
Ny Carlsberg Glyptotek,
Copenhagen
Inv. 735

This head was found together
with inscribed funerary altars for
members of the Scribonii, Licinii
Crassi and Calpurnii Pisones. This
extended clan belonged to Rome's
highest nobility. Men of the family
were involved in conspiracies
against the reigning emperors
over several generations; the first
occurred during Tiberius' reign.

The portrait seems to have been
cut from a full-length statue. Its
style and the age of the person
portrayed would fit Gnaeus
Pompeius Magnus, but this
identification remains hypothetical.
Magnus was Claudius' son-in-law
until AD 47, when he was executed
along with his parents. Two of his
brothers were exiled under Nero
(one of them later executed). After
Nero's death, Galba adopted a
third brother as his heir in AD 69,
but he was slain, alongside the new
emperor, on the Forum by forces
loyal to Otho (see p. 272).

Vespasianus (the future emperor Vespasian) and his older brother Titus Flavius Sabinus. Meanwhile Claudius' close ally Lucius Vitellius kept a watchful eye on affairs in the capital. Almost all of these men, or their close relatives, would play a prominent role at the end of Nero's reign twenty-five years later.

Following his success in Britain, Claudius returned to Rome, sending his sons-in-law ahead to inform the senate. Claudius was awarded the epithet 'Britannicus' ('Victor over the Britons'), which he passed on to his son. A year later, in AD 44, he celebrated a spectacular triumph in the capital. Crassus Frugi was awarded triumphal ornaments and rode behind Claudius' chariot; his son, Pompeius Magnus, and Silanus flanked Claudius when he ascended the Capitol to offer sacrifice.

The young Nero, now aged six, undoubtedly witnessed the spectacle. His stepfather, Passienus Crispus, had received the rare honour of a second consulship for this year from Claudius, no doubt in recognition of his marriage to the emperor's niece. He had already served as governor of the province of Asia in AD 43 (possibly accompanied by Agrippina and Nero, although the sources are silent on this).[59] Nero's education in these years was entrusted to two freedmen tutors named Beryllus and Anicetus; he seems to have been fond of them, for he later gave them important offices at court and in the military.[60] By AD 47 at the latest, Passienus Crispus died, leaving his large fortune to Agrippina and his stepson.

The same year saw the sudden downfall of Gnaeus Pompeius Magnus, who was killed, as were both his parents (Figs 32 and 33).[61] Perhaps they had been implicated in a plot, or Messalina feared their power should Claudius die. Another grandee to fall was Valerius Asiaticus, a wealthy provincial from Vienne in Gaul, whose connections and influence (at one point he was Caligula's brother-in-law) may have been a threat. Tacitus states that Messalina coveted Asiaticus' extensive *horti* or gardens in Rome, and that Asiaticus had an affair with a woman who was also Messalina's rival for the affections of the famous mime Mnester and could now be conveniently done away with as part of the purge, a tradition baffling in its malicious triviality. More to the point, Asiaticus had been yet another powerful individual named as possible *princeps* in AD 41.[62]

Clearly under pressure, Claudius assumed the consulship again in AD 47. To shore up popular support, he decided to hold spectacular *ludi seculares* ('secular games'). As part of these festivities, normally only held once a century, he also scheduled a 'Game of Troy' (see p. 145).[63] The *Lusus Troiae* was an equestrian pageant performed by Rome's gilded youth that had first been introduced by Augustus. It celebrated Rome's mythical links with ancient Troy through the Julian family's close ties to the wandering Trojan hero Aeneas, whom they claimed as their ancestor and whose descendants would bring about Rome's foundation. The main equestrian demonstration was held in the Circus Maximus in front of huge crowds. Nine-year-old Nero, who was passionate about horses from his earliest boyhood, had been selected to take part among other young nobles (Fig. 34) and he rode alongside Claudius' six-year-old son Britannicus. According to the sources, Nero performed particularly well, pleasing the crowd and attracting far greater applause and general praise than his younger relative.[64] This event showed, for the first time, Nero's confidence and performing talent in front of crowds, and it alerted Claudius to his great-nephew's potential.

Messalina, so the sources claim, observed the newly widowed Agrippina's closeness to Claudius and Nero's increasing prominence with growing suspicion,

Fig. 34
Cheek piece from a Roman military helmet
AD 1–50
Bronze, iron, remnants of white alloy
H. 18 cm, W. 15 cm
Archäologisches Museum Frankfurt
23342

The portrait on this piece of armour depicts a Julio-Claudian prince with a laurel wreath and a torc around his neck, an indication that he takes part in the equestrian *Lusus Troiae* or 'Game of Troy' in Rome.

even plotting the young boy's murder. Much of this is probably based on gossip, as the confusing accounts surrounding one of Nero's trinkets, a snake bracelet, demonstrate (Figs 35a and b). At any rate, in October of the following year, AD 48, Messalina herself became embroiled in a court conspiracy. As ever, the true circumstances are wrapped up in a lurid tale of sexual intrigue and hard to recover. In a fit of mad passion she is said to have fallen for a handsome young consul-designate, Gaius Silius, and to have 'married' him in a wild ceremony at Ostia.[65] Claudius, alerted by his freedman Narcissus, finally confronted her; Silius was executed and Messalina made to commit suicide. Nothing is certain; modern scholars who have tried to find a more rational explanation have wondered if Messalina tried to bolster her own position, in case Claudius should die or finally fall victim to a plot (yet another attempt on his life was foiled in AD 47). Silius is said to have offered to adopt her son Britannicus, which would have strengthened his claim to the throne and ensured her safety. Another possibility is that Claudius' freedmen felt threatened by her.[66] To the Roman public, these events must have come as a complete surprise as they had been surrounded by images that celebrated Messalina as dutiful wife and mother (see Fig. 27, p. 54). These were now removed or destroyed, a factor that makes the identification of her portrait difficult.

The circumstances of Messalina's death left Claudius exposed and vulnerable. A well-connected new wife might enable him to rebuild a network. He now also, perhaps for the first time, had a free choice in the matter; Caligula had probably approved, if not arranged, his previous union with Messalina. In an extraordinary passage of his *Annals*, Tacitus aims to reconstruct the arguments informing Claudius' eventual choice of wife by having the emperor's most influential freedmen advisors each present a candidate and praise her relative merits in open council.[67] While it is conceivable that there were rival factions with an interest at stake, the setting seems incongruous and primarily designed to malign every single party involved: Claudius for being a sorry puppet of his freedmen (and wives); the freedmen for their outrageous presumption and arrogance; the women for their female conceit and vulgar

Figs 35a and b
Gold snake bracelet
AD 1–79
Pompeii, Italy
Gold
H. 8 cm, W. 8.8 cm
British Museum
1946,0702.2
Donated by Mrs Marion Whiteford
Acworth JP

Jewellery of this type was popular for many centuries, as snakes were believed to have healing powers and protect the wearer.

According to Suetonius, Nero wore a golden bracelet on his right arm while he was young. Enclosed in it (at his mother Agrippina's behest) was the discarded skin of a snake that one day had been found in his bed. Suetonius refers to different rumours linked to this event: threatened by Agrippina's influence, Messalina sent henchmen to strangle Nero during his noon nap, in order to eliminate him as a rival to Britannicus. Apparently, they were scared off by a snake that darted out from under Nero's pillow (Suetonius, *Nero* 6.4). Tacitus also mentions 'a common tale' that serpents had watched over Nero's infancy, but adds that Nero himself only said that a single snake had once been found in his bedroom (Tacitus, *Annals* 11.11.1).

ambition. According to Tacitus, the freedman Pallas persuaded Claudius with his arguments in favour of Agrippina; these may have been close to Claudius' own reasoning, whether Pallas uttered them or not. Agrippina was the daughter of the popular hero Germanicus and beloved by the people for this very reason; she was a great-granddaughter of Augustus and had a young son of the same line – now the nominal head of the Domitii Ahenobarbi in his own right. By taking Agrippina (and her son) for himself, Claudius would also deny a potential rival. Importantly, Agrippina, who had been partly brought up in her grandmother Livia's household and had already received unprecedented honours at the beginning of Caligula's reign, could bring stability to the principate. Whether Claudius was driven by incestuous lust for his much younger niece (an infatuation allegedly actively encouraged by her), as the sources insinuate at length, seems questionable, and he could perfectly easily have satisfied his carnal desires elsewhere.[68]

Because of the close blood relationship between the participants, a special dispensation had to be granted by the senate. At the beginning of AD 49, Claudius and Agrippina were married. Agrippina secured Seneca's return from exile in Corsica and engaged his services as Nero's tutor. Seneca had been one of the most respected writers and thinkers of the period; in addition to teaching Nero, he was also allowed to resume his senatorial career and served as praetor, a magistrate who ranked below consul.[69] Claudius now dissolved the betrothal of his daughter Claudia Octavia to Lucius Iunius Silanus, whom he expelled from the senate. Silanus apparently had been accused of incest with his own sister, a charge dismissed by Tacitus – in itself a clear indication of how little accusations of sexual impropriety are to be trusted in general.[70] Instead, Nero became Claudia Octavia's new fiancé. In the following year, Claudius formally adopted Nero; Agrippina received the title *Augusta*, the first wife of a living emperor to receive this exceptional honour.[71] Over the next few years, she was awarded further distinctions that allowed her to appear publicly at Claudius' side, including attending ceremonies at which access for women was normally severely restricted. This was described by Dio as 'one of the most remarkable sights of the time' (Fig. 36).[72]

Claudius' manoeuvres after adopting Nero unmistakably singled the boy out as his preferred successor. By making Nero, who had just turned thirteen, assume the *toga virilis*, worn on reaching manhood, a year before the customary minimum age, he signalled that his adopted son was ready to take on additional

Fig. 36
Sestertius
c. AD 50–4
Uncertain mint (Thrace)
Brass
Weight 30.8 g
Private collection

In AD 51, Agrippina received the right to use a *carpentum* (a type of carriage), a privilege normally reserved for a very few senior priestesses. It was one of many honours that reflected the high public status Claudius accorded his new wife. The design of this coin closely copies examples issued during Agrippina's brother Caligula's reign in memory of their mother Agrippina the Elder. It shows a two-wheeled, mule-drawn cart with an ornate covering supported by four draped female statues. In Rome, wheeled traffic was not normally permitted during the day, so for Agrippina this was a significant and conspicuous distinction. The inscription around her portrait on the obverse includes her prestigious new title of *Augusta* and her affiliation: 'AGRIPPINA AUG(USTA) GERMANICI F(ILIA) CAESARIS AUG(USTI)', Agrippina Augusta, daughter of Germanicus, [wife of] Caesar Augustus (i.e. Claudius).

Figs 37, 38 and 39
Set of coins marking Nero's induction as Claudius' designated heir

AD 51–4
Minted in Rome, Italy
Gold
Weight 7.7 g (each coin)
British Museum
1864,1128.250, R.6501, R.6498
(top to bottom)
Donated by Edward Wigan (top);
Bequeathed by Clayton Mordaunt
Cracherode (middle, bottom)

These coins were issued in gold and silver, and probably handed out as official gifts to the soldiers and people. Together with the circus games that were held in Nero's name, they show that Claudius went to great lengths to introduce Nero publicly as his intended successor in AD 51.

Obverse: portrait of Nero, inscribed 'NERONI CLAUDIO DRUSO GERM(ANICO) CO(N)S(ULI) DESIGN(ATO)' – To Nero Claudius Drusus Germanicus, the Consul Designate.

Reverse: a spear and round shield with the inscription 'EQUESTER ORDO PRINCIPI IUVENT(UTIS)' – The Equestrian Order to the Leader of Youth. These objects were official gifts by the Order of Knights to heirs designated as *princeps iuventutis* (the modern term prince is derived from this title).

Obverse: portrait of Nero, inscribed 'NERO CLAUD(IUS) CAES(AR) DRUSUS GERM(ANICUS) PRINC(EPS) IUVENT(UTIS)' – Nero Claudius Caesar Drusus Germanicus Leader of Youth.

Reverse: group of four sacral implements – a *simplum* (ladle), *lituus* (augur's staff), tripod and *patera* (offering bowl); inscribed 'SACERD(US) COOPT(ATUS) IN OMN(E) CONL(EGIUM) SUPRA NUM(ERUM) EX S(ENATUS). C(ONSULTO)'. – Co-opted as a supernumerary into all priestly colleges by decree of the senate.

Obverse: portrait of Claudius with laurel wreath, inscribed 'TI(BERIUS) CLAUD(IUS) CAESAR AUG(USTUS) GERM(ANICUS) P(ONTIFEX) M(AXIMUS) TRIB(UNITIA) POT(ESTAS) P(ATER) P(ATRIAE)' – Tiberius Claudius Caesar Germanicus, Chief Priest, Holder of Tribunician Power, Father of the Fatherland.

Reverse: portrait of Nero, inscribed 'NERO CLAUD(IUS) CAES(AR) DRUSUS GERM(ANICUS) PRINC(EPS) IUVENT(UTIS)' – Nero Claudius Caesar Drusus Germanicus Leader of Youth.

responsibilities. On 4 March AD 51 the senate, no doubt prompted by the *princeps*, awarded Nero the *imperium proconsulare* outside the city of Rome. At the same time, it designated him as consul for the year 58, when he would still be only twenty years old – almost two decades before the normal minimum age;[73] the knights acclaimed Nero as *princeps iuventutis* ('the first among the young'). The following day, he was co-opted as a supernumerary into all the priestly colleges.[74] Coins with Nero's portrait were struck to commemorate these events (Figs 37–9) and in celebration circus games were given in his name. Nero presided over the games in the purple robes of a *triumphator*, whereas Britannicus attended in his child's *toga praetexta* – their relative position in the line of succession thereby made obvious to the masses. In addition, money was distributed in Nero's name to the people and to the troops. He also led the Praetorians on parade, which imbued him with a symbolic aura of military leadership and was a clear sign to the Guards that they should regard him as their future *princeps*.

Since the principate was not formally a hereditary monarchy there was no mechanism by which the ruler could simply pass on power to his chosen successor. This, therefore, was the closest Claudius could get to making his intentions clear to the senate and people, and to ensure that they would follow his wishes concerning the succession. Britannicus' position was now downgraded accordingly, as demonstrated by subtleties of court protocol. His portrait, for example, disappeared from the official coinage, although provincial mints in the Greek East continued to show him together with Nero (Fig. 40) and his image remained part of dynastic sculpture displays. For his part, Britannicus apparently resented Nero's promotion over him. He is said to have continued to greet Nero by his old name, Domitius, even after his adoption.[75] Whether or not this is true is unclear; later authors, beginning with Pliny, certainly refer to Nero disparagingly in this way.[76]

Tacitus records a major famine in Rome for the same year; a violent bread riot ensued, during which Claudius had to be saved from an angry mob by his guard.[77] The fragility of his position was exposed once more, despite the fact that he had invested in infrastructure projects and spectacles for the people. These were measures that Nero would build on.[78] Command of the Praetorians was now concentrated in the hands of a single man – a career officer, Lucius Afranius Burrus – instead of power being shared between two prefects with equal status; individual tribunes and centurions were also changed.[79] Tacitus presents this as an attempt by Agrippina to install her own men in the centre of power, and this has

Fig. 40
Coin with portraits of Nero (obverse) and Britannicus (reverse)
c. AD 50–4
Minted in Pergamon, Mysia (modern Turkey)
Bronze
Weight 3.1 g
British Museum
HPB,p104.54

Inscribed in Greek 'ΝΕΡΩΝ ΚΑΙCAP', Nero Caesar, and 'ΒΡΙΤΑΝΝΙΚΟC ΚΑΙCAP', Britannicus Caesar.

The portrait types used for the two princes on this issue are generic and nearly identical. Local mints in the Greek East continued to show Britannicus alongside Nero.

been largely accepted. Claudius may have had other motives. The following year, AD 52, saw further expulsions from the senate and men sent into exile, including Furius Scribonianus, son of the prominent coup plotter of a decade earlier.[80]

Nero was appointed *praefectus urbi feriarum latinarum causa* that same year. The rather grand title ('prefect of the city [of Rome] on occasion of the Latin holidays') was mostly ceremonial, but of great symbolic significance. It nominally put Nero in charge of the capital while the consuls and other magistrates, usually along with the *princeps*, attended an archaic religious festival in the countryside outside Rome. Suetonius states that the city's most eminent lawyers during this short period competed to bring important cases before Nero, who presided as judge for the first time.[81] This was against normal custom and suggests that they were eager to make themselves known to the heir. As Dio records that Claudius had recently fallen ill, perhaps Nero's succession appeared likely in the not too distant future. Although the exact chronology is uncertain, Dio also says that Nero addressed the senate, vowing to put on horse races should the emperor recover,[82] and that Claudius had issued a proclamation stating that Nero was capable of administering the state if he died. Nero therefore 'became a person of importance and his name was on everybody's lips'.[83] There is no mention of this in Tacitus, perhaps because it did not suit his subsequent narrative, but as a matter of public record the proclamation and letter are unlikely to be inventions.

After a betrothal of four years, Nero and Claudia Octavia were married in AD 53; the young groom was now fifteen, his bride barely thirteen.[84] As well as strengthening Nero's position, this offered Claudius much-needed dynastic reassurance, for even if his natural son Britannicus did not succeed him, he could now expect grandchildren that mixed the Claudian and Julian bloodlines. Claudius' health recovered sufficiently for Nero to hold the promised horse races in magnificent style; Suetonius talks of circus games and animal shows.[85] Nero now also gave a number of speeches before the senate, pleading on behalf of various cities throughout the Empire for reconstruction aid and tax relief, which in each case was granted. This introduced him further to the business of government and made him even better known to the senators. It also brought him the gratitude of the communities concerned.[86]

Source narratives for the following year concentrate entirely on court intrigues; their veracity and detail are impossible to confirm. Perhaps for the world beyond the palace, this was a peculiar period of limbo. Change had been in the air, the moment of succession had seemed near, but then everything settled down again. No doubt members of the various factions at court looked to the future with a mix of anxiety and impatience, depending on their individual interests. These were months rife with speculation and rumour. Tacitus begins his account for AD 54 with an unusually long series of ill omens, building up his readers' expectations towards a dramatic high point.[87]

Domitia Lepida, Nero's aunt and grandmother of Claudia Octavia and Britannicus, became yet another prominent victim of deadly accusations.[88] Tacitus mentions Agrippina as the driving force behind this, citing a general rivalry between the two women, who possessed similar wealth and status and now competed over who could exert greater influence on Nero by holding his affection.[89] However, Domitia's late husband, assigned to her by Claudius himself, had been purged in AD 42 and her daughter Messalina in AD 48, so there may have been other motives behind her downfall, even if she had initially outlasted Messalina's disgrace. She was now executed; Suetonius claims that Nero gave public evidence against her.[90]

Then Claudius collapsed during a banquet in the middle of October; the court physician was summoned, but the emperor died during the night. The sources are uniform in ascribing his death to murder by poison at Agrippina's behest.[91] Their claim has been largely accepted ever since, with some scepticism voiced only in more recent scholarship. Rumours of foul play may have circulated at the time, and the death was represented as murder immediately after Nero's downfall.[92]

According to Tacitus: Agrippina employed a certain Locusta, a woman well versed in the preparation of poisonous substances, to produce a relatively slow-acting toxin. This was administered by Claudius' food taster, the eunuch Halotus, mixed with a particularly fine mushroom that was Claudius' favourite. However, due to Claudius' drunkenness or a sudden bowel movement, the substance did not work. The physician Xenophon, already briefed and on standby, rushed in to apply a second, fast-acting poison. Under the pretence of inducing the emperor to vomit, thereby providing some immediate relief, he applied it on the tip of a feather directly to Claudius' throat. Tacitus' description of the events implies that Claudius was then taken to a different room where he passed away.[93] Suetonius, by contrast, quite openly concedes that the source texts, on which both he and Tacitus relied, gave several different versions both for where and how the poison was administered and for what effect it had on Claudius.[94] Dio similarly presents a slightly altered account.[95] None of this inspires much confidence in the story; rather, it indicates that after Claudius' death various rumours circulated and were combined and embellished in the retelling. Claudius may well have perished after consuming a dish of rare mushrooms, a prized delicacy, which could have contained a toxic specimen – similar incidents are attested for the period, with fatal outcomes but no implication of foul play.[96]

Since Claudius' recent ill health was common knowledge, the source authors needed to find a credible motive for his death being hastened by murder and Agrippina's implication in the deed.[97] They cite two reasons why Agrippina was spurred into action rather than simply biding her time. The first was a purported throwaway remark by a drunken Claudius that it was his 'fate to endure the outrages of his wives, but then to punish them', which she supposedly perceived as an imminent threat to herself.[98] The second was that Claudius had begun to express a vague concern for his natural son Britannicus and possibly had plans to enhance his official status, which might have lessened Nero's standing and Agrippina's influence.[99] However, Claudius at this point had long been committed to his succession arrangements and had signally failed publicly to indicate intentions to the contrary; had he wished to promote Britannicus, he could have done so at any time, as he had done with Nero. Arguably, the hostile tradition stems primarily from a hatred of Agrippina, whose position was already quite unparalleled and would now be enhanced further (see pp. 177–8). A quote from Pliny's *Natural History* hints at this and could not be more explicit in its vitriol. Pliny speaks of the 'notorious crime committed by Agrippina, who, through [mushrooms], poisoned her husband, the Emperor Claudius, and at the same moment, in the person of his son Nero, inflicted another poisonous curse upon the whole world, herself in particular'.[100]

II

POWER
AND
SUCCESSION

A new *princeps*

The transition to Nero's reign following Claudius' death was managed extraordinarily well, an indication that arrangements for a seamless transfer of power had long been in place and lessons from previous interregna had been learnt. Tacitus reports that the announcement of Claudius' death was delayed, so that final preparations could be made and an auspicious moment chosen for Nero's introduction as successor. Meanwhile, access to the palace was tightly controlled and fictitious bulletins of Claudius' recovery were issued. The senate was convened and prayers for Claudius' safety were offered by the consuls and priests.[1] If this account is accurate, these were all highly sensible measures that in later periods of European history became fixed elements of codified transition rituals at some courts.[2] At midday on 13 October AD 54, Nero, accompanied by the Praetorian commander Burrus, stepped outside the palace to address the Praetorian Guard unit on duty, and the men roared their approval (Fig. 41). He was then conveyed in a litter to the Guard's main barracks at the northern edge of the city (see Fig. 163, p. 216). There, Nero gave another speech to the assembled troops, promised them a cash handout equal to the one they had received from Claudius fourteen years earlier (a hefty 15,000 sesterces per head, five times their annual salary) and was duly hailed as *imperator*. The senate, already prepared, followed suit and voted Nero the necessary powers. This differed greatly to the awkward stand-off at the beginning of Claudius' reign.

Claudius' funeral was conducted with ceremony, recalling the last rites for the first *princeps*, Augustus. Specific details are lacking in the sources, but if the same protocol was followed it would have been a major public spectacle, proceeding from the Palatine to the Forum and then along a route that followed in reverse order the path taken by triumphal processions.[3] This led along the Via Sacra (Sacred Way), through the Circus Maximus and the main theatres (so that crowds could get a good view) to a cremation site on the Campus Martius, outside the old city walls. The procession was punctuated at various points by speeches and performances. Nero delivered a traditional eulogy, presumably in the Forum as was customary at such funerals, stressing Claudius' distinguished ancestry and accomplishments.[4] The funerary rites culminated in Claudius' deification by the senate. In both visual impact and political symbolism the ceremony was impressive. It formally enacted the harmony of the orders and was an emphatic reaffirmation of the principate under its young new ruler. To Agrippina, and especially Nero, this would have been an unparalleled opportunity to be observed and celebrated by the masses of the Roman *plebs*. Coins struck during the following year may allude to the event or its aftermath. They show a cart drawn by four elephants with the seated effigies of the deified Claudius and the deified Augustus, and portraits of Nero and Agrippina with their new titles: Nero was now officially the 'son of the deified Claudius' (Fig. 42). This was in stark contrast to the ignoble end of Caligula, who had been hastily buried in his gardens and suffered *damnatio memoriae*, but also of Tiberius, who pointedly had not been deified (see p. 45). Most of all, the official act of deification implied very publicly that the senators, who had not been at all well disposed towards Claudius, were willing to support the new *princeps*; it was a symbolic gesture of goodwill and trust.

Following the funeral, Nero gave a well-received speech in the senate setting out his programme and the guiding rules of his principate. Tacitus' summary of

Fig. 41
Relief with soldiers of the Praetorian Guard
AD 51–2 (the upper left corner and the heads of the three figures in the foreground have been restored)
Rome, Italy
Marble
H. 163cm, W. 134 cm, D. 28 cm
Musée du Louvre, Paris
MA 1079

The *cohortes praetoriae* (Praetorian Guard), first established by Augustus as his personal guard, were a 6,000-strong elite unit based in Rome. Apart from ceremonial duties, they maintained order in the city and formed the most powerful military force in Italy, where no legions were stationed.

Praetorians were recruited mostly from Italy and enjoyed considerable privileges, including shorter service and significantly higher pay than other soldiers. Their ornate armour, including the oval shields seen here, was based on traditional Republican-era models and emphasised their special status.

This relief has been attributed to Claudius' triumphal arch on the Via Lata in Rome, which was dedicated in AD 51 to commemorate his victory over the Britons in AD 43. Dedicatory inscriptions for members of Claudius' family linked to the arch include honours for Nero as *princeps iuventutis* and consul designate.

Fig. 42
Reverse of an aureus
AD 55–6
Minted in Rome, Italy
Gold
Weight 7.6 g
British Museum
R.6511
Bequeathed by Clayton Mordaunt
Cracherode

Four elephants draw an ornate cart on which two enthroned figures sit. The reference to 'DIVUS CLAUDIUS' in Nero's and Agrippina's titles links the scene to Claudius' funeral and deification. The enthroned figures have been interpreted as effigies of Augustus (with radiate crown, lance and offering bowl) in the foreground and Claudius (with radiate crown and eagle-topped sceptre) behind. Wax effigies were often used during imperial funerals. Alternatively, the figures might depict gods whose images were paraded through the crowds as part of the procession.

Fig. 43
Aureus of Claudius
AD 41–2
Minted in Rome, Italy
Gold
Weight 7.7 g
British Museum
R.6481
Bequeathed by Sir Hans Sloane

The portrait of Claudius on the obverse is coupled with a stylised depiction of the Castra Praetoria, the Praetorian Guard's main barracks, on the reverse. A gabled building behind a double gate contains the seated figure of Fides ('Good Faith') and a military standard. The inscription 'IMPER(IUM) RECEPT(UM)' alludes to the imperial acclamation Claudius received from the Praetorians at the beginning of his reign, which forced the senate to acknowledge him as *princeps*.

Fig. 44
Reverse of an aureus
AD 54
Minted in Rome, Italy
Gold
Weight 7.6 g
British Museum
1864,1128.252
Donated by Edward Wigan

The reverses of Nero's accession coinage prominently acknowledge the senate's authority by including an image of the *corona civica*, an oak-leaf wreath, with the formula 'EX S(ENATUS) C(ONSULTO)' and Nero's name in the dative. The senate had first awarded the *corona civica* to Augustus; it was normally given to someone who had saved the lives of fellow citizens. Seneca wrote 'no decoration is more worthy of a prince's rank than that crown [...] this power which saves men's lives by crowds and by nations is godlike' (*De Clementia* 1.26.5).

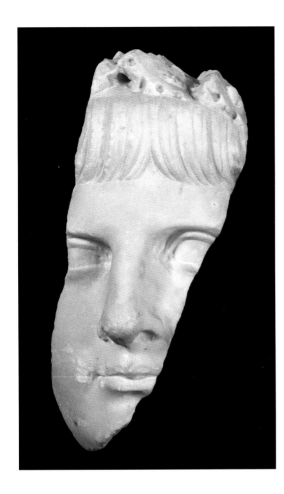

Fig. 45
**Fragment of a portrait of
a youthful Nero**
AD 54–9
Piazza d'Armi, Syracuse, Sicily, Italy
Marble
H. 25 cm, W. 11 cm, D. 14 cm
Parco Archeologico di Siracusa
6383

Nero's official portraits also
showed him with the *corona civica*.
It had been an important attribute
of imperial iconography from the
reign of Augustus, but was now
imbued with fresh symbolism and
promised a new beginning after
Claudius' reign.

the content in a mix of direct and indirect speech should be a fair reflection of
what was announced (records were undoubtedly preserved in the archives for
consultation).[5] The speech, like the funeral oration, had been drafted by Seneca,
who knew the mind and the most urgent concerns of his fellow senators and
made sure that the policies Nero announced met their highest expectations.[6]
From the outset, Nero struck the right tone by expressing his respect for the
authority of the institution he was addressing. His own youth (he was still several
years short of the normal minimum age for admission to the senate, and senators
were addressed as 'fathers'), he declared, was an advantage, as it meant that he
was not burdened by a legacy of hatred and mistrust arising from the civil
conflicts and domestic strife of previous generations. In contrast to recent
practices, he would refrain from interfering personally in legal cases, keep the
affairs of the imperial household and the state separate and restrict the influence
of certain individuals, a reference to the perceived dominance of Claudius'
senior freedmen in running aspects of the court. The senate would, he promised,
retain its time-honoured prerogatives in the administration of the Italy and
the provinces assigned to it, while he would be in charge of the armies assigned
to him. Suetonius' concise summation of the speech captures its core sentiment:
Nero 'declared that he would rule according to the principles of Augustus',
in other words, observe the agreed protocols of the 'Restored Republic'
(see pp. 28–30).[7] Nero went on to keep his promises, as even Tacitus concedes.[8]

In a demonstration of modesty, he also refused a number of honours the
senate offered him, including statues of gold and silver and additional titles,
such as *pater patriae* ('Father of the Fatherland'), for which he declared himself
too young.[9] Nero's coinage reflected his professed respect for the senate.
Whereas Claudius, and Caligula before him, had blatantly displayed an image
of the Praetorian barracks on their coins, a hint at the real source of their
power and a barely disguised threat, Nero stressed the constitutional legitimacy
of his reign by prominently acknowledging the senate's authority (Figs 43–5).[10]

Claudius' ashes were interred in the Mausoleum of Augustus on
24 October. Agrippina became priestess of the new cult for Divus Claudius,
and work soon began on a major temple complex on the Esquiline Hill, an
area designated for further development (see Fig. 163, p. 216).[11] This publicly
marked Nero's filial piety towards his adoptive father, a traditional virtue
highly rated in Roman society.[12]

A truly extraordinary text sheds light onto the real attitudes and mindsets of
senators and the court at precisely this moment. The so-called *Apocolocyntosis (divi)
Claudi*, often translated into English as the 'gourdification/pumpkinification of
(the deified) Claudius' (*apocolocyntosis* is a pun on the Greek word *apotheosis* for
deification), is a biting satire with strongly burlesque overtones (Fig. 46).[13] Most
scholars agree that it was written by Seneca, to be read out or performed in
front of a small courtly circle including Nero and his most trusted friends at the
Saturnalia festival in December AD 54, a little over two months after Claudius
had died. The action is set in heaven, just after Claudius' demise. The gods, who
initially do not recognise him, debate whether they should allow him among
their number; even the deified Augustus, who is present, considers him unworthy.
Among the many arguments against Claudius' admission into heaven is a witty
account of his political failings, ending with a long list of those he had executed
in order to stay in power. The irreverent tone of the satire is captured in

M ollia concordi descendunt stamina fuso ·

V incunt tithoni uincunt & nestoris annos ·

P hoebas adest cantuque iuuat gaudetque futuris ·

E t laetus nunc plectra mouet nunc pensa ministrat ·

D etinet intentas cantu fallitque laborem ·

D umque nimis citharam fraternaque carmina laudat ·

P lus solito neuere manus humanaque fata ·

L audatum transcendit opus nedemite parcae ·

P hoebus ait uincat mortalis tempora uitae ·

I lle mihi similis uultu similisque decore ·

N ec cantu nec uoce minor felicia lassis ·

S aecula praestabit legumque silentia rumpet ·

Q ualis discutiens fugientia lucifer astra ·

A ut qualis surgit redeuntibus hesperus astris ·

Q ualis cum primum tenebris aurora solutis ·

I nduxit rubicunda diem sol aspicit orbem ·

L ucidus & primos a carcere concitat axes ·

T alis caesar adest talem iam roma neronem ·

A spicit & flagrat nitidus fulgore remisso ·

V ultus & adfuso ceruix formosa capillo ·

H aec apollo at lachesis quae & ipsa homini formosissimo fauer & fecit illud
plena manu & neroni multos annos de suo donat claudium autem
iubent omnes ΧΑΙΡΟΝΤΑΙC ΕΤ ΦΗΜΟΙΝΤΑΙC ΚΤΕ ΙΝΑΔΟCΩ ΕΩ ·
Et ille quidem animam ebulliit et exco desiit uiuere uideri expirauit
autem dum comoedos audit ut scias me non sine causa illos timere ultima
uox eius hec inter homines audita est cum maiore sonitu emisisset illa parte qua
facilius loquebatur ueme puto concacauit me quod an fecerit nescio omnia
certe concacauit que in terris postea sint acta superuacue referre
scias enim optime nec periculum est ne excidant que memoria
gaudium publica impressit Nemo felicitati suae obliuiscitur Nec
loque attasint audita fides penes auctorem erit Nunciatur iouiue
nisse quendam bonae staturae Bene canum nescio quid illuminari Assidue

Fig. 46
**Manuscript codex containing
the text of Seneca's
*Apocolocyntosis***
AD 800–900
Possibly Fulda monastery, Germany
Parchment
H. 23 cm, W. 18 cm
Stiftsbibliothek St. Gallen
Cod. Sang. 569, p. 245

The Roman historian Cassius Dio, writing in Greek, first attributed the *Apocolocyntosis* to Seneca in his third-century text *Roman History* (61.35.3) – the proposal has been generally accepted ever since. In medieval manuscript codices, it is often bound up with other works by Seneca, and frequently entitled in Latin *Ludus de morte Divi Claudii* ('Play on the Death of the Deified Claudius').

More than forty medieval manuscripts of the *Apocolocyntosis* are known, attesting the great popularity of the text during this period. This particular codex contains the principal version, from which an important strand of the textual transmission originates. It is complemented by two other early manuscripts. The first printed edition of the *Apocolocyntosis* was published in Rome in 1513.

Fig. 47
**Detail of Seneca from the
double herm** (see Fig. 5, p. 18)
Early 3rd century AD
Rome, Italy
Marble
H. 28 cm
Antikensammlung, Staatliche
Museen zu Berlin
SK 391

Lucius Annaeus Seneca was one of the most acclaimed literary figures of his time. Born around 4 BC into an Italic family from Roman Spain, Seneca received a thorough education in Rome. Agrippina engaged him as Nero's tutor in AD 49, recalling him from a period in exile, and he was also permitted to re-enter the senate. Four years later, after Nero's accession, Seneca became one his of most influential advisors and acquired vast wealth and influence. His philosophical writings, in the tradition of the Stoic school, were widely read and admired. Over the years, he became disillusioned with power and his relationship with Nero became so strained that he was forced to commit suicide in AD 65.

This is Seneca's only extant portrait, and although it was carved more than a century and a half after his death, it is believed to be based on a portrait from his lifetime. Seneca is identified through a Latin inscription on his chest.

Claudius' supposed last words on earth, *vae me, puto, concacavi me* ('oh dear, I think I've shat myself'), and the dry summary of his life *omnia certe concacavit* ('he certainly shat on everything').[14] Behind the acerbic humour, however, lie true disgust and hatred. Claudius is sent down to the Underworld for having killed 35 senators and 221 Roman knights – a direct reference to purges under his rule; in the end, the disgraced Caligula enslaves him.

Together, Nero's inaugural speech and the *Apocolocyntosis* provide a good sense of senatorial grievances during previous reigns and expectations of the new *princeps*. Alongside these sits another of Seneca's texts, the *De clementia* ('On Mercy'), which was written a year or two later (Fig. 47). Addressed to Nero directly, it sets out Seneca's hopes for his former pupil's reign, a Stoic theory of kingship that depicts the ideal ruler in the form of a 'mirror' (*speculum*) of princes, a metaphor Seneca here introduces.[15] Mercy is viewed as the most essential virtue of a just and successful *princeps*, based not least on the example of Augustus.

A new era

After the fourteen-year reign of the elderly and frail Claudius, a man who had been given little opportunity to shine in public before his accession, expectations among the different classes for his vigorous young successor must have been high. Nero was already well known to the people, and his physical prowess projected an image of strength and dynamism that allowed him to interact with the crowds in a very different way from Claudius. His previous appearances at the 'Game of Troy', leading the Praetorians on parade and providing lavish spectacles, had given a taste of what was to come and stressed the vital role of young princes in the public image of the ruling family (see p. 61). Suetonius relates that Nero allowed even the common people to watch him exercise in the Campus Martius. This was not only a demonstration of his commitment to traditional values – the 'Field of Mars' had been a military staging area and training ground for Rome's youth – but perhaps more importantly an early sign of his *levitas popularis*, a genuine affability that endeared him to the *plebs* and contrasted with the usual senatorial insistence on *gravitas* and *dignitas*.[16] Suetonius adds, however, that Nero would 'greet members of all the orders accurately and without prompting', an important gesture of respect and mark of a good *princeps*. The phrase is the same that Suetonius used in relation to Augustus and underlines the great importance placed on formal acknowledgement of status in Roman society, even if senators seem to have regarded respect shown by the *princeps* for the lower orders as compromising their own standing and prestige.[17]

Nero's new principate, as the official rituals and speeches made clear, held the promise of a return to the golden days of Augustus. While this was a useful model overall, it certainly meant different things to different sections of society, who over the forty years that had passed since Augustus' demise would have chosen to remember him in ways that suited their particular needs. For senators and knights, the Augustan model meant respect for their rank and its privileges – a careful self-imposed restriction of the *princeps*' real powers. For the *plebs*, Augustus was probably associated more with measures such as the corn dole and projects geared towards tangible public benefit. They also expected the *princeps* to be present and approachable, ready to listen to their demands.

As Augustus' great-great-grandson, Nero offered – as Claudius had clearly recognised – the most credible personal link back to the first *princeps* in the popular imagination (see p. 63). Even his youth could be invoked positively, as Augustus had only been two years older when he set out to take on Caesar's inheritance. The connection to Augustus therefore became an important element in Nero's self-presentation in public. Official inscriptions on major monuments, for example, now often included a carefully chosen affiliation that made his reign appear as the providential fulfilment of an ideal line of succession, and also stress his descent from Augustus.

Another comparison emerged very early and was associated with a desire for a new beginning: Nero was likened to the youthful god Apollo. Already in the *Apocolocyntosis*, Seneca speaks of Nero's reign as the beginning of an 'auspicious age'; Apollo himself appears later in the text and asks for Claudius' life to be cut short, and for countless years to be added to Nero's instead. Seneca's Apollo also claims that Nero closely resembles the god himself. Like the night star, dawn or the bright morning sun, 'so Caesar does arise, so Nero shows his face to Rome before the people's eyes'.[18] Neronian panegyric took up the theme. Poems by Calpurnius Siculus that probably date to this period celebrate the return of a golden age of peace brought about by a youth of the Julian line – which must be Nero – a veritable god full of mercy.[19] In a later poem by Calpurnius, the main character describes how he glimpsed the young *princeps* from afar and saw in his likeness the appearance of Mars and Phoebus Apollo in one.[20] Another poet similarly extols the arrival of a new golden reign, that of Apollo.[21] Apollo was an appropriate model for Nero not only as a youthful god, who united both martial and more gentle aspects (the Muses were his companions), but also because he had been closely linked to Augustus. The notion of Nero-Apollo asserted in allegorical form a return to Augustan values. Metaphors of peace and references to recent civil strife must allude to Claudius' reign, which the senatorial order had experienced as a period of maladministration and persecution.

Nero's images

The start of a new principate created great demand for images of the ruler; accordingly, Nero's official portrait was now updated and widely disseminated. It was closely based on his images as the chosen heir, but with markedly more mature physical traits. The better preserved among the surviving versions provide a clear impression of the main characteristics (Fig. 48): the face appears lean, with a masculine angularity that expresses strength and vigour. Its defining features are a broad chin and well-defined jawline, deep-set eyes under sharp and slightly contracted brows, and a prominently flexed trapezoidal muscle in the centre of the furrowed forehead, a mark of concentrated energy. In many ways, this was a radical departure from the images of previous *principes*, all of whom had adapted the classical model introduced by Augustus in an attempt to suggest orderly dynastic continuity. The simplicity and naturalism of Nero's portrait broke with this tradition, which had lasted for almost eighty years. It was a good choice for someone so much younger than most of his predecessors, promising fresh beginnings, but it was also flexible enough to accommodate a full range of traditional roles (Fig. 49).[22] Many of the new statues seem to have depicted

Fig. 48
Portrait of Nero (Type II)
AD 54–9 (bust restored)
Olbia, Italy
Marble
H. 79 cm, W. 65 cm, D. 32 cm
Museo Archeologico Nazionale
di Cagliari
35533

This head was found in a building
near Olbia's ancient forum or main
square. It was worked for insertion
into a statue that would have been
draped in a toga or clad in military
armour. Angled to the left and with
a tense expression on its youthful
face, the sculpture conveys a sense
of vigour and energy. It is closely
comparable to portraits of Nero on
coins struck after his accession in
AD 54 and probably dates to the
first five years of his reign.

Nero in military garb, and in this respect the iconography harked back to the
representations of earlier Julio-Claudian princes, another reflection of his youth.[23]

A striking example of the emphatic reception of Nero's image in the
provinces comes from the city of Aphrodisias in Caria (Fig. 50).[24] The relief
shows Nero in a Greek-style military cuirass, in the act of being crowned by his
mother Agrippina. She holds a cornucopia, likening her to Tyche, goddess of
fortune. The composition seems to have been closely based on the images of
Roma and Augustus in a major temple at Pergamon, as comparisons with coins
demonstrate (Fig. 51). A statue of Nero from Tralleis (Aydın, modern Turkey)
shows the same composition as the Aphrodisias relief but fully in the round, an
indication perhaps that this was a popular way of representing the new ruler in
the Greek East (Fig. 52). As all three cities are in western Asia Minor, and since

Like the portrait opposite, this head
was fashioned for insertion into a
statue. As is clear from the hem of
the toga that is pulled over his
head, Nero would have appeared in
the act of performing a sacrifice
(compare to the statue of
Augustus, Fig. 8, p. 29). The
carving is of very high quality, as
evidenced by the sharp rendering
of the eyes and the fine detail of
the hair. It was found in a covered
walkway under the imperial palace
on the Palatine and must have been
removed from display after Nero's
death, but never altered for re-use.

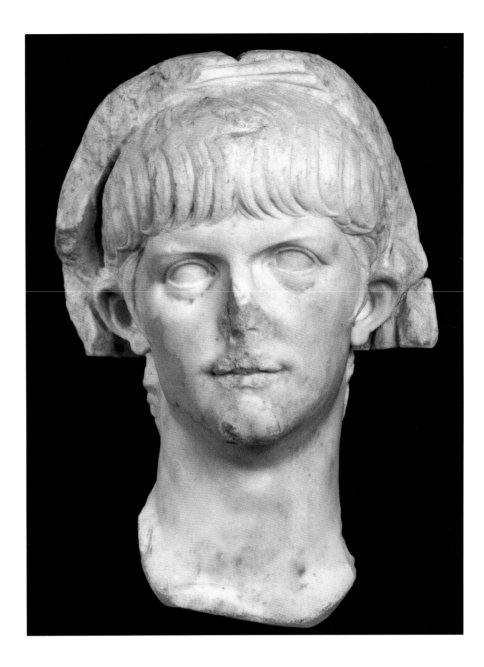

the selection of the statuary type was largely the choice of the local patron or
commissioning body, this may have reflected local expectations and a desire for
security and protection, for conflict threatened in the East (see p. 88).

Optima mater

In an unintended way, the Aphrodisias relief signifies an additional message to
the modern viewer: it was Agrippina who had made Nero. She had seen to his
education and cleared his path by assembling a powerful group of supporters and
embedding them in Claudius' court (Figs 53–5). Now she was in a position of
considerable authority. Nero responded in kind: according to Tacitus, the

Fig. 51
Cistophorus
About AD 41–2
Minted in Pergamon, Mysia
(Turkey)
Silver
Weight 11 g
British Museum
G.2216

The obverse of this coin shows a
portrait of Claudius, the reverse
a stylised depiction of the
Pergamon Temple of Roma and
Augustus, with the two cult statues
inside. Pergamon was the seat of
the provincial assembly, or *koinon*,
of Asia, whose members
congregated at the Temple.
The statues may have served as
models for the depiction of Nero
and Agrippina on the Aphrodisias
relief (Fig. 50).

Fig. 52
Statue of Nero
1st century AD
Tralleis (Aydın), modern Turkey
Marble with traces of pigment
H. 197 cm
Archaeological Museum, Istanbul
506

Although the head is now missing,
the statue is clearly identified by
the Greek inscription on its plinth
('Nero Claudius, son of the Deified
Claudius Caesar'). It shows the
statuary type used on the
Aphrodisias relief (Fig. 50) fully
in the round.

Fig. 50
Relief panel showing Nero as *princeps*, crowned by his mother Agrippina
After AD 54
The Sebasteion, Aphrodisias, Turkey
Marble
H. 171 cm, W. 141 cm, D. 40 cm
Aphrodisias Museum, Geyre
6704

The Sebasteion was a sanctuary complex dedicated to the patron goddess of Aphrodisias,
Aphrodite, and the Julio-Claudian emperors. Worshippers reached the temple along a
processional road that was flanked by two buildings containing shops and offices. The
sanctuary's construction took about four decades and was sponsored by two local families. It
was completed during Nero's reign. The buildings had richly decorated façades that extended
over three stories and were 12 m high. They were embellished with up to 200 reliefs, which
showed allegorical figures, scenes from Greek mythology, personifications of the various
nations of the Roman Empire and members of the imperial family.

This relief is from the upper storey of the north building, sponsored by the brothers Eusebes
and Menandros, and must have been designed shortly after Nero's accession. The south
building opposite, paid for by different sponsors, contained similar scenes, including Claudius,
Agrippina and a personification of the Roman Senate, flanked by the divine twins Castor and
Pollux, thought to represent the young princes Nero and Britannicus, and panels that depicted
Claudius' conquest of Britain and Nero's of Armenia, but they are much less well preserved
(see Figs 53–5). Some of the scenes may have been copied from monuments in Rome, but
they were combined with others that reflected specific local concerns in a rich expression of
Greek civic identity within the wider Roman Empire.

password he gave to the Guards on the first day after his accession was '*optima mater*' – best of mothers.[25] In his description of Claudius' funeral, Tacitus compares Agrippina's role to Livia's at the deification of Augustus, and perhaps Livia was indeed Agrippina's primary role model. Livia had been a trusted partner to Augustus and a powerful and influential dowager during the subsequent reign of her son Tiberius, a far more inspiring example than the long-suffering widows Antonia the Younger, the mother of Claudius, and Agrippina the Elder, Agrippina's own mother. Along the way, Agrippina had suffered three much older husbands. First married aged twelve, she was still only thirty-seven or thirty-eight when Claudius' death formally freed her from close male oversight and left her at the pinnacle of female Roman society.[26]

As the wife of Claudius, Agrippina had enjoyed a very prominent position in public that clearly riled traditionalists. Women were expected to remain in the background, with very few exceptions, certain priestesses for instance. In theatres, to mention but one example, even the wives of senators were forced to sit behind the lowliest free adult citizen males, among other women, children and servants. Dio reports that Agrippina, by contrast, was frequently present when Claudius carried out ordinary business, but also during more ceremonial occasions, such as for the reception of ambassadors, although she was seated on a separate tribunal. Following his accession, Nero continued to show his mother great respect in public, travelling with her in the same litter to official engagements, or, in an even stronger sign of filial deference, accompanying her on foot.[27] Arrangements were also made to enable Agrippina's continued involvement in matters of government. Tacitus claims that senate meetings were convened in the palace, so that Agrippina could discreetly listen to proceedings from behind a curtain in front of a newly created doorway.[28] Agrippina also ran her own household and received visitors, including high-ranking individuals, very much in the manner of male nobles (see p. 85).[29] Tacitus and Dio record that during the official reception of an Armenian embassy, Agrippina attempted to take her seat beside Nero on the tribunal and the situation was only saved when Nero, prompted by Seneca (Dio adds the Praetorian prefect Burrus), stepped down and walked towards her, as if thereby extending a particular honour to her. He did not retake his seat 'so that the weakness of the Empire should not be obvious to foreigners'.[30] Tacitus' language betrays his deep-seated disapproval of women in positions of power. He pours scorn on Nero, whom he accuses of 'being ruled by a woman', and aims to discredit Agrippina, calling her atrocious and false, and describing her actions as highly emotional and therefore typically female.[31] Her unusual role must have given rise to comment and rumours more generally. The later sources amplified what may have been said at the time with undisguised misogynist malice. When a woman's reputation was to be tarnished, accusations of sexual impropriety were at the forefront. In order to retain her influence over Nero, Agrippina is said to have offered herself to him for an incestuous relationship.[32] There seems little reason now to take any of this seriously, beyond what it reveals about the attitudes of the authors involved.

Another way of interpreting Agrippina's prominent role, and her continued visibility in person and within the official imagery, is that this was intended as a reassuring sign of continuity between the reigns of her late husband and son. After all, Claudia Octavia, Nero's wife, was still very young; too young perhaps to have much of a meaningful public presence yet, whereas Agrippina could lend her authority as *Augusta*.

Fig. 53
Nero(?) and horse
After AD 54
The Sebasteion, Aphrodisias, Turkey
Marble
H. 160 cm, W. 134 cm, D. 44 cm
Aphrodisias Museum, Geyre
6878

Fig. 54
Agrippina, Claudius and personification of the senate
After AD 54
The Sebasteion, Aphrodisias, Turkey
Marble
H. 159 cm, W. 164 cm, D. 38 cm
Aphrodisias Museum, Geyre
6752

Fig. 55
Britannicus(?) and horse
After AD 54
The Sebasteion, Aphrodisias, Turkey
Marble
H. 163 cm, W. 129 cm, D. 42 cm
Aphrodisias Museum, Geyre
6877

These reliefs from the Sebasteion at Aphrodisias illustrate how the imperial succession was communicated in the provinces. In the centre is a panel with Claudius. His new wife Agrippina stands next to him on the left, and on the right is a personification of the Roman senate. The fragments on either side show the divine twins Castor and Pollux, here perhaps representing the young Nero and Britannicus.

Nero and Claudia Octavia had been betrothed in AD 49, when he was eleven and she nine or ten; they were married four years later. Their youth and the arranged nature of their union seem to have stood in the way of the development of a cordial bond, let alone any notions of love. It is unclear whether Claudia Octavia was able to bear children; for many years she was probably far too young to become pregnant successfully, if any attempts to produce an heir were made. Nero instead fell in love with a freedwoman called Claudia Acte. Very little is known about Claudia Acte independently, and the story therefore relies entirely on later sources and has a whiff of vilification about it.[33] Epigraphic evidence attests that her household included enslaved people and freedmen, as well as substantial properties, but how these fit chronologically with her liaison with Nero is unclear. Acte may already have been a woman of some means, or perhaps she received lavish gifts in connection with her relationship with the emperor, as Tacitus alleges.[34] The sources claim that Seneca and Burrus encouraged the affair as a means of controlling Nero and channelling his energies; Agrippina, however, is said to have been violently opposed, out of fear that Nero might slip from her influence. For Tacitus, who only refers to Claudia Acte disparagingly,[35] the story serves mostly to discredit Agrippina further, while from the various source accounts it seems that different court factions saw the affair as a means of jockeying for position.[36] Later events suggest that it was a serious and meaningful relationship (see p. 268).

Perhaps prompted by his friends and advisors, Nero eventually took steps to limit Agrippina's influence. At the time, the imperial palace on the Palatine Hill largely consisted of interconnected older mansions (see p. 218), and visitors

Fig. 56
Denarius
AD 50–4
Minted in Rome, Italy
Silver
Weight 3.4 g
British Museum
R.9822
Donated by George IV, King of the
United Kingdom

Agrippina is prominently depicted
under her new title *Augusta*
(AGRIPPINAE AUGUSTAE,
'for Agrippina Augusta') on the
obverse. Nero's portrait is on
the reverse, with his full new name
and title of *princeps iuventutis*
(NERO CLAUD(IUS) CAES(AR)
DRUSUS GERMANICUS
PRINC(EPS) IUVENT(UTIS))
following his adoption by Claudius.

Fig. 57
Aureus
AD 54
Minted in Rome, Italy
Gold
Weight 7.6 g
British Museum
1864,1128.252
Donated by Edward Wigan

On the obverse of this aureus are
facing portraits of Nero (left) and
Agrippina (right). In an extraordinary
show of Agrippina's pre-eminence,
only her name and titles are given
here (AGRIPP(INA) AUG(USTA)
DIVI CLAUD(II) (UXOR) NERONIS
CAES(ARIS) MATER, 'Agrippina
Augusta, Wife of the Deified
Claudius, Mother of Nero Caesar').
Nero's titles are listed on the
reverse, even though he was the
reigning emperor (NERONI DIVI
F(ILIO) CAES(AR) AUG(USTUS)
GERM(ANICUS) IMP(ERATOR)
TRIB(UNITIA) P(OTESTAS), 'for
Nero, Son of the Deified, Caesar
Augustus Germanicus Imperator,
Holder of Tribunician Power').

Fig. 58
Aureus
AD 55–6
Minted in Rome, Italy
Gold
Weight 7.6 g
British Museum
R.6511
Bequeathed by Clayton
Mordaunt Cracherode

Portraits of Nero (foreground) and
Agrippina are side by side on the
obverse of this aureus. Not only is
Nero depicted more prominently, his
titles have now moved to the
obverse, with the addition of his first
consulship (NERO CLAUD(IUS)
DIVI F(ILIO) CAES(AR)
AUG(USTUS) GERM(ANICUS)
IMP(ERATOR) TRIB(UNITIA)
P(OTESTAS) CO(N)S(UL)).
Agrippina's titles (identical to those
in Fig. 57) appear on the reverse,
which has been interpreted as a
sign of her slowly waning influence.
Nero's new role as consul, however,
gave him added authority in his own
right and less of a need to benefit
from his mother's titles.

Fig. 59
Aureus
AD 55–6
Minted in Rome, Italy
Gold
Weight 7.7 g
British Museum
R.6512
Bequeathed by Clayton
Mordaunt Cracherode

Here, Nero's portrait appears
on the obverse; his titles on the
obverse and reverse (NERO
CAES(AR) IMP(ERATOR)
AUG(USTUS) PONTIF(EX)
MAX(IMUS) TR(IBUNITIA)
P(OTESTAS) II P(ATER)
P(ATRIAE),
'Chief Priest, Holder of Tribunician
Power for the Second Time, Father
of the Fatherland'). Agrippina has
now disappeared altogether.

Fig. 60
Cameo with jugate portraits of Tiberius and Livia
AD 14–29
Sardonyx
H. 4 cm
Museo Archeologico Nazionale
di Firenze
14533

Agrippina probably saw Livia as her role model. The coins with her portrait alongside Nero's (see Fig. 58), in the same jugate configuration as on this cameo, make this claim publicly. Similar representations had previously been restricted to court art.

received by Nero may have proceeded from there to pay court to Agrippina in her quarters. Nero now separated their households, and Agrippina was installed in a different mansion that had formerly been occupied by Antonia, Claudius' mother.[37] He also withdrew both Agrippina's Praetorian Guard detail and German bodyguard. Court society, ever attuned to the intricacies of protocol, took immediate note and the visits to Agrippina abruptly stopped.[38]

There is little to corroborate these stories beyond the heavily partisan source accounts. However, a remarkable series of coins issued at the time does provide some insight into how Agrippina's role was communicated to the public during this period. The prominence of her portrait in the earlier issues underlined her exalted position under Claudius; this continued into the first months of Nero's reign, to the extent that it may have suggested that she acted almost as co-regent (Figs 56, 57 and 60). Her representation then began to change (Fig. 58), until she disappeared from the coinage altogether (Fig. 59). From this, the public could deduce a gradual reduction in her status over the first year of Nero's reign.

There were other major developments at court and within the imperial family in the months after Nero's accession. The first concerned his step-brother Britannicus. Britannicus was thirteen years and eight months old when his father Claudius died in October AD 54, according to Roman law still a child. Between the end of December and the following February – he would have been fourteen on the 11th or 12th of that month – he also died. He may have suffered a fatal epileptic seizure; this was certainly how his death was announced.[39] All the extant sources, however, although they mention the seizures, claim that he was poisoned by Nero. They allege that Nero felt threatened, not least because Agrippina, after her relationship with Nero had become strained, supposedly announced that she might support Britannicus as an alternative heir in future.[40] The truth is impossible to establish, since there is no independent evidence. Modern commentators are in the same situation as their ancient predecessors – what they believe largely depends on how they judge Nero's character. Several points (though even these depend on Tacitus) give rise to speculation, certainly in retrospect and perhaps at the time: Claudius' last will had not been read out publicly, so no one knew what provisions it contained for Britannicus; the boy's burial was conducted almost immediately and with comparatively little ceremony, although he was buried in the Mausoleum of Augustus, and Tacitus, with some inconsistency, mentions crowds attending in heavy rain.[41] On his fourteenth birthday, Britannicus would have assumed the *toga virilis* and should then have played a greater role in public, which his sudden death prevented. The credibility of the poison story is undermined by the way it revels in novelistic detail of what supposedly took place in secret (including words put into Nero's mouth).[42] The sources used by Tacitus and Suetonius (neither of whom had yet been born) apparently also alleged that Nero sexually abused Britannicus in the days before his death, a sign that they were concerned chiefly with assailing Nero's character.[43]

Finally, Nero removed Claudius' senior freedmen in the palace administration, evidence that he intended to deliver on his promises to the senate who had abhorred their power and influence.[44] This act may have been prompted by Seneca and Burrus, a senator and a knight, who were now left in a strong position as the most trusted senior advisors at the court and steered policy, together with other members of Nero's governing council.[45]

III

CONFLICT
AND REFORM

Trouble in the East

Tacitus interrupts his narrative of the months immediately following Nero's accession with a dramatic account of events in distant Armenia, at the Empire's eastern frontier. Late in AD 54, rumours had suddenly begun to spread in Rome that an army from Parthia had ousted the local king and replaced him with a Parthian prince.[1] At about the same time, an Armenian delegation arrived in the city with more details about what had taken place.[2] Rome considered Armenia to be firmly within its sphere of influence, but the region remained contested between the Romans and their Parthian opponents.[3] The Parthians ruled over a vast empire centred on greater Iran; in size, power and seductive cultural reach it was Rome's equal and its only true rival.[4] Much was at stake here, and Nero's reaction was carefully observed by the Roman senate and people.[5]

Although no one could know it at the time, Nero's entire reign would be dominated by the Armenian question and its wider repercussions, along with a number of other conflicts that were left unresolved by Claudius. As a result, sustained military action ranged from Britain in the far north-west of the Empire, along the Rhine and Danube frontiers all the way to the Black Sea region, the Caucasus and greater Syria in the East. The vast distances involved stretched Roman supply lines and resources; they also necessitated complex troop movements across provinces thousands of kilometres apart. Local rebellions and barbarian incursions, first in Britain, then along the Danube and in Judaea, repeatedly hampered Roman attempts to gain the strategic initiative.

A determined effort was therefore made to reassure the Roman public and communicate an image of Nero as a competent and effective military leader. In truth, his real successes were also far more significant than the surviving literary sources indicate, and some of the monuments that extolled Nero's achievements may express genuine confidence rather than being mere propaganda. Especially in the Greek-speaking East, Nero was seen to offer protection and stability, and this contributed to his enduring popularity there. Contemporary evidence such as the relief cycles from the Sebasteion at Aphrodisias in Caria counterbalances the dominant literary record (see Fig. 50, p. 80; Figs 53–5, p. 83).[6] Although little of this type of material has survived, it reflects genuine expectations and an engagement with Nero's policies and achievements by local elites.

Modern historians have largely followed the post-Neronian source accounts and assumed that Nero had little interest in military matters and foreign affairs, but this view needs to be considerably modified if not abandoned altogether. Diplomacy and military action went hand-in-hand; the sheer number of embassies exchanged with the Parthians alone is remarkable during these years (not least given the distances involved), but Nero also regularly had to deal with delegations from numerous central European tribes or settle affairs along the frontiers. Much responsibility lay with the Roman commanders in the border provinces, but the ultimate decisions always rested with the emperor and his advisors (see p. 92).

Within the Empire's borders, but mostly beyond, there were numerous allied principalities and tribal territories – 'client kingdoms' in modern literature – whose leaders held the official title of *rex socius et amicus populi Romani*, 'Allied King and Friend of the Roman People'. This system had originally evolved during Rome's eastward expansion into the highly urbanised Greek East with its

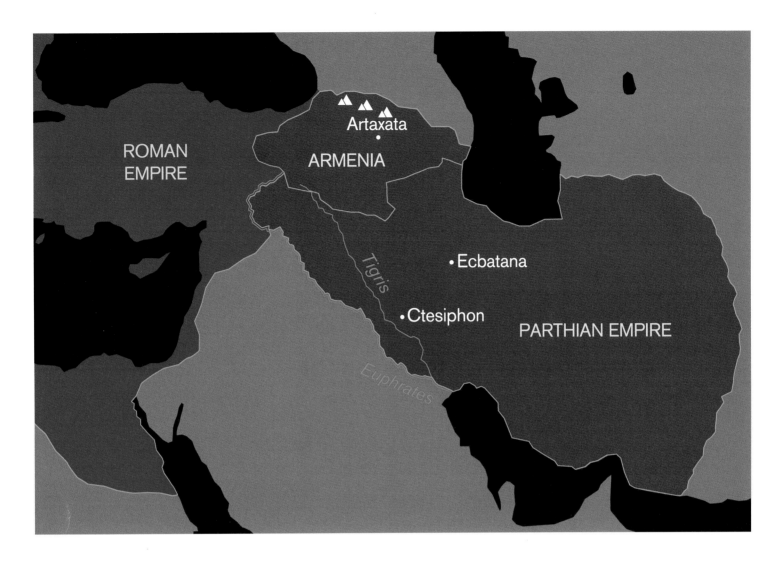

**Map of Armenia and the
Parthian Empire**

long royal traditions, but was then applied to tribal societies elsewhere.[7]
To Roman minds, the Empire – in the Augustan poet Virgil's famous phrase
– was conceptually 'without limits', and such territories were considered part of
the Roman domain even if they were not occupied as such.[8] Sometimes original
rulers were left in place, but over time Rome refused to recognise automatic
hereditary succession. At a ruler's death, or even while he was alive, his territory
could be awarded to someone else or be taken under direct Roman control.[9]
This process of control and assimilation accelerated in the mid-first century AD
and required Nero's attention.[10]

Nero and Armenia

Armenia, specifically the historical region of greater Armenia that comprised
large parts of eastern Anatolia, was at the extreme periphery of the world
known to the Romans (see Map).[11] A rugged, mountainous territory between the
Taurus and Zagros ranges and the Lesser Caucasus, it lay beyond the major
communication routes and was separated from the Mediterranean and Black

Sea by high mountains crossed by few passes. Harsh winters cut the entire region off from the surrounding lands and led to a seasonal fragmentation within, isolating local population centres in different valleys from each other. This complex geographical setting was reflected in Armenia's political organisation. Central power was weak, and local grandees enjoyed considerable autonomy in their respective domains. The few fertile plains were situated mostly along river valleys, but were not sufficient to sustain large populations, let alone substantial occupying forces. Culturally, the region looked to the East, from where it was also more accessible geographically, rather than the West. At times of internal conflict, local factions attempted to enlist outside support. Armenia's core regions were fringed by other territories that were better connected to the outside world and therefore of higher strategic value to external powers. To the south, Armenia bordered the Mesopotamian plains and greater Syria, with the Mediterranean beyond. Along the Euphrates were a number of smaller principalities that controlled major trade routes. To the north-west and north were the regions of Pontus, Iberia and Albania that stretched along the Black and Caspian seas and were bordered by the main Caucasus range to the north. The territories of Media Atropatene and Adiabene linked Armenia to the Iranian highland plain to the east. Armenia was thus both peripheral and central to a much wider region, ensuring attention from Romans and Parthians. Perhaps too remote to warrant direct control and incorporation, at the same time it was too sensitive to be left to a rival power. In Roman memory, Armenia's strategic potential lingered in the reputation of its greatest king, Tigranes II, who had expanded Armenia's borders in all directions and reached the three seas in the early first century BC (Fig. 61). This had finally drawn Roman armies to the East, and made the names and fortunes of its leading generals. Pompey the Great first established Roman power in the region at the end of the Third Mithridatic War (73–63 BC).

The prestige and enormous riches Pompey had won in the East – the theatre complex he built in the centre of Rome served as a permanent reminder – lured others now into direct conflict with the Parthians. In 53 BC the triumvir and governor of Syria Marcus Licinius Crassus perished with three legions under his command at the battle of Carrhae against the Parthians; Julius Caesar was assassinated on the eve of a planned major Parthian campaign in 44 BC. Mark Antony sought military glory against the Parthians in 36 BC in the Atropatene campaign, but found defeat. It was not until Augustus that a settlement with the Parthians was reached. Through a show of force backed by prudent diplomacy, Augustus and the Parthian king Phraates IV in 20 BC agreed their respective spheres of influence, and Augustus secured the symbolically potent return of the military standards lost under Crassus. Because of this long, entangled and troubled history, and the unrivalled significance of Parthia as a great power, the event was singled out as a major success around which a consensus could be built in Rome. It came to signify the beginning of the Augustan Golden Age, and numerous monuments celebrated the first *princeps*' achievements against the Parthians.[12]

Despite this, disputes continued to flare over Armenia and the surrounding principalities. Augustus and then Tiberius dispatched their respective heirs Gaius Caesar and Germanicus to protect Roman interests; both died in the East. The region became a place for imperial princes to demonstrate their abilities, and the distance from Rome made it desirable to have someone with senior command

Fig. 61
Tetradrachm of Tigranes II
r. 95–55 BC
Minted in Antiocha ad Orontem, modern Turkey
Silver
Weight 16.5 g
British Museum
RPK,p193A.2.Tig
Bequeathed by Richard Payne Knight

The Armenian king Tigranes II ('Tigranes the Great'), in power in the early first century BC, briefly turned Armenia into a major eastern Mediterranean power, drawing Rome into the region. Here he is shown with the Armenian royal tiara. The Parthian influence on Armenia remained strong in the centuries that followed.

authority nearby. There was little change during Caligula's brief reign, but events began to slip from Roman control under Claudius, when much attention was focused elsewhere.

In AD 51, King Mithridates of Armenia was ousted by his own nephew, Rhadamistus, son of the king of neighbouring Iberia, Pharasmanes I. To most Romans, the names of these rulers and of the territories they governed will have meant very little. Mithridates had been installed long before by Tiberius, and then restored after a short hiatus by Claudius. A small Roman garrison had not done much to protect him from his relatives; it took time to mobilise units in the adjacent provinces, and as the region was far from Rome, news travelled slowly. Perhaps because of the delay in the Roman response, the Parthian king Vologases sensed an opportunity (Figs 62–4).[13] He sent an army to oust the usurper Rhadamistus and put his own younger brother, Tiridates, on the Armenian throne instead. Parthian sympathisers among the Armenian nobility may have asked for intervention from that quarter. What followed is confused; it seems Rhadamistus attempted to return, but was ousted again. In AD 54, the year of Nero's accession, a Parthian army was in Armenia.[14]

Our knowledge of subsequent events relies entirely on Roman sources, chiefly Tacitus and Cassius Dio. They in turn used accounts written closer to the time, including ones by participants in Rome's military campaign.[15] It is unclear whether Claudius planned a major Roman response before his death, but if he had, Nero may already have been acquainted with the circumstances in broad terms. Tacitus provides a plausible sense of how the uncertain situation of AD 54 may have played out in Rome. He imagines some voicing concern that the young and inexperienced *princeps* was confronted by a major crisis so soon in his reign, while others trusted in his vigour and senior advisors.[16]

Modern scholars have argued that Nero engaged in an Armenian war out of choice, mainly to prove himself an energetic leader at the outset of his principate. Subsequent reactions by the senate and people, however, perhaps suggest that the weight of expectations, based on the Augustan precedent, may have been an overwhelming factor that left him little alternative. It is probably safe to say that there was such a broad consensus that individual motivation mattered relatively little.[17]

Fig. 62
Obverse of a tetradrachm with a portrait of Vologases with diadem, necklace and embroidered Parthian robes
AD 52–3
Minted in Seleucia ad Tigrim, modern Iraq
Silver
Weight 9.8 g
British Museum
1878,0301.408

Fig. 63
Reverse of a drachm showing Vologases enthroned with bow
AD 51–78
Minted in Ecbatana, modern Iran
Silver
Weight 3.6 g
British Museum
1917,0204.126
Donated by Sir Evelyn Grant Duff

Fig. 64
Reverse of a tetradrachm on which a female deity hands the enthroned Vologases a wreath or diadem
AD 51–2
Minted in Seleucia ad Tigrim, modern Iraq
Silver
Weight 13.2 g
British Museum
1878,0301.407

Vologases I (Parthian: Walagaš) ruled the Parthian Empire as powerful 'King of Kings' of the Arsacid dynasty from AD 51 to 78. In a military and diplomatic stand-off with Rome, he secured Armenia for his younger brother Tiridates, in a manner that was acceptable to Nero. Parthia controlled the middle section of the trade routes known as the Silk Road, and both empires benefited from mutual trade. Vologases' coinage combined Iranian and Western motifs (including traditional royal titles in Greek), acknowledging the cultural traditions of his subjects.

For Nero, the first important task was the choice of commander. The *princeps*, barely seventeen, had not yet had an opportunity to gain any military experience himself. Young men of equestrian or senatorial families might serve as tribunes in a legion for a year or so aged nineteen or twenty before embarking on their senatorial career. Had Claudius still been alive, perhaps Nero would now have been sent to become acquainted with military matters on the staff of a senior general. Just months into his reign, it was politically inadvisable for Nero to leave Rome. He therefore had to select a suitable military man whose loyalty he could count on to lead the campaign; it was also a good opportunity to make a significant political gesture. Nero undoubtedly received prudent advice from his council – Seneca would have provided guidance on political aspects and Burrus on military matters. The choice of a senior senator would be seen as a further conciliatory measure and set the tone for the new principate. Nero needed to be able to trust these aristocrats and he had to give them a chance to shine if he was to rule according to the principles of Augustus' 'Restored Republic', while managing any risk that might arise from a successful officer's growing reputation.[18]

In consequence, and to general approval, Nero appointed Gnaeus Domitius Corbulo to a special command for the Armenian campaign.[19] Corbulo was a distinguished and extremely well-connected senator; a former consul and governor of the province of Asia, he had made his name under Claudius and been awarded triumphal honours for successes in Germany (see p. 118).[20] His orders now were to 'retain Armenia' for Rome.[21]

Corbulo must have reached the East early in AD 55. He had been assigned half the *exercitus Syriae*, the Roman army in Syria, so now commanded two legions and their associated auxiliary units. In addition, he was allocated all the auxiliary cohorts stationed in Cappadocia.[22] Nero in the meantime made other arrangements to bolster the campaign. He ordered the eastern legions to move closer to Armenia and added to them new recruits from neighbouring provinces as reinforcements; he also instructed the allied kings Agrippa of Cilicia and Antiochus IV of Commagene to mobilise their native contingents and be at the ready. Furthermore, he assigned two new client kings to smaller regions bordering Armenia: Aristobulos of Chalcis to Lesser Armenia and Sohaemus of Emesa to Sophene. This was designed both to bring in additional local troops and expertise, and ensure that the situation in Armenia could be closely monitored during the build-up of Roman forces. Bridges were constructed over the Euphrates in advance of planned offensives.

The Parthian army apparently had left Armenia during the winter, though Tiridates and his followers remained. In Rome, news of the Parthian army's withdrawal was interpreted as a direct result of Nero's actions and the senate immediately discussed far-reaching honours for the *princeps*. As a national act of thanksgiving, Nero should enter the capital with an ovation and wear triumphal robes. Even more symbolically significant, he should be honoured with a statue in the Temple of Mars the Avenger that would be the same size as the existing image of Mars there.[23] This proposal aligned Nero's Parthian action directly with Augustus' diplomatic success more than seventy years earlier – the Temple of Mars the Avenger had been dedicated on the Capitoline to display the standards recovered from the Parthians during his principate (Fig. 65).

Further good news followed. The Parthian king Vologases' attention was diverted by a rebellion by his son Vardanes and he therefore chose not to escalate the nascent conflict with Rome unnecessarily at this time. Prompted by the Roman commanders on the ground, he agreed to hand over hostages and defuse the situation.[24] There followed an unseemly squabble over the hostages between Corbulo and the governor of Syria, Ummidius Quadratus, who each wanted to claim this success for themselves. It was a sign of the excessive aristocratic competition that developed if more responsibility was delegated by the *princeps*, as was evident elsewhere, too. Regardless, the Parthian move was duly celebrated in Rome as a further success. Nero, who seems to have refused the senate's earlier honours in a well-received gesture of modesty, now accepted an imperial acclamation.[25]

For a while, little of note happened in the East and after these initial achievements Nero's attention was mostly focused on domestic matters. The underlying causes of the conflict had not gone away, however, and planning continued. Corbulo seems to have found the Syrian legions assigned to him below strength and ill-prepared for war; many months were spent bringing them up to scratch. With Nero's consent, he discharged elderly and physically frail soldiers from service (in order to save money on discharge bonuses, previous emperors had extended the period of service or otherwise kept veterans from being released). Nero settled many of these veterans in Italy, an important aspect of a *princeps*' care for his soldiers, and new men were recruited in the provinces of Galatia and Cappadocia. Tacitus, apparently erroneously, reports that an entire legion with its associated auxiliary infantry and cavalry units was sent east from Germany. There was little military action, but it seems smaller Roman detachments closer to the border were routed by the Parthians.

By AD 58 Corbulo had completed his preparations and advanced in force. Following fruitless negotiations with Tiridates, the Romans finally pushed into Armenia. Suppressing local resistance as they advanced, the Romans marched on the Armenian capital, Artaxata, and took it after a short siege. As he had insufficient troops to hold the city, Corbulo razed it and its fortifications to the ground; Tiridates was driven out of Armenia. In Rome, the news was received with jubilation. Nero was awarded another imperial acclamation; the senate decreed that days of thanksgiving should be held and voted to award Nero statues and arches, as well as successive consulates. The dates of the victory, of its announcement and of the decrees in celebration were to be made into annual festivals. These honours aligned Nero's successes firmly with those achieved by Augustus; furthermore, Nero's Parthian Arch on the Capitoline echoed Augustus' on the Forum (Fig. 68). The exact location of this new monument is unknown as it has not survived, but it may have formed part of a symbolic route that connected markers of Parthian victories, including the Temple of Mars the Avenger (Figs 66, 67 and 69). Nero's coinage put a particular focus on his Parthian Arch, with issues including its image minted over several years. These coins give a good idea of the single-span monument, richly decorated with reliefs and free-standing sculptures and crowned by a statue of Nero in a triumphal chariot (Figs 70–2).[26] At the city of Aphrodisias, Nero's success in Armenia was likened to Claudius' conquest of Britain, demonstrating the broad spectrum of positive responses across the Empire (Figs 73–5).

Fig. 66
Aureus showing the Temple of Mars Ultor ('Mars the Avenger') on the Capitoline in Rome on the reverse
18 BC
Minted in Andalucía, Spain
Gold
Weight 7.9 g
British Museum
1867,0101.594

Fig. 67
Reverse of a denarius with the Temple of Mars Ultor ('Mars the Avenger') on the Capitoline in Rome
18 BC
Minted in Andalucía, Spain
Silver
Weight 3.9 g
British Museum
R.6093
Donated by George IV, King of the United Kingdom

The Temple of Mars Ultor housed an image of the war god (Fig. 67, right) and was used to display the standards retrieved from the Parthians (Fig. 66, left). After Nero's first successes in Armenia, the senate proposed erecting a statue of him next to the one of Mars.

Fig. 68
Denarius showing Augustus' Parthian arch in the Forum in Rome
16 BC
Minted in Rome, Italy
Silver
Weight 3.9 g
British Museum
R.6038

Augustus' Parthian arch in the Forum in Rome formed a monumental backdrop to Nero's investiture of the Parthian prince Tiridates as king of Armenia in AD 66. The senate honoured Nero with a corresponding arch on the Capitoline Hill in AD 58 (see Fig. 70).

Fig. 69
Reverse of a denarius with a depiction of a kneeling Parthian handing over a Roman standard
19–4 BC
Minted in Rome, Italy
Silver
Weight 4.1 g
British Museum
1920,1102.1
Donated by Sir Henry Hoyle Howorth

Parthia was Rome's equal, even if Roman imagery presented the Parthians as defeated enemies.

Fig. 70
**Hypothetical reconstruction
of Nero's Parthian Arch on the
Capitoline Hill**

Nero's Parthian Arch on the Capitoline Hill became the central monument to celebrate his achievements as *princeps* in the early part of his reign, and images of it were widely propagated on coins minted between AD 64 and 66.

Fig. 71
**Pilaster with remains of
winged figures in front of an
architectural façade**
After AD 58
Campidoglio, Rome, Italy
Marble
H. 150 cm, W. 110 cm, D. 80 cm
Musei Capitolini, Centrale
Montemartini, Rome
AC 11123

This fragment has been attributed to Nero's Parthian Arch, which is otherwise lost.

Fig. 72
Sestertius
AD 65
Minted in Lugdunum (Lyon), Gaul
(modern France)
Copper alloy
Weight 28.9 g
British Museum
1872,0709.453

This coin gives a good sense of the rich decoration of the arch with its reliefs and free-standing sculpture and stresses the role of the senate in dedicating the monument. At the top, Nero is seen in a triumphal chariot flanked by the goddesses Victory and Peace.

Figs 73, 74 and 75
**Three relief panels from the
Sebasteion at Aphrodisias:
Claudius and Britannia; the
goddess Victory floating to
earth; Nero supports Armenia**
After AD 54
The Sebasteion, Aphrodisias, Turkey
Marble
H. 167 cm, W. 136 cm, D. 45 cm
(left); H. 164 cm, W. 158 cm,
D. 38 cm (middle); H. 162 cm,
W. 132 cm, D. 42 cm (right)
Aphrodisias Museum, Geyre
6755, 6713, 6754

This set of three relief panels
from Aphrodisias aligns Nero's
military actions with those of
earlier Julio-Claudian rulers. The
central scene shows the winged
goddess Victory floating to earth
with a *tropaeum,* a physical marker
of triumph on the battlefield.
On the left, a heroic Claudius
strikes down a personification of
Britannia, while on the right, Nero

supports Armenia. The emperors'
and provinces' names were
inscribed in Greek below. Nero's
name was erased after his death
as part of a campaign of *damnatio
memoriae.* Also noteworthy in light
of the later literary source tradition
is the natural progression from
Claudius to Nero as his adopted
son and successor.

Probably in the next campaigning season of AD 59, Corbulo advanced
on Armenia's second city, Tigranocerta. Here, the local garrison surrendered
without a fight. An attempt by Tiridates to return in the following year was
repelled. Nero now appointed a different Armenian prince, Tigranes, who had
spent many years in Rome, as new client king for Armenia. It proved a poor
choice. Misreading the situation, Tigranes soon began raiding neighbouring
Parthian territories, ultimately provoking the Parthians into retaliatory action.
In the spring of AD 61, Tiridates returned with a large Parthian contingent and
besieged the Roman garrison that had been installed at Tigranocerta. For Rome,
the timing could not have been worse; a fierce rebellion had in the meantime
wrought havoc at the opposite end of the Empire, in Britain.[27]

Britain

Just over seventeen years after Claudius' conquest of Britain, anti-Roman sentiment in the new province exploded in a violent insurrection that quickly engulfed the core of the Roman-held territory.[28] The events leading up to the rebellion starkly expose the harsh reality of Roman occupation and the frequent unwarranted alienation of previously cooperative tribal elites (Figs 76–8). Disregard for local sensibilities and widespread exploitative practices by Roman officials, such as tax farmers and military contractors, but also soldiers and newly settled veterans, were to blame. The province was still in a formative period of transition. Only a small part of the south-east was under civilian administration, and this was bordered by allied client kingdoms and a military zone that secured the Roman-occupied areas against the unconquered tribal lands beyond, in those days principally in Wales and the Pennines (see Map, opposite). Roman policy to a large extent depended on the 'men on the ground', the senatorial governors – all former consuls – whose approach in these decades veered between consolidation and expansion. Much rested on the character and personal ambition of the individual aristocrats.[29]

Over the decade and a half after the conquest, Britain had seen near-constant warfare.[30] The initial invading force in AD 43 under Aulus Plautius, who stayed on as first governor, had sailed from northern Gaul and landed unopposed.[31] Its objective from the beginning was the most powerful native kingdom in eastern Britain. The Catuvellauni tribe, led by its chief Caratacus, had its centre at Camulodunon (later Camulodunum; Colchester), by then a well-established *oppidum* (fortified town) and trading centre protected by extensive defensive dykes.[32] In two hard-fought battles, the Romans had forced river crossings, including one over the Thames, and then – joined by Claudius himself – quickly overwhelmed Camulodunon's resistance. Claudius accepted the surrender of eleven kings and departed from Britain after a short stay of only sixteen days.[33] Some of the defeated chiefs were subsequently recognised by the Romans as client rulers; the most important leader, Caratacus, however, had escaped. The Roman force now split into three main battle groups to consolidate its gains. One legion remained at Camulodunon to secure the centre and supply lines, pacifying and disarming the neighbouring Trinovantes. The other legions fanned out in different directions: north and north-west against the Corieltavi; west towards the Dobunni; to the south-west into the territory of the Durotriges.[34] Fighting in this last area was particularly dogged and involved the storming of several hill forts.[35] A Rome-friendly southern kingdom that comprised Atrebates, Regni and Belgae, centred on Silchester, Chichester and Winchester, was re-established under the ruler Togidubnus, who would soon prove a staunchly loyal ally.[36]

By AD 47, the incoming governor, Publius Ostorius Scapula, found the lowlands mostly under Roman control, but the island's main mineral resources – the real prize of conquest according to Tacitus – still lay just beyond in the highlands to the west and north.[37] Scapula decided to extend direct Roman control further outwards by establishing Roman garrisons, and forcefully disarmed the nearer client kingdoms. Among the Iceni in Norfolk, until then never in battle against the Romans, this led to a fierce but short-lived rebellion. In AD 49, Scapula renewed his attack against the Silures of southern Wales.

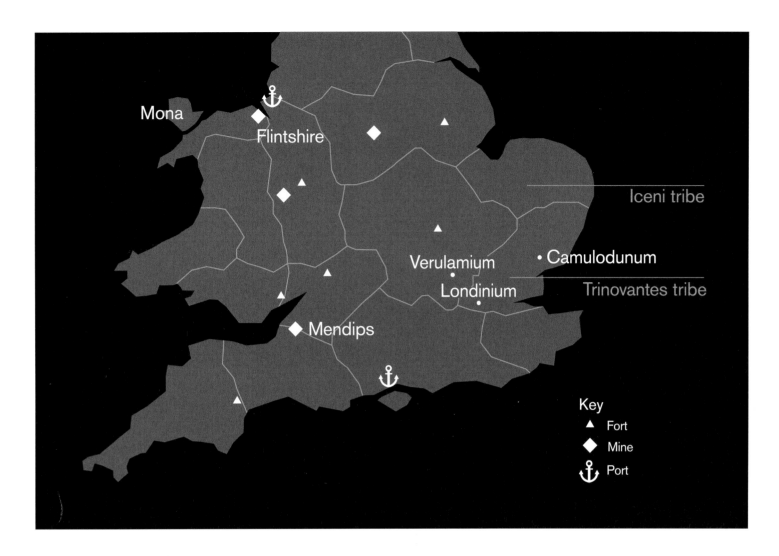

Mona

Flintshire

Iceni tribe

Verulamium

• **Camulodunum**

Londinium

Trinovantes tribe

Mendips

Key
▲ Fort
◆ Mine
⚓ Port

**Map of Roman Britain, showing
the position of tribal boundaries,
major Roman settlements and
forts, ports and lead mines**

Close contact between Britain and the Roman world preceded the Claudian conquest of AD 43. Caesar's short-lived invasions of 55 and 54 BC established a network of treaty relationships with local rulers; cross-channel trade with northern Gaul was now taxed by Rome. Roman recognition of rulers and their territories profoundly influenced elite dynamics and artificially ascribed fixed tribal identities, a process that intensified after the conquest. Access to Roman imports and control over their distribution became an important marker of power and status. In parallel, Roman and local tastes began to influence one another, and a new artistic identity, particularly evident in jewellery and decorated military objects, emerged.

Fig. 76
The 'Meyrick helmet'
AD 50–100
England
Copper alloy
H. 16.5 cm, W. 17 cm
British Museum
1872,1213.2
Donated by Sir Augustus
Wollaston Franks

The 'Meyrick helmet' may be a local version of a Roman auxiliary helmet. It combines a Roman shape with traditional Celtic decoration. The two flat bosses on the neck-guard originally held red glass studs and a plume would have been inserted into the hole at the top. The side straps or cheek pieces are now lost.

Fig. 77
Neck collar
AD 50–150
Portland, Dorset, England
Brass and enamel
Diam. 15.6 cm
British Museum
1963,0407.1

This hinged neck collar displays Celtic motifs. Holes in the metal once held glass inlays. It was an evolution of earlier gold and silver torcs that had traditionally expressed the wearer's status and may now have been used to express opposition to Rome, as these were found exclusively at the edges of the province. The more affordable metal used may in part reflect Rome's exclusive control of local gold and silver deposits after the conquest.

Fig. 78
Dragonesque brooches
AD 75–175
Faversham, Kent, England
Copper alloy and enamel
L. 5.6 cm (each)
British Museum
.1088.70a–b
Bequeathed by William Gibbs

Named for their distinctive shape, brooches such as these first appeared after the Roman conquest. They fuse an existing local artistic taste for s-shaped ornaments with Roman enamelling techniques.

Fig. 79
The tombstone of Marcus Favonius Facilis, centurion of Legion XX
AD 43–63
Camulodunum (Colchester), England
Freestone
H. 199.5 cm, W. 86 cm, D. 24 cm
Colchester Museums
JOSLIN.46

Facilis is shown in full regalia, holding the *vitis*, a centurion's swagger stick (a short cane that symbolised his authority), in his right hand. He was probably born in northern Italy (in Nero's day still considered part of Cisalpine Gaul). This had been the traditional recruiting ground for the legions since Augustus, later complemented by the descendants of Roman settlers from southern France and Spain. Facilis' legion was transferred from Lower Germany in AD 43 to form part of the invading force that entered Britain.

The style of the carving is very similar to Roman legionary tombstones in the Rhine region, suggesting that the sculptor had come from there together with the army and used familiar material. Analysis has revealed that the stone was imported from Gallia Belgica. The monument was dedicated by Facilis' freedmen Verecundus and Novicius. As he is not described as a veteran, Facilis may have died before AD 49 when the colony at Camulodunum (Colchester) was founded, but this is not certain. His tombstone – one of the earliest preserved examples of Roman sculpture from Britain – was toppled during the Boudican rebellion.

The legion until now stationed at Colchester was moved forward, but its veterans were settled in a newly established *colonia* that replaced Camulodunum's previous military garrison and converted the old fort to civilian use (Fig. 79).[38] Caratacus, still leading the resistance, was thereby forced to move on from his refuge with the Silures. In a pitched battle with Roman forces in AD 51, he was defeated and escaped, but his wife, daughter and brothers were captured. He fled to the Brigantes, but was handed over by their Rome-friendly queen Cartimandua and taken to Rome to be paraded in public.[39] Claudius honoured Scapula with triumphal insignia; it was at this point that Claudius' own triumphal arch in Rome was dedicated.[40] Many of the major mining sites were now within Roman reach (Figs 80–3).[41]

However, Caratacus' capture did not end tribal resistance; the Silures, against whom Scapula seems to have ordered a brutal campaign of extermination, fought particularly hard.[42] They overwhelmed a large Roman detachment left behind in their territory, which suffered heavy losses, including numerous senior officers. Other units engaged in plunder – Tacitus mentions the greed of their commanders – were also overwhelmed.[43] Roman booty and prisoners were traded among the tribes and this spurred further unrest. Amid these setbacks, Scapula died in post in AD 52. The next governor, Aulus Didius Gallus, focused on consolidation.[44] He was an experienced commander, who previously had received triumphal insignia for his action in the Balkans. When Nero succeeded Claudius as *princeps* two years later he initially left Didius Gallus in post. Roman attention, and Nero's main focus, was now firmly on the emerging threat in Armenia.[45]

Nero appointed a new governor of Britain in AD 57, Quintus Veranius.[46] Veranius had been the governor of Lycia from AD 43 to 48, when this territory had been converted from a client kingdom into a Roman province. During this time he also suppressed a rebellion there. With his experience and his first-hand knowledge of warfare in Lycia's rugged mountains, he was now considered the right man to take up the offensive against the Silures. In this he seems to have been successful, but he died at the end of his first year in office. According to Tacitus, he flattered Nero in his will and boasted that he would have conquered the whole island for him, if only he had two more years.[47] It is a revealing claim that illuminates both the relationship between senatorial governors and the *princeps*, and the highly competitive spirit among the aristocracy.[48]

In AD 58, the year of Corbulo's victories in Armenia, Nero appointed Gaius Suetonius Paulinus as governor of Britain.[49] Paulinus had a reputation to rival Corbulo's as a military commander. Early in Claudius' reign, he had been tasked with the suppression of a revolt in Mauretania in North Africa, and in the process became the first general to lead a Roman army across the Atlas Mountains and into the fringes of the Sahara Desert beyond, a glorious feat that he seems to have promoted in his dispatches or other writings (as Corbulo would do for his exploits in Armenia).[50] By AD 58, the military situation in the British tribal belt had become tense, and Nero probably chose Paulinus precisely because of his formidable reputation as a soldier. Whether this included explicit orders to expand Roman-held territory or whether Paulinus acted on his own initiative in the pursuit of glory is not known. The four legions and large numbers of auxiliaries under his command certainly provided Paulinus with options, and as an island, Britain offered clearly defined objectives for territorial

Britain's rich mineral resources were an important factor in Rome's economic exploitation of the province. The army's westward push into Wales after the initial conquest was partly motivated by a desire to control further mining assets. Export-geared production from British mining sites began under Claudius (the first ingots are dated to AD 49) and expanded rapidly under Nero. It was not long before British lead production rivalled that of Roman Spain. Lead extraction was often a by-product of silver mining, as both metals can occur in the same ore. Mines were under direct government control and often under military supervision (Fig. 80), but could be leased out to private contractors (Figs 81 and 82). While some of the work required specialist skills, the bulk involved arduous, and often dangerous, manual labour, usually by enslaved individuals, prisoners or convicts (*damnatio ad metalla,* 'condemnation to the mines', was a common form of punishment). For administrative purposes, ingots were produced to a standard size and weight (averaging 78 kg, perhaps to prevent pilfering), and mould-cast with inscriptions giving information on the production authority and date. Lost in transit, these lead pigs provide information on mining and processing sites, as well as transport routes (Fig. 83).

Fig. 80
Ingot
Romano-British
Blagdon, Somerset, England
Lead
H. 9.2 cm, L. 61 cm, Weight 73 kg
British Museum
1854,0506.1
Donated by James Williams

Inscribed in Latin: (PLUMBUM) BRITANNIC(U)M AUG(USTA) LE(GIO) II – 'British (lead) (produced by) Legion II Augusta'.

This ingot came from the Mendip mines in Somerset, which were among the earliest under Roman control and initially operated by the army. A similar ingot, mentioning the same legion but also inscribed with Nero's name, was found in a northern Gaulish port.

Fig. 81
Ingot
AD 60
Stockbridge, Hampshire, England
Lead
H. 11.4 cm, L. 58.4 cm, Weight 75.3 kg
British Museum
1861,0218.1

Inscribed in Latin: NERONIS AUG(USTI) EX K(ALENDIS) IAN(UARIIS) IV CO(N)S(ULIS) (PLUMBUM) BRIT(ANNICUM). EX ARGENT(ARIIS) C(AI) N[I]PI ASCAN[II] XXX – 'British (lead) (property) of Nero Augustus, from the first January of his fourth consulship. From the lead-silver works of Gaius Nipius Ascanius 30.'

Nero's titles date this ingot to AD 60. Gaius Nipius Ascanius seems to have been an official in one of the Mendip mines. The ingot was lost en route to a port on the south coast.

Fig. 82
Ingot
AD 60–70
Carmel, Flintshire, Wales
Lead
H. 9.5 cm, L. 59.5 cm, Weight 61 kg
Amgueddfa Cymru – National
Museum Wales
50.188

Inscribed in Latin: C(AI) NIPI
ASCANI – '(product) of Gaius
Nipius Ascanius'.

Roman expansion brought northern
Welsh mining sites in Flintshire
under Roman military control. It
appears that Ascanius, formerly
active in the Mendip mines, now
set up as a private contractor and
leased a Flintshire mine.

Fig. 83
Ingot
AD 63–9
Rossett, Flintshire, Wales
Lead
H. 11 cm, L. 53 cm, Weight 63.4 kg
Wrexham County Borough Museum
and Archive
1446

Inscribed in Latin: [NERONIS]
CAES(ARIS) AUG(USTI)
(PLUMBUM) BRIT(ANNICUM)
(E)X MAGUL(…) FUSUM
OP(ERIBUS) IN PROV(INCIA)
TREBEL(LIO) MAXIMO
LEG(ATO) AUG(USTI) –
'(Property) of Nero Caesar
Augustus, British (lead) from
Magul(…), smelted at the works
in the province when Trebellius
Maximus was imperial legate'.

Trebellius Maximus brought stability
to the province after Boudica's
revolt. This ingot, discovered only
in 2019, is the first attestation of
Trebellius' name in Britain. Lead
from the Flintshire mines was
probably exported along the River
Dee estuary.

expansion. Corbulo's successes in Armenia and victories in Germany will have stirred Paulinus' aristocratic pride and sense of rivalry further.[51] He may also have felt considerable pressure not to remain inactive, both in his own province and compared to other commanders elsewhere.[52]

Paulinus immediately took up the offensive and subdued the Ordovices of mid-Wales within two years. At the start of his third campaigning season, his army faced the last symbolic stronghold, the island of Mona (Anglesey). Mona was the main centre of Druidism in Britain and was in addition crowded with refugees from the mainland. Druids, influential native priests, had long been targeted for fostering resistance against Rome. With his force of two legions and associated auxiliaries, Paulinus staged an amphibious landing and massacred the native population (Fig. 84).[53]

While Paulinus was thus occupied, Prasutagus, the prosperous client king of the Iceni, had died. In his will he named Nero as his joint heir together with his two daughters, perhaps seeking in this way to safeguard his family's prominent position. However, Nero resolved to abolish the client kingdom and impose direct Roman control, in line with established Roman policy. The decision may have not have been anticipated by the Iceni, and its implementation certainly seems to have been badly mishandled by the province's financial procurator, Catus Decianus. Tacitus states that Roman centurions pillaged Iceni territory, the king's relatives were exploited and abused and other Icenian nobles stripped of their estates. Cassius Dio additionally records that Decianus unexpectedly called in long-standing loans to members of the local elite who had considered them grants awarded by Claudius; he also alleges that Seneca had invested on a grand scale and lent large sums at a heavy rate of interest, which he suddenly reclaimed.[54]

With the governor and the bulk of the Roman army engaged far to the west, Prasutagus' widow Boudica (Tacitus calls her 'Boudicca') now led an uprising in AD 60–1.[55] The Trinovantes, in the same region, had many grievances of their own and quickly joined the rebellion, as did others. Boudica must have been a powerful woman who commanded great authority, but she is hard to grasp as a historical character. Her name, in the authentic Celtic form of 'Boudica', means 'victory'. Evidence from elite burials of the period confirms that women could hold prominent positions in British tribal society.[56] Apart from that, the Boudica of the Latin and Greek written sources is entirely a Roman literary construct designed to bring the qualities and flaws of certain Roman actors into sharper focus (see p. 180).

The uprising took Camulodunum's Roman settlers and their families by surprise and gave them little time to react. Decianus sent a negligible relief force of 200 men – either they were all the troops he could spare or he misread the rebellion as a minor, localised riot. Camulodunum was not only the closest Roman settlement to the Iceni territories, but also a highly symbolic prize. Refounded as Colonia Claudia Victricensis ('The Claudian City of Victory'), it was the administrative capital of the whole province and the centre of its civilian Roman citizen population. A major temple dominated the settlement, perhaps begun by Claudius but then completed by Nero after Claudius' deification and dedicated to his memory. It served as the provincial focus of the imperial cult – a place for the native population and their elite to demonstrate their loyalty to Rome. To the local Trinovantes, who had been forced to make financial contributions to its construction and maintenance, it seemed – in Tacitus' words

Fig. 84
Gang chain
100 BC–AD 78
Llyn Cerrig Bach, Anglesey, Wales
Iron
W. 20 cm, L. 310 cm
Amgueddfa Cymru – National
Museum Wales
44.32/59

This chain would have held five enslaved people, convicts or prisoners of war. It is extremely heavy and its wearers would have been forced tightly and painfully together. It was ritually deposited in the lake of Llyn Cerrig Bach, on Anglesey, a stronghold of the druids and an important religious centre where people had left metal offerings for centuries. Violence between different communities accompanied the establishment of kingdoms in late Iron Age Britain, and enslaved men and women were exported to the Continent even before the Roman conquest. After the Roman invasion, captive Britons had to serve the occupiers, and a significant number would have done so in the mines. During the subsequent conflicts, many Roman soldiers were taken prisoner and passed between tribal communities, including the Silures and Ordovices.

Fig. 85
The 'Fenwick Hoard'
AD 60–1
Colchester, England
Copper alloy, emerald, ivory, glass,
gold, pearl, silver
Hooped armlet: Diam. 7.6 cm; ring
with emerald (centre): Diam. 1.6 cm;
silver armlet with roundel: Diam.
8 cm
Colchester Museums

This remarkable hoard was found beneath the floor of a Roman house in Colchester. It seems to have been buried for safekeeping by settlers fleeing for their lives during Boudica's attack. The building was destroyed by fire and the objects never retrieved. Its owners, perhaps a couple, most likely perished during the onslaught. The woman's gold jewellery – a pair each of hollow ball and pearl earrings, two hooped armlets and a bangle, and the gold rings (three of them still set with green emeralds) – is very similar to finds from Pompeii and Herculaneum and may have been

imported from Italy (or brought from there as personal belongings). Among the silver items is a solid chain with a hoop for a pendant. Four ivory feet represent the remains of a small *pyxis* or box. A beautiful armlet, the strap of which is decorated with a hunting scene of panthers stalking deer, features a central roundel showing Jupiter seated between Fortuna and Victory – a common military motif. There are two further silver *armillae* (armbands) that may have been awards for bravery in battle, fitting for a retired soldier. In addition, there is a bronze *bulla* and twenty-seven coins.

Fig. 86
Bone fragments
AD 60–1
Colchester High Street, England
Bone
Tibia: W. 6.5 cm (approx. max.);
mandible: L. 11.5 cm (approx. max.)
Colchester Archaeological Trust

These burnt human bone fragments, part of a mandible (jawbone) and tibia (shin) were found in Camulodunum's Boudican destruction layer. The front of the tibia – this is the upper part of the bone just below the knee – was sliced off by a ferocious blow with a sharp blade while the leg was flexed. The back of the jawbone similarly shows cut marks along the raised inside edge, consistent with a downward blow through the cheek, between the left eye and ear. The existence and shape of the third molar suggest that the victim was an older individual.

– *quasi arx aeterna dominatione*, 'like a citadel of eternal servitude'. Particular hatred was directed towards the veteran settlers, who had driven the locals from their lands and enslaved the native population.[57] Recent excavations provide a sense of the settlers' prosperity and the savagery of the attack by the British rebels (Fig. 85). As the city had no defensive wall, the Romans withdrew to the temple precinct and the soldiers and others barricaded themselves inside. After a two-day siege, the temple was torched and stormed. Dio records gruesome atrocities against any survivors; while his account is partly a stock description, there can be little doubt about the brutality of what happened (Figs 86 and 87).[58]

By now, a detachment of a legion under the commander Petilius Cerealis had rushed to the scene, but was beaten back with catastrophic losses among the infantry. Only Cerealis' cavalry managed to escape to the security of a fortified camp (Fig. 88).[59] Paulinus had meanwhile quickly moved back east from Mona towards Londinium (London) on the Thames, already the commercial centre of the province and thronging with traders and merchants (see Fig. 90, p. 115).[60] Warned by Cerealis' experience and with insufficient troops, he decided to abandon the settlement and withdraw westwards, allowing the able-bodied civilian population to join him. Many others were left behind and killed by the natives, who now torched Londinium. The *municipium* of Verulamium (St Albans) soon after suffered the same fate.

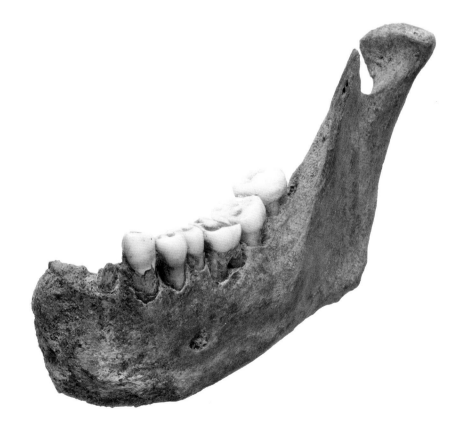

Fig. 87
Bronze head of Nero
AD 54–61
River Alde at Rendham,
Suffolk, England
Copper alloy
H. 31.5 cm; W. 24.5 cm; D. 25 cm
British Museum
1965,1201.1
Purchased with support from
Art Fund

Statues of Nero were erected
throughout the Empire. This bronze
head (long mistaken for Claudius)
shows his characteristic accession-
period hairstyle of the mid-fifties AD,
with its simple fringe and central
parting (see Fig. 49, p. 79). The
eyes were originally inlaid in a
different material. It was probably
produced in the north-west
provinces, perhaps Gaul. The slight
incongruity between the frontal and
profile views (see image p. 86),
often found in imperial portraits
from this region, may reflect limited
access to three-dimensional
models from Rome – images were
based on coin impressions instead.
The head was found in the River
Alde in Suffolk, on the boundary
between Iceni and Trinovantes
tribal land, which suggests that
it may have been purposefully
deposited there as an offering.
The complete statue was likely
torn down in nearby Camulodunum
during the Boudican rebellion.

Paulinus eventually drew together a force consisting of about 10,000 soldiers according to Tacitus, and committed to meeting Boudica's forces.[61] He chose terrain that suited his troops and neutralised his opponents' vast numerical superiority. The ensuing battle turned into a rout. The tribal force, swelled by many non-combatants, was annihilated; Boudica committed suicide. Tacitus records 80,000 Britons slain, as against 400 Romans soldiers.[62]

Perhaps the most remarkable aspect of Tacitus' account is his unquestioning exoneration of Paulinus; while he refers to the events as *gravis clades*, a grave defeat, he offers no further qualification.[63] In its associations and magnitude, the near loss of a recently conquered province must have conjured up traumatic memories – the scale of civilian deaths, put by Tacitus and Cassius Dio at a staggering 70–80,000 Roman victims overall, recalled the infamous 'Asian Vespers' of 88 BC, when Mithridates VI of Pontus had incited a massacre of all Roman and Italic citizens in the province of Asia during the First Mithridatic War.[64] More recent was the spectre of Varus' defeat in Germany (*clades Variana*); by rights, the British *clades* should have been recorded as *clades Pauliniana*, even if Paulinus had not been personally defeated in battle.[65]

Nero had meanwhile authorised the transfer of reinforcements from the Rhine frontier: a detachment of 2,000 legionaries, eight cohorts of auxiliaries and 1,000 auxiliary cavalry – a total of 7,000 men (Fig. 88, Figs 91 and 92).[66] The legionaries were used to bring the troops that had suffered defeat under Cerealis back up to strength. If the prior Roman losses corresponded to the reinforcements, their dreadful scale becomes apparent (not far off a fifth of the original invasion force).[67] Paulinus now continued the war against other groups of the native population. He pursued excessive punitive measures – bystanders were treated as traitors and, in Tacitus' words, 'the tribes which had shown themselves dubious or disaffected were harried with fire and sword'.[68] A direct result of this ongoing warfare and destruction was widespread famine.

The next events may be far more significant than Tacitus' highly partisan account indicates. Nero replaced the hapless procurator Catus Decianus (who had fled to Gaul as the rebellion unfolded) with a new man, Gaius Iulius Alpinus Classicianus. Classicianus must have witnessed the smouldering ruins of the province's urban centres and the devastation of the surrounding countryside at first hand and reported back what he found. Vital infrastructure and nearly two decades' worth of investment into the new province had been lost, with the tax base correspondingly eroded. According to Suetonius, Nero briefly considered abandoning the province altogether.[69] If this was the case, he quickly decided against it, as it would undoubtedly have tarnished his prestige as *princeps* only six years into his young reign. According to Suetonius, he did so out of respect for his adoptive father, Claudius, who had conquered the province. In truth, the enormous cost of maintaining a large Roman garrison probably meant that the province was never profitable even during peacetime.[70]

In order to salvage the situation Classicianus seems to have advocated a far more conciliatory policy towards the native population, and this brought him into conflict with Paulinus almost from the outset. Nero now dispatched Polyclitus, one of his senior freedmen, from Rome to investigate the matter. As a result, in AD 62 Paulinus was replaced as governor by Publius Petronius Turpilianus, a man loyal to Nero, and policy changed accordingly.[71] The financial aspects of the provincial rebuilding programme must have been overseen by Classicianus.

Londinium appears to have served as the major logistics hub and centre of a large-scale army-led recovery operation.[72] A major quay structure was built on the north bank of the River Thames, in work involving Thracian auxiliaries.[73] A large fort was constructed here in about AD 63 in order to protect the site and provide facilities for army personnel.[74] It also guarded a piled wooden bridge over the Thames, creating an important north–south transport link. It has not yet been confirmed when exactly Londinium became the province's official capital, but if it was not under Nero, then the foundations of its future pre-eminence were certainly laid in this decade.

Classicianus died in post in AD 65 and was buried at Londinium. His tomb provides important details about his background and career (Fig. 89).[75] A provincial from north-eastern Gaul, he was a Romanised member of the local Treviran elite – presumably much more attuned to provincial sensibilities than senatorial officials from Rome. Tacitus, however, presents Polyclitus' replacement of Paulinus by Turpilianus very much as the wrongful ousting of a successful senatorial commander by social inferiors, an early hint of his prevailing bias. This is also the first time that he singles out a prominent freedman for negative comment during Nero's reign.[76] In reality, the transition was managed tactfully. Paulinus does not seem to have suffered any further censure, although, in contrast to the majority of his predecessors he did not receive the triumphal honours he may have hoped for at the outset of his term. His successor Turpilianus was the nephew of Britain's first governor, Aulus Plautius, and had just served as consul – his appointment therefore was a conciliatory gesture to the senate at a time of crisis more than a reprimand for his predecessor.[77] Turpilianus, however, remained for only a year, returning to Rome to take up another senior post. His successor in AD 63 was Marcus Trebellius Maximus, who had served as *consul suffectus* with Seneca during the second year of Nero's reign. (A *consul suffectus* would sometimes take over from a *consul ordinarius* part way through a year. It was a role with less prestige than the latter position, the holder of which was elected at the start of a year and after whom that year would be named.) Trebellius Maximus had also been a member of an important commission in AD 61 that revised the census lists and tax assessments for Gaul.[78] His financial expertise may have played a major part in his new appointment. The wider context arguably was Nero's attempt to rectify uncontrolled extortion and other abuses by Roman officials and tax farmers in those years, which also saw a number of official trials involving former governors of various provinces (see p. 135). For Britain these measures were unfortunately not implemented in time to avoid the rebellion that caused such destruction.

Togidubnus' and his southern kingdom's loyalty during the Boudican rebellion seems to have been an important factor in Paulinus' ability to turn the military situation around, and it may now have been rewarded. At Calleva Atrebatum (Silchester), locally produced tiles stamped with Nero's name suggest significant imperial investment in the town, on a scale so far not attested elsewhere in the north-western Roman provinces (Fig. 93). Preliminary excavation results indicate the existence of a high-status domestic building in stone architecture west of Calleva's timber forum, plausibly interpreted as a town residence for Togidubnus and his family. Perhaps this complemented the palatial residence at Fishbourne near the south coast, which was enhanced in this period to a luxurious standard with a range of imported material, including

Fig. 89a
Partial reconstruction of the tomb of Gaius Iulius Alpinus Classicianus
After AD 65
Trinity Place, City of London, England
Stone
H. 218 cm, W. 230 cm
British Museum
1852,0806.2
Donated by W.J. Hall

Fig. 89b
Reconstruction sketch of the tomb of Gaius Iulius Alpinus Classicianus with restored inscription

Nero's procurator, Gaius Iulius Alpinus Classicianus, was appointed to rebuild and reform the financial administration of the province of Britain after the devastation of the Boudican revolt. Classicianus was a well-connected provincial knight, most likely from Augusta Treverorum (Trier) in Gallia Belgica, where his family seems to have belonged to the local elite. He died in post in AD 65. His wife, Iulia Placata Induta, dedicated this imposing tomb to him. The tall, altar-shaped monument was probably raised on a high plinth above shallow steps, with the inscription carefully laid out in fine *scriptura monumentalis* (literally 'monumental script'). It was crowned by an ornate antefix between lateral bolsters, most likely above an ornamental cornice, similar to contemporary tomb monuments in Italy (preserved, for example, in Pompeii). In post-destruction Londinium, it must have been particularly conspicuous in its expensive stone architecture and Continental refinement.

Fig. 90
Writing tablet
AD 57
Walbrook, London, England
Silver fir
H. 5.6 cm, W. 13.7 cm
Bloomberg collection
WT 44

'In the consulship of Nero Claudius Caesar Augustus Germanicus for the second time and of Lucius Calpurnius Piso, on the sixth day before the Ides of January (8 January AD 57). I, Tibullus the freedman of Venustus, have written and say that I owe Gratus, the freedman of Spurius, 105 denarii for the price of the merchandise which has been sold and delivered. This money I am due to repay him or the person whom the matter will concern…'

The text gives a lively sense of the atmosphere in the busy commercial centre of Londinium (London) at the beginning of Nero's reign. It belongs to a cache of wooden writing tablets discovered in the City of London between 2010 and 2013. The 'Bloomberg Tablets' are among the very earliest examples of Latin writing in Britain. This was a stylus tablet. The original wax writing surface in the recessed section is now lost, but the tip of the stylus penetrated into the wood, in such a way that with the use of special imaging techniques the outlines of the letters can still be made out.

Fig. 91 (above left)
Writing tablet
AD 65–70
Walbrook, London, England
Silver fir
H. 4.4 cm, W. 13.6 cm
Bloomberg collection
WT 33

'… Classicus, prefect of the Sixth Cohort of Nervii.' The text may refer to the equestrian Julius Classicus, a Treviran nobleman and most likely a kinsman of Nero's procurator Classicianus, who perhaps recommended him as commander of an auxiliary cohort. The Sixth Cohort of Nervii may have been one of eight auxiliary units sent from Germany to Britain to provide reinforcements after the Boudican revolt in AD 61.

Fig. 92 (left)
Writing tablet
AD 67
Walbrook, London, England
Silver fir
H. 11.2 cm, W. 14.2 cm
Bloomberg collection
WT 48

'In the consulship of Fonteius Capito and Iulius Rufus (AD 67) […] of the First Cohort of Vangiones […] son […] all […].' The text marked on the tablet seems to be a legal document, perhaps a will, drafted by a member of the Sixth Cohort of Vangiones. The date and find context suggest that this was another of the auxiliary groups transferred from Germany to Britain in AD 61.

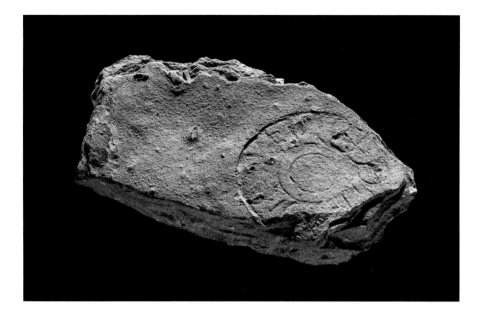

Fig. 93
Roman tile stamped with Nero's name
AD 54–68
Silchester, Hampshire, England
Ceramic
L. 13.2 cm, W. 7.2 cm
British Museum
1925,1212.1
Donated by Lieutenant Colonel
J.B.P. Karslake

This tile was discovered at
Silchester (Calleva Atrebatum
during Nero's reign) in the south
of England. It is stamped with
the *princeps*' name: NER(O)
CL(AUDIUS) CAE(SAR)
AUG(USTUS) G(E)R(MANICUS).
Many more tiles of this type were
found during recent excavations,
as well as the kilns that produced
them. They attest significant
imperial investment in the
town's infrastructure during
the Neronian period.

expensive marble. At Calleva, there was also a Neronian bath building in the south-eastern part of the city, and the simple earth and timber amphitheatre just outside may have first been built in the Neronian period.[79] In the nearby town of Noviomagus Reginorum (Chichester) a dedicatory inscription to Nero was discovered, most likely associated with a building.[80] At Aquae Sulis (Bath) further to the north-west, there is evidence of Neronian work on the Temple of Sulis-Minerva and its associated sacred spring and thermal baths, presumably mostly for the benefit of nearby Roman army units.[81]

The post-rebellion change in policy, with its momentary halt to further expansion and more accommodating treatment of the population, stabilised the province sufficiently for Nero to order one of its four legions east in preparation for his planned Caucasus campaign in AD 67, along with its associated eight cohorts of elite Batavian auxiliaries.[82]

The Rhine and Danube frontiers

Nero's measures along Rome's central European and Balkan borders received scant attention from ancient authors, and until relatively recently this was echoed in modern scholarship. By necessity, demands on Roman manpower elsewhere limited offensive options in this vast region, but while individual generals may have cherished battle honours against Germanic and other tribes, in a wider context there was little to be gained here. For these areas, Nero's reign largely constituted a continuation and consolidation of Claudian policies.

At the beginning of Claudius' principate, the Rhine frontier had seen a number of major campaigns, perhaps in part stemming from his predecessor Caligula's unrealised plans for a Germanic war. In AD 41, the new governor of Upper Germany, Servius Sulpicius Galba (who had been appointed by Caligula after Gaetulicus' conspiracy against him; see p. 47), defeated the Chatti; his colleague in Lower Germany, Publius Gabinius, the Chauci. These were large and powerful tribes between the Rhine and Weser rivers, and along the North Sea coast. During the latter operation the last remaining eagle of one of Varus'

Figs 94a and b
Horse trappings
c. AD 50–5
Xanten, Germany
Silvered bronze
H. 140 cm (approx.), W. 160 cm
(approx.), as mounted
British Museum
1854,0717.1–55, 1868,0220.1
(1854,0717.53 pictured right)
Donated by Joseph Mayer

These silvered horse trappings are
from the Roman fort Castra Vetera
(Xanten) in Lower Germany, a key
military base from which Roman
power was projected across the
Rhine into the north-west German
plain. Depictions on military
gravestones give a good sense of
how these ornaments were fitted
to the mounts. Among the set are
four roundels with portrait busts,
perhaps of Nero or Claudius.
One is inscribed 'PLINIO
PRAEF(ECTO) EQ(UITUM)'
(property, or unit of 'Pliny, prefect
of cavalry') and may have belonged
to Pliny the Elder during his
service there, or a soldier under
his command.

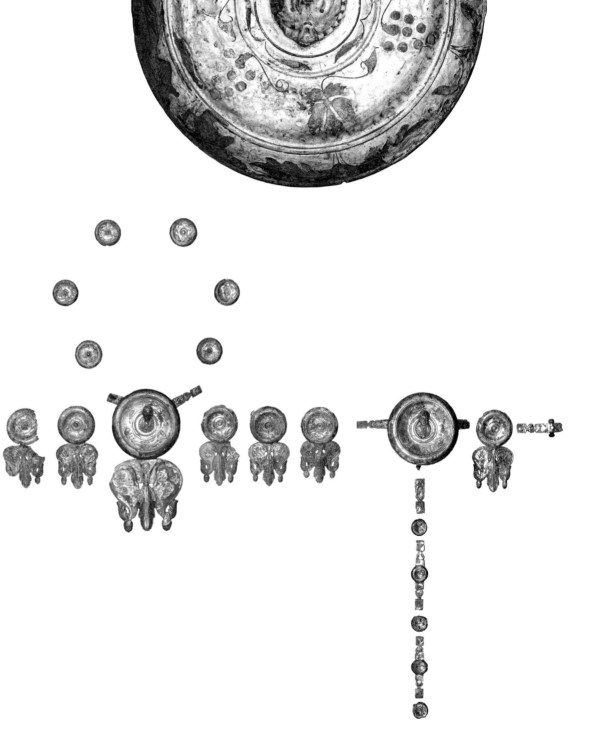

lost legions was recovered, a great propaganda success.[83] Afterwards, Claudius installed various Rome-friendly chiefs as client kings, with mixed success – individual leaders could generally only maintain limited authority within Germanic tribal society.[84]

In AD 47 the Chauci raided the Gaulish coast with their fleet.[85] Gnaeus Domitius Corbulo, then newly installed as governor of Lower Germany (and later in command in Armenia under Nero), took action. Despite having some success, his measures threatened to bring together a major coalition of Germanic tribes. Claudius ordered Corbulo to cease further offensive action and withdraw across the Rhine. Still, he did grant Corbulo triumphal insignia.[86] Corbulo is said to have uttered *beatos quondam duces Romanos* – 'happy the Roman generals of old'. The quote, related by both Tacitus and Cassius Dio, perfectly encapsulates the fundamental incompatibility between the old Republican senatorial military ethos and the new political realities of the principate.[87]

Pliny the Elder, author of the *Natural History* and an important source on Nero's reign, was stationed in Germany at the very beginning of his equestrian military career during the reigns of both Claudius and Nero.[88] He first served in AD 46 under Corbulo as the *praefectus*, commanding officer, of an auxiliary infantry cohort in Lower Germany and probably took part in Corbulo's defeat of the Chauci. Pliny later returned to the province to become a *praefectus alae*, the commander of an auxiliary cavalry unit, under the incoming governor Pompeius Paulinus (Figs 94a and b). His service coincided with that of Vespasian's older son Titus.[89] During this time, Pliny composed his first treatise, *De Iaculatione Equestri*, on the use of javelins by cavalrymen, and later a *History of Rome's German Wars* in twenty-two books, an important source for Tacitus' *Annals* and *Germania*. In AD 57, two and a half years into Nero's reign, the Frisii, another Germanic tribe, tried to settle on a strip of borderland on the right bank of the Rhine, an area out of bounds to tribesmen. The new governor of the province, Lucius Duvius Avitus, demanded that they should withdraw or seek permission from Nero in Rome. Tacitus mentions a visit by their tribal leaders to the capital, when Nero awarded them Roman citizenship but refused their people permission to settle in the disputed territory.[90] As the Frisii did not leave, they were forcefully expelled by auxiliary cavalry in bloody skirmishes. These horse units were the type Pliny had commanded; whether he was still present and involved is unclear – he may have left military service around this time to return to Rome. The action appears to have been considered significant enough for Nero to accept his third imperial acclamation.[91] A year later, in AD 58, another tribe, the Ampsivarii, moved into the same borderlands after they had been pushed out of their own territory by the Chauci. Avitus did not allow them to settle either and an attempt by the Ampsivarii to assemble a Germanic tribal coalition was defeated by the swift action of the armies of Lower and Upper Germany.[92]

These examples demonstrate the active use of both diplomacy and force required of the Roman commanders, and perhaps they may at times have felt tempted to expand their mandate in the pursuit of glory, even if the big decisions had to be referred to Nero in Rome.[93] Pliny hints at the wealth of these men and their desire to demonstrate their status as members of the senatorial elite. Pompeius Paulinus travelled with 12,000 pounds of silver tableware even 'when confronting the most ferocious tribes', while Duvius

Fig. 95
Inscribed tombstone
AD 74–9
Tomb of the Plautii, Ponte Lucano,
near Tivoli, Italy (in loco)
Marble

This remarkable inscription details
the career of Tiberius Plautius
Silvanus Aelianus. It comes from
the tomb of his family, the Plautii,
near Tivoli outside Rome. As Nero's
governor of the province of Moesia,
Plautius Aelianus established
settlements of various tribal peoples
and expanded Roman influence
along the Black Sea coast. None of
these actions are mentioned in the
extant literary record.

Avitus owned two chased metal drinking cups by the classical Greek artist
Kalamis, prized antiques once owned by Germanicus. The possession of such
artworks mattered; Nero himself never travelled without a statuette of an
Amazon by the Greek master Strongylion.[94]

Following the Boudican rebellion, numerous units of the German army had
to be sent across the channel as reinforcements to the British garrison. Strong
detachments were later despatched east to the Parthian borderlands. This left the
Rhine frontier exposed. In the early AD 60s, Nero gave orders to rebuild in stone
Castra Vetera (Xanten), one of the main legionary bases in the north-west. Not
only did this turn it into a strong fortress but it also sent a clear signal of Roman
might to the tribes east of the river.[95] In parallel, archaeological finds from
greater Germany attest a marked intensification of diplomatic contacts with
these tribes around the middle of the first century AD.[96] Perhaps in consequence,

conditions were stable enough for a Roman knight to travel through central Germany to the Baltic region in order to secure an extraordinary and plentiful supply of precious amber for Nero's displays in Rome (see p. 145).

The Danube frontier, all the way to the Black Sea and its northern shores, was similarly affected by tribal movements. In this case, however, the literary sources are entirely silent about events – a stark reminder about how selective their authors were, mostly in order to construct a highly focused, anti-Neronian narrative that suppressed anything more positive. It is only through the chance survival of a lengthy inscription from the tomb of one of the main protagonists that we have any knowledge of events (Fig. 95).[97] In about AD 60, Nero appointed a new governor, Tiberius Plautius Silvanus Aelianus, to the province of Moesia on the lower Danube.[98]

The region, linking Europe and Asia, had great strategic value, so Claudius had fully incorporated the client kingdom of Thrace into the Roman Empire in AD 46, some of which was included in Moesia. Nero made his first significant speeches in the senate in AD 53 and must have been briefed on the recent unrest and wars in the region. In response, the senate granted the city of Byzantium a five-year remission of tax to relieve its financial burden. Some three years later, in AD 56/7, during Nero's reign, the city of Tyras, an old Greek foundation on the Black Sea shore near the mouth of the Dniestr River, issued coins that suggest it had just become part of the province of Moesia. Originally this had extended only south of the Danube but now seems to have been expanded northwards beyond the Danube delta to incorporate more of the coast of the Black Sea, perhaps including the city of Olbia.[99] The governor in those years was Titus Flavius Sabinus, Vespasian's older brother; perhaps in recognition of these accomplishments, Nero next appointed him *praefectus urbi* ('prefect of the city') in Rome, a prestigious post he held throughout the remainder of Nero's reign.

Fig. 96
Detail of a silver cup
Late 1st century BC–early
1st century AD
Boscoreale, Italy
Silver
H. 9 cm, W. 19.5 cm, Diam. 12.5 cm
Musée du Louvre, Paris
BJ2366

Augustus, seated, extends his right arm to receive submissions from captives (this part of the cup is now lost). A small bronze figure of Nero shows the *princeps* in a strikingly similar pose (Fig. 97).

Fig. 97
A small bronze figure of Nero in full military dress
AD 54–9
Opitergium (Oderzo), Italy
Bronze
H. 11 cm, W. 9.2 cm
Museo Archeologico Nazionale
di Venezia
n.402 Inventario 1887, n.276
Inventario dei Bronzi 1952

Nero, wearing full military dress including body armour and *paludamentum* (military cloak), is depicted seated, his right hand extended to accept the submission of captives or receive envoys. His pose is similar to that of Augustus on the Boscoreale silver cup (Fig. 96).

The figure is hollowed out in the back and similar finds suggest that it was originally an attachment to a bronze monument and almost certainly part of a multi-figure group.

Plautius, Sabinus' successor, faced similar challenges to his colleagues along the north-west frontier. Significant pressure on his province came from large groups of restive tribesmen across the Danube. The exact chronology is unclear, but in AD 61 Plautius had to relinquish one of his legions, which was sent east to reinforce the troops of Lucius Caesennius Paetus who was then in Armenia (see p. 122).[100] Perhaps because military options were now limited, around 100,000 tribal people were allowed to settle south of the Danube. There was similar strain on the Bosporan Kingdom, an important client state along the northern Black Sea shore, partly in eastern Crimea. Here, Plautius relieved a siege of the city of Chersonesus by Scythian tribesmen. As these incidents demonstrate, Nero, and his governors, had to deal with the first ripples of the great tribal migrations,[101] events perhaps reflected in the iconography of certain Neronian statuary, relief sculptures and other imagery (Figs 96 and 97).

Further measures followed to strengthen the Roman position in the Black Sea. In AD 64, Nero recalled Polemo II, the ruler of Pontus, and turned his realm over to direct Roman control.[102] Pontus comprised much of the southern and south-eastern Black Sea coast, and its ports were crucial for trade with the northern shore. It may be that Nero's advisors judged Polemo's performance in securing the shipping lanes and coastal hinterland insufficient and urged change. Polemo's royal fleet, some forty vessels operating out of Trapezus (Trabzon), was turned into a new unit of the Roman navy, the *classis Pontica*. Similarly, his guard was taken into Roman service as a new auxiliary formation.[103] Roman interest seems mainly to have been in securing the maritime routes, but a few road links that connected across the mountains with Armenia were also important. The region remained a high priority for Nero's military planning over the remaining years of his reign.

Crisis in Armenia

At the height of the Boudican rebellion in Britain, the Parthian prince Tiridates had re-entered Armenia with the support of Parthian troops. He laid siege to Tigranocerta, the city captured by Corbulo two years previously where Rome's hapless new client king Tigranes now held out with a contingent of Roman soldiers. The Parthian great king Vologases meanwhile assembled a large army along the Euphrates River, threatening the Roman province of Syria.

Corbulo's special command had come to an end, but he remained in the region as governor of Syria, having taken over the province from Ummidius Quadratus, who had died in office. The precise nature and sequence of the following events is not easy to establish, and may have been contested in the partisan accounts Tacitus used as his sources. In light of the Parthian show of strength, Corbulo negotiated with Vologases, who was still interested in securing Armenia for his younger brother Tiridates as part of a peaceful settlement with Rome (their other brother, Pacorus, ruled over the Iranian region of Media). Corbulo therefore agreed that a Parthian delegation should travel to Nero in Rome for further discussions. However, in a serious setback after Corbulo's earlier military successes, the besieged Tigranes and the entire Roman garrison had to withdraw from Armenia.[104] At Corbulo's request, Nero appointed a new commander for the Armenian war, and in an important political gesture to the senate, Nero chose the consul of AD 61 Lucius Caesennius Paetus, whose term of office ended in June (his fellow consul Publius Petronius Turpilianus was assigned to Britain). Nero was clearly not yet prepared to relinquish Armenia. The Parthian delegation was sent back without having secured any Roman commitment. Immediately after his arrival in the East, Paetus prepared an offensive, even though winter was approaching. He crossed with two legions into Armenia, aiming to recapture Tigranocerta and devastate – in retaliation and a quest for booty – the areas spared by Corbulo previously.[105] While he took a few fortified places, the onset of colder weather soon forced him back to his quarters in eastern Cappadocia. Yet he seems to have extolled his modest exploits in a glowing despatch to Nero in Rome.[106]

In the following spring of AD 62, Paetus renewed his offensive.[107] Corbulo had in the meantime moved his forces in Syria up to the Euphrates, whereupon Vologases' army turned towards Armenia, threatening Paetus instead. Paetus first moved as if to offer battle, but then drew back and left 3,000 chosen infantry and his Pannonian auxiliary cavalry to hold the nearest passes over the Taurus Mountains and the adjacent plain against the pursuing Parthians (Figs 98–101). The Roman troops were decisively routed. Paetus and his two legions tried to hold a fortified camp at a place called Rhandeia near Tigranocerta, where they were surrounded and besieged by Vologases' vastly superior forces. Corbulo marched to his aid with part of the Syrian army, but under heavy pressure Paetus initiated negotiations for a truce with Vologases. The result amounted to Roman surrender; Paetus and his army were allowed to retreat, but all Romans had to vacate Armenia and hand over their strong points and supplies to the Parthians. Another Parthian delegation was sent to Rome, presumably to reiterate Vologases' demands now that Paetus had been humbled, and no Roman was to enter Armenia in the meantime. A lack of close coordination between the Roman commanders, due in part to their fierce rivalry, clearly played a major part in the Rhandeia setback.[108]

In Rome, the news must have come as a resounding shock and surprise. The timing, so soon after the debacle in Britain, was also unfortunate – Nero's Parthian Arch had been completed in record time and had only just been dedicated. Nero and his council now at last decided to accept a diplomatic solution, but only after a renewed show of Roman strength.[109] The Parthian emissaries were sent back with presents, and perhaps already with Nero's counter-proposal. To the public, however, it looked as if the war would continue with renewed vigour; Nero may even have given the impression that he would join the army himself.[110] Paetus was recalled, Corbulo reappointed to his special command and given additional reinforcements: a legion was sent east from Carnuntum in Pannonia (a distance of some 3,000 km away) and additional troop detachments followed from Illyria and Egypt.[111]

Probably in AD 64, with his new army ready and assembled, Corbulo re-entered Armenia. He destroyed the domains of those Armenian nobles who had switched their allegiance to the Parthians and threatened widespread devastation, but soon received envoys from both Tiridates and Vologases. It was agreed that a conference would be held at Rhandeia, the site of Paetus' defeat. After preliminary negotiations, a major ceremony was enacted in front of the assembled armies: Tiridates symbolically put down his crown in front of an image of Nero and undertook to travel to Rome and there receive it back from Nero's hands (Fig. 102).

In the eyes of the Roman public, Nero would therefore, seemingly of his own volition, crown the new Armenian king. While this may not have been the outcome originally intended, it ultimately proved surprisingly successful in improving relations with the Parthians and bringing stability to the region. This opened up possibilities for other campaigns in the future, which were set in motion some years later. A different assessment of the Armenian war was

Cavalry underpinned Parthia's military might. These terracotta figurines
(Figs 98–100), all from domestic contexts in Mesopotamia, show riders in
characteristic Parthian dress, mounted on light horses and with composite
bows. Two are in full gallop. A Parthian tactic, used to devastating effect,
was to feign retreat, only for the horse archers to turn their bodies and
shoot at the pursuing enemy. The square plaque (Fig. 101) shows a heavy
Parthian *cataphract* rider in plate armour.

Fig. 98
Mounted Parthian archer
AD 1–300
Syria
Terracotta
H. 17 cm, W. 15.6 cm, D. 4cm
British Museum
1972,0229.1

Fig. 99
Parthian horseman
AD 1–300
Iraq or Syria
Terracotta
H. 22.5 cm, W. 16 cm
Museum für Islamische Kunst,
Staatliche Museen zu Berlin
I. 3684

Fig. 100
Parthian horse-archer
AD 1–300
Iraq or Syria
Terracotta
H. 17 cm, W. 14.5 cm
Museum für Islamische Kunst,
Staatliche Museen zu Berlin
I. 3685

Fig. 101
Relief of Parthian *cataphract*
300 BC–AD 200
Iraq
Limestone
H. 15.2 cm, W. 19 cm
British Museum
.91908

formulated and circulated only after Nero's death. Suetonius speaks of *ignominia ad orientem*, 'a humiliation in the East', ascribing to Nero personally the failure of his commanders.[112] Yet at the time, and in the immediate aftermath, a fierce debate seems to have raged only between the respective followers of Paetus and Corbulo.

The ardent reception by the senate and people of the early successes against the Parthians suggests that Nero fully met their expectations as *princeps* when it came to military matters. In all likelihood, there were many more monuments like the Aphrodisias Sebasteion relief cycle that enthusiastically celebrated his victories and aligned them with earlier Roman triumphs. To create such a mood of widespread optimism and contentment was a major achievement in itself, for Nero's position was not without serious contradictions. As *princeps* he was expected to merit his authority by outshining all other senators in *virtus* (valour) and old-fashioned martial glory. Yet any attempt to monopolise such activities, as some of his predecessors had done, would be seen as denying senators an opportunity to gain the same honours and dignity their forefathers had enjoyed. Nero did his utmost to accommodate such senatorial desires, appointing senior consulars (an experienced former consul) to important commands and leaving them in post for unusually long periods of time. It turned out to be a delicate balancing act. The potential downside of allowing these military men too much

Fig. 102
Photograph of an inscription of Legion III Gallica dating to AD 64/5
June 1909
Mezreh, Elazig, Turkey
Gertrude Bell
Gertrude Bell Archive, Newcastle University
N_122

Inscribed: 'NERO CLAUDIUS CAESAR AUG(USTUS) GERMANICUS IMP(ERATOR), PON(TIFEX) MAX(IMUS), TRIB(UNICIA) POT(ESTATE) XI, CO(N)S(UL) IIII, IMP(ERATOR) VIII, PAT(ER) P(ATRIAE), CN. DOMITIO CORBULONE LEG(ATO) AUG(USTI) PRO PR(AETORE), T. AURELIO FULVO LEG(ATO) AUG(USTI) LEG(IONIS) III GAL(LICAE).'

'Nero Claudius Caesar Augustus Germanicus Imperator, Chief Priest, Holder of Tribunician Power eleven times, Consul four times, Imperator eight times, Father of the Fatherland, under the Governorship of Gnaeus Domitius Corbulo, and Titus Aurelius Fulvus as commander of Legion III Gallica.'

The wording on this inscription indicates that some Roman troops remained in southern Armenia after the Rhandeia agreements.

Fig. 103
Sestertius
AD 64
Minted in Rome, Italy
Copper alloy
Weight 28.4 g
British Museum
R.6442

These two sestertii (see also
Fig. 104) show Nero in his
role as military commander.
On the reverse, the emperor,
on horseback, leads a parade
(*decursio*). Behind him is a
cavalryman with a standard
(*vexillum*). A *decursio* was a public
demonstration of military might and
individual skill. Nero had already
led the Praetorians on parade as
crown prince.

A similar coin showed Nero in the
same pose, but surrounded by
two soldiers on foot. His attire
would have been comparable to
that visible in the small bronze
statuette (see Fig. 97, p. 121).

Fig. 104
**Sestertius showing Nero
addressing the troops
(*adlocutio*)**
AD 64
Minted in Rome, Italy
Copper alloy
Weight 30.3 g
British Museum
R.9923

On the reverse of this coin, Nero
(in toga and with laureate crown)
stands next to a Praetorian prefect
on a low platform. His hand is
raised as he addresses the three
soldiers on the left.

room to act on their own initiative was a dangerous re-emergence of aristocratic
pride and competition, the very evils that had caused the downfall of the
Republic. Overzealous ambition played a major part in the British and
Armenian disasters of AD 60 to 63 and may have led Nero to reconsider his
approach. It coincided with the death of Burrus and the subsequent waning
influence of Seneca as Nero's main advisor.

For the time being, carefully choreographed martial demonstrations in
Rome had to substitute for new military successes over external enemies. Nero's
coinage both commemorated these events and made them accessible to people
throughout the Empire. The Parthian Arch, that great symbol of a new
Neronian Golden Age echoing Augustus' own monument, appeared on coins
minted in Rome and Lugdunum (Lyon) for several years, up to AD 64. It was
now complemented by other depictions that showed Nero addressing the troops
and leading the Praetorians on parade, a potent reminder of his power (Figs 103
and 104). With this, it is time to turn to Nero's domestic policies and his activities
in Rome and Italy.

IV

SPECTACLE
AND
SPLENDOUR

Discordia: social tensions

Upon his accession in AD 54 Nero was confronted with a deeply divided citizenry and the looming threat of disorder and social unrest. Conflicts that weakened the cohesion of Roman society had built up gradually under Augustus' successors and reached a dangerous impasse under Claudius. In many ways they were the result of a dynamic generated by the principate itself (see pp. 31–3). Tacitus captures some of the slogans propagated by the opposing factions: there was *vis* on one side, and *avaritia* on the other: (mob) violence and (elite) greed.[1] The reason Nero was welcomed so warmly as new *princeps* probably lay precisely in this sharp polarisation of Roman society; the different groups – with their vastly diverging expectations of the young ruler – were eager to maintain the *princeps'* support or otherwise wanted to win him over to their cause. Initially, they all vied for his goodwill and attention.[2] This story of underlying civic strife is rarely told, but at the time it influenced a number of Nero's domestic policies, including measures that were considered to be controversial. Matters were further complicated by escalating conflicts within the elite, especially between the *iuvenes*, the younger generation of knights and sons of senatorial families, and their elders, among them the most senior senators. The particular conditions of Roman culture meant these disputes were often contested publicly in the theatres and other entertainment venues, in ways that are not intuitive from a modern perspective and need careful exploration.

Like nearly all *principes*, including Claudius and Caligula before him, Nero began his reign with an attempt to reconcile these often contradictory demands. He aimed to realise the traditional, if elusive, ideal of *concordia ordinum*, a paternalistic notion of harmony between the different status groups in Roman society. Nero's accession promise, a return to the principles of Augustus, partly expressed this aspiration. The policies during the first half of his reign consequently appear to be scrupulously even-handed. Yet some powerful antagonists emerged very soon in the senate, and, by the end of his first decade in power, it was abundantly clear that any real form of concord under the benign guidance of the *princeps* was almost impossible to achieve.

Conciliation and reform

Nero's initial interventions as ruler were concerned with correcting some of the problems that had occurred under his predecessor, while also addressing wider social imbalances. Within the first months of his reign the new *princeps* introduced a number of measures to this effect. So as to suppress corruption and discourage legal cases brought for political and financial gain, while also making recourse to the law more affordable, he stipulated that no one should receive a fee or gift for pleading a case in court.[3] A direct consequence of this initiative was that Nero almost immediately had to shield a senator from prosecution by an enslaved servant, an event that must have rattled the elite in its audacity.[4] Additionally, he freed quaestors designate from the obligation of putting on gladiatorial fights in order to further their senatorial careers, a task that had become so costly that all but the wealthiest candidates were barred from seeking office. In another significant move, Nero banished a notorious *delator*, or prosecutor, who for his own profit had revived old claims against individuals for monies owed to the treasury.[5] The man's account books were ordered to be burnt, presumably in a public ceremony in the Forum – a clear signal that Nero would forgive some outstanding debts.[6]

Expressions of respect towards the senate that echoed Nero's accession speech continued in subsequent years. The *princeps* personally assumed the consulship in deference to traditional, Republican-style governance, but ensured that a record number of senators could share the honour.[7] In an early example of his avowed policy of clemency (advocated so eloquently by Seneca), he symbolically reinstated a prominent senator excluded under Claudius.[8] Other gestures were directed towards the *plebs* (and possibly the knights). Near the end of AD 55 Nero withdrew the cohort of soldiers that supervised the crowds in theatres and other entertainment venues. This was meant to encourage *theatralis licentia*, best translated as freedom of expression (see p. 158), which had been tightly circumscribed by previous *principes*, starting with Tiberius.[9] There followed apparently tumultuous scenes in the theatres and violence soon spilt out onto the streets. Tacitus' description of events recalls closely the notorious 'pantomime riots' of AD 14 and 15, when a dispute ostensibly about public funding for these performances had led to a fierce eruption of simmering social and political discontent.[10] Now, there was a flurry of interventions by enraged senior senators, many of them directed against more junior magistrates suspected of abetting the rioters.[11] By contrast, a high-ranking financial official was the subject of a tribune's unsuccessful litigation, accused of pursuing his right of confiscation too mercilessly against the poor.[12]

Questions of social hierarchy loomed large. In the senate, there was a heated debate about the status and rights of *liberti*, or freedmen. Some hardliners bemoaned their 'insolence' and moved that it should be possible to revoke the liberty of those who disrespected their former masters.[13] The consuls, mindful of the consequences of such a momentous change to the fabric of society, did not immediately put the matter to a vote (though Tacitus maintains it would have carried a majority), but first consulted the *princeps*. Nero decided against adopting the measure and recommended that each individual case should be examined on its own merit according to existing legislation. Tacitus' summary of the deliberations in Nero's council demonstrates how important *liberti* had become in Roman society; by the mid-first century AD, even some senators and knights were descended from freedmen, and the upward mobility of *liberti* underpinned much of the progress and economic development of the early principate. Conversely, the increasing influence and wealth particularly of imperial freedmen, who operated within the parallel world of the imperial administration and court, threatened old senatorial privileges and elicited undisguised hatred. Suetonius states that Nero did seek some form of compromise: he 'refused for a long time to admit the sons of freedmen into the senate and denied office to others who had been admitted by previous emperors', whereas he subsidised 'senators of noble family who had lost their ancestral fortunes'.[14]

Perhaps emboldened by Nero's reluctance to interfere in matters of the senate, its leaders significantly curtailed the powers of tribunes and aediles, public officials, and limited their ability to act independently or interfere with the legal initiatives of more senior, and perhaps more conservative, praetors and consuls. To Tacitus, this was evidence that there remained 'some shadow of the

Republic'.[15] His account provides very few details and at times deliberately appears to obscure what really happened, but the rioting and unrest, and the abuse directed towards senators and their families, must have been significant.[16] It seems that Nero allowed the people more freedom to vent their anger and concerns than many senators thought tolerable; after a period of several weeks or months, the military presence was finally reinstated and the actors involved were expelled from Italy.[17] Tacitus implies that Nero had actively encouraged the exchanges in the theatres or even participated (although he presents them merely as brawls devoid of political significance). This seems hard to credit; it is linked to a strange tale of other corrupt escapades, also relayed in altered form by Suetonius and Cassius Dio, in which Nero roamed the streets at night disguised as an enslaved man or freedman and molested senators and other honest citizens. Most of this must be pure fabrication, reflecting much later tensions between the *princeps* and the senate, but introduced early to characterise Nero as a criminal from the outset.[18]

The year AD 56 saw a first wave of impeachment trials against former governors and procurators accused of financial misconduct during their terms of office. The number of such cases peaked under Nero, probably a reflection of the scale of abuse that had built up over the years and of a new determination to act against it.[19] Further governors were impeached in AD 57 and Nero introduced additional measures to curb corruption among officials in the provinces.[20] The trials involved men appointed by the *princeps* as well as the senate; the details are difficult to reconstruct, but it seems that the senate was generally lenient towards its own, whereas imperial appointees faced greater scrutiny.[21] Instead, the senate considered new measures against freedmen. A draconian law of AD 10, the *senatus consultum Silanianum*, stipulated that if someone was murdered by his *servus*, all the enslaved servants in his household should suffer the death penalty. This was now amended to include all those who stood to be freed under the terms of the dead owner's will and who had previously been exempt.[22] Nero meanwhile distributed 400 sesterces a head to the *plebs*, and transferred 40 million from his privy purse into the exchequer (Figs 105 and 106).[23]

In AD 58 there were major riots in Puteoli, the Empire's main commercial port in the Bay of Naples. Relations between the populace and the wealthy local elite had broken down. There were violent incidents involving stonings and arson, and a further escalation seemed likely. Deputations of both groups were heard by the senate; an eminent jurist, the former consul and proconsul of Asia, Gaius Cassius Longinus, was dispatched to Puteoli to resolve matters. His harsh and uncompromising approach made matters worse; at his own request, a pair of new officials eventually replaced him. They brought with them a cohort of armed Praetorians who inflicted heavy punishment on rebellious individuals. Some form of order was quickly restored through this heavy show of force; Tacitus merely states that 'harmony (*concordia*) was returned to the townspeople'.[24] Nero's role in this is difficult to assess; the matter was largely dealt with by the senate, but the dispatch of a unit of the Praetorian Guard would have required the *princeps*' approval. Longinus, it is worth noting, belonged to a powerful and extremely conservative faction of the senate. He was related by marriage to the Iunii Silani (see p. 177) and his daughter was married to Domitius Corbulo (see p. 118). His word carried weight, and Nero would have been in a tricky position had he favoured a more conciliatory approach.[25]

Nero's reintroduction of brass coinage after a twenty-year hiatus primarily served practical needs. It increased the supply of low denomination coins – a fraction of the value of the silver denarius – that were required for mundane, everyday transactions. The sestertius, worth a quarter of a denarius, was used by a much broader section of the population. Its relatively large size provided a means of communicating messages to a wide audience through high-quality and complex imagery. Nero's concern for the people was a major theme of the sestertii issued between AD 64 and 66, which recalled a number of achievements during his first decade in power. In his portraits on the obverse he now regularly appeared wearing a laurel wreath or radiate crown.

Fig. 105
Sestertius
AD 64
Minted in Rome, Italy
Copper alloy
Weight 26.3 g
British Museum
BNK,R.133
Donated by Bank of England

This sestertius celebrates a cash handout given to the people in AD 64. Nero, on the right, is seated on a magistrate's chair placed on a high podium. An official stands by his side. Below, another official in a toga hands a *tessera* (token) to a plebeian in a short tunic. Behind them is a columned building; a statue of Minerva dominates the central background. The inscription is a reminder that this was the second instance of Nero's generosity towards the *plebs*: 'CONG(IARIUM) II DAT(UM) POP(ULI) S(ENATUS) C(ONSULTUM)', 'a cash handout given to the people for the second time, [issued by] decree of the senate'. A first handout had been made in Nero's name by Claudius in AD 51.

Fig. 106
Sestertius
AD 66
Minted in Lugdunum (Lyon), Gaul (modern France)
Copper alloy
Weight 25.9 g
British Museum
R.10032

A second series varied the scene slightly. Nero is on the left, an official on a second podium hands money to a citizen in toga with a little boy behind him. Next to Minerva is a personification, perhaps *Liberalitas* (Generosity).

NERO

Meanwhile in Rome, the complaints of the people about the greed of the *publicani*, or tax farmers, led Nero to consider the abolition of *vectigalia*, the indirect taxes.[26] Their demands were almost certainly made in the theatres, when the crowds were able to appeal directly to the *princeps*.[27] The senate apparently welcomed Nero's 'noble sentiment', but argued that such a measure would jeopardise state revenue, as further demands for the abolition of direct taxes would inevitably follow. It also reminded the ruler that many of the tax-farming companies had been formed by senators and tribunes, but conceded that 'the greed of the *publicani* should be tempered'. Nero withdrew his plans, but he issued an edict that the regulations for each tax should be made public, a measure intended to prevent future abuse. Claims older than a year should lapse; officials should give precedence in court to all cases against tax farmers.[28] He also stipulated that soldiers should retain their exemptions, except when they traded for profit. Furthermore, at Nero's instigation the cost of transporting grain in the overseas provinces was made less expensive and grain ships were made exempt from tax to reduce costs further. It is hard not to view some of these measures as a response to the severe abuses that were cited as direct causes of the Boudica rebellion in Britain two years later (see p. 106). Such malpractice seems to have been far more widespread; however, provinces with long-established urban and legal traditions were more successful at seeking official recourse against these irregularities than the recently conquered territories.[29] Nero introduced a number of other fair and sensible changes. While some were later abandoned, others remained in force in Tacitus' day.[30]

In parallel, the impeachment trials continued.[31] In what must have been a much-observed cause célèbre of the day, two very prominent individuals publicly traded insults: Publius Suillius Rufus and Lucius Annaeus Seneca, Nero's chief minister. Suillius, a notorious informer in the days of Claudius and blamed for

Fig. 107
The Pompeii amphitheatre riot of AD 59
AD 59–79
House of the Riot in the Amphitheatre, Pompeii, Italy
Plaster and paint
H. 170 cm, W. 185 cm
Museo Archeologico Nazionale di Napoli
112222

This extraordinary fresco almost certainly illustrates the unrest at Pompeii mentioned by Tacitus in his *Annals*. A violent clash between Pompeians and visiting supporters from neighbouring Nuceria during a local gladiatorial show led to 'atrocious bloodshed' with many dead, including children. The realistic depiction of a historic event in this manner is remarkable, as is the level of detail in the painting.

The scene was originally flanked by further images that each showed a pair of gladiators fighting. The frescos decorated the peristyle courtyard of a small house in the south of Pompeii, in a block next to the theatre and a colonnaded square.

In a highly accurate representation of Pompeii's urban topography, the fresco shows a view of the south-east quarter of the town from the north-west. The amphitheatre is in the centre, a corner of city wall with its watch towers is visible behind, and the main Palaestra, or exercise ground, is seen to the right. Spectators fight inside the amphitheatre and in the surrounding streets. Many victims appear to be dead or lie injured on the ground. Under the trees in the foreground are various market stalls. The sun-sails of the amphitheatre are clearly depicted, as are painted notices on the walls of the Palaestra. The painter used an effective composite perspective with frontal façades and a tilted bird's-eye view, an artistic

innovation of the period, that allowed more of the interior spaces behind to be presented.

The riot must have been of great significance to the owner of the house onto which this fresco was painted – it covered an earlier image with an athletic theme.

The façade of the house preserves a graffito mentioning the pantomime actor Actius Anicetus, the leader of a troupe that performed at Pompeii and the neighbouring towns and had its own group of fanatical supporters, the *Anicetiani*. Tacitus' description of the theatre riots in Rome at the beginning of Nero's reign evokes similar scenes of civic strife to the one seen here.

the downfall of many senators and knights, was accused of having taken on court cases for profit, in contravention of the recent law. After a lengthy trial and much background briefing by the opposing parties, he was convicted and banished to the Balearic Isles. However, during his defence he levelled serious accusations against Seneca, pointing out that he had managed to amass, by unethical and criminal means, an immense fortune of 300 million sesterces in the four years since Nero's accession. Seneca, whom the sources describe repeatedly as *praedives*, or fabulously wealthy, had indeed used his position of influence with Nero to further the careers of his close relatives and friends and establish an extensive patronage network. In this manner, the impeachment and other trials elucidated how widespread corrupt practices were among broad sections of the elite.[32]

The violent death of Agrippina occurred in AD 59 (see p. 181), but successes in the Armenian war (see pp. 92–4) and Nero's great spectacles quickly diverted public attention. Later in the year, a serious riot broke out in Pompeii, as local supporters clashed with those from neighbouring Nuceria during a gladiatorial show in the city (Fig. 107). While Tacitus blames petty small-town rivalry, there may have been other factors at play; army veterans, whom Nero had recently settled in Nuceria (as well as in Capua), must have had an impact on local life. Nero again allowed the senate to investigate and implement appropriate disciplinary measures without his intervention.[33]

In AD 61 there was a major disturbance in Rome. The *praetor urbanus* Lucius Pedanius Secundus, a high-ranking magistrate, was murdered in his house by one of his enslaved servants.[34] After the debate in AD 57 concerning the *senatus consultum Silanianum*, the senate was now eager to set a stern example, and it decreed that all 400 of Secundus' household *servi* should be executed in line with the law (Fig. 108). In response, and in an extraordinary show of solidarity, the *plebs* gathered to protect the innocent. In a mood of violent protest and defiance (Tacitus uses the word *seditio*), they blockaded the senators in their assembly.[35] In a city with an enslaved population that may have approached 30–40 per cent, this case had an enormous impact.[36] Even among the senators, a strong minority opposed the full application of the law and argued for a different form of punishment. However, Gaius Cassius Longinus, who had dealt so harshly with the earlier protests in Puteoli (see p. 132), insisted on the death penalty as a powerful deterrent, even if this meant that a great number of innocents would lose their lives; his fearsome reputation was such that no individual senator dared raise his voice in opposition, but there was a joint clamour for clemency (the original law had been introduced by a member of the Silani family to which Longinus was affiliated). All the while, the people, armed with stones and firebrands, prevented the death sentences from being carried out.[37] Finally, Nero issued an edict to the populace that endorsed the senate's decision; the condemned were led to their deaths through streets lined by soldiers to prevent further disturbances.

The grain supply, ever precarious in the eyes of the *plebs*, continued to be high on Nero's list of priorities. After a storm in AD 62 sank 200 grain ships in port and 100 more burnt in a fire upriver, Nero kept the price stable; to reassure the populace, he even had grain that had spoilt in storage thrown into the Tiber to demonstrate there was no shortage.[38] In the same year he appointed a number of former consuls to supervise contributions to the exchequer, claiming that he provided a subsidy of 60 million sesterces annually from his own funds to make up for the ruinous expenditure of previous *principes*.[39] Tacitus' sparse account of these measures for once can be cross-checked against other evidence. An inscription from Ephesus in Asia Minor preserves the text of a customs law for the province (*lex portorii Asiae*) that sheds light on Nero's wider economic measures.[40] Nero's claim of fiscal frugality has some merit, despite claims to the contrary by later authors who accused him of spending far too lavishly on spectacles and other amusements.[41] To facilitate trade and simplify the exchange of currency, he introduced major monetary reforms that included a reduction of the gold and silver content in aureus and denarius coinage.[42]

Seneca's position, already compromised, was further weakened by the death in AD 62 of Sextus Afranius Burrus, commander of the Praetorian Guard. The two had formed a close partnership as Nero's most influential advisors. Seneca sought permission to retire, which Nero refused, but his former tutor now stayed away from court. At around the same time, there was a trial under the charge of *maiestas* (treason), the first in Nero's reign, against a praetor who had circulated a

Fig. 108
**Statue of a *lanternarius*
or lantern-bearer**
AD 1–100
River Tiber, by the Ponte Palatino,
Rome, Italy
Marble
H. 63 cm, W. 29 cm
Terme di Diocleziano, Museo
Nazionale Romano, Rome
125587

A *lanternarius*, or lantern-bearer, was an enslaved young boy, or day labourer, whose duty it was to light his owner's way at night – Roman cities normally lacked any other form of street lighting. He is depicted, barefoot and dressed in a short tunic and hooded cloak, having nodded off while waiting dutifully for his master to return, a lantern by his side. Such scenes were common; *lanternarii* were obliged to spend long hours loitering outside houses until their masters emerged from a late night dinner or similar social engagement.

As representations of selfless devotion beyond death, statues of this type were sometimes used to decorate tombs. Yet their romanticised depiction of servitude was deeply misleading. Young and enslaved members of households were subject to physical abuse and sexual exploitation. The draconian law enforced after the murder of Rome's city governor in AD 61 led to the execution of hundreds of innocent men and women, no doubt including blameless children like the boy here.

Fig. 109
Sestertius
AD 64
Minted in Rome, Italy
Copper alloy
Weight 29.8 g
British Museum
R.6445

Fig. 110
Reverse of a sestertius
AD 65
Minted in Lugdunum (Lyon), Gaul
(modern France)
Copper alloy
Weight 28.9 g
British Museum
R.10028

This sestertius celebrates the new harbour at Ostia (Portus), construction of which was begun under Nero's adoptive father Claudius. Together with a series of related coin reverses, it demonstrated the dynasty's ongoing concern for the security of the food supply and welfare of the people. The harbour basin appears in a daring bird's-eye perspective. On the left is a quay with porticoes and warehouses, and, on the right, a colonnaded breakwater. In the upper centre is Claudius' lighthouse (crowned by a statue of Neptune), which guided ships into port. Below, a reclining male figure with a dolphin and ship's rudder personifies the sea or the River Tiber. He might also represent the harbour, which bustles with vessels of all sizes, from large commercial ships under sail to oared galleys. The inscription reads: 'POR(TUS) OST(IENSIS) AUGUSTI S(ENATUS) C(ONSULTUM)', 'The emperor's harbour at Ostia, [issued] by decree of the senate'.

The image on the reverse of this sestertius commemorates the free provision of grain to Rome's population (those entitled constituted the *plebs frumentaria*, a privileged segment of the *plebs*). Seated on the right is Ceres, the goddess of agriculture. Annona, the personification of the corn dole, stands opposite her on the left holding a horn of plenty. Between them is a *modius* (a measure for a grain ration) on a garlanded altar; the stern of a grain ship is visible behind. The grain was transferred onto smaller riverboats at Ostia and ferried to warehouses along the River Tiber in Rome.

Fig. 111
Reverse of a dupondius
AD 63
Minted in Rome, Italy
Copper alloy
Weight 17.7 g
British Museum
R.9974

Coins of the Rome and Lugdunum
mints celebrated one of Nero's
important construction projects,
the Macellum Magnum, a central
food market completed in AD 59
(labelled here 'MAC(ELLUM)
AUG(USTI)' – 'the emperor's
market'). For these sestertii, the
Neronian die-cutters again created
an image of remarkable clarity and
sophistication. In the centre is a
two-storey domed rotunda, with
steps leading up to its colonnade.
The ground floor holds a statue of
Neptune with dolphins on either
side. Behind are columned
porticoes that frame the market
square (the structure on the left
may be the pillared entrance).

number of libellous verses against Nero. The proceedings were dominated by
the senator Publius Clodius Thrasea Paetus, who managed to garner a majority
for the accused's relegation while the consul designate had argued for the death
penalty. Paetus thereby emerged as a leading voice of a dissenting faction in the
senate. Such a shift in the political climate was perhaps the first public reflection
of a nascent conspiracy against Nero (see p. 256).

Great projects

Nero's concern for the people of Rome found its splendid expression in a
number of major building projects that provided new amenities for the welfare
and entertainment of the population and were, in part, a response to the events
described above.[43] Planning for some of these structures must have begun
almost immediately after his accession and in a few cases may already have
been considered under Claudius. The first decade of Nero's reign thus saw the
completion of a significant project every two to three years. Construction at this
scale, for the benefit of the people and the beautification of the city, had become
the prerogative of the emperors during the reign of Augustus. *Providentia* (care for
the citizens) and *publica magnificentia* (public splendour) became important policies
that ensured the acceptance of the principate and were soon expected of every
new ruler. At these, Nero excelled. The little attention that authors like Tacitus
later devoted to these projects (or the negative manner in which they singled out
particular aspects) partly reflects senatorial frustration with this shift in patronage
and the prestige it provided.

A secure and heavily subsidised food supply for the *plebs* was among every
princeps' highest priorities; the bread riots under Claudius had illustrated how
quickly the public mood could change (see p. 65).[44] Nero acted accordingly
and his coinage, in beautiful new-style brass issues in low denominations that
circulated among the wider population, served as a potent reminder of his
efforts.[45] Claudius' new harbour at Portus near Ostia with its extensive facilities
was depicted prominently in a stunning aerial perspective (Fig. 109).[46]
Sometimes this is interpreted as a sign that Nero completed or expanded
Claudius' project, but the evidence for this is not conclusive. Dynastic
continuity mattered here, and the sheer number of merchant vessels in
the harbour basin could be seen to reflect Nero's successes in encouraging
trade, through economic reforms and the securing of new sources of grain.
Engineering projects outside Rome complemented these efforts. A new
harbour was built at Antium, Nero's birthplace on the coast south of Rome,
perhaps intended to complement that of Claudius at Portus.[47]

Further Neronian coin issues illustrated additional elements of the
food-supply chain: the *cura Annonae* celebrated the free distribution of grain
(Fig. 110); another beautiful series advertised Nero's new food market, the
Macellum Magnum ('great market'), which opened in AD 59 near the Temple
of Claudius on the Esquiline Hill (Fig. 111).[48] It was an elegant rectangular
square flanked by two-storey porticoes that enclosed a domed rotunda in the
centre.[49] By chance, the funerary altar for an auctioneer working there has
survived, with a fine depiction of the man himself and two market porters
(Fig. 112).[50] The market seems to have offered luxury foods, perhaps in addition

to wholesale supplies, and its location may reflect Nero's wider urbanistic ambitions in this part of the city (see p. 217).

Around AD 62 Nero opened his magnificent new baths in the Campus Martius (Fig. 113).[51] They surpassed everything of this type built in Rome to date and became a model for later imperial baths, with a central axis of warm, tepid and cold rooms around which a variety of spaces were grouped symmetrically. Their sheer size and the sequence of light-filled halls, with high ceilings flanked by colonnaded courtyards and other outdoor areas, set a new standard. Bathers were encouraged to spend time at these generous facilities and engage in additional exercise and leisure pursuits. The costly marble decoration, and the abundant amount of water and firewood for the heating systems, provided a level of luxury hitherto unattainable to the masses, let alone at this scale. The fame of the baths outlived Nero; the poet Martial, writing under the next dynasty and hostile towards the late *princeps*, still put it thus: 'Who was ever worse than Nero? Yet what can be better than Nero's warm baths?'[52] Nero could build here on the work of his predecessors, stressing the continuing care of the Julio-Claudian family for the city of Rome and its people. His baths adjoined those of his great-grandfather Agrippa, small by comparison, but similarly exceptional at the time of their construction some eighty-five years earlier; the water was supplied by aqueducts built under Claudius, completing a project first conceived under Caius. Nero's baths were linked to a gymnasium inaugurated in AD 60 in connection with newly instituted games, the *Neronia* (see p. 167). Both structures may have been planned together; the gymnasium finally brought sophisticated and permanent Greek-style exercise complexes to Rome. Architecturally, it complemented the elegant colonnaded squares that had risen all over the Campus Martius in previous centuries. While traditionalists may have resented the cultural implications of this building, the type of sports and training regimes housed there had long been established. Recent excavations have unearthed what are thought to be traces of the gymnasium.[53]

The long series of Nero's building projects began with the construction in AD 56 of a large new amphitheatre, an emphatic marker of a uniquely Roman identity. Hunts and gladiatorial fights, along with the execution of convicts, were still staged in other venues, such as the Circus Maximus (Fig. 114) and the Saepta (a large colonnaded square in the central Campus Martius), but all of these involved compromises when it came to visibility and the use of specialist machinery, as they were not designed for this kind of entertainment and its rapid evolution. The only existing permanent, purpose-built amphitheatre in Rome was that of Statilius Taurus, the first to be constructed in stone (albeit with a mostly wooden interior) and dedicated in 30 or 29 BC.[54] In Nero's day, it had probably started to show its age; it also offered limited seating capacity and appears to have been used relatively rarely for imperial *munera*, or gladiatorial shows.[55] Nero's uncle Caligula had begun construction of a new facility in the Campus Martius. However, work did not progress very far during his short reign. The project was abandoned by Claudius and what little had been built was dismantled.[56]

Perhaps in order to speed up the building process, Nero opted for a largely wooden construction for his own amphitheatre: the entire new structure was completed within a year, a feat that appears to have been considered remarkable.[57] The building was clearly astonishing in its engineering, scale and splendour, rich in

Fig. 112
A funerary altar for the moneylender and fish auctioneer Lucius Calpurnius Daphnus
After AD 59
Rome, Italy
Marble
Palazzo Massimo alle Colonne, Rome

Daphnus worked at the Macellum Magnum and is represented in the centre. He holds a money box in his left hand and a fish in his right. Two market porters in short tunics, weighed down by heavy baskets, stand on either side. All three sport the fashionable hairstyle made popular by Nero from AD 59 onwards.

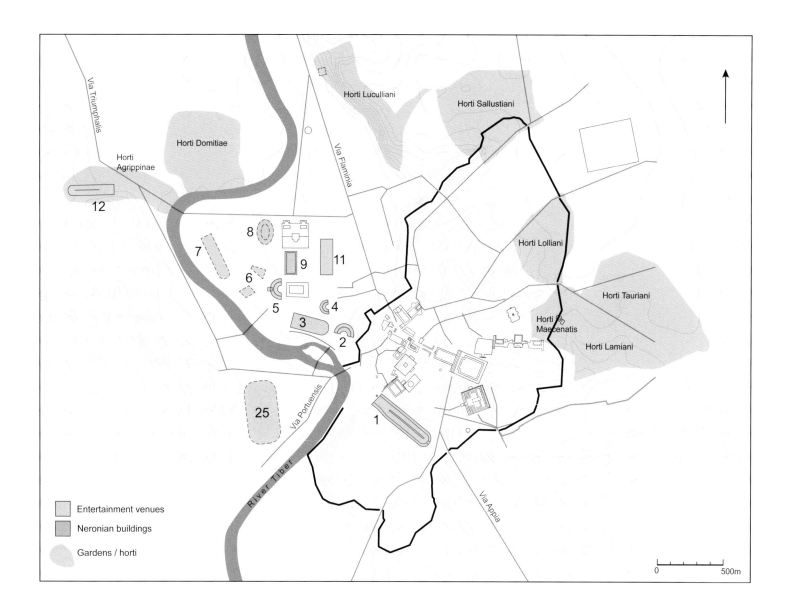

Fig. 113
**Map of Rome's main entertainment
venues and gardens (*horti*)**
(see also Fig. 163, p. 216)

1   Circus Maximus
2   Theatre of Marcellus
3   Circus Flaminius
4   Theatre of Balbus
5   Theatre and porticus of Pompeius
6   Stables of the Circus factions
7   Trigarium
8   Nero's Amphitheatre (possible location, before AD 64)
9   Stagnum
11 Saepta
12 Nero's Circus (and gardens)
25 Naumachia

gilding and marble veneer that made it look like a permanent stone structure, and full of technical innovations. Pliny remarks on an extraordinary tree used in its construction that must have been one of the amphitheatre's many talking points; it was the trunk of a larch, originally brought to Rome by Tiberius and displayed as a curiosity, for it was thought 'the largest tree ever seen'.[58]

Ludi and Roman society

It would be hard to overstate the significance of *ludi*, or (sacred) games, for Roman culture. *Ludi* had a marked impact on daily life in the capital for members of all classes. People came to see the games, but in doing so also became performers in a structured social group ritual that affirmed their individual place in society. The *princeps* and the leading senatorial magistrates

Fig. 114
**A *venatio* (beast hunt) in
the Circus Maximus**
AD 40–70
Campania, Italy
Terracotta
H. 52.1 cm, W. 52 cm
Museo Nazionale Romano, Terme
di Diocleziano, Rome
62660

Two trained hunters fight a lion
and lioness in the arena, another
figure appears to be already dead
on the ground. The man on the
left is attacked by two animals
simultaneously, while his comrade
on the right comes to his aid. In the
centre is one of the ornaments of
the Circus' central barrier: an
egg-shaped lap counter for the
chariot races. To the left are
spectators in the stands, to the
right a column topped by a statue.
Beast hunts usually opened the
programme on circus days,
followed by executions of criminals
at lunchtime and gladiatorial fights
thereafter. This relief comes from
the same series as the scenes
with chariot races (Figs 122 and
123, p. 150).

simultaneously took on multiple roles as consumers, active participants and
providers of games in a complex ceremony played out in front of a keenly
observant community. Ideally, the joint ritual strengthened the community
spirit, but, at times of tension, it also highlighted discord between the orders.
This could turn *ludi* into highly politicised events, a function that was clearly
recognised (and to an extent encouraged), but also carefully controlled under
the principate, as it had been during the Republic. The *princeps* could try to
manipulate this process, usually appearing in concord with the senators and
knights, but on occasion siding with the *plebs*; yet he himself was equally exposed
to the demands of the people, which could be refuted or tacitly supported by
the upper orders. The *ludi* gave the people of Rome a high degree of relatively
immediate access to their ruler, a peculiarity of Roman society with few parallels
in world history.[59]

Ludi had their origin as extensions of major religious ceremonies, and they
kept this religious aura throughout their existence, however much spectators may
have come to enjoy them purely as entertainment. Many had been initiated or
were turned into regular events in the later third century BC, as a way of securing
divine assistance during a crucial period of Rome's imperial expansion,
including the wars against Carthage. Some of the sacred and sacerdotal games
had been established as annual ceremonies from the outset; others started as
ludi votivi, vowed for specific events. They were often tied to the consecration
of a temple, originally dedicated for delivery from frequent plagues and other

diseases, or to invoke divine assistance against foreign threats in war and conflict. This was reflected in the associated ritual. *Ludi* began with a *pompa*, or religious procession, from the temple of the deity in whose honour they were celebrated to the place outside the old city walls where the games were held, usually the Circus Maximus or the Campus Martius. The processions were led by high magistrates, then the Roman youth, followed by the performers, which could include charioteers and jockeys (with their horses), athletes, dancers and musicians, and finally images of the gods, borne on carts or litters. Sacrifices were performed before the games started.

Days of the *ludi* were considered public holidays; they grew steadily in number from a few dozen during the Republic to about a third of the year during the Empire.[60] This alone demonstrates their importance, and the heavy investment of resources they required. Tens of thousands of people were employed to service the games. The impact was profound, particularly for the lower classes, whose lives evolved around the *ludi*. 'Really I think that the characteristic and peculiar vices of this city, a liking for actors and a passion for gladiators and horses, are all but conceived in the mother's womb', is how Tacitus puts it.[61]

By their very nature, *ludi* recalled important events from Roman history. In other ways, too, they reflected Rome's intensifying relationship with the outside world. Exotic cults were imported from abroad, such as the worship of Magna Mater. Actors and musicians initially came from Etruria. The different types of gladiators maintained the names and armour of foreign peoples the Romans had successively encountered, such as 'Samnite' or 'Thracian', or the Spanish-style sword, the *gladius*. *Ludi* thus reinforced a sense of Rome's dominance and the increasing integration of the Mediterranean, and the territories beyond, into the Empire. Yet at the same time, all these foreign influences could be perceived by some (usually conservative aristocrats) as deeply ambiguous dilutions of authentic Roman culture, and this applied in particular to the scenic performances.

The popularity of the games turned them into a major field of aristocratic competition during the later years of the Republic. One of Augustus' initiatives effectively prevented other nobles from organising spectacles that rivalled his own in size and splendour, thereby thwarting any intentions they may have had to curry favour with the *plebs* in this way. Later Caligula, and then Claudius, lavished resources on the games. This was the situation Nero inherited, and a trajectory he would follow over the course of his own reign.

Nero's spectacle entertainments and their venues

Claudius invested heavily in games and made a point of engaging passionately, on one reported occasion joining the crowds in counting a winner's prize money on the fingers of his hand.[62] Whether he genuinely enjoyed particularly bloody fights and showed little compassion for defeated fighters, as some sources report, can be debated – since he was hated by the senatorial and equestrian class for the trials and executions carried out during his reign, this may have been a literary embellishment to underline his brutal character traits.[63] The young Nero would have witnessed in the Campus Martius the fights performed by captives from the war in Britain, and he and Agrippina are explicitly mentioned as being by Claudius' side during the spectacular mock sea battle (*naumachia*, see p. 155) at the Fucine Lake that surpassed anything comparable in scale and the number of participants. Nero therefore came to know the power of these events early on, an experience heightened through his own participation in the *Lusus Troiae* ('Game of Troy') and the spectacles given first in his honour by Claudius and then organised by Nero for his adoptive father while still crown prince (see pp. 65–6).

The ancient literary sources provide some detail on Nero's games as *princeps*, but to which particular spectacles they refer is a much more complex question than is evident from most modern discussions. This leaves their chronology and programmatic evolution open to interpretation.[64] However, there can be no doubt as to their scale and ambition.

The construction of his new amphitheatre was an early high point of Nero's reign. The poet Calpurnius Siculus captured beautifully a sense of the awe the venue and the spectacular games held there inspired, perhaps in reference to the opening ceremony in AD 57. In one of his eclogues, a young shepherd returns to the countryside and describes to his companion the marvels he has just witnessed in the capital: the beams of the amphitheatre seemed to rise to the sky, surpassing in height Rome's mightiest hill, the Capitoline; the arena and seating reminded him of a valley surrounded by steep slopes. Finding his seat among the poorer people high up, next to an elderly Roman who noticed his marvel and astonishment, he heard confirmation that nothing so magnificent was ever seen before. Amid a sea of knights and white-robed tribunes, there in the distance down below was the youthful *princeps*, god-like, resembling both Mars and Apollo. What a joy to be young in such an age![65]

If the poem deployed typical elements of panegyric, other authors confirmed much of the detail, and the effect the amphitheatre's luxurious finish and novel technical facilities had on spectators. Pliny the Elder, for example, records that there was netting around the arena, studded with precious amber, which was secured in unprecedented quantities by a knight sent to the distant Baltic, far beyond the Empire's borders.[66] This alone demonstrates the enormous logistical effort and advance planning required for the new venue and the spectacles it hosted. In a comparable manner, acquiring the exotic animals for the wild beast hunts, designed to demonstrate the Empire's dominance and global reach, was a vastly complex enterprise. Pliny furthermore mentions novel awnings, extended with the aid of ropes, to provide shade for the spectators. They were 'dyed azure, like the heavens, and bespangled all over with stars'.[67] Seneca, in turn, refers to the hydraulic engineering of the arena's mighty fountain jet.[68]

These accounts contrast sharply with Tacitus' surly remarks about the amphitheatre, which are worth quoting in their full hostile menace:

> In the consulate of Nero, for the second time, and of Lucius Piso, little occurred that deserves remembrance, unless the chronicler is pleased to fill his rolls with panegyrics of the foundations and the beams on which the Caesar reared his vast amphitheatre in the Campus Martius; although, in accordance with the dignity of the Roman people, it has been held fitting to consign great events to the page of history and details such as these to the urban gazette.[69]

The *ludus Neronianus*

To ensure a steady supply of well-trained fighters, the emperors maintained a large school of gladiators at Capua in Campania, the *ludus Iulianus* (named after Julius Caesar, its one-time owner). Under Nero, there is also epigraphic evidence for a *ludus Neronianus*. It is not quite certain whether Nero simply gave the existing training centre his name or founded his own, perhaps to cater for increasing demand. Notices from Pompeii for fights with elite gladiators supplied by the agent Marcus Mesonius mention both *Iuliani* and *Neroniani*, which could suggest that the two *ludi* existed in parallel.[70] Gladiator armour belonging to members of Nero's troupe was found in the Palaestra of Pompeii that served as temporary barracks next to the local amphitheatre (Figs 115–19 and 120). Various local graffiti depicted famous *Neroniani* gladiators (Fig. 121). However, the *ludus Neronianus* provided fighters throughout Italy and the western provinces, where branches were established. One of these regional training centres is attested at Arausio (Orange) in Gaul, and another may have existed at Cordoba in Spain.[71]

Training facilities and barracks also existed in and around Rome, in order to supply the capital. For reasons of security they were dispersed, so as not to concentrate too many fighters in a single location. However, around AD 64 there was an attempted breakout of gladiators in Praeneste, less than 40 km east of Rome. It immediately sparked fears among the populace, 'allured and terrified as always by revolution', of a wider uprising of the type led by Spartacus in 73 BC.[72] On this occasion, however, the unrest was quickly suppressed by a local detachment of soldiers, perhaps an indication that the gladiators belonged to the imperial *ludus* and the military had been there as a precaution. Evidently, little had changed with regard to the men's abject living conditions in the century since that major revolt. Seneca describes suicides that demonstrate the still desperate circumstances of many of these individuals in Nero's day. In one instance, a gladiator, carted with other prisoners to one of the morning shows, deliberately allowed his head to be caught in the spokes of the wheel until his neck was broken; in another incident a wild-beast hunter went as if to relieve himself, the only opportunity to be alone and unguarded before a show, and rammed a sponge-stick down his throat to choke himself.[73] References to the arena abound in Seneca's writings. His own attitude to spectacles, including hunts, executions and gladiatorial combat, was complex; in a famous letter he deplores the senseless bloodlust of the masses, but otherwise felt there was much to be learnt from a brave gladiator's equanimity and contempt for death.[74]

The supply of elite gladiators from the imperial *ludus* was a way for Nero to show favour to officials in charge of games and to exercise considerable patronage.[75] Tellingly, some of his own freedmen sponsored spectacular events, a fact that must have appeared as unwelcome and even outrageous competition to many members of the local and senatorial elites. Pliny the Elder mentions that one of Nero's freedmen exhibited lifelike portraits of all the gladiators and assistants of a show he gave at Antium in the town's public porticoes.[76] Tacitus rages about a widely attended gladiatorial contest given by the freedman Vatinius at Beneventum, in his words a man 'sprung from a shoemaker's shop' and 'one of the foulest prodigies of Nero's court', dangerously wealthy and influential.[77] Nero's mere presence at Vatinius' spectacle could thus be perceived as an affront to the traditional social order.

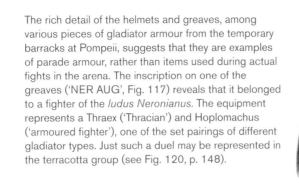

The rich detail of the helmets and greaves, among various pieces of gladiator armour from the temporary barracks at Pompeii, suggests that they are examples of parade armour, rather than items used during actual fights in the arena. The inscription on one of the greaves ('NER AUG', Fig. 117) reveals that it belonged to a fighter of the *ludus Neronianus*. The equipment represents a Thraex ('Thracian') and Hoplomachus ('armoured fighter'), one of the set pairings of different gladiator types. Just such a duel may be represented in the terracotta group (see Fig. 120, p. 148).

Fig. 115
Gladiator's helmet
AD 1–100
Pompeii, Italy
Bronze
H. 48.2 cm, W. 37 cm, L. 38 cm
British Museum
1946,0514.1
Bequeathed by Miss H.R. Levy

Fig. 116
A Hoplomachus shield
AD 1–100
Pompeii, Italy
Bronze
Diam. 36.5 cm
British Museum
1772,0303.141

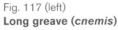

Fig. 119
Thraex gladiator's helmet
AD 50–79
Pompeii, Italy
Bronze
H. 38 cm, W. 40 cm
Musée du Louvre, Paris
BR1108

Fig. 117 (left)
Long greave (*cnemis*)
AD 50–79
Pompeii, Italy
Bronze
H. 52.8 cm, W. 19.7 cm
Museo Archeologico Nazionale
di Napoli
5648

Fig. 118 (right)
A pair of greaves
AD 50–79
Pompeii, Italy
Bronze
H. 57.5 cm, W. 17 cm (each)
Musée du Louvre, Paris
BR1169 and BR1170

Fig. 120
**Statuette of two gladiators,
a Hoplomachus and Thraex,
fighting**
AD 1–200
Turkey
Terracotta
H. 13.5 cm, W. 13 cm, D. 4 cm
British Museum
1907,0518.4

Nero occasionally used gladiators as discreet, well-trained bodyguards, a fairly common practice among the wealthy. He eventually appointed one of the most renowned fighters of the day, a man named Spiculus, as *decurio Germanorum*, or commander of his horse guard, an elite force of Germanic warriors famed for their strength and fierce loyalty.[78] According to Suetonius, he bestowed on Spiculus a fortune 'worthy of a triumphant general'.[79] This may have happened while Spiculus still fought to great acclaim in the arena (Suetonius mentions similar rewards for the lyre player Menecrates in the same sentence) and before he gained his freedom under the name of Tiberius Claudius Spiculus. The details are lost; Spiculus' emancipation, itself of uncertain date, and his rewards may reflect Nero's own fascination with the arena and would have pleased the crowds just as much as they upset certain members of the senatorial class. Nero could easily demonstrate his overwhelming power both as patron and ruler whenever he chose to do so; on one occasion he had his mounted guards perform publicly during a major spectacle, where they slew 400 bears and 300 lions with javelins in a fearsome show of equestrian and military skill.[80]

Once installed as commander of the horse guards, Spiculus became an important and trusted member of Nero's inner circle, demonstrating exemplary loyalty to the emperor until the very end (see p. 269). His lavish rewards may also refer to this period of his life; the fact that later authors describe him as 'gladiator' throughout is a telling social slur, aimed at Spiculus and Nero equally (see p. 152).

Fig. 121
Graffito of a gladiatorial duel
Line drawing. Original found at House of the Faun, Pompeii, Italy (in situ)

The victorious fighter on the left is labelled 'SPICULUS NER(ONIANUS) TIRO'. Above the defeated gladiator on the ground to the right are the words 'APTONETUS P(ERIIT) LIB[E]R(TUS) XVI'. Spiculus therefore was a gladiator from Nero's troupe, the *ludus Neronianus*, performing here in his first public contest ('tiro' means novice). His opponent Aptonetus, a veteran of sixteen fights (who had already gained his freedom), perished. This sensational debut must have contributed to Spiculus' early fame. Characters labelled Spiculus are also depicted on numerous gladiator cups, often in (fantasy) duels with other famous gladiators of the period. He may well be the renowned fighter who rose to become the loyal commander of Nero's bodyguard, although many others probably adopted his evocative stage name (derived from spiculum, 'little sharp point').

The Circus Maximus

The Circus Maximus, 'great(est) circus', was at the very centre of the Roman *ludi*. It formed by far the most important element of the elaborate physical performance infrastructure that had evolved over the centuries around their religious ceremonies and became a model for similar facilities elsewhere. With a capacity estimated at 150,000 people in Nero's day, it dwarfed in size all other venues for spectacle entertainments: the crowds assembled in the circus during the *ludi* would have surpassed in number the inhabitants of all but a very few cities of the Empire, which must have contributed to the fame and overpowering aura of the space.[81]

The Circus Maximus was located just beyond the central part of the city in a long and narrow valley (the Vallis Murcia) between the Aventine Hill and the Palatine Hill (Fig. 113). The parallel slopes on either side of the valley floor turned the area into a natural assembly and viewing space, a function it fulfilled from the time of Rome's first kings.[82] The vale and its immediate vicinity contained numerous ancient cults; these located the circus at the core of a sacred landscape and early on made it the venue for important religious rites. There were ancient shrines to the goddess Murcia and the god Consus, who may have been honoured with the first chariot races, and a temple to Sol and Luna (sun and moon), all of which over time were integrated into the very fabric of the circus.[83] Even the distant vista to the south-east led to the sacred Mons Albanus, the mythical mountain seat of Iupiter Latiaris. Because of its unmatched capacity for accommodating vast crowds, the route of all important state processions also traversed the circus.[84]

A number of related facilities stretched from the Circus Maximus in a north-westerly direction along the Tiber (see Fig. 113, p. 142). Just outside the city walls on the southern Campus Martius was the Circus Flaminius, a venue for horse races, but also a flexible staging and assembly area. The Trigarium, a track for three-horse chariots, followed further to the west. Both were related to particular cults. Beyond the river, on private ground belonging to the imperial family on the alluvial plain known as the Ager Vaticanus, or 'Vatican Field', was a smaller circus constructed under Caligula. During the major religious festivals, spectacles were distributed between these venues and the city's nearby theatres.[85]

The Circus Maximus was steadily upgraded, and it gradually became more monumental in its architecture, a process that reached a first climax under Julius Caesar.[86] Agrippa and Augustus added further elements: the central reservation (*euripus* or *spina*) received a series of rectangular water basins, and new dolphin-shaped lap counters complemented the existing egg-shaped ones – both becoming iconic visual symbols of the circus. Augustus turned the *pulvinar*, a platform on the Palatine side where images of the gods were kept during ceremonies in the circus, into an impressive shrine. He also brought a tall obelisk from Heliopolis in Egypt and added it to the eastern end of the *spina*. Originally erected by Pharaoh Rameses II in 1280 BC, it now glorified Rome's conquest of Egypt and celebrated the circus's link to the sun god Sol-Helius, who in ancient belief traversed the skies in his chariot, just as the charioteers circled the arena during their races.[87]

A major fire under Tiberius in AD 36 (one of many to afflict the circus) caused much damage to the still largely wooden structure. Reconstruction took place during Nero's infancy under Caligula and Claudius. The latter, keenly aware of the role of spectacles in maintaining his popular appeal, concentrated much of his investment in physical entertainment infrastructure here. He had the starting gates rebuilt in marble and the *metae*, or turning posts at either end of the *spina*, elaborately sheathed in gilded bronze. These, too, came to be potent visual symbols for the dramatic action during races (Figs 122 and 123).

Racing was big business and supported a complex, powerful industry involving many hundreds, if not thousands, of specialists and other staff at all levels. The industry was organised into four main teams, or *factiones*: the Reds, Whites, Blues and Greens (Fig. 124).[88] The factions themselves comprised numerous smaller units, so-called families, or *familiae quadrigariae*. With the steady increase in races, the factions could hold considerable sway over the *editores*, the magistrates who had to stage the games as part of their official duties. By Nero's reign, the stable managers (*domini factionum*) allegedly refused to provide their teams unless they were engaged for the entire day, not just for individual races, a process that must have begun with a substantial expansion in the number of daily competitions under Caligula.[89] As a means of attracting the best performers, Nero raised the prize money.[90] During the first century AD, the racing industry was administered as a private enterprise, with financial investments by knights but also senators.[91]

The stables of the circus factions were located in the southern Campus Martius, between the Circus Flaminius and the Trigarium. Together, they formed an extensive *vicus stabularius* ('stable quarter'), a whole area of the city devoted to the facilities of the racing teams (additional training grounds and stud farms were situated in the countryside). The headquarters of the Greens and

Fig. 122 (opposite, above)
Relief panel showing a racing scene in the Circus Maximus
AD 40–70
Italy
Terracotta
H. 30.5 cm, L. 40.6 cm, D. 3.5 cm
British Museum
1805,0703.337

A charioteer gets ready for the sharp left-hand turn at the end of the long straight, always the most dangerous moment in a race. Ahead of him is a *hortator*, an outrider who supported the chariot team during the race. On the ground between them are the poorly preserved remains of a third figure, perhaps a *sparsor*. His job would have been to douse the sand with water and keep the dust down – a very exposed and dangerous task. The turning-post (*meta*) with its three conical pillars probably dates to Claudius' upgrade of the Circus. He replaced the old stone posts with new *metae* sheathed in richly ornamented, gilded bronze.

These reliefs (Figs 122 and 123) were produced as architectural decorations. Originally brightly painted, they could probably be customised with a favourite team's colours. The maker's mark names the workshop owner, Annia Arecusa – a woman.

Fig. 123 (below)
**Relief panel showing an
accident during a chariot race**
Mid-1st century AD
Rome, Italy
Terracotta
H. 31.5 cm, W. 40.5 cm
Kunsthistorisches Museum, Vienna
Antikensammlung, V 49

This scene dramatically illustrates
a crash (*nauphragium* – literally
'shipwreck') during a turn. The
horse team is in disarray, the
charioteer helpless on the ground
(one set of reins would have been
wrapped around the charioteer's
body, so there was a high risk that
he might be dragged by the
animals during such an incident).
Various helpers have stepped into
the arena to free the horses and
remove the wreckage. Behind is a
turning post and a dolphin-shaped
counter marking the seven laps of
a typical 5-km race. A pillar
crowned by a statue is further in
the background. The stands for
the visitors (or perhaps the more
elaborate starting gates) are visible
on the right.

Blues have left some archaeological traces.[92] Nero's uncle Caligula, a fanatical supporter of the Greens, is said to have dined regularly at their stables and spent the night there. He also furnished his favourite horse Incitatus ('Flyer') with a lavish marble box and ivory manger, purple blankets and a collar of precious stones.[93] Popular passions could be attached to factions (supporters often wore clothes in team colours), to particular horses or to famous charioteers, the heroes of the racetrack.

Charioteers, especially the *agitatores* who handled four-horse teams, needed experience, technical and tactical skill, physical stamina and incredible bravery for what was an inherently dangerous activity.[94] They required many years of specialist training, a major investment by their owners or employers. Some charioteers became popular idols and could accrue vast sums of prize money over the course of their careers (see Figs 128 and 129).[95] Yet in one of the deep contradictions of Roman society, like actors, gladiators and other performers, they were classed as *infames*, men and women of reduced social and legal standing that withheld from them the normal rights of Roman citizens, even if they were freeborn. While some such professionals were foreign-born citizens or other members of the lower classes, most were drawn from the enslaved population, although many continued to race even when freed.[96] Their celebrity status could lead to raucous behaviour (at least in the eyes of the elite); Suetonius states that Nero 'put an end to the diversions of the chariot drivers, who from immunity of long standing claimed the right of ranging at large and amusing themselves by cheating and robbing the people'. Whatever this meant in detail, it clearly signified that Nero was determined to uphold the traditional social order, despite claims to the contrary by his later detractors.[97]

By the time he was fifteen Nero was intimately familiar with the operation of the *ludi* and their effect on the population, including the intense emotions, the *furor circense*, they aroused (Figs 125–7). Suetonius claims that Nero constantly

Fig. 124
Fresco fragment depicting a chariot race
AD 62–79
House of the Quadrigae,
Pompeii, Italy
Museo Archaeologico Nazionale
di Napoli
9055

A total of five four-horse chariots or *quadrigae* are preserved on this fresco fragment (only three horses of one remain in the upper left corner). The vivid scene captures the excitement of a race and contains many closely observed details. The charioteers, in helmets and protective leather corsets, wear tunics in the team colours of the four main circus factions: Greens, Blues, Reds and Whites. In the foreground, a charioteer of the Blues spurs on his horse-team with his raised whip; his path seems blocked by the Reds' chariot. The figure in green reins in his horses to avoid a collision, while the Whites appear to be racing ahead. The lightweight construction of the chariots is realistically rendered (see Fig. 143, p. 173). Pompeii did not have a racecourse. The fresco is testimony to the wide appeal of chariot races in the Roman world.

Figs 125, 126 and 127
Three oil lamps
AD 30–100
Puteoli (Pozzuoli), Italy;
Italy (far right)
Terracotta
W. 9.1–9.7 cm, L. 12.5–14.4 cm
(min.–max.)
British Museum
1856,1226.417, 1856,1226.479
and 1868,0804.1
Bequeathed by Sir William Temple;
Donated by John Henderson
(far right)

These oil lamps served as cheap
keepsakes that captured the
glories of the circus games in
iconographic vignettes. The scenes
show (from left to right): a
four-horse team at full gallop; the
winning charioteer parading down
the Circus Maximus, a wreath and
victory palm in his hand (behind
him is the *spina* with dolphin-
shaped lap counters and other
monuments); and a victorious
horse being paraded through the
streets and cheered by supporters.
One member of the crowd holds a
sign that may have given the
horse's name, others carry victory
palms. The horse harnessed to the
left of a chariot was the most
important animal, as it was closest
to the tight inner corner of the
turning-posts and crucial for a
successful manoeuvre.

talked about the circus performances, although he was forbidden to do so by his teachers. In one anecdote, Nero was bemoaning with his fellow pupils the fate of a charioteer of the Greens, who was dragged by his horses after an accident. When caught by his teacher, Nero supposedly pretended that he had been talking about Hector, the Trojan hero from Homer's *Iliad* that may have been the lesson's official subject – a story one would like to believe, even if it may be pure invention.[98] As *princeps*, 'he came from the country to all the games, even the most insignificant' or so Suetonius claims, a passion that would have endeared Nero to the people, but also a courteous gesture that honoured the aristocratic *editores* of the *ludi* in question.[99] Whether or not Nero played 'every day with ivory chariots on a board' at the beginning of his reign, as Suetonius alleges, the planning of such spectacles required much consideration, even if all the practical detail was delegated to a *curator ludorum*.[100] Nero was an avid supporter of the Green faction. Pliny records that he regularly had the arena's sand strewn with greenish chrysocolla, or gold-solder, and later wore a green coat in the circus when he himself performed as charioteer.[101] The Greens were by far the most popular faction, attracting a wide mass following (Figs 130a and b). It is not quite clear whether they were especially favoured by the *plebs* (as opposed to the Blues), as has sometimes been thought. One of Nero's successors, Aulus Vitellius, by contrast, was an ardent adherent of the Blues.[102]

Among the diverting innovations to the programme of lavish games expected of every emperor, Nero introduced races in which the *quadrigae*, or four-horse chariots, were drawn by teams of camels instead of horses, and there must have been many more such novelties for the entertainment of the crowds.[103] He also organised significant changes to the physical appearance of the Circus Maximus that were directly related to its formal use. Around AD 63, he ordered Caesar's old ring channel to be filled in. This had surrounded the racetrack and provided both drainage and a security barrier for the protection of the spectators,

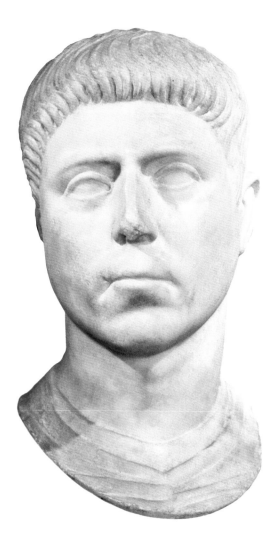

Figs 128 and 129
**Portraits of two charioteers
of the Neronian period**
AD 50–70
Italy
Marble
H. 36 cm; H. 38 cm
Palazzo Massimo alle Terme, Museo
Nazionale Romano, Rome
290, 281

These busts belonged to a group
of monuments dedicated in a
sanctuary of Hercules Cubans in
the Horti Caesaris on the far side
of the River Tiber in Rome. The
quality of the carving hints at the
wealth and prestige successful
charioteers could gain. For such
men, often drawn from the
enslaved population, this was an
emphatic statement about their
place in society.

NERO

particularly during beast hunts. The main purpose must have been to create additional space for the knights, to whom Nero now assigned dedicated seats in front of those for the commoners, similar to the arrangement brought in by Augustus in theatres.[104] This measure, often only treated in passing, is linked to Nero's consistent efforts to accommodate this order. It likely also facilitated the deployment of the *Augustiani* (see p. 167), essential if their chants were to be effective in the incredible din of a circus filled to capacity.

Another result of this measure must have been an increase in the seating capacity of the circus; the innermost seats were now much closer to the arena. Undoubtedly, arrangements were made to protect these seats from the action in the arena (perhaps not quite as extravagant as in the new amphitheatre), but all the detail is lost due to the almost complete destruction of the circus in subsequent fires (see pp. 197, 202).

Naumachia

An extremely costly and therefore rare spectacle were *naumachiae*: realistically staged sea battles that could involve thousands of participants and dozens of ships.[105] For best effect, these required a substantial body of water, so that the replica war galleys could be of reasonable size and the water deep enough for combatants to drown when they were injured in battle or their ships went under, an element of gruesome realism. According to Cassius Dio, Nero gave a *naumachia* that represented a historic naval battle between Athenians and Persians.[106] This echoed a similar-themed show given by Augustus many decades previously, and with its propagandistic reference to what was traditionally presented as a clash between western civilisation and eastern barbarism, may have vaguely alluded to the ongoing conflict with Parthia over Armenia.[107] Again, Seneca provides some detail about the fate of the involuntary performers at such shows, usually convicts or captives whose lives were regarded as expendable; he mentions that during the build-up of a particular mock sea battle, one of the men took his own life by sinking a spear into his throat, thus determining his own fate and demonstrating that 'it is more honourable for men to learn to die than to kill'.[108] Given that the largest ever *naumachia* had been staged by Claudius and that there was a certain expectation that imperial *spectacula* should always surpass what had gone before, Nero's show must have involved considerable effort and expense. Both Suetonius and Dio report that the basin was filled with fish and 'sea monsters'.[109] Dio continues that, after the sea battle, the water was immediately drawn off and the ground dried, and Nero 'once more exhibited contests between land forces, who fought not only in single combat but also in large groups equally matched'. If this was accurate, then an important element of the display was the quick change between environments and the technical feat of flooding and emptying the basin accordingly. Augustus had constructed a venue for such spectacles (also called *naumachia*, after the mock battles performed there) on the opposite bank of the Tiber, and it may be that Nero utilised it now for his own show.[110] The sequence of different fights suggests a long and carefully choreographed programme.

The most significant year for which a dense sequence of Nero's spectacles can be reconstructed is AD 59, followed by AD 60. In September AD 59 Nero celebrated the *ludi Romani* with particular largesse. Renamed *ludi maximi*

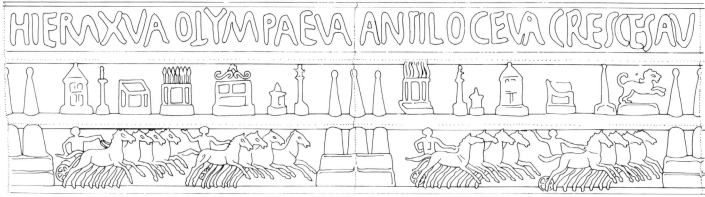

Figs 130a and b
The 'Colchester cup'
AD 41–75
Camulodunum (Colchester),
England
Glass
Diam. 7.7 cm, H. 8.4 cm
British Museum
1870,0224.3
Bequeathed by Felix Slade

The 'Colchester cup' is a mould-blown glass beaker that depicts a race in the Circus Maximus. Such 'spectacle cups', with scenes of gladiatorial fights or chariot races, made use of a relatively recent glass-manufacturing innovation and were popular during the third quarter of the first century AD. The Circus is represented here by the central barrier with its lap counters, obelisk and other monuments. Four chariots race along the arena, separated into two pairs by the oversized *metae* or turning-posts. A continuous band of text along the upper register relates some of the crowd noise: 'HIERAX VA(DE), OLYMPAE VA(LE), ANTILOS VA(DE AGE), CRESCES AV(E)' ('Hierax go! Olympus be strong! Antilos go on! Hail Cresces!'). The prefix 'va-' could stand for different words and 'vale' might also be translated as 'farewell', in the sense that the spectators jeer Hierax, Olympus and Antilos, but hail the winner, Cresces. The four charioteers may represent an all-star cast of the four different racing factions. Claudius Olympus, for example, was a famous charioteer for the Greens.

The cup's findspot in Britain indicates that an avid follower of the races had brought this fragile item as a precious reminder of life in the Roman capital.

('Greatest Games'), he dedicated them to the 'eternity of the Empire', in all likelihood for his recent salvation from Agrippina's alleged assassination plot or else in anticipation of his imminent *quinquennalia*, or five-year anniversary on the throne (see p. 181).[111] Stretching over several days, performances took place 'in five or six theatres at once', as well as the Circus Maximus.[112] 'Every day presents of all kinds were thrown to the crowds; these included a thousand birds of every kind each day, various kinds of food, tokens to be exchanged for grain, clothing, gold, silver, jewels, pearls, paintings, slaves, working animals, and even tamed wild ones, and finally ships, apartment buildings, and farmland.'[113] The effect of this munificence, particularly on the *plebs*, can easily be imagined. The new central market was also opened at around this time. The *ludi maximi* were followed by the *Iuvenalia* (*ludi Iuvenales* – 'Youth Games'), a celebration of the twenty-one-year-old Nero's ceremonial first shaving of his beard. It is a striking reminder of his youth upon accession that this ritual transition into adulthood should occur almost five full years into his reign.[114]

A radical new portrait of the *princeps* seems to have been introduced to coincide with Nero's *quinquennalia* (Fig. 131).[115] Whereas his accession portrait retained an almost austere simplicity, the new version projected a very different image that marked a major departure from previous imperial likenesses. The most obvious difference was in the hairstyle, where the simple strands now made way for a refined, voluminous coiffure that reflected the height of contemporary fashion. Its main characteristic was a series of long curls that framed the forehead, emanating in opposite directions from a parting above the corner of the right eye – a look that could only be achieved with the use of curling irons. The new style combined the traditional iconography of heroic vigour with luxurious sophistication.[116] It quickly became widely imitated and remained popular for the next half-century (see Figs 128 and 129, p. 154).[117]

Among Nero's other entertainments in this period were lavish banquets held in the city's public squares, presumably very generously funded versions of the traditional *epula*, or communal feasts, that also formed an important element of the *ludi* and their religious ceremonies. Suetonius mentions that Nero dined in public in the Circus, the Campus Martius and in Augustus' *naumachia*, which had been drained for the purpose, always surrounded by the people (the *naumachia* and its grove were also the setting of the *Iuvenalia*).[118]

Tacitus, offended perhaps by the luxury enjoyed here by the *plebs* and their access to the *princeps*, singles out a particular feast given by Nero's new prefect of the Praetorian Guard, Ofonius Tigellinus, in AD 64. He styles it as a typical example of these sumptuous festivities and what he considers their hallmark of wasteful prodigality and resultant moral decay. For this *epulum*, held either at an ornate pool in the Campus Martius or at Augustus' *naumachia*, the banqueters were positioned on rafts, drawn by vessels gleaming with gold and ivory and 'oars manned by male prostitutes'.[119] Birds and exotic wild beasts as well as marine animals formed a striking backdrop. Around the basin, so Tacitus states, stood makeshift brothels, filled with women of high rank; on the opposite side were naked prostitutes, gesturing and dancing obscenely. The festivities continued into the night, glittering with lights and echoing to song.[120] It has long been recognised that Tacitus may have described here an especially opulent version of the traditional *Floralia* festival; the *Floralia* always included prostitutes in prominent roles, a sacred custom of obscure antiquity.[121] By omitting this reference, Tacitus radically changes the perceived character of the *epulum*, allowing him to follow up with a direct attack on Nero's morals and then present later events as expressions of divine retribution.[122]

In the surviving source accounts, two elements of Nero's *spectacula* in this period stand out: his mixing with the common crowds; and the active participation, in the arena and on stage, of performers drawn from the highest orders of senators and knights and members of their families. Together with Nero's own public performances (albeit still limited at this point), this blurring of traditional status hierarchies enraged later authors, who highlighted it as the most overt sign of the deeper failings of Nero's reign – Tacitus' heavily manipulated account of the 'banquet of Tigellinus' is a prime example.

Theatralis licentia, pantomimes and the *ordo equester*

The chance find of a small first-century bronze tablet in a town in south-east Italy, first published in 1978, has transformed the understanding of some crucial features of Roman performance culture during the Julio-Claudian period and the controversies they caused with regard to the traditional social order.[123] It does much to complement and balance the sparse literary accounts of the period, and, most importantly, it puts some noteworthy aspects of Nero's spectacles, and his own performing activities, in perspective.

The Latin text of this tablet, the so-called *Tabula Larinas*, contains parts of an official senate decree of AD 19, including references to closely related earlier legal provisions (Fig. 132). In essence, the decree tightened the existing law in order to prevent male and female descendants of senators, knights (*ordo equester*) and their relatives of either sex from becoming professional actors, gladiators or other performers. Previous regulations had banned knights and the sons of senators (who counted as knights before their formal entry into the senate) from these professions. Violations of the law were to be punished with banishment and the loss of various privileges. Yet the regulations concerned other activities as well: senators were forbidden from visiting the houses of pantomime actors, knights from joining their public processions and pantomime actors from performing privately in the homes of the wealthy.[124] This prominence of pantomime actors hints at their seductive star appeal and easy access to the elites. The new decree is testimony to the inventiveness and determination with which young aristocrats had circumvented the earlier restrictions so that they could continue to perform, even if they had to relinquish their formal rank in order to do so (Fig. 133).[125]

The *Tabula Larinas* thus opens a window into a profound change in cultural attitudes within the Roman aristocracy during the last decades of the Republic and the early principate. It seems astonishing that elite men and women would still want to engage in these activities, and in numbers that warranted repeated legislation, given that such occupations came with the social and legal stigma of *infamia* (see p. 152). Yet the presence of knights, and even senators, in the arena and on stage is well attested. The first appearance of a knight as a gladiator is recorded in the extant sources in connection with a festival given by Julius Caesar in 46 BC, and perhaps a display of sword skills was something more easily reconciled with aristocratic ethos. Under Augustus, seventeen years later in

Fig. 131
Portrait of Nero (Type III)
AD 59–64
Palatine, Rome, Italy
Marble
H. 31 cm, W. 23 cm, D. 25 cm
Parco Archeologico del Colosseo,
Museo Palatino, Rome
618

This portrait-type, Nero's third, is attested on coins from AD 59 onwards and may have been created to coincide with his *quinquennalia*, or fifth anniversary on the throne. Nero's hair reaches far down the neck. Towards the front, the dense, voluminous strands are arranged in long curls that frame the forehead – an elaborate look that required the use of curling irons. The coiffure recalls Suetonius' description of Nero's supporters, the *Augustiani*, who may well have imitated his style, with their 'pinguissima coma' ('very thick, luxurious hair'). Their chants ('beautiful Caesar, Apollo') also hint at the way Nero's new portrait was intended to be read by the Roman public, a combination of vigour and refined elegance.

This portrait head was found in one of the covered passageways underneath the imperial palace, where it may have been stored for safekeeping or later re-use. It is remarkably well preserved with no sign of deliberate damage.

29 BC, a senator fought in public at the dedication of a temple (something previously forbidden). However, in 23 BC, again with Augustus' explicit approval, a knight appeared as a pantomime dancer.[126] Nero's paternal grandfather, Lucius Domitius Ahenobarbus, similarly organised scenic performances as consul in 16 BC (and previously as praetor) in which he gave the stage to knights and women of the higher orders, who acted in a mime.[127] Further instances followed in quick succession, with repeated legislation hinting at divisions within the senate and a continuing concern to maintain traditional class distinctions. The reasons behind these changes in attitudes and behaviour were complex, but linked to the fame, public adulation and substantial wealth star actors, as well as gladiators and charioteers, could paradoxically acquire despite their lowly status. Whereas previous generations of senators and knights may have sought fame on the battlefields, economic hardship in the wake of the civil war was widespread, and their sons and grandsons turned to the arena or stage, attracted by the prospect of winning back their fortunes through performing as paid professionals (where their unusual background automatically garnered them greater attention). This radical shift in mindset must have been the cause of major rifts within many elite families.[128] In subsequent decades, the more limited opportunities for gaining personal glory under the political conditions of the 'Restored Republic' provided a different incentive.[129] Ultimately, the moral permissibility of their appearances hinged on the question of pay (*quaestus*). While voluntary performances were considered acceptable (if still undesirable by the conservatively minded), pay continued to evoke the spectre of *infamia*. It seems that this matter was clarified again under Nero in legal regulations introduced by Cocceius Nerva the Younger.[130] Yet the definition remained contested, particularly when gifts in kind rather than money were involved.

The prominence of a small number of performers naturally raised the suspicions of the senatorial aristocracy. If pantomime processions attracted greater crowds than their senatorial equivalents, this threatened the senators' prized dignity.[131] It is equally apparent that in the intensely politicised atmosphere of the theatre, crowd reactions to performers from the higher orders appearing alongside those from a lower-class background could easily get out of hand and become an additional means of venting political and social discontent. The knights had a particular interest in manipulating these dynamics. The *lex Roscia* of 67 BC, later complemented by the *lex Iulia theatralis* of about 20 BC, had assigned them the first fourteen rows in the theatres. Since the knights lacked any formal assembly equivalent to the senate, it was here that they could make their collective opinions and demands known, and for this reason also they became heavily involved with theatrical claques (organised groups that would attempt to influence the audience by applauding or deriding a performance as one).[132]

As a consequence, wider conflicts evolved mostly around pantomime (see p. 131), which quickly became the popular lead genre of the performing arts and had the most profound impact on the established social order (pantomime actors performed predominantly in the theatres, where the knights sat as a coherent block).

Augustus' role in these developments was ambivalent. While the first *princeps* became socially more conservative over the time of his reign and passed legislation to this effect, he and his close confidant Maecenas had firmly established and popularised fully fledged Greek-style pantomime in Rome through two of their freedmen, the celebrated dancers Pylades and Beryllus.

Fig. 132
The *Tabula Larinas*
AD 19
Larinum (Larino), Italy
Bronze
H. 47 cm, W. 31.2 cm, D. 1 cm
Museo Sannitico di Campobasso

The *Tabula Larinas* is an inscribed bronze tablet from the ancient town of Larinum in Italy. It preserves lines of a senatorial decree of AD 19, passed under the consuls Marcus Iunius Silanus Torquatus and Lucius Norbanus Balbus. The decree aimed to restrict the public appearances – as actors, gladiators and other entertainers – by men and women from senatorial and knightly families. It is an important testimony to the cultural conflicts fought within the senior orders during the Julio-Claudian period, the result of a gradual shift in upper-class social values that continued into Nero's reign.

Text of important legislation passed by the senate was disseminated throughout the Empire and made available for consultation through copies, such as this, inscribed locally in stone or bronze.

The powerful attraction of these performances and their intense hold over Roman audiences of all classes are hard to comprehend from a distance of two thousand years. The immersive group ritual of the ancient theatre must have been a major factor. Pantomime actors were a type of ballet dancer whose art combined expressive grace with vigorous athletic training. They wore masks that allowed them to adopt a broad repertoire of male and female roles, a gender fluidity which must have held additional appeal (all roles in Roman theatre were normally performed by male actors, but pantomime performers had to use their bodies as the prime means of artistic expression) (Figs 134 and 135). Some of their dances could be highly eroticised.[133] Latin texts use the terms *pantomimus* and *histrio* (actor in a more general sense) interchangeably, leading to occasional ambiguity. Pantomime professionals seem to have referred to themselves mainly as 'actors of tragic rhythmic movement', reflecting their athletic training and elevated subject matter. They mostly performed as soloists, which added to their star attraction (although there was always another actor who recited the storyline mimed by the dancer, and there could be a supporting chorus) and facilitated

Fig. 133
The 'actor king'
AD 30–40
Palaestra at Herculaneum, Italy
Plaster and paint
H. 39 cm, W. 39 cm
Museo Archeologico Nazionale
di Napoli
9019

The fresco depicts an actor in regal attire on an ornate throne. He holds a long sceptre and sword and gazes towards the right, where a kneeling woman writes out a dedication below a tragic mask. Behind the mask is another attendant. The composition seems to capture something of the star allure of famous performers; the noble appearance of the actor contrasts markedly with the nominal status of *histriones* (theatrical performers) in Roman society, but reflects the prestige they could attain in real life.

their performances in private houses of the aristocracy (Fig. 136). The primacy of pantomime as artistic genre is becoming ever more evident. For example, recent research indicates that Seneca's tragic plays, long considered almost impossible to perform on stage, were in fact libretti for pantomimes that only sketched out the plot, while any detail was interpreted through dance.[134]

The titles and outlines of individual plays (and, in some cases, their preserved texts), as well as the visual representations of actors and other performers, alongside the sparse literary descriptions of shows and crowd reactions, can only provide a faint glimmer of the intense emotional experience these occasions must have offered (see Fig. 139). Actors in tragic plays dominate the iconographic record, but the ubiquity of frescos with theatrical themes and ornate stage architectures, so well preserved in the Vesuvian cities, is testimony to the commanding appeal of the theatrical world (Figs 137 and 138).

Much of Roman performance practice led to a gradual convergence of the different genres, with common mythological themes across conventional tragic plays, *tragoedia cantata* ('sung tragedy', or aria-like recitals sung by soloists who accompanied themselves on the cithara, or lyre) and *tragoedia saltata* ('danced tragedy' or pantomime). The reduction of extended tragic plots to shorter pieces and the increasing focus on solo performers, who often appeared in direct competition for prizes, added to the mass appeal particularly of the latter format. Equally popular were their primary media of music and dance, which could be appreciated even by those who may have struggled with the lyrics (especially if performances were in Greek).[135] The elevated subject matter and the relative exclusivity that came with the years of training required to perform in these roles may have held additional attraction for those from knightly and senatorial families.

Figs 134 and 135
Two ornaments carved in the form of tragic theatre masks
AD 1–79
Pompeii, Italy
Marble
H. 31 cm (left); H. 37 cm, W. 32 cm (right)
Museo Archeologico Nazionale di Napoli
6611, 6613

These masks, which would have been suspended between columns, may have served to decorate a peristyle garden (see the staged reconstruction, Fig. 136). They closely resemble real tragic masks, an impression undoubtedly heightened by their original painted finish. Pantomime masks, by contrast, featured a closed mouth.

Aristocratic performers

Nero did not compel members of senatorial and knightly families to perform at his spectacles. On the contrary, it seems that he responded to an existing demand among such persons for public appearances at prestigious events and thereby returned to a policy adopted by several of his predecessors. There evidently was a perception that voluntary performances by men and women of high social standing honoured the sponsor and provided a much nobler prospect than lower-class characters acting out of compulsion could offer.

At the splendid *munus*, or gladiatorial show, that Nero gave in his new amphitheatre, probably at its AD 57 inauguration, four hundred senators and six hundred knights fought in the arena according to Suetonius.[136] If these numbers are to be trusted, this would constitute two-thirds of the senate. Even the beast fights that complemented the gladiatorial combat were performed by members of the two orders. Suetonius adds, perhaps with the incredulity of someone writing two generations after these events (when attitudes had changed considerably), that 'wealthy men of good reputation' were among them. In light of this, Nero's unusual decision to put no one to death, 'not even criminals', could be interpreted as a measure intended not to divert attention from the participating senators and knights. Executions, often staged as highly inventive mythological tableaux, were supremely popular entertainments and might otherwise have upstaged the displays of martial and hunting prowess offered by the high-born amateurs.[137] Perhaps the mass participation of senators and knights should also be seen in connection with the exceptional honours the senate proffered Nero in those years. In this case, it could be regarded as an extension of the appearances of individual aristocrats at events given by their peers, but now they collectively represented the two senior orders in a show of homage and respect towards the young *princeps*.[138]

Fig. 136
Photograph of the House of the Golden Cupids, Pompeii
c. 1900
Glass plate
H. 21, W. 27 cm
Fratelli Alinari

This is the colonnaded garden courtyard of the House of the Golden Cupids (Casa degli Amorini Dorati) in Pompeii. It was richly decorated with sculptures that alluded to the world of the theatre (including images of the god Bacchus, or Dionysus, and representations of theatre masks). Many scholars believe that one wing of the colonnade (seen here in the centre) may have served as a stage for private performances. The famous Augustan-era pantomime Pylades visited the city; the celebrated dancer Paris also did so in the Neronian period. Pantomines routinely gave performances and lessons for enthusiastic high-status amateurs in the houses of the wealthy.

Fig. 137
Polychrome stucco panel
AD 62–79
House of Meleager, Pompeii, Italy
Stucco and paint
H. 159 cm, W. 285 cm
Museo Archeologico Nazionale
di Napoli
9596

This vibrant, polychrome stucco panel depicts an elaborate theatre stage (steps leading up to the podium are visible on the left). The rich, architectural stage wall of Roman theatres (*scenae frons*) was meant to evoke the façades of royal palaces of the Greek world, the setting of many myths and classical plays. The panel was part of a continuous frieze that decorated the upper wall of the *tablinum* ('study', or privileged reception room) of a Pompeian house. It would have been prominently visible across the atrium from the entrance. Mythological scenes, perhaps reflecting famous plays, were painted on the walls below.

Fig. 138
Two tragic actors on stage
AD 62–79
House of the Dioscuri, Pompeii, Italy
Plaster and paint
H. 58 cm, W. 51 cm
Museo Archeologico Nazionale
di Napoli
9039

The elaborate costumes, platform shoes and distinctive masks worn by these actors, along with their pronounced gestures, give a good sense of a performance in progress. The white colour of the mask of the actor on the right indicates that he portrayed a female character; perhaps he performs the role of the mythical heroine Auge, holding her infant son Telephus.

Fig. 139
Statuette of a tragic actor
AD 1–200
Via Appia, Rome, Italy
Ivory
H. 16 cm
Petit Palais, Musée des Beaux-Arts
de la Ville de Paris
DUT 192

This intricately carved figure preserves strong traces of its polychrome finish, highlighting the rich and delicate patterns of the actor's costume. Behind the mask, the actor's eyes and mouth are wide open as he recoils during a scene. He wears high platform boots (*cothurni*) like those in the fresco (Fig. 138).

Similarly, at the unspecified spectacle that involved beast hunts performed by Nero's horse guards, thirty knights fought as gladiators, and again, there is no sign of compulsion.[139] There were several gladiatorial shows in AD 63, 'equal in magnificence to their predecessors', according to Tacitus, 'though more women of rank and senators disgraced themselves in the arena'.[140] From the context, it is quite clear that these were fights organised by the praetors or other officials, not the *princeps*, and they therefore must be testimony to a broader cultural shift.[141]

At Nero's *ludi maximi* of AD 59, parts in the theatrical plays 'were taken by several men and women of both the orders', and, in a noteworthy cameo highlight, a 'well-known Roman knight mounted an elephant and rode down a rope'.[142] Suetonius mentions the participation of high-born performers in a relatively neutral way, but regrettably he provides little detail about the actual entertainments, perhaps because it could all be found in his lost monograph treatise on Roman spectacles and games. Dio is more expansive, stating that 'men and women not only of the equestrian but even of the senatorial order appeared as performers in the orchestra, in the Circus, and in the hunting-theatre, […] some of them played the flute and danced in pantomimes or acted in tragedies and comedies or sang to the lyre; they drove horses, killed wild beasts and fought as gladiators'.[143] Both Dio and Tacitus are furious in their disapproval, yet on close reading of their texts, there is no convincing evidence that these performances were anything but voluntary.[144] On the contrary, they may have been intended as public displays of loyalty and gratitude for the salvation of the *princeps*, a continuation of the numerous sacrifices, thanksgivings and extraordinary honours Nero had received over the previous months (see p. 164). In turn, the *princeps* demonstrated his obligation to the equestrian and senatorial performers with lavish gifts. At any rate, Dio's list of participants reads like a roll call of the old Roman nobility, and Tacitus stresses that some of the knights were very well known.[145]

The *Iuvenalia*, held a little later in the same year, followed a similar pattern. According to Suetonius, Nero allowed 'even old men of consular rank and aged matrons [to] take part'.[146] Again, Dio may have had recourse to a more detailed source; after stating that members of the most noble families – as well as others – took part, he cites the example of Aelia Catella, 'a woman not only prominent by reason of her family and her wealth but also advanced in years (she was an octogenarian)' who danced in a pantomime. Others sang in choruses.[147] Even Tacitus had to concede with regard to the high-born performers that 'a crowd of volunteers enrolled themselves'.[148] It was at the *Iuvenalia* that Nero's personal claque, the *Augustiani* ('supporters of the Augustus'), made its first appearance. The *Augustiani* were sturdy young knights, modelled on existing Roman claques but trained in the rhythmic chants and applause practised with great effect by Alexandrian theatre factions.[149] Suetonius' description of these young men, with their 'thick hair and most refined appearance', brings to mind Nero's own new portrait style, which may have served as their model.[150]

The *Neronia*, another new festival first held in the following year, formally introduced Greek-style contests to Rome.[151] They were intended to be held in every fifth year. Augustus had introduced a similar festival, the *Sebasta*, at Naples in AD 2, which now served as a model for Nero's competition. Like its Greek counterparts, the *Neronia* were divided into three sections, comprising music, gymnastics and equestrian displays. It seems that Nero again responded to popular demand, as he had with the construction of his amphitheatre. The modern notion that philhellene emperors introduced such contests to a reluctant Roman public, which was much more interested in gladiatorial combat and other blood sports, is wholly mistaken. On the contrary, Tacitus, in a short aside, explicitly refers to the populace demanding Greek-style contests, *certamina Graeca*, from the magistrates.[152] Previous *principes* had already integrated individual elements of Greek games into earlier spectacles, even if moralising senatorial prejudice may have prevented them from going further.[153] Nero's devotion of an entire festival to Greek *certamina* was but a logical next step. Even the name, *Neronia*, need not be something chosen by the emperor unilaterally – it is reminiscent of the senate's offer in AD 64 to rename the fourth month of the year Neroneus in honour of the *princeps*.[154] The first *Neronia* purposefully coincided with the dedication of Nero's new baths and gymnasium, which were as popular (see p. 140) as the contests themselves (the adjacent Baths of Agrippa and their ancillary structures had essentially fulfilled functions of a gymnasium already, but the term had been cautiously avoided).[155] The gymnasium was aimed primarily at the *iuvenes*, among whom young knights were prominent.[156]

The musical programme of the *Neronia* took place in the nearby theatres of the Campus Martius (the Theatre of Pompeius, the largest, was in the immediate vicinity). Former consuls, chosen by lot, presided over the contest. According to Suetonius, the most eminent men contended for the prize in Latin oratory and poetry. Although Nero did not participate himself, the competitors unanimously agreed to award the first prize to their *princeps*. Nero graciously accepted, receiving the award amid the assembled senators in the theatre. The entire contest was marked by these mutual gestures of honour and respect between the *princeps* and the orders of senators and knights; Nero, in turn, provided them with free oil for their exercises in the baths and gymnasium.[157] As a further nod to the dignity of the event, pantomimes had been explicitly excluded, thus avoiding the usual boisterous behaviour of their supporters. Seneca's nephew, the young poet Lucan, first came to public attention with a recitation of his *laudes Neronis*, or praise of Nero, for which he was awarded a prize (Fig. 140). The judges also offered Nero first prize for playing cithara (again he had not performed at the contest). This he declined, although he knelt before it and ordered that it be laid at the feet of a statue of Augustus – a revealing link back to the first emperor and his interests.[158]

The second *Neronia*, in AD 65, included performances by Nero himself.[159] It seems that Aulus Vitellius presided over one of the competitions and encouraged the *princeps* to play the cithara.[160]

Nero: the performing prince

Nero's natural peer group in terms of age and social background were the young knights and sons of senators, those singled out by the senatorial decrees mentioned earlier (see p. 158). These men were the most conspicuous occupants of the first fourteen rows in the theatres, heavily involved with the various groups of claques and supporters, and in many cases keen to perform themselves. Inevitably, Nero shared their interests and enthusiasms, and his role as *princeps iuventutis* had made him their semi-formal representative. His early passions for equestrian sports and for the stage were wholly in line with those of many aristocrats of his generation. By the time Nero was crown prince, he must have come across numerous determined dilettantes of the higher orders who practised their arts in their own houses or those of aristocratic friends, and clearly he would have seen some of them perform publicly as well.

A degree of musical training formed part of Nero's early education, as seems to have been the norm at the time. Among those brought up with him at Claudius' court, Britannicus moved participants of a palace banquet with his singing voice, while the future emperor Titus Caesar Vespasianus, instructed by the same palace tutors, 'was not without talent' in music and 'could sing and play the cithara with grace and skill'.[161]

After his accession, Nero was in a position to gather the best performers at his court. Terpnus, the leading master of the cithara in those days, gave frequent private recitals at the palace, which may have inspired Nero to invest time and effort in his own musical exercises, just as many other wealthy amateurs seem to have done. Suetonius claims that he followed a professional exercise and practice regime; whether he also adopted the more eccentric and superstitious habits of famous citharodes is perhaps moot.[162] He certainly attained a level of competency that required serious commitment.[163] Suetonius describes his voice as *exigua et fusca*, often translated as 'thin and indistinct', or 'weak and husky'. Quintilian is perhaps more useful, in stating that a *vox fusca* was suitable for stirring emotions, soothing listeners or rousing them to pity, all likely to have been utterly appropriate reactions in the context of a performance of *tragoedia cantata*.[164] After some five years of practice and private recitals in the palace among a close circle of friends, at his AD 59 *Iuvenalia* Nero first performed in front of a larger crowd (albeit in a context that could still be termed private) a piece entitled 'Attis or the Bacchantes'.[165] Over the following years he performed publicly in Naples, mingling freely with the crowds in the local theatre. Finally, at the second *Neronia* he sang 'Niobe' in public in Rome.[166]

In order to assess Nero's activities in the context of his own times, even the briefest look at a few other prominent individuals is illuminating. Nero's most outspoken critic in the senate, Thrasea Paetus, for example, pointedly did not participate in the *Iuvenalia*; however, he had previously performed publicly in full tragic robes at a religious festival in his native Patavium.[167] Another leading

Fig. 140
Semis
AD 64
Minted in Rome, Italy
Copper alloy
Weight 3.5 g
British Museum
1906,1103.2827
Donated by Dr Frederick
Parkes Weber

The semis was among the lowest denominations of coin minted during the Empire, its value equivalent to half an as, or one eighth of a sestertius. The reverse here carries a reference to Nero's new games, the *Neronia*, labelled here as 'CERT(AMEN) QUINQ(UENNALE) ROM(AE) CO(NSTITUTUM)', 'five-yearly contest established at Rome'. The image highlights the Greek character of the *Neronia*. It shows a prize table (richly decorated with griffins or sphinxes), on which are an urn for the judges' ballots and a laurel wreath (sacred to Apollo) for the winner. A discus leans against one of the table legs, representing the athletic contests that formed part of the programme alongside music and recitals. The *Neronia* ceased after Nero's death, but were essentially re-constituted in slightly modified form as the *Capitolia* (*ludi Capitolini*) under Domitian in AD 86. Coins struck under Domitian, and later Trajan, reproduced the reverse image of Nero's semis unaltered.

member of the so-called senatorial opposition, Gaius Calpurnius Piso, apparently also sang in tragic costume and was an accomplished cithara player.[168] The former consul Cluvius Rufus, later author of a history of Nero's reign, even shared a stage with Nero for many years, without any harm to his reputation.[169] If anything set Nero apart, it was his role as *princeps*, and his inability to accept that this meant he would never be judged, particularly in competitions, as a mere performer, despite his attempts to cast off the trappings of power and assume the persona of a devoted professional. However, the seemingly genuine delight of the populace, the delicate position of the judges and the extreme sycophancy of the senate only reinforced this delusion. All these factors contributed to the lasting image of Nero as imperial citharode, a notion of such powerful agency that his later biographer Suetonius was convinced a Neronian coin type of the god Apollo Citharoedus really showed a portrait of the *princeps* in the flowing robes of a professional cithara player (Fig. 141).[170]

The evidence for Nero's tragic stage performances relates exclusively to the years after AD 66 and his tour of Greece. Suetonius and Cassius Dio record some of the plays and Nero's roles, at first glance an odd mix of often troubled characters.[171] Modern scholarship has overwhelmingly treated the relevant source accounts as reliable, and the more sensitive interpretations provide a fair attempt at exploring a possible rationale behind Nero's choices.[172] This seems especially convincing in relation to one of the core themes of ancient tragedy: the conflicting demands often placed on individuals. Incompatible obligations towards the gods and fellow humans lead to moments of profound crisis. In Nero's case this could be understood metaphorically to reflect irreconcilable choices between family bonds and matters of state. Nero's role as Orestes, for example, might have alluded to his strained relationship with his own mother Agrippina and the fateful decisions that were forced on him against his will (Fig. 142). Nero would thus have tried to communicate some of his personal actions to the wider Roman public.[173] Attractive as this may be, however, serious problems remain. Given the evident manipulation of facts so clearly noticeable elsewhere in the source record, there is no particular reason to consider the references to Nero's performance repertoire any more reliable. The preserved catalogue of Nero's roles may be inaccurate or have had the less controversial roles carefully edited out so as to depict the *princeps* in a negative light. A more direct reading of Nero's purported catalogue of stage personas merely suggests that the source authors wanted to characterise him as deluded, frenzied, culpable and effeminate. They did so by insinuating, with little sophistication, that Nero as performer shared the negative traits of the characters he adopted, many of whom are linked to incest and matricide.[174]

Nero's artistic talents found other outlets as well. A good rhetorical education was mandatory for Roman upper-class males, and with Seneca as his tutor, Nero achieved a high level of competency that allowed him to deliver creditable speeches in the senate in his early to mid-teens. Tacitus repeatedly states that Nero even after his accession merely read out what Seneca had composed.[175] These remarks were uncharitable and perhaps intended to distract from the fact that the young *princeps* was a confident public speaker – surely a marked contrast to Claudius' long-winded speeches and occasional stammer. The same holds true for Nero's poetry. Tacitus maintains that Nero's *carmina*, or poems, showed 'no vigour or inspiration, or unity in their flow' and were composed or improved

Fig. 141
Sestertius
AD 62
Minted in Rome, Italy
Copper alloy
Weight 12 g
British Museum
1921,0612.5

The portrait of Nero on the obverse
of this sestertius is coupled with
an image of Apollo Citharoedus
(Apollo the cithara player) on the
reverse. A fillet (diadem) is tied
around the god's head. His long,
flowing robes reflect the ornate
stage attire citharodes wore during
their performances. The size and
weight of the instrument are also
apparent in his posture.

Suetonius claimed that these coins
showed Nero as a citharode, but
the god has no recognisable
portrait features.

with the help of many others. Yet in a fascinating vignette, Suetonius explicitly defends the *princeps*, who in his words 'wrote verses with eagerness and without labour and did not, as some think, publish the work of others as his own'. As evidence, he refers to some original notebooks and papers in Nero's handwriting that he had in his possession. Apparently, they showed clear signs of original composition through frequent erasures, additions and other alterations that indicated work in progress.[176] According to Suetonius, Nero recited his poems not only in private but also publicly in theatres 'to widespread delight'. After one particular event, a public thanksgiving was voted and the passage he had read out was inscribed in gold letters and dedicated to Iupiter Capitolinus.[177] This is in line with other honours and prizes the senate and various judges awarded the *princeps*. It is little wonder that Nero felt encouraged in his creative endeavours. He later began work on a longer epos on the Trojan War and recited selected passages publicly (see p. 211). Collections of Nero's poems were in circulation after his death and appreciated for their quality (the poet Martial in this context referred to Nero as 'learned'). Vitellius even asked for some of Nero's well-known and popular works to be read out at a palace banquet, but it must always have been difficult to judge these compositions on their own merit, without making political points.[178]

In the field of sporting activities, Nero's passion for horses soon encompassed a range of equestrian disciplines. As an amateur sport, chariot-racing was a privilege of the wealthy; the later rulers Galba and Vitellius are known to have driven chariots, as did Nero's grandfather and father, and his uncle Caligula.[179] Nero raced two-, three- and four-horse teams (*bigae*, *trigae* and *quadrigae*), and later even a ten-horse chariot (Fig. 143).[180] He first practised his skills on the racetrack in his gardens across the Tiber, the Circus Vaticanus constructed by Caligula. Claudius had frequently invited the people to shows in this circus, perhaps during repair and construction works on the Circus Maximus. Nero now also invited the public to observe him racing, to the great delight of the *plebs*. Suetonius contemptuously describes those attending as in servitude and the lowest class of people (*plebs sordida*, 'a filthy mob'), and Tacitus, in a similarly disparaging manner, refers to the 'common crowd' (*vulgus*), 'craving amusements' and 'rejoicing when the *princeps* moved in the same direction'. The people were full of praise for Nero, encouraging him to go further.[181] Tacitus alludes to these

Fig. 142
A scene from *Iphigenia in Tauris* showing Orestes and Pylades
AD 30–40
House of the Citharist, Pompeii, Italy
Plaster and paint
H. 166 cm, W. 177 cm
Museo Archeologico Nazionale di Napoli
9111

The fresco depicts a key scene from Greek myth, dramatised in Euripides' fifth-century BC tragic play *Iphigenia in Tauris*. The Greek hero Orestes, in a quest for redemption, had to retrieve a sacred image of the goddess Artemis from the Taurians, a tribe on the remote shores of the northern Black Sea. Here he is depicted on the left with his

companion Pylades, standing captive in front of the Taurian king, who sits on the right. Orestes' long-lost sister Iphigenia is the partially preserved female figure clad in white.

According to the literary sources, Orestes was among the roles Nero performed on stage. In ancient myth, Orestes had slain his mother,

Clytemnestra, and her lover to avenge the murder of his father Agamemnon. It was a profound ethical dilemma that continued to haunt him.

Fig. 143
Model of a two-horse chariot (*biga*)
AD 1–100
River Tiber, Rome, Italy
Bronze
H. 20.3 cm, W. 10 cm, L. 25.4 cm
British Museum
1894,1030.1

The horse that would have been harnessed to the left of this two-horse chariot is now missing. The body of the chariot itself is rendered in astonishing detail – even the wheels show slight differences. Specific modifications have been made to the left wheel, which would, in real life, have enabled the *biga* to execute tight left-hand turns on the racetrack more quickly. The chariot's pole ends in an ornate ram's head. The accuracy, scale and material of this *biga* suggest that it was not a toy, but perhaps a precious offering or a prized scale model, owned by a wealthy racing enthusiast or high-ranking professional. Few ancient representations are as detailed, so it has formed the basis for many modern chariot reconstructions.

spectacles not as 'public' but 'promiscuous', a clear hint of what he perceived as a destabilising effect and potential threat to the senatorial class if the *princeps* found common cause with the people. The same notion was behind his criticism of Nero's participation in feasts and amusements for the *plebs*. When Nero later raced publicly in the Circus Maximus, this became even more acute.

It seems that towards the mid-60s AD the character of Nero's performances changed, as did the attitude of parts of the senate. In parallel, the *Augustiani*, from small beginnings, became a substantial force organised into different groups that now comprised knights as well as five thousand men drawn from the *plebs*. Their leaders' salaries were equivalent to the highest-paid equestrian posts in the imperial administration.[182] With this, the *Augustiani* took on an almost paramilitary character, accompanying Nero on his abortive tour of the East, alongside the Praetorian Guard.

The crucial question here is one of chronology, or rather of cause and effect. Senatorial actions may have been prompted by Nero's behaviour, and his performances may have given rise to such deep unease and controversy that they came to symbolise his unsuitability for holding imperial power. Conversely, Nero's later performances may have reflected a changed attitude towards the senate and an attempt to garner support from elsewhere, including the *plebs*.

V

PASSION
AND
DISCORD

Women of the Julio-Claudian dynasty became highly visible in Roman society, through their physical presence at important state events and the unprecedented number of their images in the public sphere.[1] In what was perhaps a sign of the traditionalist backlash that followed Nero's reign, the ability of female members of the imperial family to influence politics was not matched again until the very late second and early third centuries AD. Some of the reasons for their prominent position during the first century, chiefly to do with Augustus' bloodline, have been discussed above (see p. 37). Yet even for the early principate it is frustratingly difficult to gauge what real impact these imperial women may have had, and to what extent such an impression is mostly due to a misrepresentation of their agency by deeply hostile male authors, who adhered to traditional moral codes that strictly circumscribed acceptable female behaviour in a male-dominated society.[2] Modern readers, much more attuned to the ways in which language reflects power structures and inherent prejudices, and perhaps less in awe of the reputation of Classical authors than previous generations, will quickly note this profound bias.[3]

Following Nero's accession as emperor, a number of women were of great importance to him. This was, however, portrayed in an overwhelmingly negative way in later literary accounts, which were exclusively concerned with their authors' own political agendas. They were framed by concomitant moralistic judgements and therefore require careful scrutiny. Nero's mother Agrippina remained a powerful presence, even after her access to her son and the court was restricted. For the first half of Nero's reign his wife Claudia Octavia continued to be dynastically significant, but she was soon eclipsed by Poppaea Sabina, who would become his second wife in AD 62 and to whom he seems to have been genuinely devoted (see p. 190). Nero's third wife, Statilia Messalina, never quite attained the same status, but she married him only about a year and a half before his death.

In their narratives, the source authors allude only obliquely to matters of state; instead, they concentrate on the deeply personal, with recourse to invention and topical invective, so that the court appears as a hotbed of petty jealousies, intrigues and sexual perversions. This may have been a deliberate strategy to hide some of society's underlying issues; a coded language that never really revealed the names and motives of the political actors involved. Most of the claims advanced are so exaggerated and contradictory as to be highly dubious (see, for example, p. 59, pp. 82–4 and p. 190). Also, as some of the first generation of authors – Pliny the Elder, Fabius Rusticus, Cluvius Rufus, all filtered through Tacitus – were not of the same social class as those they described, their access to information was more limited than often credited. Therefore, rather than relying on these sources for what might have happened to certain members of the senatorial and equestrian class, they should be used to discover what seems plausible (or true in a metaphorical sense), and what this reveals about their wider expectations and attitudes. Cassius Dio, writing over a century and a half after these events and less invested in judging individual personalities in the same way, hints at his own doubts about these earlier texts. Concerning the tedious reports of incest between Agrippina and Nero, for example, he states: 'Whether this actually occurred, or whether it was invented to fit their character, I am not sure'.[4]

In order to understand the organising principles of such a conviction-led narrative, its compositional consequences deserve attention. Most of these authors undoubtedly resented Agrippina's position near the centre of power and they approved of Nero's subsequent actions, as did the vast majority of their peers and the general populace at the time. Because their overall intention, however, was to demonstrate Nero's fundamental unsuitability as emperor, they had to find a way to censor his actions regardless. They achieved this by ascribing to him motives different from their own and those of his senatorial and equestrian advisors, ranging from the petty and personal to the outright perverted. Once they had embarked on this path, these elements had to be applied to all of his relationships, both for narrative consistency and escalating dramatic tension.

Matricide: Agrippina's death and its aftermath

Agrippina was clearly perceived as the crucial force during the transition to Nero's rule, maintaining in the mind of the source authors the same sinister background role she had played under Claudius (Fig. 144). Tacitus accuses her of inflicting 'the first death under the new principate' by instigating the poisoning of the senator Marcus Iunius Silanus in AD 54, but he explicitly states that this happened without Nero's knowledge.[5] The evidence is thin, either way. Serving as proconsul of Asia, Silanus seems to have died after a dinner attended by two officials in charge of imperial revenues, the knight Publius Celer and the freedman Helius, who supposedly administered poison very openly.[6] Significantly, Marcus Iunius Silanus was the eldest brother of Lucius Iunius Silanus, who had for many years been betrothed to Claudia Octavia and was later driven to his death under Claudius (see p. 63). Tacitus refers to 'rumours' related to the Silani's high birth and descent from Augustus that made them appear as plausible rivals of Nero and prompted Agrippina into action.[7] While such rumours may have arisen, particularly after the purges late in Claudius' reign, Tacitus' sources may also have projected later events backwards. However, it seems perfectly credible that members of the families who had come so close to power under Claudius continued to harbour ambitions for the principate at the very beginning of Nero's reign, and Agrippina's actions may not have been without justification (Tacitus writes that Agrippina referred to the Silani as a 'hostile house', succinctly capturing the relationship between these rival clans).[8] Pliny the Elder – at the time based far away from such events, at a military garrison in Germany – bluntly blames Silanus' poisoning on Nero, but like most of his anti-Neronian statements, this is merely evidence of his intense hatred for the *princeps*.[9]

While Nero's accession was widely accepted and enjoyed popular support, there were events that suggested ongoing tensions within the nobility and between different factions at court, an atmosphere still rife with conspiracies, real or imagined, similar to those that had marred Claudius' reign. Iunia Silana, a relative of the two doomed Silani, in turn now accused Agrippina of involvement in a plot against Nero, claiming that she intended to replace him on the throne with Rubellius Plautus, another descendant of Augustus slightly older than the *princeps*.[10] In this, Agrippina supposedly had the support, or acquiescence, of Burrus, who owed his position as Praetorian prefect to her patronage. Tacitus' account here is difficult to assess and loose with its chronology. Earlier he had mentioned Agrippina's 'respect for the names and virtues of the nobility' and insinuated that she was 'in quest of a leader and a faction'.[11] Silana apparently advanced her denunciation through two of her clients, and a trusted freedman of Nero's surviving aunt Domitia reported the alleged plot to the young *princeps*. Tacitus aimed to create here a sense of petty female rivalry, but the reason he gives for the animosity between Agrippina and Silana hints at a much deeper political background: Agrippina had prevented a marriage between Silana and the young noble Sextius Africanus, 'to keep a wealthy and childless widow from passing into the possession of a husband'.[12] The clear implication is that an ambitious man might have used Silana's blood link to Augustus to strengthen political claims of his own; similarly, Tiberius had denied Agrippina's mother permission to remarry, because a potential husband of Germanicus' widow and stepfather to her children inevitably would have asserted his own part in running the affairs of state.[13] In the same manner, Silana seems to have implied that Agrippina planned to marry Rubellius Plautus and regain her share in government through him: a fascinating reversal of the usual gender roles, charged with impropriety.

According to Tacitus, on hearing the accusation Nero was shocked and enraged; he instantly resolved to kill Agrippina and replace Burrus. Yet in the end, Agrippina was given an opportunity to defend herself and the whole plot was quickly dismissed as an intrigue spun by Silana, who was duly banished. The relative ease with which the affair was settled raises doubts about Nero's purported initial reaction, and the reliability of Tacitus' sources.[14] On the contrary, Tacitus implies that Agrippina's position remained strong enough for her to exercise considerable patronage and gain some key appointments for her allies.[15] Tacitus also refers to more general rumours and hostile gossip about Agrippina, including that she openly mourned Britannicus' death and was supportive of Claudia Octavia. As Claudius' dutiful widow (and priestess of his cult), she most likely did all of this, not least in the interest of orderly dynastic continuity. Other evidence, like the Aphrodisias relief cycle (see Figs 50, 53–5, pp. 80–3), demonstrates how her role in this regard was perceived in a positive light throughout the Roman Empire. Any suggestion that these gestures were directed against Nero seems like a biased, retrospective interpretation based on the dramatic events of several years later.

Further accusations against Agrippina followed shortly after. Yet another informer accused Claudius' still influential freedman Pallas, routinely described as one of Agrippina's allies, of having conspired with Burrus to put Faustus Cornelius Sulla Felix, the husband of Claudius' elder daughter Antonia and thereby Nero's brother-in-law, on the throne.[16] In this case, too, the accuser was exiled; this was a certain Paetus, who was notorious for seeking financial gain from buying up the confiscated property of those convicted on the basis of his accusations.[17] For now, Sulla suffered no ill consequences, but this would change in the future. These events were all recorded for AD 54 and 55; there follows a long gap until the beginning of AD 59, which the source authors clearly struggled to fill with meaningful content. Tacitus' account for the crucial year AD 59 therefore essentially begins with a repetition of what he had noted previously.[18]

In consequence, it is nearly impossible to gain any sense of Agrippina as a real person, beyond the stereotyped invective propagated by the surviving literary sources. It may have been in those years that she wrote her history of the Julio-Claudian family, referred to as 'Comments' (*commentarii* – a standard term

Fig. 144
Statue of Agrippina performing a sacrifice
AD 54–9 (the head is a cast of the original now in the Ny Carlsberg Glyptotek, Copenhagen)
Caelian Hill, Rome, Italy
Basanite
H. 2.1 m
Musei Capitolini, Centrale Montemartini, Rome
MC 1882/S

This imposing statue was carved from Egyptian basanite, a rare hard stone worked to imitate the metallic sheen of bronze. The sculpture was found on the Caelian Hill, in an area with a number of sanctuaries, including the Temple of Divus Claudius. Agrippina is seen here performing a sacrifice, with her head veiled and wearing a diadem (compare this image to the Via Labicana Augustus, Fig. 8, p. 29). As priestess of Claudius' cult, she enjoyed various privileges, among them the right to be accompanied by two *lictors* (ushers and bodyguards assigned to senior magistrates and priests). Images like this added to the public's sense of Agrippina's importance.

for such works), in which she recorded for posterity her own life and the fate of her relatives. It included information not accessible to earlier writers of annalistic histories. That Agrippina did so as a woman in a male-dominated society was remarkable, a testimony both to her education and strong belief in herself and her position within the ruling family; Augustus and Tiberius had composed similar memoirs. Agrippina's account was an important source for later Roman writers, such as Pliny the Elder and Tacitus.[19] In all likelihood, the work was intended to convey her view of events and to counter rival texts already in circulation, as well as various rumours about conflicts between the different branches of the imperial family and its affiliated clans; this was mixed with personal detail, perhaps where it was linked to omens (for example, according to Pliny she stated that Nero was born breech).[20]

Agrippina's lifestyle after AD 55, following the allegations, continued to be regal. Tacitus writes that she moved between her suburban gardens in Rome and her estates at Tusculum and Antium; she also owned a villa by the exclusive Lucrine Lake near Baiae on the Bay of Naples.[21] The measures Nero had taken to restrict her access to court merely limited the occasions on which she could exercise official power independently and firmly established his own pre-eminence in terms of protocol. The loss of her Praetorian and Germanic guards (see p. 85) was one significant element of this (it also deprived her of a routine daily exchange with officers and soldiers, and the opportunity to create exclusive bonds of loyalty that this might entail).[22] As *Augusta*, *Mater Augusti* and *Flaminica Divi Claudi* she still far outranked all other Roman women in prestige, but these privileges were now more in line with the highest honours available to women traditionally.[23] Her office as priestess of Claudius was particularly important in this respect.

Yet Nero's active part in these decisions and the following events is obscured rather than elucidated by the sources. They depict him throughout as a disinterested, self-indulgent youth, only concerned with his own pleasures, a hapless prince torn between his dangerously ambitious mother and his senior advisors, who at least consider the well-being of the nation. The main reason advanced for the gradual breakdown of Nero's relationship with his mother is her interference in his emotional involvement with other women, first the freedwoman Claudia Acte (see p. 83), then the aristocratic Poppaea Sabina, with whom he first seems to have been linked around AD 58 (see pp. 183–4). Just as these authors attack Agrippina for inappropriately taking on a male role and morphing into a dangerous *dux femina* or female leader – tolerable perhaps among 'barbarians' (see p. 106), but shockingly outrageous for a Roman woman – so they characterise Nero correspondingly as submissive, childlike and effeminate, because he is dominated by successive women.[24] In Roman discourse, such dynamics were frequently articulated in sexual terms. Agrippina's transgressive appropriation of male roles is therefore accompanied by tales of her active and often adulterous promiscuity, while Nero's alleged lack of manly vigour finds its narrative expression in highly questionable descriptions of his sexual perversions and passive homosexual encounters.[25] The result is strangely dissonant, for these were also the years of Nero's great successes, filled with the excessive honours proffered in turn by the senate. The *princeps'* public perception was therefore fundamentally different from his private life in the palace as painted so evocatively, and almost certainly misleadingly, by the sources.

At some point before AD 59 Nero decided to remove his mother. His motives and the precise details must remain speculative, because the only evidence comes from later literary sources. It is possible to strip out some elements of topical *vituperatio* (sustained verbal attacks on moral grounds), and occasionally to read between the lines, but ultimately various scenarios are plausible. What matters here is that a consistent case can be made for Nero as a rational actor interested in maintaining a broad acceptance of his reign, even if this required extreme measures. Nero's own differences with Agrippina may have arisen mainly from her insistence that he should retain his Claudian links, primarily by staying married to Claudius' daughter Octavia, whatever his attraction to other women. This may have carried weight not just in terms of his dynastic legitimacy, but more importantly as a means for ensuring the loyalty of Claudius' old allies against rival clans.[26]

Nero clearly acted with the acquiescence of his senior male advisors, chiefly Seneca and Burrus. These two had most to gain personally from Agrippina's removal, as this cemented their practical hold over Nero against his mother's influence, a position they used to acquire great wealth and build extensive patronage networks (see pp. 83–5; see also p. 136). Cassius Dio explicitly states that Seneca incited Nero to action; as elsewhere, he followed an anti-Senecan source tradition that Tacitus chose to ignore and which is now completely lost to us.[27] Seneca may have chiefly pointed out that the antipathy towards Agrippina's prominence, exacerbated by her close association with the perceived excesses of Claudius' reign, tarnished Nero's reputation with the senate and stood in the way of any reconciliation with important rival families. It was an argument with some merit, which may have swayed a possibly reluctant Nero. Tacitus, in this sense, may accurately reflect the majority view of the senatorial and equestrian elite at the time, perhaps as conveyed by his sources, but certainly as it appeared plausible to him more than half a century later. He refers to 'the anger of the nation against the pride and greed of his [Nero's] mother' and states that 'all men yearned for the breaking of the mother's power'.[28] What doomed Agrippina was, in the end, most likely an intersection of different interests that was best served by her death. By the time the decision was taken to remove her, Nero's standing was finally strong enough to dispose of Agrippina without undermining his own dynastic claims. He was nearing his *quinquennalia*, his five-year anniversary on the throne, and Corbulo's successes in Armenia made his position as *princeps* seem unassailable (see p. 94) . Suetonius' statement that Nero over the years had attempted to kill Agrippina with poison on three occasions lacks any credibility.[29] Instead, a plan was set in motion to eliminate her quietly, away from Rome, and to give the impression that it was a necessary measure for the safety of state and *princeps*.[30]

Nero invited Agrippina to the resort town of Baiae, during the time of the local Quinquatria festival of Minerva, around the middle of March AD 59. Agrippina arrived by boat from the coastal city of Antium south of Rome, was greeted by Nero with great deference and asked to join a lavish banquet, all gestures intended to signal an imminent reconciliation between mother and son. Yet by the end of the night, Agrippina lay dead in her villa, forced to commit suicide or slain by officers led by Nero's loyal prefect Anicetus, commander of the Misenum fleet.[31]

Nero informed the senate about events in a formal letter. It stated that an attempt on his life by Agrippina's closely trusted freedman Agimus had been foiled, and that Agrippina, conscious of her guilt as instigator of the crime, had paid the price. The existence of the letter is only known through Tacitus, who paraphrased its content. His wording is ambiguous, probably echoing the official record: it may have suggested that Agrippina took her own life.[32] For once, it is at least possible to find corroborating evidence for this official version and the way it was communicated to the public. Inscriptions of the Arval Brethren, a prestigious order of priests in Rome, note sacrifices they performed as part of a thanksgiving for Nero's salvation following the failed assassination plot.[33] According to Tacitus, the senate letter had been drafted by Seneca; rather than a valiant effort to justify retrospectively the gruesome crime of a matricidal master, as it is sometimes presented, it may well have summarised the reasoning that lay behind Agrippina's execution from the very beginning. For this purpose, it apparently blamed every crime committed during Claudius' reign on the woman who had now finally been silenced, perhaps a signal that a conciliation of the senatorial elite formed a major element of the decision to eliminate her.[34]

Yet the source accounts reported events very differently. The tragic play *Octavia*, written soon after Nero's death, clearly set the dramatic pattern followed by other authors later. It plainly accused Nero of murder and introduced a highly theatrical motive: with her final breath, the dying Agrippina exhorts her killer to strike her womb, uttering 'this is the place, this is the spot that must be pierced with your sword, the place which gave birth to that monster of a son!'[35] Cassius Dio simply copies the stage play's scenic device. In his version, on seeing Nero's prefect Anicetus and his men, Agrippina, 'leaping up from her bed, [...] tore open her clothing, exposing her abdomen, and cried out: "Strike here, Anicetus, strike here, for this bore Nero."'[36] Tacitus adopts a slightly shorter form: 'Then, as the centurion drew his sword for the death-blow, thrusting forward her womb she shouted, "Strike the belly", and was despatched with many wounds.'[37] It seems that not even the play that inspired the 'historical' accounts was particularly innovative: the lines in *Octavia* in turn closely echo one of Seneca's earlier tragedies. In Seneca's *Oedipus* the tragic hero's mother Iocasta (who had become Oedipus' wife and mother to his children, not knowing his true identity) commits suicide with the words: 'Target this, my hand, this, the fertile womb that bore me sons and husband'.[38]

The sources present this execution as an act of almost panicked improvisation, after a different plan earlier in the evening had failed. This supposedly involved an assassination attempt at sea, disguised as a shipwreck or accident aboard a manipulated vessel. Agrippina survived and safely swam to shore. Yet these accounts are so contradictory as to raise serious doubts about their veracity; most intriguing in this regard is Cassius Dio, who claims that the inspiration came from a theatrical stage prop, a vessel that opened to release wild animals and then closed up again. In this light, it is worth considering whether the descriptions of the first attempts on Agrippina's life were not a novelistic literary trope derived from such a noteworthy performance, just as the details of her last moments were freely embellished on the basis of tragic plays (see p. 170).

Many of the contemporaries, including authors like Pliny, Fabius Rusticus and Cluvius Rufus, must have been taken by complete surprise; there was nothing that indicated a change in Agrippina's status before her sudden and brutal removal. With hindsight, they drew on gossip and rumour to describe the lead-up to this event, based heavily on the content of Nero's letter to the senate.

The process can still be detected even in Tacitus' text, where elements of Nero's justification are presented as facts over the previous years. Dramatic invention and novelistic narrative made up for the lack of real information.

Following Agrippina's death, Nero remained in Campania for several months, presumably to gauge the reaction in Rome under the protection of the loyal Misenum fleet and its marines. Officers of the guard, and then deputations from the local towns, arrived to congratulate him on his salvation and performed numerous sacrifices. In the capital, the senate voted days of thanksgiving; in gratitude for the goddess Minerva's protection, a golden statue of her was to be erected in the senate house, flanked by a statue of the *princeps*; and annual games were to be added to the celebrations in Minverva's honour. Agrippina's birthday was from now on to be counted among the days of ill omen, on which no official business could be conducted. The Arval Brethren had carried out annual sacrifices to mark Agrippina's day of honour; according to their records, these now ceased.[39]

Nero's subsequent entry into Rome was spectacular. According to Tacitus, the citizenry came to meet him on the way: the tribes, women and children segregated into age groups, the senators in festive dress. Tiered wooden seating had been set up, so spectators could get a better view, as was done for triumphal processions. Agrippina's statues were torn down or removed. The magnificent *Neronia* festival was held for the first time soon after (see p. 167). It had probably been planned long in advance, but may now partly have been associated with Agrippina's demise. In the public perception, the events of the year, Nero's *quinquennalia*, new victories in Armenia and the state's 'liberation' from Agrippina presumably all blurred into one.

Poppaea Sabina and the demise of Claudia Octavia

Nero's association with Poppaea Sabina is perhaps the one relationship through which it is possible to get closest to the *princeps* as a person, although here, too, the source tradition is hostile in the extreme.[40]

Poppaea came from a family that had emerged with the principate and later paid a heavy price for its proximity to the centre of power. Her grandfather Gaius Poppaeus Sabinus made his way as a *homo novus*, or 'new man' (a first-time senator without senatorial ancestors), under Augustus. He rose to become consul in AD 9, then served for many years as governor in Greece and the Balkans, for which he was granted triumphal ornaments by Tiberius in AD 21.[41] His daughter, Poppaea Sabina the Elder (Poppaea's mother), was known as the foremost beauty of the age.[42] She married an ambitious knight, Titus Ollius, who was closely associated with Sejanus, Tiberius' ruthless commander of the Praetorian Guard who came to run affairs in Rome on his behalf (see p. 43). Their daughter Poppaea was born around AD 31, making her five or six years older than Nero. Shortly after, Ollius lost his life in the wake of Sejanus' downfall. Young Poppaea, born as Ollia, thereupon assumed her grandfather's name. Poppaea's mother remarried; her new husband was a former consul, the distinguished *nobilis* Publius Cornelius Lentulus Scipio. Under Claudius, he served as proconsul of Asia.[43]

Poppaea was first married to an influential equestrian, Rufrius Crispinus, a commander of the Praetorian Guard with whom she later had a son of the same name. Yet in AD 47 Poppaea's mother was driven to suicide by Messalina, while her husband Crispinus was rewarded for putting down a conspiracy against Claudius, to whom Messalina had been married previously. Tales of the elder Poppaea's promiscuity abound, but, again, given this context it is hard not to see them as entirely politically motivated.[44] In AD 51 Crispinus was finally replaced by Sextus Afranius Burrus, allegedly at Agrippina's behest because she suspected Crispinus of continuing loyalty to the late Messalina and her surviving children (see p. 62).[45] When exactly Poppaea came to Nero's attention is unknown; her stepbrother at any rate served as consul in the second year of Nero's reign. According to Tacitus, she had inherited her mother's beauty and wealth, and her new family links to the Cornelii Scipiones may have provided an additional attraction (Figs 145 and 146).[46] At some point she had been divorced from Rufrius Crispinus; the source accounts not only vary, but are as usual contradictory.[47] All involve Marcus Salvius Otho, Nero's companion during the first years of his principate. The least salacious version, and therefore perhaps the most believable, is that Nero became infatuated with Poppaea and asked Otho to wed her in a sham marriage, so that he could be with Poppaea in secret while remaining with Claudia Octavia for dynastic reasons (Seneca's relative Annaeus Serenus had supposedly provided similar cover for Nero's relationship with Claudia Acte).[48] Nero's love for Poppaea, and Agrippina's repeated admonitions that he should let her go, is given as the most important reason for the break between mother and son. The source authors ascribe to Poppaea a cold, insatiable ambition for power, leading her to manipulate and control Nero for her own gain – a younger, seductive version of Agrippina.[49] She is depicted as one of the decisive voices behind Agrippina's murder and Octavia's dismissal, in order to free her way to marry Nero and become his empress. In this version, Nero committed matricide out of sheer selfish besottedness, without a care for the state.[50]

If Messalina, Agrippina and Poppaea emerge from the sources only as extreme stereotypes of depraved females, the opposite is true for Octavia. Yet she similarly appears entirely as a literary construct. Whereas the other women are described as cruelly ambitious and therefore sexually transgressive, Octavia became a model of long-suffering virtue, piety and chastity. The Flavian rehabilitation of Claudius found in her an ideal anchor, an embodiment of all the ills endured under Nero's regime and his most innocent victim. The pattern was set almost immediately after Nero's death with the stage play already mentioned and Octavia as its eponymous, demure heroine (see p. 182).[51]

Claudia Octavia and Nero were betrothed as children and were barely adults when they got married (see p. 83). When Nero finally divorced her in AD 62, it was initially on the grounds that Octavia, now in her early twenties, was barren (Fig. 147).[52] In a Roman context, this was a perfectly acceptable reason for divorce, but it may have been a mere pretext.[53] The claim was followed up with charges of adultery, which were unanimously rejected by the sources as completely unfounded – strong evidence for the political nature of such accusations and the cynicism of authors who levelled them freely against other women.[54] Octavia was relegated to Campania and her supporters in Rome rioted on learning of the decision. Whether this was a sign of Octavia's

Fig. 145
Dupondius with portrait of Poppaea Sabina on the obverse
AD 64–5
Uncertain mint
Brass
Weight 13.2 g
Private collection

This is a rare example of Roman imperial coinage featuring Poppaea Sabina's portrait. Poppaea's image, usually alongside Nero's, appears more frequently on coins from provincial mints.

Fig. 146
Portrait of Poppaea Sabina (?)
AD 59–68
Rome, Italy
Marble
H. 41 cm, W. 22 cm
Palazzo Massimo alle Terme,
Museo Nazionale Romano, Rome
124129

With her intricate coiffure of
ringlets, rows of elaborate curls
and long tresses, all crowned by
a diadem, the woman depicted
here was clearly a member of the
elite, in the orbit of the imperial
court. The head was worked for
insertion into a draped body.
The identification is debated:
Poppaea's images (like Agrippina's
and Octavia's after their deaths)
were removed or destroyed after
Nero's fall, but there are similarities
between this and her coin portraits
(see Fig. 145).

Fig. 147
Portrait bust of a
Julio-Claudian princess (?)
c. AD 63–8
Villa of Anteros and Heracles,
Stabiae, Italy
Marble
H. 60 cm, W. 36 cm, D. 28 cm
Museo Archeologico Nazionale
di Napoli
6193

This high-quality portrait was found
in a Roman villa at Stabiae, on the
coast south of Pompeii. The bust
is draped in a *stola*, a long gown
reserved for married citizen women
that served as an equivalent to
the male toga. The elaborate band
of jewellery in her hair marks the
sitter as a member of the elite and
the woman bears a strong facial
resemblance to female members
of the Claudian family – she might
be a princess rather than a private
citizen. A number of identifications
have been proposed: Livia,
her granddaughter Livia Julia
(Tiberius' daughter-in-law), great-
granddaughter Julia (mother of
Rubellius Plautus), and finally
Claudius' daughter, and Nero's
first wife, Claudia Octavia. Despite
achieving prominence during their
lifetimes, portraits of all of these
women (with the exception of Livia)
have not been securely identified
– a direct result of the persecution
most of them suffered as a result
of dynastic conflicts within the
ruling family.

popularity among the people, as suggested, or an orchestrated political
demonstration by old Claudian loyalists, who mobilised their extended
household and client networks, cannot be determined.[55] At any rate, it must have
been the kind of reaction Agrippina had warned about when she advised Nero
against separating from Octavia (see p. 181).[56] Soon after, probably as a direct
response, Nero ordered Octavia's transfer to the island of Pandateria. This had
been the place of exile for several Julio-Claudian women, an important reminder
that Nero's harsh actions did not mark him out as exceptional. In truth, all of his
predecessors had banished close female relatives for political reasons in this
manner. Augustus had set the precedent with the relegation of his own daughter
Julia in 2 BC and Tiberius had followed with the exile of Agrippina the Elder.
Caligula deported his sisters Agrippina, Nero's mother, and Livilla, and, after
both had been recalled by Claudius, he soon expelled Livilla again.

Several months after her arrival on the island, Octavia was either forced to
commit suicide or was executed. Nero finally married Poppaea; she had already
proven that she could conceive (recommending her as the official consort of a
princeps who may have felt that he needed offspring to strengthen his position),
and was now pregnant with Nero's long-desired child.[57] A girl was born on
21 January AD 63, at Antium, like her father. Nero, now aged twenty-five, was
overjoyed, a sympathetic trait since there must have been some pressure to
produce a male heir. The birth was treated like an affair of state, and indeed

Fig. 148
**Portrait statue of a young girl,
perhaps Claudia Augusta** (?)
AD 63–8
Baiae, Italy
Marble
H. 120 cm, W. 36 cm, D. 31 cm
Museo Archeologico dei Campi
Flegrei nel Castello di Baia
222740

This statue of a young girl
was found during underwater
excavations at a Roman villa in
the elite coastal resort of Baiae
on the Bay of Naples. The girl's
attire recalls sculptures from
classical Greece. Her right hand,
worked separately and preserved
in fragments, held a butterfly – a
symbol of the soul that lends the
piece a funerary air. She wears a
unique piece of jewellery in her
hair. The head and chest were
carved in high-quality Parian
marble and inserted into the
body. The girl has traditionally
been identified as a daughter
of Claudius (especially Claudia
Octavia), but elements of the
coiffure so deliberately copy Nero's
hairstyle of the early AD 60s that
the girl might be an idealised
portrait of his young daughter
Claudia Augusta, who died aged
only three months.

the little princess was the first child born to a reigning *princeps* in more than twenty years. The senate had proffered solemn vows for the baby's safe delivery. Sacrifices were now made and public days of thanksgiving proclaimed, and the entire senate travelled to Antium to congratulate the emperor and his wife. Nero named his daughter Claudia, in filial deference to his predecessor and adoptive father, a clear political gesture of dynastic continuity even after his divorce from Octavia. The senate voted Claudia the title *Augusta* at birth; it was now also granted to Poppaea, who thereby received the same honour as Agrippina had twelve years earlier (see p. 63). In addition, a Temple of Fertility was decreed together with a quinquennial festival, golden effigies were placed on the throne of Jupiter in his temple on the Capitoline, and circus games were instated at Antium in honour of the Claudian and Domitian families, modelled on those for the Iulii at Bovillae.[58] The cumulative effect of these measures was extraordinary and amounted to a significant expression of the senate's loyalty and deference to the *princeps*, at a time of clear political and dynastic tension.[59]

However, Claudia Augusta died in April, having lived less than four months. Although infant mortality in ancient Rome was high and parents regularly had to endure the loss of babies and young children, Nero was beside himself with grief.[60] Again the senate extended its sympathies, voting the princess the honour of deification, along with a temple and a priest. A rare portrait statue of Claudia Augusta may have survived from Baiae (Fig. 148).[61] It was discovered in 1981 during underwater excavations off the coast, in the submerged room of a lavish Roman villa for which the area was famous in antiquity.[62] The sculpture, originally identified as Claudia Octavia and more recently as another unnamed daughter of Claudius who may have died prematurely, represents a very young girl with precious jewellery that marks her out as a member of an elite family. Her coiffure shows an unusual combination of different elements: while the curly locks at the back and sides are fairly generic, the forehead fringe deliberately and very precisely copies Nero's own hairstyle of the period (see Fig. 131, p. 159). It is not simply a common Claudian or Neronian coiffure and the empress would have served as a much more obvious model.[63] If Claudia Augusta received a temple and cult, she must have had statues; and since an infant of three or four months could not readily be depicted, these must have been highly idealised portraits that tried to evoke her appearance had she lived into childhood.[64] Copying the most characteristic element of Nero's coiffure may have been a convenient way to suggest a blood relationship between father and daughter.

Poppaea and Nero remained close; the Jewish writer Flavius Josephus describes meeting Poppaea on a delegation to Rome in AD 64 and states that she successfully intervened with Nero on behalf of some Jewish priests.[65] Meanwhile, intriguing evidence from Pompeii suggests that the imperial couple visited the city together and dedicated precious offerings in the local Temple of Venus, the goddess of married love (Fig. 149). Perhaps this was part of an inspection tour following the earthquake in AD 62 (see p. 204). Poppaea's family or some of their freedmen seem to have had business interests in the area and owned property there; a large villa at nearby Oplontis is often ascribed to her.[66] Nero's popularity in Pompeii, attested through graffiti and painted inscriptions, may therefore have had some link to Poppaea. A local group of supporters at spectacles appreciatively named themselves *Nero-Poppaenses* after the first couple. A rare official coin type may show the *princeps* with his wife (Fig. 150).

This scattered evidence complements (and partly contrasts with) the literary sources that otherwise focus on Poppaea's luxury and excess. Pliny, for example, claims that she had her favourite mules shod in gold. He also alleges that Poppaea always travelled with 500 asses and their foals, so that she could regularly bathe her entire body in their milk. This was meant to whiten her skin

Fig. 150
Aureus
AD 64–5
Minted in Rome, Italy
Gold
Weight 7.3 g
British Museum
1864,1128.248
Donated by Edward Wigan

On the obverse of this aureus is a portrait of Nero (NERO CAESAR AUGUSTUS). The reverse features two upright figures: a male in toga with a radiate crown, holding a lance and offering bowl, and a female with offering bowl and horn of plenty. The iconography is purposefully ambiguous. The figures could be images of gods, but the inscriptions 'AUGUSTUS' and 'AUGUSTA' also allow them to be interpreted as Nero and his wife, probably Poppaea Sabina.

and maintain its suppleness. He similarly declares that Poppaea introduced a fashion among society ladies for washing their faces many times a day in asses' milk to prevent wrinkles and preserve their elegantly pale complexions.[67] Since Poppaea was considered a great beauty, she may well have been regarded as a model to be followed. The fact that similar habits were ascribed to Cleopatra, however, should sound a note of caution.[68] Nero apparently composed various poems for Poppaea; in one known to Pliny, he adoringly described her hair as amber-coloured and this, too, set a new fashion.[69]

By AD 65, Poppaea was pregnant with her and Nero's second child, but tragically died before she could give birth. The sources blame Nero directly, the most extreme version stating that he kicked her in the stomach while in a wild fit of rage, thus causing her death.[70] However, this is such a well-known literary topos associated with tyrants that scholars more recently have rightly dismissed it as another anti-Neronian invention. It seems more likely that Poppaea died from complications during pregnancy, an all too frequent cause of death in Roman society across all classes.[71] Other sources appear to allege that Nero poisoned her, a claim that even Tacitus found absurd, given Nero's obvious love for his wife. He states that they asserted this 'out of hatred rather than belief', but in a similar vein coldly adds that her death was welcomed because of her 'immodesty and cruelty'.[72]

Nero was inconsolable.[73] The senate dutifully voted to deify his wife as Sabina Aphrodite and to dedicate her a temple and cult (Fig. 151).[74] She received a ceremonial public funeral; Nero himself gave her eulogy in the Forum. Poppaea's embalmed body was buried in the tomb of the Iulii. According to Pliny, Nero burned more incense at the ceremony than southern Arabia produced in an entire year, presumably a literary exaggeration intended to castigate Nero for his excess, but at least a glimpse of what must have been an elaborate state funeral and apotheosis ritual.[75] A third-century papyrus preserves fragments of a poem describing Poppaea's apotheosis, which was probably written shortly after the event to console the *princeps* over the death of his consort (Fig. 152).[76] Modelled on Hellenistic deification rituals for Ptolemaic queens, the

Fig. 151
Aes
c. AD 65
Minted in Caesarea Paneas, Judaea
Alloy
Weight 6 g
British Museum
1908,0110.1711

The obverse of this aes shows a gabled rectangular shrine with two columns on a stepped podium. Inside is an enthroned female with a horn of plenty, identified as 'DIVA POPPAEA AUG(USTA)'. On the reverse is a standing female in a small round temple with six columns and domed roof, inscribed 'DIVA CLAUDIA NER(ONIA) F(ILIA)' ('The deified Claudia, daughter of Nero'). Nero's daughter Claudia Augusta, like her mother after her, was deified after her premature death. The cults of both were annulled or lapsed after Nero's fall.

The coin was struck under the client king Herod Agrippa II of Judaea, a loyal supporter of Nero and Rome.

Fig. 152
Papyrus fragment with a poem celebrating Poppaea Sabina's apotheosis (deification) as Diva Poppaea Augusta
AD 200–300
Oxyrhynchus, Egypt
Papyrus
H. 26 cm, W. 9.6 cm
Papyrology Rooms, Sackler Library, Oxford
POxy.v0077.n5105

The text of this papyrus, in Greek hexameter, describes Poppaea's arrival among the gods as 'Diva Poppaea Augusta'. It draws on Hellenistic precedents and provides important information on Poppaea's cult and links to Venus. It is unclear whether the composition was copied, as a rhetorical or poetic exercise, from a poem written soon after Poppaea's death in AD 65, or if the text was composed some years later. Nero's positive memory in the Greek East may have contributed to the copying of such works.

Fig. 153
**Obverse of a coin showing
Statilia Messalina facing Nero**
AD 66–8
Minted in Hypaepa, Lydia
(modern Turkey)
Bronze
Weight 8.2 g
Private collection

Fig. 154
Portrait of a Roman lady
AD 50–70
Rome, Italy
Marble
H. 45 cm
Musei Capitolini, Rome
MC 424/S

This woman's elaborate coiffure
reflects fashions at the imperial
court during the Neronian period.
The ornate locks required the
use of curling irons, just like
Nero's own hairstyle at the time
– an expression of luxury and
refinement. The portrait exists in
two copies, indicating that this was
an important woman (though not
necessarily the wife of an emperor).
Historically, she has been identified
as Statilia Messalina, Nero's third
wife, but this association remains
hypothetical. None of the coin
portraits of Neronian empresses
(almost exclusively from the
Greek-speaking provinces) match
any surviving sculptures precisely,
and some appear to use generic
variations of hairstyles current at
the time.

touching poem praises Poppaea as a devoted wife, led by Aphrodite to the heavens where she will guard her children with Nero for eternity and await his eventual arrival as another *divus*.

Nero clearly mourned Poppaea deeply and had great difficulty accepting her death, for which he was cruelly mocked by various later authors. One of the more outrageous claims was that he found a freedman, Sporus, who resembled the late Poppaea, had him castrated and married him in a bizarre ceremony as his official wife. Although the alleged event is said to have taken place in Greece two years after Poppaea's death, it is part of a catalogue of Nero's sexual perversions. These form a standard element of vituperative invective, but nevertheless were widely believed into the present. Little of this bears closer scrutiny.[77]

Dynastically, Poppaea's death was a disaster. Now more than a decade into his reign, Nero needed an heir. He supposedly considered marrying Claudius' surviving daughter, Claudia Antonia, but was refused. Early in AD 66, he wed the aristocratic Statilia Messalina (Figs 153 and 154), who would outlive him (see p. 272). Nero's third wife remains a shadowy figure in the source accounts, which instead turned their attention to political events.

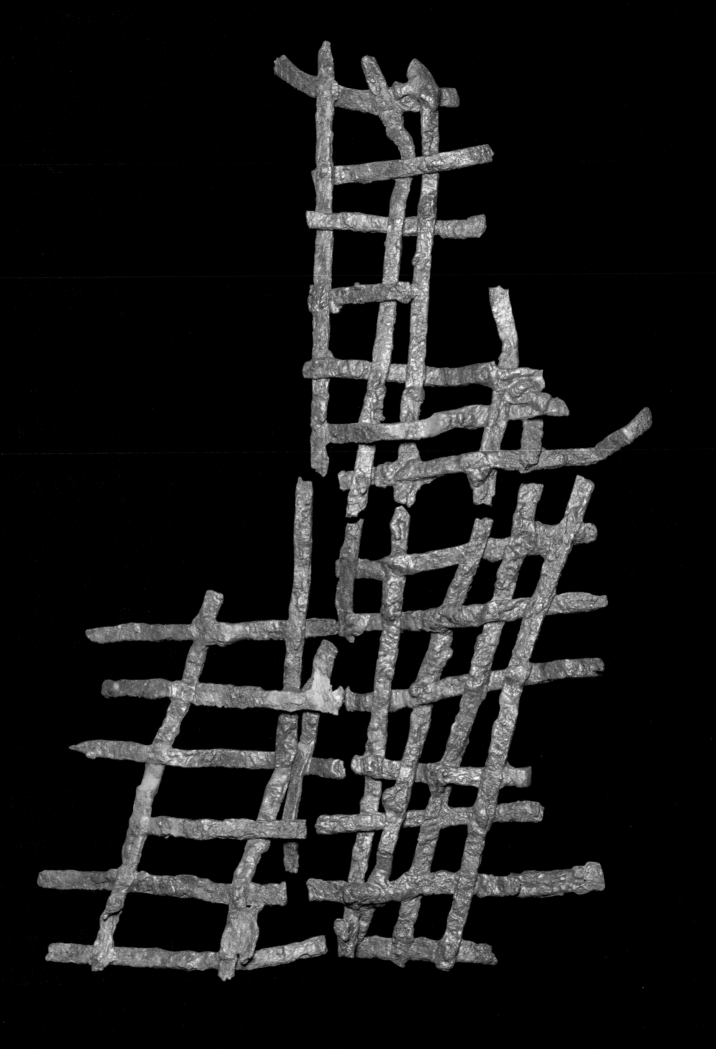

VI

INCENDIUM: THE GREAT FIRE OF ROME

In the summer of AD 64 – three months before Nero's tenth anniversary on the throne – Rome suffered a catastrophic fire that laid waste to large parts of the city.[1] Fires raged frequently in the capital, but this conflagration was unprecedented in its scale. Extensive excavations in recent years have revealed stark evidence of its ferocity and impact.[2] The circumstances surrounding the disaster reveal much about living conditions in the city, the gulf between rich and poor, and the role of emperors as protectors of the *plebs*. Had Nero's reign lasted longer, his large-scale relief and reconstruction effort and the 'striking beauty of the rearisen city' undoubtedly would have dominated later memories of the Great Fire (see p. 209).[3] As it was, Nero's adversaries (a major conspiracy had been building for two years already) and his later detractors seized upon the events to establish a powerful counter-narrative that shaped Nero's reputation for nearly two millennia.[4]

'A savage city'

The literature of late Republican and early imperial Rome is full of references to the perils of urban life.[5] Fire hazards and the poor state of cheaply constructed housing blocks were on everybody's mind. 'Such is the height of buildings and so narrow are the streets, that there is no protection from fire' was a typical lament.[6] The 'constant collapses of buildings and the thousand dangers of this savage city' made even wealthier Romans wish they could live 'where there are no fires, no fear at night'.[7] The imposing, 30-m high firewall built by Augustus at the back of his Forum is a lasting testimony to these fears. Its protective tufa-stone masonry doubled as a social-distance barrier against the notorious Subura quarter behind, where the *plebs* lived in poor housing at constant risk of disaster.

History and topography had forced Rome down an unusual path of urban development, notably different from the planned cities of the Greek world. The steep hills and small valleys within Rome's tight circuit of fourth-century BC city walls exacerbated a severe lack of space and suitable building ground. As it grew into the largest city of the ancient Mediterranean (approaching perhaps a million inhabitants), Rome therefore had to expand upwards. Soon, ever taller buildings crowded around narrow and irregular lanes. This lent Rome a distinctive character: to its citizens a source of pride and concern in equal measure.[8] Pliny the Elder glories in the unequalled size of the capital, readily apparent not least in the towering height of its many buildings.[9] Before him, the architectural writer Vitruvius stressed that, despite their drawbacks, these 'tall piles' created much-needed living space for the people of Rome.[10] Also in the Augustan period, the writer Strabo commented on Rome's incessant growth and constant metamorphosis: 'the construction of houses [. . .] goes on unceasingly in consequence of the collapses and fires'.[11] The city thus was a sea of *insulae*, large mixed-use multi-floor apartment blocks, and a few interspersed *domus*, the single- or double-storey houses of the wealthy. Cheap construction, with wooden frames, floors, ceilings and stairs, helped unscrupulous landlords to maximise profits, as did the piling on of additional storeys and extensions. The use of the cost-saving wattle-and-daub *opus craticium* technique for upper floors in particular posed a notorious fire risk, with its relatively lightweight combination of wood, reeds and stucco. Vitruvius condemned this type of construction, 'for it is made to catch fire, like torches'.[12] Yet even in brick buildings, the sheer amount of timber used in the roofs, with projecting beams and wooden cornices, seems to have been a serious hazard and often contributed to the rapid spread of fires between houses.[13]

Emperors and fires

Given this perilous nature of Rome's dense urban housing, acts of carelessness, neglect or deliberate arson, in addition to the usual natural causes (such as lightning strikes), could easily lead to conflagrations. The frequent devastation they wrought punctuated historical accounts and imperial biographies of the early principate.[14]

Under Augustus alone, there were a significant number of major fires. In 31 BC riotous freedmen set off a fire in the Circus Maximus that spread to destroy the temples of Ceres and Spes and the nearby Forum Holitorium. In 14 BC a severe conflagration devastated much of the Forum, leaving in ruins the Basilica Aemilia, the Basilica Julia, the Temple of Castor and Pollux, and the Temple of Vesta. Two years later, in 12 BC, parts of the Palatine Hill suffered and the venerable hut of Rome's mythical founder Romulus caught fire. Even members of the imperial family regularly lost their homes to the flames. It might have been on this occasion, too, that Augustus' own house on the Palatine burnt down. Not long after, in AD 6, much of the city at large suffered. There was little change under Tiberius: in AD 21 the Theatre of Pompeius in the Campus Martius went up in flames; in AD 27 the entire Caelian district; in AD 36 the Circus Maximus again and with it much of the Aventine Hill. Two years after, under Caligula in AD 38, a fire consumed the district around the Horrea Aemiliana, the grain warehouses by the River Tiber that were of immense importance for Rome's food supply. In AD 53 or 54, shortly before Nero's accession, the Horrea Aemiliana area caught fire again and continued to burn for two nights and a day.

In light of these recurrent disasters, certain expectations arose when it came to the emperor's response to such emergencies. Augustus had set a precedent by taking full personal control during blazes and supervising the relief effort, often accompanied by his wife Livia.[15] Tiberius, in a gesture of concern, and out of a sense of foreboding, on one occasion dispatched units of firefighters from Rome to nearby Ostia, when a dull glow could be observed in the night sky that seemed to signal a major fire there.[16] Indeed, when he 'made good the losses of some owners of blocks of houses on the Caelian mount, which had burnt down' in AD 27, and thereby relieved great hardship, Suetonius maintains this was one of only two acts of generosity towards the general public during his entire reign.[17] Tacitus describes the way rumours and discontent could spread rapidly during such times of distress, if the *princeps* did not keep them in check through appropriate actions. On this occasion, the people had already begun to express their deep dissatisfaction, because Tiberius had been far away on Capri, leaving the city to its own devices. He recovered by offering compensation to all affected.[18] Nine years later, after much of the Aventine had been destroyed, Tiberius again enhanced his reputation 'by paying the full value of the mansions and tenement-blocks destroyed'. According to Tacitus, he provided 100 million sesterces for this act of munificence, which was all the more remarkable as he had not hitherto spent much on construction works in Rome.[19] Fire insurance did not exist: to estimate the losses of the various claimants, Tiberius appointed a commission comprising the four husbands of his granddaughters. They included Nero's father, Gnaeus Domitius Ahenobarbus, who had been consul four years earlier in AD 32.[20]

Perhaps it was during one of these major conflagrations, or in one of the frequent isolated fires not otherwise recorded, that Tiberius' nephew, the future *princeps* Claudius, lost his private mansion to the flames. The senate voted to rebuild the house at public expense.[21] A few years later, in AD 38, the new emperor Caligula personally 'helped the soldiers to extinguish a conflagration and rendered assistance to those who suffered loss by it', possibly when the Horrea Aemiliana were threatened.[22]

Under Claudius, a fire damaged the Temple of Salus on the Quirinal Hill. The sole record of this incident is in Pliny's *Natural History*, of interest to him only because several highly regarded paintings by the artist Fabius Pictor perished in it – a reminder that most incidents went unmentioned.[23] Towards the end of his reign, Claudius took charge of a major firefighting effort in person, as Augustus and Caligula had done. Again, the threat to the grain warehouses by the river forced his direct involvement. He remained near the affected area for two consecutive nights, and when his guards and enslaved servants could not extinguish the flames, called on the people to help, 'placing bags full of money before them' and 'paying each man on the spot a suitable reward for his services'.[24] It was probably during this incident that Claudius' wife Agrippina, Nero's mother, accompanied him to supervise the rescue effort, as Livia had done with Augustus.[25] Perhaps in the same conflagration, if not in an isolated fire earlier, the Temple of Felicitas between the Forum Boarium and the main Forum burnt down with the loss of a celebrated statue of Venus by the Greek sculptor Praxiteles.[26]

Even this brief survey of major incidents demonstrates the frequency of fires, although the sources were clearly very selective in their reporting. Certain hotspots emerge, buildings or areas that burnt repeatedly, such as the Forum and the Palatine. However, these were important politically and therefore thought worthy of mention, whereas the vast majority of domestic fires in the poorer regions did not register, unless they turned into district-wide conflagrations. It is also worth noting the long time it took to reconstruct some fire-damaged buildings. This could stretch over decades and successive reigns, as was the case with the Theatre of Pompeius and the Temple of Castor and Pollux. Utilitarian structures and tenement blocks, by contrast, were rebuilt quickly and often with little regard for fire prevention. In buildings six or seven storeys high, this put the tenants' lives in peril, particularly those on the upper floors.[27]

Firefighters

Despite these dangers, firefighting was originally left to individual landlords and their servants. All too often, it was closely linked to property speculation.[28] Early in the reign of Augustus, the magistrate Marcus Egnatius Rufus established a dedicated fire brigade from the enslaved members of his own household, augmented by hired men. The unit tackled numerous fires free of charge, to the

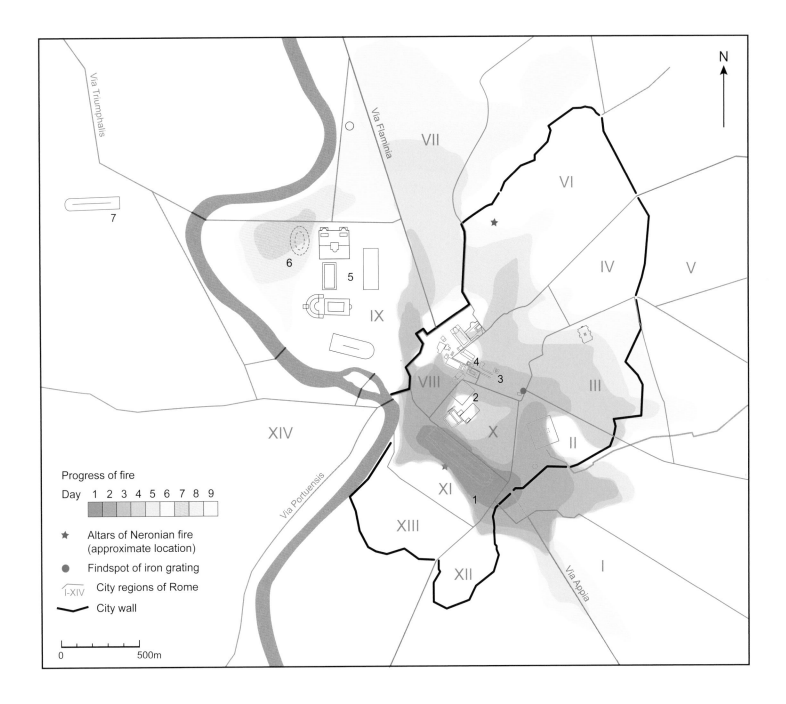

Fig. 155
Map showing the progress of the Great Fire of AD **64**

On 18 July AD 64 a fire broke out in Rome's Circus Maximus, which at the time was predominantly constructed of wood. Over nine days, the fire blazed and moved through the city. By the time it was finally extinguished only four of the city's fourteen regions had been spared.

The following labels appear within the map:

Via Triumphalis

Via Flaminia

N

VII

VI

IV

V

7

6

5

IX

III

4

3

VIII

2

XIV

X

II

XI

1

Via Portuensis

XIII

XII

I

Via Appia

Progress of fire

Day 1 2 3 4 5 6 7 8 9

★ Altars of Neronian fire
   (approximate location)

● Findspot of iron grating

I–XIV City regions of Rome

City wall

0   500m

benefit of landlords and tenants alike. This soon brought Egnatius Rufus such popular esteem that the *princeps* came to consider him a dangerous rival.[29] Augustus therefore assembled his own troop of 600 enslaved men and formed a standing corps of firefighters under the supervision of civic magistrates.[30] The severe fires of 14 BC and AD 6 demonstrated this was still not sufficient, so in AD 6 he resolved – perhaps under renewed public pressure – to radically transform the new fire service, raising the necessary finances from a 4 per cent tax on the sale of enslaved individuals. With this funding he set up the *vigiles* or *cohortes vigilorum*, units of a (night)watch that were recruited from the *liberti* and organised along paramilitary lines. The officers were mostly military men, the commander a prefect from the order of knights. There were seven cohorts, each taking responsibility for two of the fourteen regions into which Augustus had divided the city in AD 5. Each cohort comprised seven centuries of eighty men, making a cohort 560 men strong and the whole corps of *vigiles* just under 4,000. Compared to the previous arrangements, this constituted an almost sevenfold increase in manpower. The *vigiles* soon evolved into a highly efficient, professional firefighting force with watch houses, or *stationes*, in each of Rome's fourteen regions.[31] Their focus was on active fire prevention through regular patrols, particularly at night-time, when the danger of undiscovered fires spreading out of control was greatest. To this end, they could enforce adherence to basic fire-safety rules and punish any infringements. The men out on patrol also carried fire buckets (*hamae*) and pickaxes (*dolabrae*), so that they could deal with small incidents on the spot. They soon came to be known as *sparteoli*, from the ropes or rope ladders made of esparto grass they carried wound across their bodies.[32]

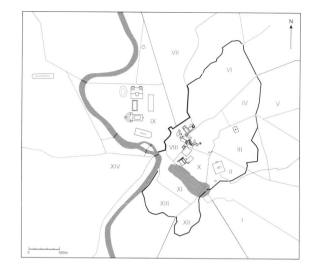

For larger fires, the bigger units had numerous specialists: *aquarii*, who knew the location of the nearest aqueducts and fountains and could therefore quickly organise men into efficient bucket chains; *centonarii*, who would try to smother fires with mats; and *siphonarii*, mechanics and engineers who supervised fire pumps. Given the density and great height of buildings, the efficacy of these was limited, so *fulciarii* and *unciarii* were tasked with tearing down burning structures and creating firebreaks with grappling irons and demolition hooks, often the only efficient way of preventing the flames from spreading further. *Ballistarii* could even use military-style siege engines for this purpose. Early containment of fires was crucial, and as there were no hoses, sufficient manpower was required to set up multiple bucket chains, as well as to maintain good area coverage by the patrols throughout the night. The service was physically demanding and dangerous, so that most *vigiles* served for only about six years. In addition to the hardship entailed, opportunities for promotion from the ranks were very limited, not least because the officers had to be freeborn citizens. However, after three years of service the *vigiles* were rewarded with enrolment among the *plebs frumentaria*, thereby joining a more privileged section of the common people's *plebs urbana*.[33]

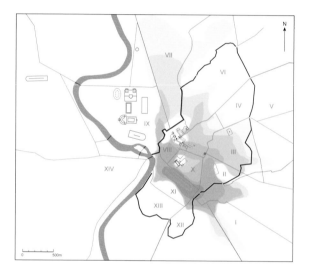

It is perhaps a tribute to the bravery of these men and the efficiency of the new system that the number of very major conflagrations remained relatively limited.[34] In time, units of the *vigiles* were detached on rotation to provide a similar fire service for the vital harbour towns of Ostia and Puteoli.

Augustus had passed new building legislation (the *lex Iulia de modo aedificiorum urbis*) as an additional precaution. It restricted the height of houses to 70 Roman feet (20.7 m), the equivalent of five or six storeys. However, over the following decades these regulations were routinely disregarded, to devastating effect.

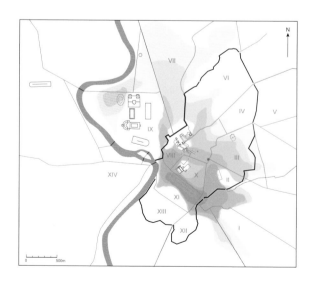

Fig. 157
The steps leading up to the sanctuary of the Curiae Veteres below the Palatine

The scorch marks on the burst travertine blocks attest the enormous heat and ferocity of the Neronian fire. In the background are fragments of a temple wrecked in the conflagration. Recent excavations have revealed destruction layers linked to the AD 64 fire over wide parts of the city.

Fig. 156 (opposite)
Maps showing the spread of the fire on the first, sixth and ninth days of the conflagration

The findspot of the burnt grating (Fig. 159) is indicated.

●   Findspot of iron grating

‾I-XIV   City regions of Rome

⌣   City walls

The great conflagration: July AD 64

The disastrous Neronian fire began to unfold in the night of 18 July AD 64 (Fig. 155). The most detailed surviving account is by Tacitus, who would have been around ten years old at the time (but did not live in Rome).[35] As a guide for his very carefully and deliberately composed text, he could draw on earlier written sources and 'oral history', a mix of individual eyewitness accounts and general hearsay passed on over generations. These had already solidified into a strong, politically inflected narrative.

Tacitus' vivid description makes strikingly engaging reading. It has become a classic text of disaster literature (comparable to the younger Pliny's description of the eruption of Mount Vesuvius in AD 79) and acquired a powerful agency that has dominated all later accounts of the Great Fire to this day.

There followed a disaster [. . .] graver and more terrible than any other which has befallen this city by the ravages of fire. It began in the part of the circus touching the Palatine and Caelian Hills; where, among the shops packed with inflammable goods, the conflagration broke out, gathered strength in the same moment, and [...] swept the full length of the circus [. . .]. The flames in full force overran the level ground first, then shot up to the heights and sank again to the lower parts, keeping ahead of all countermeasures. The destruction travelled fast, and the town was an easy prey due to the narrow, twisting lanes and formless streets [. . .]. Only on the sixth day was the conflagration brought to an end at the foot of the Esquiline, by demolishing buildings over a vast

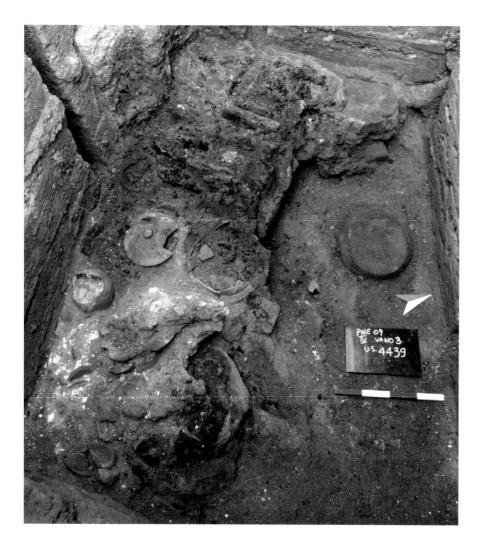

Fig. 158
Traces of destruction in the back room of a domestic building west of the Curiae Veteres

The flames here travelled along an important thoroughfare that linked the Circus Maximus to the Via Sacra and Via Labicana.

area and restricting the unabated fury of the flames through clear ground and an open sky. But the plebs' fear had not yet abated, nor hope returned, when the fire resumed in the more spacious areas of the city.[36]

This part of Tacitus' description is perfectly clear and closely fits the pattern of earlier disasters. Recent archaeological excavations in the centre of Rome have confirmed many details. As in the conflagrations of 31 BC and AD 36, the fire started in the Circus Maximus, this time at its eastern end. In Nero's day, most of the structure – the stands, but also the food stalls and shops below and around – was still built almost entirely from wood. July can be a period of strong summer winds, sometimes reaching storm force, that bring dry, hot air all the way from the Sahara Desert in North Africa.[37] The origin of the fire, perhaps an unsupervised open flame in a stall full of combustible material, appears utterly plausible. Fanned by the southerly winds, the flames rapidly turned into a powerful firestorm. From the eastern end of the circus, they spread north along the valley that separates the Palatine and Caelian Hills, destroying everything in their path on either side of the road (Fig. 156). There, at the bottom of the Caelian, was a venerable Temple of Fortuna Respiciens of the second century BC;

archaeologists found the remains of its pedimental sculptures broken into many fragments, lying where they had fallen on the ground during the fire. Further north, at the north-eastern edge of the Palatine Hill, a small sanctuary of great antiquity, the Curiae Veteres, was overcome. It was the oldest sacred precinct serving the thirty *curia*-units into which the citizenry was divided, by tradition going back to the time of Romulus. A small temple had recently been dedicated there by Claudius. Excavations here revealed the full force of the blaze: scorched paving slabs covered in layers of ashen debris, burst architectural blocks and fragments of statues and bases from a small shrine dedicated to members of the imperial family (Fig. 157). Only burnt floors with the scorch marks of fallen wooden beams and some badly damaged objects survived of a shop building next door (Fig. 158); higher up the slope, behind the Curiae, the burnt remains of a mansion dating to the Republican era were discovered. Augustus had been born in the vicinity in 63 BC. An important landmark, the ornate Meta Sudans fountain dedicated by the *princeps* in 7 BC at the nearby crossroads, was damaged by the falling debris of surrounding houses. Particularly striking are the remains of a heavy iron grating that was found on the road, twisted and bent out of shape by the incredible heat of the blast (Fig. 159).

From here, the fire spread in all directions along the converging valley floors and then up the slopes. Burnt floors of late Republican mansions have come to light in several locations in this area. The blaze moved east along the Via Labicana, north up the lower slope of the Esquiline Hill, and south-east up the Caelian Hill, where further remains of buildings destroyed by the flames are attested archaeologically (see Figs 163 and 164, pp. 216–17). The Claudianum, Nero's temple for the deified Claudius atop a high platform, at the time still unfinished, may also have been affected.

To the west and north-west, the flames overcame the Velian Hill with its houses, shrines and commercial buildings. The remnants of several burnt-out grand mansions have been discovered along the northern slope of the Palatine Hill. On the Via Nova, the blaze seems to have consumed the Temple of Vesta, the house of the Vestal priestesses next door, and the Regia, monuments that had already been rebuilt repeatedly after previous fires, but were still of considerable cultural and religious significance. Here the flames seem to have stopped, sparing the Forum. However, they made their way along the Clivus Palatinus road up to the Palatine, destroying mansions and parts, at least, of Nero's palace, including the newly built Domus Transitoria. Towards the north and north-west of the Via Sacra, they devastated the Argiletum area beyond the Forum, where recent excavations have brought to light the burnt remains of houses going back to the late Republican period. Presumably large tracts of the nearby Subura district were also laid to waste. This is where the loss of life must have been greatest, with people unable to evacuate tall buildings and escape through congested lanes.

At the same time, the flames spread west of the Circus Maximus, destroying a vast area including the Forum Boarium, Velabrum and Forum Holitorium, as in several previous fires. This was a tightly built-up commercial district, full of warehouses, shops, workshops and low-grade housing, but also some very old and important monuments, such as the Temple of Hercules Victor mentioned by Tacitus as being among the significant buildings lost in the disaster.

The fire raged unchecked over five days and nights; only on the sixth day did the rescue forces, *vigiles* and hastily drafted-in soldiers of the urban cohorts and Praetorians, finally manage to control the flames by creating a successful firebreak through extensive demolitions at the foot of the Esquiline. There may have been several unsuccessful attempts to achieve this in other locations earlier, but the fury of the flames would easily have leapt smaller fire barriers.[38] All along, the *vigiles* must have been severely obstructed in their efforts by the fleeing and injured masses who blocked the narrow roads with their belongings. These people were confused and increasingly disoriented by the multiple blasts that

Fig. 160
A relief from the House of Lucius Caecilius Secundus
AD 62–79
Pompeii, Italy
Marble
H. 16.5 cm, L. 97 cm
Parco Archeologico di Pompei
20470

This relief is believed to show the earthquake that hit Pompeii and the Vesuvius region in February AD 62. Visible left of centre is the Capitolium (main temple) on the northern end of Pompeii's forum. Two equestrian monuments on tall plinths are in front, and a triumphal arch stands to the left. The sculptor has captured the tremor in the dramatically slanting lines of the buildings.

Seneca described the earthquake in his treatise on natural phenomena, *Naturales Quaestiones*: 'Pompeii, the celebrated city in Campania, has been overwhelmed by an earthquake, which shook all the surrounding districts as well […] involving widespread destruction over the whole province of Campania.' Nero visited the city in the years after the tremor. Eleven years after his death, Pompeii and the neighbouring towns were destroyed in the eruption of Mount Vesuvius.

were caused by leaping flames, with sparks and embers carried some distance by the wind. Modern scholars have furthermore reinterpreted scattered references in the source texts as evidence for attempts by the *vigiles* and others to set controlled counter-fires. Together with targeted demolitions these were the only feasible means of fighting large fires once they had spun out of control and could no longer be tamed with bucket chains and simple pumps. Tacitus, for example, mentions that '[Men] were openly throwing firebrands and shouting that "they had their authority"'.[39] Suetonius similarly states that 'several ex-consuls did not venture to lay hands on [Nero's] servants although they caught them on their estates with kindling and torches, while some granaries [...] were demolished by military machinery and then set on fire, because their walls were of stone'.[40] The military machinery probably referred to the heavy equipment routinely used by the *vigiles* for emergency clearances. Finally, Cassius Dio declares that 'many [houses] were set on fire by the same men who came to lend assistance; for the soldiers, including the night watch [...] instead of putting out fires, kindled new ones'.[41] It is perhaps not difficult to imagine that distressed property owners or panicked fugitives may have misread the *vigiles*' intentions or even opposed them. The way the source authors presented these actions out of context is a different matter.

However, while these demolitions eventually halted the fire in the Esquiline area, their overall success was limited. As Tacitus states, the blaze soon restarted and raged on elsewhere in the city, where it caused fewer deaths but more destruction of important monuments. He claimed that this second phase began in 'property of Tigellinus in the Aemiliana district', somewhere near the Forum Holitorium and the southern Campus Martius. Tigellinus was Nero's close associate and commander of the Praetorian Guard and had been prefect of the *vigiles* until AD 62. Perhaps what people saw (and may have misinterpreted) was an attempt to create a further firebreak through a targeted counter-fire in this area, albeit without success. While some landmark buildings in the Campus Martius, like the Theatre of Pompeius, the Saepta and Nero's new baths, seem to have been spared (due mostly to the prevailing wind direction and the large open squares with their marble architecture that offered less combustible material to the flames), the area to the north burnt for a further three days. Another prominent victim of the blaze was Nero's splendid wooden amphitheatre, likely located somewhere in this sector and only completed seven years before.

Nero and the Great Fire

Nero was away from Rome when the disaster unfolded in the Circus Maximus. He stayed in his coastal residence at Antium, like most aristocrats who relocated to their country or seaside villas in cooler climes to escape Rome's insalubrious summer heat. On hearing of the fire, Nero immediately hastened back from Antium to Rome.[42] Perhaps he was then in direct contact with the commanders of the firefighting units, because some decisions about the location of firebreaks may have required his personal authorisation, particularly if they involved significant properties.

Like every inhabitant of Rome, Nero must have been alert to the dangers of fire from an early age. The disasters of AD 36 and 38 would still have been talked about when he was growing up, their consequences visible for many years (see p. 197). He witnessed the fire of AD 53/4 as crown prince, together with the elderly Claudius' and Agrippina's spirited response. In AD 53 he had also given one of his first speeches in the senate and pleaded on behalf of the Roman colony of Bononia (modern Bologna), which had recently been devastated by a major conflagration, securing a grant of 10 million sesterces for the relief effort.[43] Together, these experiences gave him a clear sense of how a ruler should respond to such incidents, both through personal intervention and administrative measures.

No major fires were reported in Rome for almost the entire decade following Nero's accession. However, in AD 62 a hundred grain ships burnt in a blaze in Rome's river port, presumably when they were moored together by one of the warehouses along the Tiber. Nero quickly calmed the people's concerns about the safety of the food supply (see p. 136). In the same year, his newly built gymnasium in the Campus Martius was struck by lightning and burnt down, a fate suffered by a number of prominent buildings over the previous centuries. Yet again, this seems to have been dealt with swiftly and reconstruction started almost immediately. A series of earthquakes that hit the Vesuvius region around this time and caused heavy damage to Pompeii and other cities was of far greater consequence (Fig. 160).[44] The visits Nero and his wife Poppaea Sabina paid to the area, only attested through chance graffiti, may have been partly in response (in AD 53, Nero had also appealed to the senate on behalf of the earthquake-struck Greek city of Apameia) (see p. 120).[45]

Nero's response to the Great Fire was similarly competent. As before, it is best to look at relevant sections of Tacitus' report in isolation, without the more negative context into which he embeds this information. He describes Nero's actions thus:

> As a relief to the homeless and fugitive population, he opened the Campus Martius, the buildings of Agrippa, even his own Gardens, and built a number of improvised shelters to accommodate the helpless crowds. The supplies necessary for daily life were brought up from Ostia and the neighbouring towns, and the price of grain was lowered to three sesterces.[46]

These measures must have been taken in the fire's immediate aftermath, some perhaps even while it still burnt itself out. It is not hard to imagine Nero's personal involvement in any of this, even if his physical presence is not explicitly attested. However, this may have been a purposeful omission by authors eager to promote a very different narrative.

Aftermath

The level of destruction was immense. Undoubtedly Region Eleven was among the three city regions that were completely levelled to the ground, since it contained the Circus Maximus (where the fire had started) and the commercial fora to the west. One of the four regions spared must have been Region Fourteen, which was located across the Tiber and probably safely upwind as well. The identification of the remaining regions is disputed among scholars,

Fig. 161
An altar on the Quirinal Hill dedicated to the god Vulcan after the Great Fire
1935
Ernest Nash
Fototeca Unione, American Academy in Rome
FU.3504

According to inscriptions, Nero had vowed the erection of altars such as this during the conflagration, but they were only completed under Emperor Domitian several decades later. Visible are a number of paving slabs of the altar precinct that, according to ritual, was to be kept free from construction, and the altar itself on a stepped platform. The exact number of altars is unknown, but archaeological and epigraphic evidence points to the existence of at least three or four. According to one theory, they may have marked the outer limits of the area devastated by the fire.

including the seven of which only a few 'relics of houses' were left.[47] At any rate, the lists of destroyed monuments indicate they were spread over a wide area, reflecting the scale of devastation and the enormous loss of historically and culturally significant buildings, trophies and works of art (see Fig. 155, p. 199).[48]

The fire caused deep anxiety and distress among the population. In a profoundly religious (and superstitious) society there must also have been a genuine fear that the catastrophe signalled divine displeasure, or even Rome's abandonment by the heavenly powers. Nero therefore led the citizenry in public acts of reconciliation towards the gods, many of whose temples and sanctuaries had perished in the flames. According to Tacitus, Nero ordered a ritual consultation of the Sybilline books, ancient oracular texts that provided guidance in times of distress. Special prayers and sacrifices were then offered to the gods Vulcan, Ceres and Proserpina, while married women from well-to-do families ritually propitiated their patron goddess Juno.[49] Again, archaeological evidence corroborates elements of Tacitus' account. Throughout the city, Nero vowed to dedicate altar precincts sacred to Vulcan, whose placation seems to have been of particular significance. Associated inscriptions confirm they were set up following a 'vow undertaken [. . .] for the sake of repelling fires, when the city burnt for nine days in the time of Nero' (Fig. 161).[50] Specific religious buildings took priority in the reconstruction effort. The Temple of Vesta, crucial in cultic terms as the ritual hearth of Rome and centrally located near the Forum, was rebuilt in record time. Nero celebrated the fact on coins issued in AD 65/6, and the archaeological evidence seems to confirm that the new temple was completed

during his reign, along with the house of the Vestals and other parts of the Atrium Vestae, apparently part of a wider project to reorganise the area east of the Forum (Fig. 162; see also p. 227).

To reassert his authority, Nero also had to establish the causes of the fire and publicly discipline those responsible, as was customary.[51] Large numbers of undesirables, guilty or not, were rounded up and convicted.[52] Their punishment seems to have followed standard practice, whereby the retribution mirrored the nature of the crime. In the case of arson, this meant that the culprits would die by fire. Later legal commentaries, reflecting much earlier practice, illustrate precisely this: 'persons who deliberately set fire to a house or a heap of grain are to be bound, whipped, and put to death by fire'.[53] Another type of punishment is also attested: 'Those who deliberately start a fire in a city, if they are of more humble status, are usually thrown to the beasts.'[54] The culprits' gruesome end was meant to inflict maximum humiliation and was often staged as an elaborate quasi-mythological pageant.[55] Tacitus says of those convicted: 'derision accompanied their end – they were covered with wild beasts' skins and torn to death by dogs. Or they were fastened on crosses and, when the daylight faded, were burnt to serve as lamps by night.' In a passage that later took on great significance for quite different reasons, Tacitus questions Nero's motives and provides further details:

> But neither human help, nor imperial munificence, nor all the modes of placating Heaven, could [. . .] dispel the belief that the fire had taken place by order. Therefore, to stop the rumour, Nero substituted as culprits, and punished [. . .], a class of men, loathed for their vices, whom the crowd styled Christians [. . .] vast numbers were convicted, not so much on the count of arson as for hatred of humankind.[56]

This statement was of tremendous historical consequence, as it seemed to attest the first official, state-sponsored persecution of Christians under the Roman Empire. It was an account of events adopted by later Christian authors that was to have major practical repercussions. Yet Tacitus' specific reference to

Fig. 162
Aureus
AD 65–6
Minted in Rome, Italy
Gold
Weight 7.3 g
British Museum
R.6534
Donated by George IV, King of the
United Kingdom

The reverse of this aureus shows
Nero's new Temple of Vesta. It was
one of the first monuments
reconstructed after the fire.

Christians along with his usage of that term may have been an anachronistic back projection. Christians in Nero's day were regarded as one of many diffuse Jewish sects, and if singled out at all among them, were usually referred to as 'Nazroans', or Nazarenes.[57] The monotheism that formed the basis of Jewish belief was at odds with the expected ceremonial worship of the emperor, and its followers had already been expelled from Rome on several occasions, most recently under Claudius in AD 49. Subsequent events involving Jewish communities in Egypt and Judaea had stirred up further trouble and elicited a strong Roman response that involved the arrest and eventual execution of the Christian leader Paulus, possibly a few years before the fire.[58] 'Christians' may therefore have formed a significant group among those convicted, viewed as suspicious outsiders of doubtful belief. After all, any form of monotheism could be considered a dangerous insult to the gods (Tacitus refers to their faith as 'superstition') that had brought about the disaster.[59]

According to Tacitus, 'Nero had offered his gardens for the spectacle, and gave an exhibition in his circus, mixing with the crowd in the habit of a charioteer, or mounted on his car.'[60] The chronological frame for this is uncertain, but it is likely to have happened relatively soon after the fire. The location is significant; executions of this type usually took place in the Circus Maximus, which was presumably still a smouldering ruin, and all other suitable venues had been destroyed. The reference to his appearance in a charioteer's attire or mounted on his chariot may indicate that a full programme of races was included. The fire had started less than a week after the *ludi Apollinares*; other *ludi* normally followed towards the end of July and in September, so perhaps they were now held in an improvised manner. If Nero mingled freely with the *plebs urbana*, as Tacitus relates, this should be another indication that his actions were seen by the majority as a sign of his exemplary care for his people, along with providing food supplies and emergency shelter, and that he had nothing to fear from the crowd.

The *Urbs Nova*

In parallel to these religious ceremonies and retributions, an immense clean-up operation began, firstly to clear the major roads and recover bodies, then to prepare for rebuilding. Tacitus once more provides fascinating detail: Nero undertook 'to hand over the building-sites, clear of rubbish, to the owners […] As the receptacle of the refuse he settled upon the Ostian Marshes, and gave orders that vessels which had carried grain up the Tiber must run down-stream laden with debris.' This demanded a coordinated effort that far exceeded the means of private landlords. Given the enormity of the task, it may also have been a welcome way to employ masses of the urban poor, many of whom had become homeless and lost their livelihoods.[61]

To prevent future conflagrations, Nero set new guidelines for urban planning that finally brought Rome in line with other major cities. According to Tacitus, the rebuilt parts of the city had orderly 'lines of streets, with broad thoroughfares, buildings of restricted height, and open spaces'. Colonnades, paid for by the *princeps*, were 'added as a protection to the front of the tenement-blocks'. New legislation specified that the buildings had to be 'solid, untimbered structures', incorporating fireproof stone and that there were to be no shared partition walls.[62] Concrete vaulting may also have been introduced to replace wooden floors and ceilings.[63] Further measures safeguarded the public water supply from private misappropriation and provided additional outlets; householders had to keep firefighting equipment at the ready. Many existing rules, such as those introduced by Augustus, had clearly been flouted over previous reigns, exacerbating the effects of the fire (see p. 200).

To encourage speedy rebuilding, Nero incentivised landowners by offering subsidies to reconstruct houses and buildings, which were made available only if the work was completed within a fixed timeframe.[64] This was a prudent and much more measured alternative to Tiberius' indiscriminate cash handouts after the Caelian and Aventine fires several decades before. It may have been accompanied by other arrangements, such as tax relief and the cancellation of arrears that eased the financial burden on property owners. Investment in the reconstruction effort was encouraged in a number of ways. Nero stipulated that any person of Latin right (a form of qualified or restricted citizenship often granted to provincials) and in command of a fortune of 200,000 sesterces (half the census required for knights, so not insubstantial) would obtain full citizenship if they invested half that sum in construction projects in Rome.[65] Financial help arrived from other sources as well. The wealthy city of Lugdunum (Lyon) in southern Gaul gave a contribution of 4 million sesterces towards the relief effort. Nero reciprocated in the following year, when Lugdunum in turn was destroyed by a devastating fire.[66] In a consolation letter to a wealthy friend from the city, Seneca expressed the hope that it would rise from the ruins more beautiful than before, a sentiment no doubt felt by many in relation to Rome as well.[67]

Tacitus, otherwise so hostile to the *princeps*, gives a positive assessment of Nero's reconstruction measures: 'These reforms, welcomed for their utility, were also beneficial to the appearance of the new capital', and he even went on to speak of the 'striking beauty of the rearisen city', although he quickly tempered this praise with devastating criticism of Nero himself.[68]

'Gaudete, ruinae' – Rejoice, O ruins: Nero as instigator of the Great Fire

Nero's opponents established a resolute tradition that accused the *princeps* of having started the fire and delighted in its devastation. Whether rumours arose genuinely out of the confusion that accompanied the blaze, or were deliberately spread to malign the ruler, is hard to determine. The desperate countermeasures during the fire, and the rekindling of the inferno after it already seemed to have subsided, may have provided fertile ground for such suspicions to take hold. Tacitus and others claim that conspirators involved in a failed plot of AD 65 blamed Nero for the fire. However, as with almost every other of Nero's reputed outrages, the tragic play *Octavia* provides the first firm record of such an allegation. The Flavian poet Statius similarly portrays Nero as an arsonist, referring to 'the guilty lord's monstrous fires sweeping Rome'.[69] The extant literary sources repeat this charge largely without subtlety or internal consistency. Little seems to withstand close examination.

Dio puts it bluntly: 'Nero set his heart on accomplishing what had doubtless always been his desire, namely to make an end of the whole city [. . .] he secretly sent out men [. . .] and caused them at first to set fire to one or two or even several buildings in different parts of the city'.[70] Suetonius writes that when someone once quoted a line from a play, 'When I am dead, let earth be consumed by flames', Nero ominously retorted 'No, while I live.' *Octavia*'s plot may have been his main inspiration. With dramatic flourish, it had Nero utter, 'Very soon, the homes of the citizens shall fall a prey to the conflagrations which I will set going! Fire, utter ruin, shall weigh down this hateful rabble, extremest privations, bitter starvation with weeping and sorrow!' At least Suetonius also provides a motive, claiming that Nero scorched the city because of the 'ugliness of the old buildings and the narrow, crooked streets'. Tacitus similarly remarks that Nero had 'sought the glory of founding a new capital and endowing it with his own name'.[71]

Tacitus' account, by far the longest surviving description of the fire, is perhaps the most damning because it ostensibly appears to be more balanced. Yet from its first sentence ('There followed a disaster, whether due to chance or to the malice of the *princeps* is uncertain, for there are authors who assert either'), it skilfully manipulates the reader in a way that leaves little doubt of Nero's guilt, at least in a moral sense. Leading on rather abruptly from a description of Nero's stage performances and promiscuous mingling with the crowds, the Tacitean conflagration is presented as inevitable retribution for a misguided ruler and the rabble that cheered him on.

Having conceded that the ruler was not in Rome when the fire broke out, Tacitus scorns Nero's response by claiming that he did not return to the city until the flames began to encroach upon his palace, even if it then 'proved impossible to stop it from engulfing both the Palatine and the palace and all their surroundings'. Given the speed with which the flames travelled north from the circus, there is, however, no reason to assume any delay on Nero's part. Antium was some 60 km away, the distance between the Circus Maximus and the eventual firebreak on the Esquiline maybe 1,600 m, the lower slopes of the Palatine even closer.[72] Tacitus follows with an even more disturbing accusation, described as anonymous rumour, that came to dominate later reports of the fire: 'At the very moment Rome was aflame, [Nero] mounted his private stage and sung of the destruction of Troy, likening the ills of the present to the catastrophe of the past.'[73] This deeply distressing claim was also adopted by other authors. 'Viewing the conflagration from the tower of Maecenas and exulting, as he said, in "the beauty of the flames", he sang the whole of the "Sack of Ilium", in his regular stage costume', as Suetonius puts it. Similarly, Cassius Dio: 'While the whole population was […] crazed by the disaster [. . .] Nero ascended to the roof of the palace, from which there was the best general view of the greater part of the conflagration, and assuming the lyre-player's garb, he sang the "Capture of Troy".' Rather than reflecting actual rumours, these claims were probably based on a purposeful later fabrication that drew on events dating to before and after the fire.[74]

Nero's interest in Troy is well documented. It stemmed in part from his position within the Julio-Claudian imperial family and its particular tradition and pageantry. This in turn may have concentrated his intellectual and artistic energy, and made him explore further what was otherwise a fairly conventional topic of the elite cultural canon.[75] In the years before the fire, Nero began to compose an *Iliou Halosis*, a description of the fall of Troy, and he may have given recitals of finished sections at his palace during this period. An allusion to such a performance is perhaps reflected in Neronian court panegyric, from which it could have become more widely known. An anonymous poet here likened the Palatine to Mount Helicon, a place sacred to the Muses, and compared Nero to Apollo. He then suggested, in hyperbolic praise, that Troy's fall was justified – by the sheer beauty of Nero's description of its demise. This culminated in the verse *Gaudete, ruinae et laudate rogos: vester vos tollit alumnus*, 'Rejoice, O ruins; praise your funeral pyres: it is the man you nursed that raises you again!'[76] Such lines and their setting would require little adjustment to arrive at the later story. Furthermore, Nero continued to perform and elaborate the topic after the Great Fire, notably at the second *Neronia* of AD 65. Perhaps at this point he also tried to console the people and rouse their spirits by suggesting that as Rome metaphorically had been born out of the ruins of Troy, so a new, more beautiful city would arise from the ashes of the old. Again, such a sentiment could easily be turned on its head by those hostile to the *princeps*. Romans of all classes may also have remembered a particular play performed five years before the conflagration, at the *ludi maximi* festival of AD 59. This was a comedy by the second-century BC playwright Lucius Afranius, entitled *Incendium* ('Fire'). It apparently involved highly realistic pyrotechnic effects, for the actors were allowed to salvage and keep the furnishings of a house that burnt on stage, as Suetonius records. Here Nero may indeed have watched and cheered a fire, along with most of the audience. Suetonius claims that Nero observed these performances from the top of the stage wall (which after all symbolised the roof or towers of a palace), a likely model for the later tales that only had to mix in references to Nero's performances.[77]

In addition, these authors associated the desperate firefighting efforts of the *vigiles* (alongside other troops and Nero's palace staff) with looting. Tacitus states that people laying fires did so 'possibly in order to have a freer hand in looting, possibly from orders received', while Cassius Dio maintains that the soldiers and *vigiles* set fires with 'an eye to plunder'.[78] While there may have been individual instances of looting under cover of the conflagration, the main background to these claims was really literary. In his manual for aspiring orators, the rhetorician Quintilian gives striking examples for how the capture and sacking of a city should be described in order to touch the audience's emotions: 'flames racing through houses and temples', the 'blind flight of some' while 'others cling to their dear ones in a last embrace', the 'shrieks of children and women', 'the pillage of property, secular and sacred' and 'the frenzied activity of plunderers carrying off their booty and going back for more'.[79] Quintilian's instructions read like a blueprint for the relevant sections of Tacitus' and Dio's texts. This association of the Great Fire with a generic *urbs capta* ('captured city') motif was heightened by evoking the memory of a disaster deep in Rome's historical past, its sacking and burning by invading Gauls four and a half centuries earlier. Tacitus and other sources claim that references were soon made to the fact that the Gaulish assault had supposedly also started on a nineteenth of July.[80] There were other fires that could have been recalled instead, such as the blazes that destroyed much of Rome in 111 BC and 86 BC. Yet a comparison with the Gaulish sack (instead of more relevant civic disasters) could serve to besmirch Nero: like the barbarian invaders of old, he had purposefully destroyed the city, a true enemy within. Suetonius, in a telling variation of the theme, transfers the allegations of plunder to the aftermath of the fire and blames Nero directly. The *princeps*, he asserts, 'while promising the removal of the debris and dead bodies free of cost, allowed no one to approach the ruins of his own property', in order to 'gain from this calamity all the spoil and booty possible'.[81]

The same authors polemically liken the heavy financial burdens that had to be imposed on individuals and the provinces to further ill-disguised plunder. Tacitus states, 'meanwhile, Italy had been laid waste for contributions of money; the provinces, the federate communities, and the so-called free states, were ruined'. Suetonius adds, 'from the contributions which he not only received, but even demanded, he nearly bankrupted the provinces and exhausted the resources of individuals', whereas Dio claims that Nero 'now began to collect vast sums from private citizens as well as from whole communities, sometimes using compulsion, taking the conflagration as his pretext, and sometimes obtaining it by voluntary contributions, as they were made to appear'.[82] There can, however, be little doubt that circumstances legitimately required the raising of additional revenue. In addition to the reconstruction effort in Rome, money was urgently needed for other purposes, including the aftermath of the wars in Britain and Armenia and long-planned military action in the East.[83]

While it is not implausible that rumours and suspicions circulated among the population about the causes of the fire and possible culprits, it seems doubtful that Nero was widely blamed at the time in the manner the key authors suggest. There is no indication of unrest or of any divide between Nero and the *plebs*, who were otherwise quick to signal their discontent. The hatred, however, with which some members of the senatorial elite came to blame Nero personally for the fire may have been caused in part by a chance circumstance of Roman topography (see p. 227). A wing of the imperial residence was located at a key junction where the Palatine, Velia and Esquiline Hills merged. As the flames rapidly approached from the circus, this suddenly became the focal point of frantic firefighting activities aimed at protecting both the palace and the Forum area beyond (probably the explanation for the involvement of Nero's *cubicularii*, or chamberlain, as reported by Suetonius[84]). These desperate countermeasures may have led to the destruction of grand elite mansions central to their owners' aristocratic identity.[85] The subsequent reconstruction and enlargement of Nero's residence must have vindicated and hardened misgivings among sections of the elite. This new palace complex was the Golden House or Domus Aurea.

VII

THE NEW APOLLO

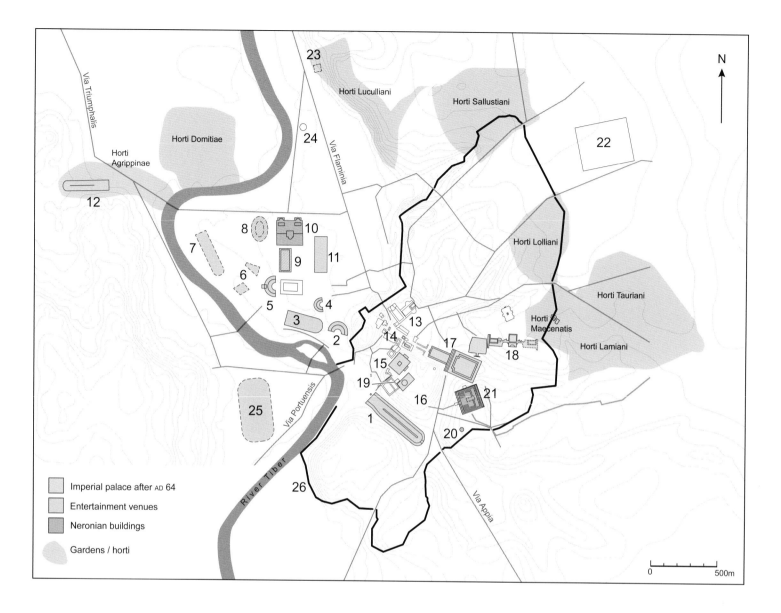

Fig. 163
Map of Rome showing significant buildings and public venues in the latter half of Nero's reign

1 Circus Maximus
2 Theatre of Marcellus
3 Circus Flaminius
4 Theatre of Balbus
5 Theatre and porticus of Pompeius
6 Stables of the Circus factions
7 Trigarium
8 Nero's Amphitheatre (possible location, before AD 64)
9 Stagnum
10 Nero's Baths
11 Saepta
12 Nero's Circus (and gardens)

13 Fora of Caesar and Augustus
14 Forum Romanum
15–18 Imperial Palace (after AD 64, see Fig. 169b, p. 225)
19 Temple of Apollo Palatinus
20 Macellum Magnum
21 Temple of Claudius
22 Praetorian Guard barracks
23 Tomb of the Domitii Ahenobarbi (Nero's family)
24 Mausoleum of Augustus
25 Naumachia
26 City walls

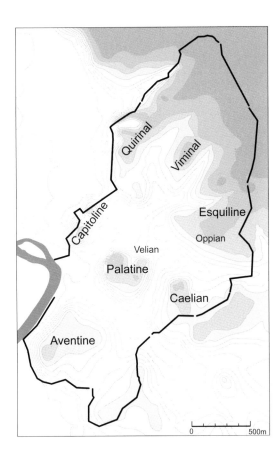

Fig. 164
The hills of Rome within the city walls

Among the gestures intended to soften and disguise the true nature of Augustus' 'Restored Republic' was the notion that the *princeps*' residence should not fundamentally exceed the houses of other leading senators in size and sumptuousness. Over the following decades, this balance became ever harder to maintain, as the rulers' evolving obligations and the growing imperial household (the *familia Caesaris*) could no longer be adequately accommodated in this manner. The crowds at the emperor's morning receptions, the multitude of high-status guests at his regular banquets, and the number of staff tasked with expanding administrative duties soon exceeded those of the largest senatorial households, even if a *princeps* scrupulously respected the conventional norms of aristocratic behaviour (see pp. 36–7). Contemporary language reflected this evolution in the appearance and function of the imperial residence: the word *aula* came to denote the imperial 'court' as a more expansive architectural space (and also a large community of servants, officials, friends and advisors), alongside the established term *domus*.[1]

While Tiberius initiated little, his successors gradually rebuilt and extended the imperial residence to reflect these changing requirements. Yet the principate's complex nature meant that there were no immediate architectural models upon which to draw. The basic template of the *domus*, the traditional Roman aristocratic town house, was socially acceptable but functionally limiting. Fully developed Greek-style palace architecture, however, seemed improper because of its regal associations, even though it had long influenced the Roman elite's leisure villas outside the capital.

By the time Nero acceded to the throne, the existing imperial residence on the Palatine Hill no longer fulfilled the growing needs of the emperor and his court. Nero's situation differed from his predecessors' in that he had also inherited the Ahenobarbi's ancestral mansion, the Domus Domitiana, on the Velia Hill between the Palatine and the Esquiline, next to the Forum. Over time, this became part of his expanding vision for the imperial palace and its integration into the urban fabric of Rome (Figs 163 and 164).

The resulting buildings were marvels of their age, mostly short-lived, but disproportionately influential in their design. Beginning with the new Domus Palatina, they evolved in a series of successive construction projects over much of Nero's thirteen-year reign, culminating in the Domus Transitoria just before the Great Fire of AD 64 and its even grander successor thereafter, the Domus Aurea, or 'Golden House'. The latter was the first imperial residence in Roman history for which the names of the supervising designers are known, the architect-engineers Severus and Celer, a reflection of its innovation, scale and impact.

The construction of these palatial buildings occurred during a period of ultimately destabilising, highly competitive luxury consumption among the elite, in which the growing gulf between the *princeps*' means and those of the senatorial class became ever more obvious. This strained relations at a time when the ruler was expected to treat senators as his social equals, despite their differences in rank. It also coincided with a dramatic period that saw the spectacular state visit of a large royal Parthian delegation to Rome, Nero's long-postponed tour of the East that came to a premature end in Greece, and a series of major conspiracies against his rule.

No contemporary descriptions of Nero's palaces have survived. Instead, our knowledge of the Domus Aurea in particular is shaped almost entirely by heavily distorted post-Neronian Flavian accounts that served to legitimise a new dynasty under its own heavy pressures and set the tone for later authors such as Suetonius and Tacitus.[2]

The beginnings and significance of Nero's palaces

It is not quite clear what kind of imperial residence Nero found in place at the outset of his reign. There are literary references to the houses of his predecessors, but few archaeological traces to give a real sense of their layout and architectural detail. Much of the later palace area on the Palatine Hill still seems to have been a cluster of interconnected and expanded mansions that had belonged to individual members of the imperial family. The fact that Agrippina maintained her own household on the Palatine and held separate morning receptions in the early months of her son's principate seems to confirm this.

From the days of the Republic, the Palatine and its slopes had formed the most prestigious residential area for the leading families of the senatorial elite; some still retained houses there early in Nero's reign. This came from the Hill's association with Rome's mythical founder Romulus, and its prominent position and vicinity to the Forum, the political and administrative centre of the city and Empire.[3] Grand Palatine mansions were prized heirlooms: ancestral strongholds that expressed the reputation and historical standing of important family clans.[4] The prime area within the Palatine was its north-western sector, where the cultural memory of Romulus' fabled *urbs quadrata* was maintained in the physical layout of local streets and housing plots over many centuries. Yet high regard was also attached to aristocratic houses in other locations 'adjoining the Forum', for example on the lower slopes of the nearby Arx and Velia Hills.[5]

Augustus had been born in 63 BC in a small family property on the Palatine's north-eastern slope. With his rise to political eminence, he gradually moved closer to the Hill's prime area, where he eventually acquired a number of large mansions near the house of his wife Livia, a member of the Claudian family.[6] He later built a temple to Apollo Palatinus on his new property, while the senate in turn gifted him a new mansion next door, the Domus Publica. Parts of this house, temple and adjacent area were subsequently used for senate meetings and other state functions, lending the *princeps*' residence a distinctive character that merged public and private roles.[7] The domestic section seems to have remained relatively modest and did not exceed other senatorial mansions in terms of luxury.[8] Its exterior was distinguished by public marks of honour rather than architectural splendour, including a civic crown and laurels above the entrance similar to the insignia added to the houses of those given a triumphal ceremony during the Republic.[9] The Palatine maintained its public character, particularly around the sanctuaries, where the general population regularly gathered for festivals.[10]

Little change is evident under Tiberius, who seems to have been content with the continued incorporation of other properties associated with his ancestral clan, the Claudii, through structural alterations and underground passageways, a process that may have been initiated under Augustus already. Different branches of the imperial family (led by influential dowagers like Livia, Antonia and the elder Agrippina) continued to maintain individual households with all their attendant social functions, such as the important morning *salutatio*. At any rate, Tiberius concentrated his efforts on his palatial villa on the island of Capri, where he spent the final decade of his reign.[11]

A first departure from this conservative pattern occurred during the short reign of Nero's young uncle Caligula from AD 37 to AD 41.[12] According to the later literary sources, he extended the palace down the north-western slope of the Palatine to link it to the Forum area, where it now incorporated the Temple of Castor and Pollux, which effectively became its vestibule. Furthermore, he is said to have built a bridge linking the Palatine to the Capitoline Hill and to have started the foundations of a new mansion next to the Temple of Iupiter Capitolinus.[13] These building projects starkly expressed the difference between the *princeps*' status and that of the senatorial elite and echoed the allusions to the supreme god Jupiter that began to appear in contemporary court poetry and in Caligula's portrait iconography. They were a direct and largely symbolic response to the complete breakdown of his relationship with the senate, after a major senatorial conspiracy against him was foiled in AD 39.[14] Caligula's assassination in AD 41 put an end to any construction he may have initiated on the Capitoline (no traces have been identified). The literary accounts of his last moments provide valuable insights into the physical character of the Palatine quarter at the time.[15]

Claudius reversed his predecessor's most controversial measures, closing the link to the Temple of Castor and Pollux and abandoning the Capitoline project, if it had ever been started in earnest. It is hard, however, to see how his developing court ceremonial, particularly the regular *convivia* that involved ever larger numbers of the aristocracy (a process that had started under Caligula), would not have necessitated substantial modifications to the Palatine residence, including a degree of monumentalisation. Suetonius, for example, mentions a pediment above the main entrance, decorated with a naval crown to celebrate Claudius' conquest of Britain, and, upon his accession, the young Nero is said to have greeted the Praetorians from the grand stairs of the palace.[16] Perhaps Claudius had commissioned some additions to the existing fabric of buildings or changes to their internal layout. Nero grew up in the Claudian residence from AD 49, when he was aged twelve, and was familiar with its potential and shortcomings.[17]

Nero's new palace

Nero's first project completely transformed the prestigious old western quarter of the Palatine with its surviving cluster of interlinked individual houses (Figs 163 and 164). In their place, it created a uniform, grand palatial structure that rose from a monumental podium high above the hallowed ground of the *urbs quadrata*, along with the Republican and later mansions that had occupied the area since. With this bold architectural statement, the new Neronian Domus Palatii both appropriated and suppressed the historical memory associated with the area.[18]

Only the main dimensions and basic plan of the building can at present be deduced from its scant archaeological traces. The vast podium measured approximately 130 × 150 m. It rose 6–9 m in the east and 16–24 m in the west to create an extensive level terrace, from which the imperial residence dominated the skyline like no secular building before. The new *domus* appears to have been a large peristyle mansion with rooms arranged around a colonnaded central courtyard and geometrically laid-out garden areas around.[19]

Other buildings dating to the first decade of Nero's reign were located further south, away from the podium mansion and immediately to the south-east of the Temple of Apollo Palatinus (No. 19, Fig. 163).[20] They included a large and magnificent basilical hall, some 30 m wide and divided by two parallel rows of columns into three aisles. It had a well-preserved and extremely lavish *opus sectile* floor with inlays in exotic marble, of a staggering refinement not attested before. The hall seems to have linked the Apollo sanctuary to a building further to the south-east, of which only a part below ground is preserved.[21]

This comprised a sumptuously decorated set of dining rooms, arranged around a sunken nymphaeum, or fountain court, that was open to the sky and included a small stage and elaborate water displays (Fig. 165).[22] While their wider architectural context is unclear, these rooms provide the best evidence of Neronian palace interiors and their possible use, complete with painted ceiling frescos, and walls and floors bedecked in colourful marble *opus sectile* that have not survived anywhere else (Fig. 166).[23] The court could be reached from the higher ground above by two symmetrical staircases. The main area was orientated towards an ornate façade with a central water feature, flanked by small niches that may have held statues. In front was a narrow stage platform accessed by two short flights of stairs at either end, its decoration echoing the *pulpitum* of Roman theatres. The stage was embellished with revetments and miniature columns in coloured marble, their capitals and bases made of gilded bronze. Given its location and size, it may have been particularly suited to intimate musical performances or poetry readings.[24]

A shallow podium, in all likelihood the elevated setting for three dining couches in a traditional triclinium configuration, abutted the opposite wall. It was screened by columns of precious porphyry that supported a baldacchino-type roof structure. There were two spacious barrel-vaulted rooms on either side of this central area, each linked to two interconnected anterooms. Their wall decoration comprised ornamental panels with figurative inlays and additional metal embellishments. The barrel-vaulted ceilings were richly painted with an array of star patterns and intricate plant ornaments, in places in combination with light-reflecting glass gems. Figurative mythological friezes extended below, lending a particular narrative theme to each room. They contained scenes from the Trojan War in the large rooms, and Amazons and Dionysiac groups, including the Muses, in the anterooms (Fig. 167).[25]

Apart from its costly marble floor and wall decoration, the main feature of the fountain court was its carefully engineered infrastructure. From a large storage tank, water entered the court via a stepped cascade in the central niche of the north façade, where it was collected in a smaller lead tank and conducted below the stage platform. It re-emerged through a row of vertical fountain jets set in a long rectangular water basin in front of the *pulpitum*, and from a square basin set into the triclinium podium opposite. Similarly, the back walls of the two

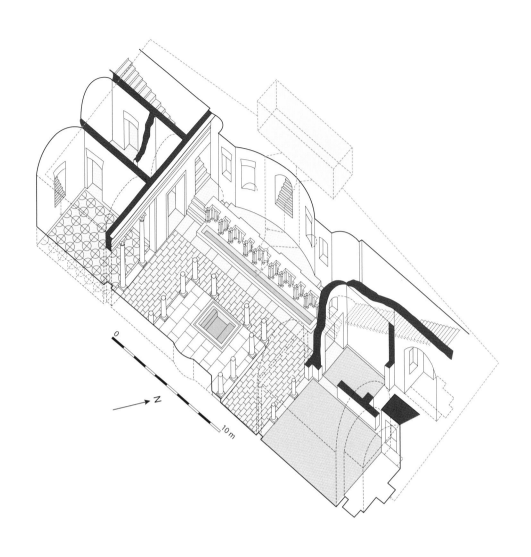

Fig. 167
Vault fresco from Nero's Palatine palace
AD 54–64
Rome, Italy
Plaster and paint
H. 21 cm, W. 42.8 cm
Parco Archeologico del Colosseo,
Museo Palatino, Rome
381404

This fresco fragment is from the ceiling vault of the large room to the left of the sunken court of Nero's Domus Transitoria (see Fig. 165). It shows various Homeric scenes. Inset glass elements reflected the light like precious gems. The rich scroll-work with vignettes of sphinxes and wild animals foreshadows the decoration of the Domus Aurea's Esquiline building.

lateral rooms contained stepped cascades. The combined effect of these hydraulic displays must have been mesmerising. The court was a most luxurious setting for intimate dinner parties and performances, particularly in the hot summer months, when the shaded location and cooling effect of the water provided a pleasant ambient temperature.[26]

The Domus Transitoria and the Great Fire

As *princeps*, Nero had access to extensive *horti* (parklands) on the outskirts of the city in addition to the imperial residences on the Palatine. They included the *horti* (gardens) of Agrippina in the Ager Vaticanus (alluvial plain) on the far bank of the Tiber to the north-west, and the Gardens of Maecenas and Lamia on the Esquiline Hill to the east (see Figs 163 and 164, pp. 216–17). Nero frequently opened the Vatican gardens to the people, as his Circus was located there. The Esquiline *horti*, much closer to the Palatine, seem to have had a more private character. Caligula had already commissioned a number of exquisite buildings and spent much time there.[27]

At some point before AD 64, Nero developed a plan to link the imperial properties on the Palatine and Esquiline Hills through a new palace building (or set of buildings): the Domus Transitoria, literally the 'Transit Mansion' or 'House of Passage'. The literary sources (principally Suetonius) mention the Domus Transitoria only briefly, as a short-lived, pre-fire predecessor to the Domus Aurea, and provide little clarity on how far the mansion referred to by this name extended up the slopes, particularly on the Palatine side. This detail mattered little to them; more important was that the building provided the impetus for the later Domus Aurea with its perceived encroachment on public space and private property. In his account of the Great Fire of AD 64, Tacitus seems to differentiate between the Palatine *domus* and the Domus Transitoria, without specifying where one ended and the other began.[28]

If Nero was the only emperor to conceive of this idea, it was almost certainly because the ancestral home of his paternal family, the Domitii Ahenobarbi, lay right between the imperial properties on the Palatine and Esquiline, one of the grand senatorial mansions that abutted the Forum along the Via Sacra. Nero's father had added a set of lavish baths to this *domus* and his family seems to have owned commercial warehouses nearby, part of larger property holdings in the area (see Fig. 169a).[29] Nero proudly retained his childhood home after he had become emperor. Regular public sacrifices in honour of his late father and the family's ancestral household gods (*Di Penates*) were performed outside the house and are attested epigraphically.[30] In all likelihood, this family property made the idea behind the Domus Transitoria appear both technically feasible and emotionally significant.

There are indeed architectural remains of considerable refinement and complexity in this area of the Velia, some 5 m below the modern ground level, which have been linked by a number of scholars to either the Ahenobarbi mansion or the Domus Transitoria, even though only a small section has been explored. At its centre was a rotunda, normally reconstructed as domed and lit by a central oculus, located at the intersection of two barrel-vaulted corridors set at right angles. Column screens and ornate floor inlays hint at the original splendour of the structure (Fig. 168).[31] Its wider context, however, is uncertain.[32]

Fig. 168
Axonometric drawing of a building on the Velian Hill that may have formed part of the Domus Domitiana or Domus Transitoria

Two barrel-vaulted corridors crossed under a central dome.

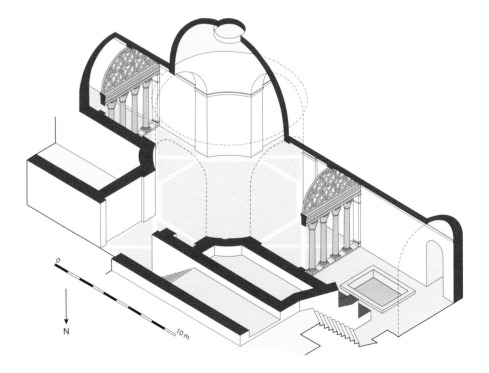

The Great Fire seriously damaged, perhaps even destroyed, the Neronian buildings on the Palatine and the Domus Transitoria, along with other private houses that remained on the Hill and its lower slopes (Fig. 169a). These included the mansion of the late Gaius Caecina Largus, consul of AD 42, previously the property of Marcus Aemilius Scaurus and the wealthy triumvir Licinius Crassus before him. Pliny the Elder mentions the destruction of this house in passing in his *Natural History*, as six highly prized ancient lotus trees perished with it in the flames.[33] It was a good example of the imposing historic mansions full of treasured heirlooms that were of such importance for the senatorial aristocracy's class identity. Tacitus and other writers devote substantial parts of their fire narratives to this area, particularly the passages accusing Nero's palace staff and others of deliberate arson (see pp. 204–5 and 210–11). Another nearby private residence, not mentioned in the literary sources but attested through an inscribed water pipe, belonged to Gaius Licinius Mucianus, suffect consul at the time of the fire.[34] Some senatorial *domus* may have remained on the Palatine after the fire (the evidence at present is inconclusive), but it is thought that Nero now took over several fire-damaged and ruined senatorial properties on the Hill and its lower slopes, presumably financially compensating their owners. For decades, senators had moved from the old centre around the Palatine to districts further out; this process now came to a rapid conclusion. Grand senatorial mansions were from then on concentrated particularly on the Viminal, Caelian and Aventine Hills; the Palatine was left to the emperors.[35]

Post-fire reconstruction

While the extent of the direct damage caused by the Great Fire to the imperial palace is hard to quantify, its consequences were grave. Only the Forum to the north-west of the Palatine had been spared by the flames – whatever buildings on the Palatine that had survived the inferno likely stood isolated. The area around the palace's main access road, the Clivus Palatinus, had burned down. The residence may have been rendered largely unusable. Perhaps in consequence, Nero seems to have spent much of the following year in temporary accommodation in his gardens outside the centre of Rome and in properties further away.[36]

Although speedy reconstruction was an obvious priority, it is significant that Nero's reign ended three years and eleven months after the fire, and that he spent more than a year towards the end of this period on his tour of Greece. This had a major impact on how much of the new palace could be completed and put to use while the *princeps* lived, and needs to be balanced against the picture evoked by the source accounts.

Nero's first palace in the north-western part of the Palatine, apparently damaged, was remodelled and extended (Fig. 169b). The new building was surrounded by a columned portico along the outer edge of the platform, while at its centre was a square residential block more than 80 m wide on each side, set around a rectangular inner courtyard of 32 × 45 m. Further porticoes may have linked the outer halls with the central block, with the areas in between planted as raised gardens. A monumental staircase was added to the north-west, rising above the Forum. Another staircase probably served the main entrance in the

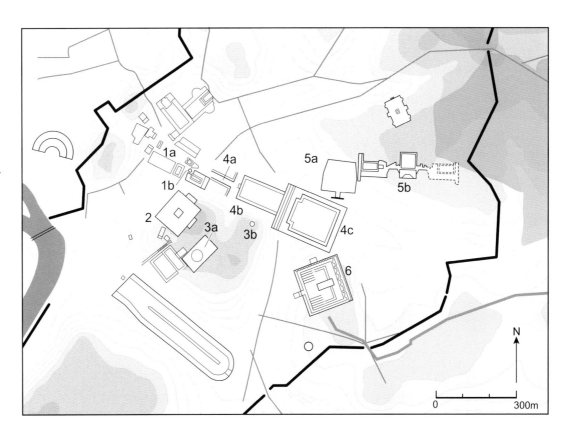

Fig. 169a

Map showing the location of imperial palace buildings in Rome before the Great Fire

1 Forum of Augustus
2 Subura quarter
3 Argiletum quarter
4 Domus Transitoria
5 Via Sacra
6 Main palace building (Palatine, pre-fire)
7 Temple of Apollo Palatinus
8 Nymphaeum
9 Meta Sudans fountain
10 Curiae Veteres
11 Porticus Liviae

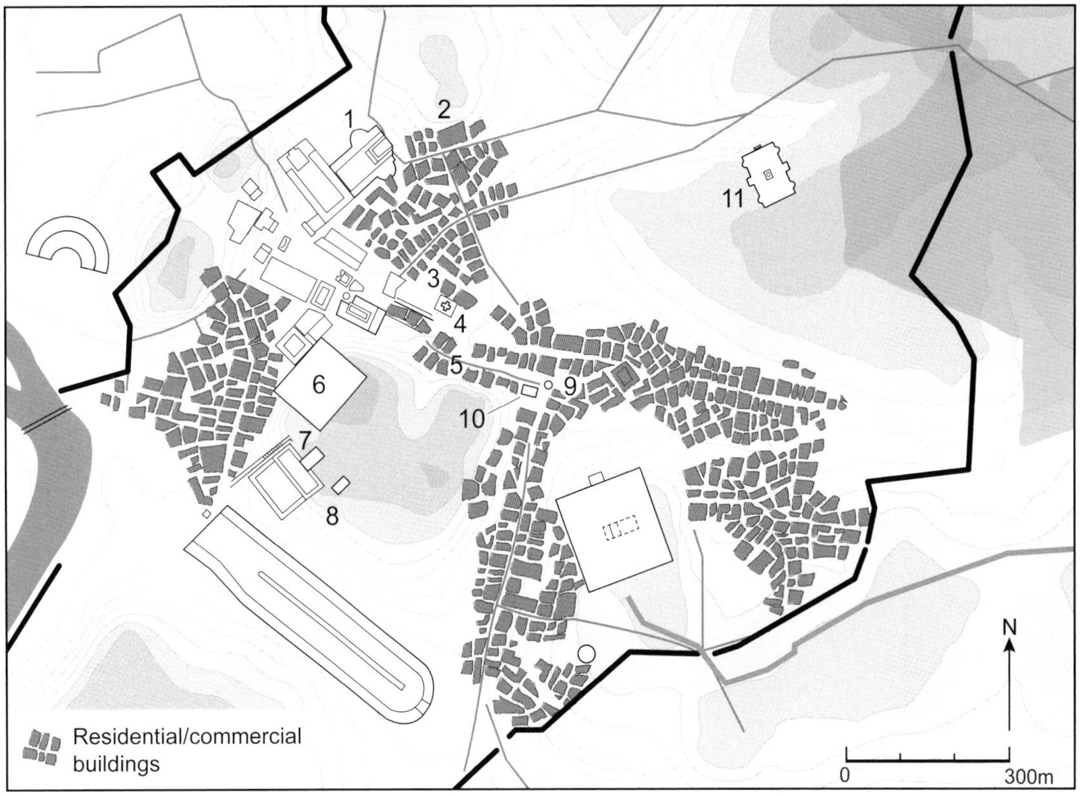

Residential/commercial buildings

Fig. 169b

Map showing the expansion of imperial palace buildings and monumental squares after the fire of AD 64

1a Forum Romanum
1b Temple of Vesta
2 Main palace building (Palatine, post-fire)
3a New palace building (Palatine)
3b Cenatio Rotunda?
4a Neronian Porticoes
4b Vestibule with colossus of Sol
4c Stagnum
5a Baths (later Baths of Titus)
5b Esquiline building
6 Temple of Claudius with nymphaeum façade

east, facing the Area Palatina square. With its high podium, grand staircases and gabled entrances, this imposing palace building dominated the Palatine and stood in a visual dialogue with the temples and official buildings in the Forum below and the Capitoline opposite. Isolated fragments hint at its original splendour (Figs 170 and 171). It seems likely, if not from its architectural form alone, then from the building's role in the moments after Nero's downfall, that some administrative functions were concentrated here, too, including the imperial secretariat and possibly other offices.[37] With modifications by later emperors, it remained an integral part of the palace over the following centuries.

Among the other Neronian buildings on the Palatine, the sunken triclinium to the south-east and the hall above seem to have been abandoned and swiftly replaced, with no attempt to salvage their costly marble decorations.[38] A large circular structure of disputed function rose in their place at ground level. Its detailed articulation and wider architectural context are unknown, but it surely would not have sat in isolation. The area may again have been damaged by fire in AD 80; at any rate, everything was then buried under Flavian emperor Domitian's great new palace, leaving only scant traces. A late Neronian palace wing, however, may have preceded the Flavian buildings in this area.

Nero's architect-engineers Celer and Severus, now put in charge of the post-fire rebuilding effort, carried out significant new construction along the north-eastern slope of the Palatine, the Velia and the valley to the east.[39]

Fig. 170
Corinthian capital
AD 54–68
Palatine, Rome, Italy
Marble
H. 70 cm, W. 84 cm, D. 68 cm
Parco Archeologico del Colosseo,
Museo Palatino, Rome
12484

This Neronian capital from the Palatine stands out for its quality, the precision of its workmanship and the fine Corinthian-style ornamentation. It can be linked to examples from Nero's villa at Subiaco, east of Rome, and other more fragmentary capitals and pilasters from the Palatine. Together, they demonstrate the high standard and innovation of Neronian marble decoration. This was widely imitated, for example in the scroll-work of contemporary tomb altars commissioned by private patrons (see for example Fig. 209, p. 269).

Fig. 171
Detail of wall *opus sectile*
AD 54–68
Palatine, Rome, Italy
Marble
H. 77 cm, W. 77 cm, D. 5 cm
Parco Archeologico del Colosseo,
Museo Palatino, Rome
12510

Nero's palatial residence made
more extensive use of exotic
marbles than those of his
predecessors, a trend also
followed in contemporary elite
villa architecture. This lavish *opus
sectile* panel was part of a wall
decoration. It combines marble
tiles in contrasting colours, drawn
from different parts of the Empire,
into a beautiful geometric pattern.
Fragments of this type have
survived on the Palatine, whereas
the Esquiline building was
completely stripped of its marble
decoration during the later
Flavian period.

This area greatly exceeded the space previously occupied by the Domus
Transitoria, and work here attracted much greater public attention than on the
Palatine. It amounted to a major urbanistic remodelling of this part of the city.

Before the fire, the valley between the Palatine, Esquiline and Caelian had
been a densely settled commercial and residential district, dissected by major
roadways that followed natural communication lines between the Hills. The
extensively terraced lower slope of the Oppian (the Esquiline's southern spur)
contained commercial buildings, including *horrea*, or warehouses. In between
these were numerous smaller residential and mixed-use structures. Further to
the west, the Via Sacra, a busy traffic artery as well as an important ceremonial
route, led towards the Forum, lined by temples but also many shops and other
commercial buildings (see Fig. 169a).[40] So much had been destroyed here that
Nero and his planners were presented with an opportunity to intervene in a
manner completely unthinkable before the catastrophe.[41] Through extensive
levelling and terracing, they created a series of expansive portico-lined squares
linked by colonnaded streets that equalled or even surpassed in size the *fora*
of Caesar and Augustus and some of the plazas in the Campus Martius,
radically changing the character of the area. As imperial builder, it put
Nero on a par with Augustus.[42]

The first phase of this ambitious building programme started immediately
east of the Forum, where the flames had finally come to a halt. Along with the
reconstruction of the Temple of Vesta, the Via Sacra was slightly realigned and

widened and given a much grander character through new porticoes that flanked it on either side.[43] In this way, the majestic architecture of the Forum, with its temples, public buildings and commemorative monuments, was carried eastwards up the Velia to the first new square that extended over a large artificial terrace created on the Hill's eastern side and overlooked the valley beyond.[44] To the south of this junction, the Clivus Palatinus led up to the Palatine and was now also framed by new porticoes. The Via Sacra, meanwhile, continued down the eastern slope of the Velia, where it met a street leading north to south. East of the Velia plaza, on lower ground in the valley floor, Nero's architects built a second, even larger square, surrounded by colonnaded halls and almost entirely taken up by a vast pool similar to the *stagnum* of Agrippa in the Campus Martius. Nero's new *stagnum* covered an area of almost 4 hectares (see Fig. 169b, p. 225).[45]

To the south-east a vast nymphaeum-fountain with an ornate, multistorey columned façade was added to the eastern front of the Claudianum's podium (see p. 204). It was fed from a Neronian extension of Claudius' Aqua Virgo aqueduct. The podium platform itself was laid out as a large garden square.

The Domus Aurea: the Golden House and the Golden Day

Nero also commissioned a successor for the short-lived Domus Transitoria. In its place rose a new, even more ambitious building, the Domus Aurea. A well-known passage in Suetonius' Nero biography provides the most detailed evocation of the palace:

> There was nothing however in which he was more ruinously prodigal than in building. He made a palace extending all the way from the Palatine to the Esquiline, which at first he called the House of Passage, but when it was burned shortly after its completion and rebuilt, the Golden House. Its size and splendour will be sufficiently indicated by the following details: […] There was a pond too, like a sea, surrounded with buildings to represent cities, besides tracts of country, varied by tilled fields, vineyards, pastures and woods […]. In the rest of the house all parts were overlaid with gold and adorned with gems and mother-of-pearl. There were dining-rooms with fretted ceilings of ivory, whose panels could turn and shower down flowers and were fitted with pipes for sprinkling the guests with perfumes. The main banquet hall was circular and constantly revolved day and night, like the heavens. He had baths supplied with sea water and sulphur water.[46]

Tacitus' brief description concentrates on the Domus Aurea's landscape setting (Fig. 172). He states that Nero built a mansion 'in which the marvels were not so much the jewels and gold, long familiar and quite vulgarised by our extravagance, but the fields and lakes, like a wilderness with woods and open spaces and extensive views'.[47] Yet it seems that, in many ways, the Domus Aurea, as we have come to imagine it, was already the polemical invention of a small number of earlier authors, such as Pliny the Elder and Martial, who overstated its expanse as a means of political invective. Pliny twice declares that it 'encircled

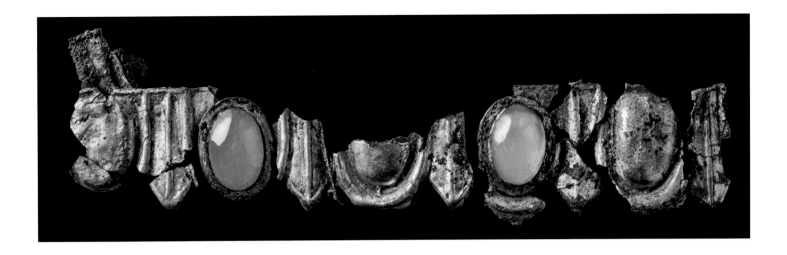

Fig. 172
**Decorative element from
the Horti Lamiani**
Date uncertain
Horti Lamiani, Esquiline Hill, Rome
Gilded copper and chalcedony
H. 3.1 cm, L. 16.5 cm
Antiquarium Comunale
del Celio, Rome
AC 10606

Julio-Claudian frescos depict
architectural components, such
as columns, decorated with inset
gemstones and other ornaments
of the type shown here. These
fragments are from the Horti
Lamiani, where Caligula
commissioned lavish garden
buildings that later became part
of the Domus Aurea's parklands.
Tacitus' reference to the 'gold and
gems' of Nero's *domus* may refer
to such elements.

the entire city', as Caligula's palace had once before, while Martial in a slight variation professes that 'one house took up the entire city'.[48] Suetonius mentions a similar slogan, allegedly from Nero's day, that admonished citizens to flee to the neighbouring city of Veii, 'lest all of Rome be turned into the emperor's house'.[49] To claim that villas reached the size of towns and cities was of course a long-established rhetorical ploy.[50]

Together, these authors conjured a vast palace precinct that stretched from the Palatine to the Velia, Esquiline and Caelian Hills, an area now estimated to have extended over 50 to 80 hectares.[51] But the boundaries were never very clearly defined, and much depended on whether Nero's new colonnaded streets and squares between the Hills were considered part of the new *domus*, a question open to subtle rhetorical manipulation, as will become clear.[52]

There is one structure, however, that seems to have formed the core of Nero's Domus Aurea. This was a magnificent edifice that now rose from a large artificial terrace cut into the southern slope of the Esquiline.

The new building was laid out symmetrically around a central pavilion with two lateral wings. It unfolded over two levels, the lower set deep into the hillside and partially hidden, while the upper merged into the surrounding parklands. The two-storey south-facing façade originally measured some 360 m, more than double the length of the Palatine mansion's podium. A colonnade, perhaps continuous, ran along its front. The rooms here enjoyed fine views across the valley below to the Caelian Hill opposite.[53] Further terraces, linked by ramps and staircases, may have extended towards the valley floor.[54]

The building's lower level was organised around a majestic, domed octagonal hall (see Figs 173b, Room 1, and 174). It had five radial extensions, was flanked by symmetrical apartments on either side and was open to the façade. Behind, in the central axis of the entire building, was a nymphaeum with a stepped water cascade, even grander than its earlier Palatine twin. The suites to the left and right of the octagonal hall were each dominated by large apsidal rooms, with barrel-vaulted ceilings richly decorated in painted stucco. After their

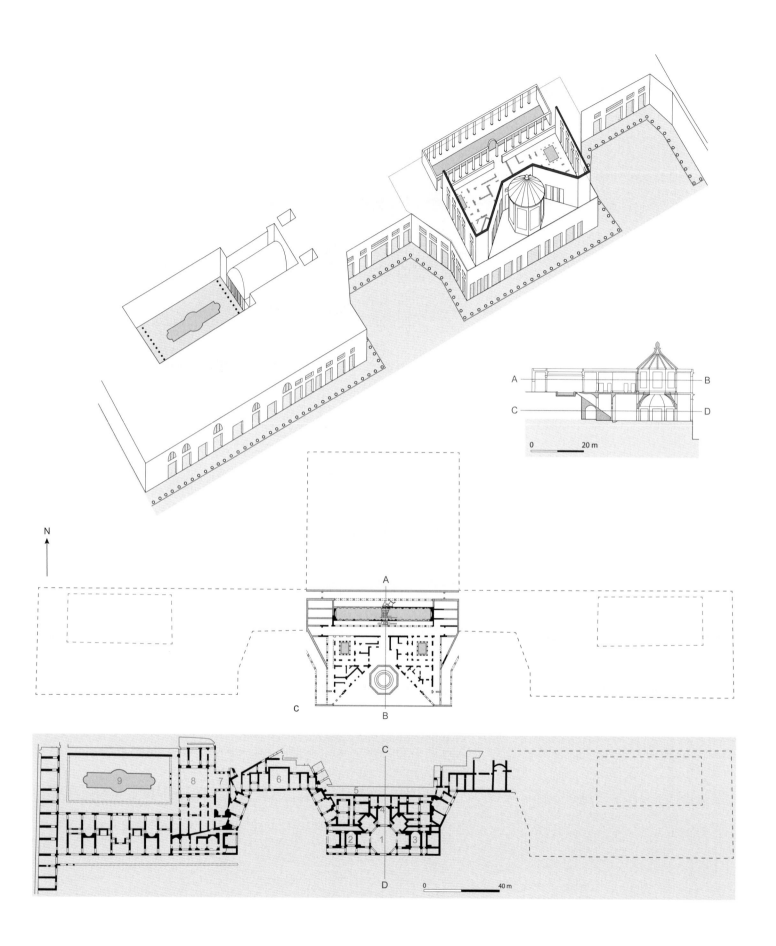

N

A B

C D

0   20 m

A

C   B

C

D

9   8   7   6   5   4   2   1   3

0   40 m

Fig. 173a (opposite top and middle)
Axonometry and section of the Esquiline building

Only the central section of the upper level has been explored archaeologically.

Fig. 173b (opposite below)
Floor plan of the Domus Aurea's Esquiline building

1 Octagonal Room
2 Hall of Achilles
3 Hall of Hector and Andromache
4 Nymphaeum
5 Service Corridor
6 Hall of the Golden Vault
7 Nymphaeum
8 Hall
9 Peristyle courtyard with central fountain

Some 150 rooms and corridors have been documented so far at the lower level, although new discoveries continue to be made – an additional room, the 'Hall of the Sphinxes', was recently revealed (behind Room 1). Most of the rooms were barrel-vaulted, with ceiling heights of 10 to 11 m. The shell of the Domus Aurea burnt out during a fire of AD 104. The entire building was subsequently buried under Trajan's new baths.

Fig. 174 (above right)
Photograph of the 'Octagonal Room' at the centre of the Esquiline building

The 'Octagonal Room' formed the core of the Esquiline wing's central pavilion (Fig. 173b, Room 1). To the north was the nymphaeum with its cascade fountain. The walls were originally faced in marble, with pairs of columns in front of the pilasters.

central mythological ceiling frescos, they are known as the 'Hall of Achilles on Skyros' and the 'Hall of Hector and Andromache' respectively (Fig. 173b, Rooms 2 and 3, and Figs 175–7).

The level above comprised a set of rooms with lavish *opus sectile* floors, smaller colonnaded fountain courts and a large rectangular pool, or *euripus*, towards the back. This marble-lined basin alone measured approximately 50 × 5 m.[55] Beyond it extended a large peristyle; traces of its southern colonnade are preserved over a length of 63 m. At this higher level, the building communicated with the parkland of the imperial gardens on the upper slope of the Esquiline, and this area provides the best fit for Tacitus' description of the *domus'* landscape setting, including further ornamental pools.[56]

The two side wings were visually separated from the central pavilion by open hexagonal courts that formed deep recesses in the façade. Sets of interconnected rooms ran along their front. In the central axis of the western hexagon was a stunning hall (now named 'Hall of the Golden Vault' (Fig. 173b, Room 6) after its ornate ceiling), flanked by subsidiary rooms of decreasing size. The same arrangement was followed along the court's other sides, creating clear hierarchies between the rooms.[57]

The west wing was laid around a large rectangular interior peristyle with a central fountain and may originally have supported an upper floor similar to the central pavilion (Fig. 173b, Room 9). It was dominated by a hall at its eastern end, with an elaborate nymphaeum behind that had a ceiling of artificial stalactites to emulate the appearance of a natural grotto and was interspersed with mosaic emblems. The central emblem depicted Ulysses with Polyphemus, a Homeric motif that became popular in imperial villas (Fig. 173b, Rooms 7 and 8).[58]

A series of rooms corresponded to this suite at the western end.[59] The southern range was divided along the middle into two beautifully articulated room sequences, opening respectively to the peristyle in the north and the main

Figs 175a and b

Fragments of a stucco panel from the Domus Aurea's 'Hall of Achilles' showing a pair of sphinxes among acanthus plants

AD 64–8
Esquiline, Rome, Italy
Plaster and paint
H. 16.5 cm, W. 39 cm; H. 21.7 cm, W. 51.5 cm
British Museum
1908,0417.5, 1908,0417.2

A pair of winged sphinxes among acanthus scrolls can be seen on this fragment (top), which would originally have sat above a floral border (bottom). The centres of the large open flowers on either side show the mythical figures of Leda and Zeus (in the form of a swan). The fragments are from the lower border of the ceiling vault (see Fig. 177). They contain traces of gold leaf and expensive pigments like cinnabar and copper-based green. According to Pliny the Elder's *Natural History*, costly 'florid' pigments like cinnabar were usually provided by the patron commissioning the work, whereas the cheaper ones were supplied by the painters and included in their fee.

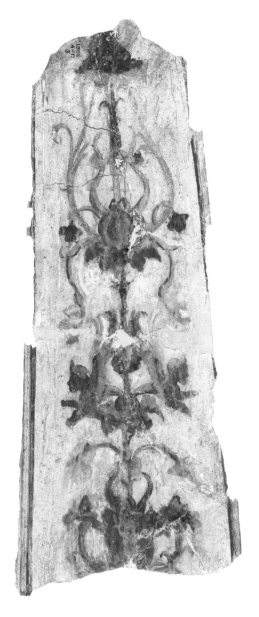

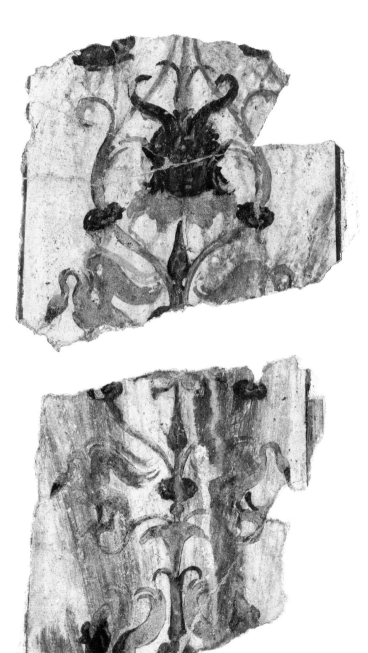

Figs 176a–d
**Fresco fragments from the
upper section of the apse in
the Hall of Achilles**

AD 64–8
Esquiline, Rome, Italy
Plaster and paint
H. 48 cm, W. 22 cm; H. 22 cm,
W. 22.3 cm; H. 18.6 cm, W. 22.7 cm;
H. 17 cm, W. 19.6 cm
British Museum
1908,0417.3; 1908,0417.12;
1908,0417.13; 1908,0417.14

façade in the south.[60] Towards the back, cut into the slope, were more irregularly shaped subsidiary rooms and long service corridors. The corridor behind the central block (Fig. 173b, Room 5) ran over a length of 70 m; originally it was lit through large windows in the northern section of its vault, admitting sunlight from the peristyle above (Fig. 178).

After completion, the Esquiline building must have been dazzling in its splendour. The amount of costly coloured marble used to line the walls and floors of the main apartments would have been unprecedented, a gleaming testimony to the Empire's far reach and Nero's command of its resources. The painted decoration of walls and ceilings, in the so-called Fourth Style, followed more familiar patterns, although it may in itself have sparked off some of these trends. They included elaborate stage architectures, masks and landscapes, but mostly mythological tableaux focused on Dionysiac and Homeric themes. The ceilings of the main halls had particularly rich stuccoed patterns with multilayered painted scenes and ornaments.[61] By contrast, some of the fragmentarily preserved ceiling decorations in the rooms adjacent to the central octagon give the impression of precious fabric canopies held in place by wooden struts and hoops.[62] This would have evoked luscious awnings and tented pavilions, familiar from the descriptions of the luxurious dining tents of

Fig. 177
Photograph of the 'Hall of Achilles' in the Domus Aurea, showing the original positioning of fragments now in the collection of the British Museum

The so-called 'Hall of Achilles' was one of the principal rooms of the Domus Aurea's Esquiline wing, located to the west of the Octagonal Room. The upper walls and ceiling vault were richly decorated in polychrome stucco. The central panel showed the Greek hero Achilles on the island of Skyros, one of the episodes leading up to the Trojan War. Below, the walls were lined in marble. This decoration was later removed for reuse elsewhere, leaving the bare brick exposed.

Fig. 178
The long service corridor along the back of the Esquiline building's central pavilion

The 'bridge' in the centre conducted water from a large basin on the upper level down to the nymphaeum. Large windows (seen here on the left) cut into the ceiling vault would originally have admitted light from the garden peristyle above.

Hellenistic kings that recalled the feasts of Homeric heroes and historical figures like Alexander the Great. Apparently, Nero possessed just such a tent, octagonal like the room and 'a huge structure which was a sight to be seen because of its beauty and costliness'.[63] Expensive portable wall hangings, curtains and soft furnishings would have been an important part of the room decorations throughout the building. Pliny mentions that the Domus Aurea contained many works by the artist Famulus, 'a painter in the florid style', and a great number of sculptures by famous Greek masters, although this need not necessarily refer to the Esquiline building alone.[64]

The variation in size and decorative detail between the rooms suggests clear hierarchies. The floors and walls of the main halls were clad in coloured marble *opus sectile*, with ceiling vaults of richly decorated stucco. These were flanked by smaller apartments, with walls lined up to two thirds of their height in marble and painted friezes and stuccoed ceiling vaults above. Ancillary rooms had painted walls with marble base mouldings, whereas the service rooms and corridors had walls and ceilings entirely of painted plaster, with simple black-and-white mosaic floors (Figs 179–81). The rooms, especially those along the building's façade, could therefore be assigned according to a finely graded social ranking of visitors, for example during banquets at which Nero might assemble

Fig. 179 (above)
Fresco fragment thought to belong to the Domus Aurea's service corridor
AD 64–8
Esquiline, Rome, Italy
Plaster and paint
H. 32 cm, W. 72 cm, D. 7.3 cm
British Museum
1908,0417.1

Service areas like the long corridor (see Fig. 173b, Room 5, p. 230) had simple fresco decoration, without extensive marble elements. The pigments used were also much less costly than those in the more important rooms. The walls were painted with elaborate stage architectures, interspersed with a wide variety of mythical creatures. This fragment shows two sea monsters flanking a mask above a plant motif.

Fig. 180 (above, right)
Fresco fragment attributed to the Domus Aurea's service corridor
AD 64–8
Esquiline, Rome, Italy
Plaster and paint
H. 30 cm, W. 18 cm
British Museum
1908,0417.8

A winged horse (Pegasus) emerges from an ornate acanthus scroll. This fragment probably belonged to the corridor's vaulted ceiling.

Figs 181a and b (below)
Fresco fragments attributed to the service corridor
AD 64–8
Esquiline, Rome, Italy
Plaster and paint
H. 16.1 cm, W. 26 cm; H. 24.8 cm, W. 35.3 cm
British Museum
1908,0417.10; 1908,0417.6

Fig. 182
**Altar dedicated to Sol and
Luna by the servant Eumolpus**
After AD 64
Rome, Italy
Marble
H. 59 cm, W. 30 cm, D. 30 cm
Museo Archeologico Nazionale
di Firenze
86025

This is a small altar dedicated
to the gods Sol and Luna by
Eumolpus, an enslaved chamberlain
in charge of furnishings at the
Golden House ('A SUPELLECTILE
DOMUS AURIAE' [sic]), and his
daughter Claudia Pallas. The
radiate bust of Sol echoes the
physiognomy and coiffure of Nero's
last portrait type and stresses the
close link between *princeps* and
god. High-ranking enslaved men of
the imperial household frequently
married freed- or even freeborn
women, and the name of Eumolpus'
daughter suggests that her mother
belonged to this category. The altar
was originally dedicated in a
sanctuary of the sun god in the
Transtiberim (Trastevere) district.

hundreds if not thousands of high-status guests.[65] The Domus Aurea's staff accordingly must have been vast. An altar dedicated by a palace chamberlain provides the only epigraphic testimony for the new palace's Neronian name, aside from the later literary sources (Fig. 182).

Despite the building's opulence and imposing layout, its construction involved astonishing pragmatism. The fabric incorporated remains of earlier residential and commercial edifices, dominated by a set of warehouses whose angled outer façade closely determined the shape of the western hexagonal court. In this way, Nero's engineers could utilise an existing terrace, from which the debris of old buildings had been cleared. Its supporting back wall partly consisted of the front of the former warehouse, while the storerooms behind were filled in. In order for construction to advance quickly, work gangs progressed simultaneously from different points and used large numbers of reclaimed bricks. This first construction phase included the octagonal hall complex, the central and corner rooms around the hexagonal court, and the corners of the west wing peristyle. Then the sections in between were completed.[66] The painted decoration similarly seems to have been divided between several workshops that proceeded in parallel. Three of these have so far been identified on stylistic grounds.[67] It appears that Nero expected rapid results from his architects and possibly did not envisage regular, year-round domestic use of the entire building.[68]

In spite of this, the rooms on the Esquiline building's lower level stand out through a very competent adoption of recent construction techniques and even more so through their innovative conception of spatial volumes. This made them highly influential for the further development of Roman palace and villa architecture.[69] The remarkable octagonal room and its satellites were particularly significant in this respect, and there have been many speculative attempts to identify it with the Domus Aurea's famous rotating dining hall, Suetonius' *coenatio rotunda*.[70]

Modern readings of the Domus Aurea have largely depended on the literary source record, which has come under critical scrutiny only more recently.[71] A number of scholars have stressed the influences of Eastern palace architecture on the Esquiline building, suggesting that in embracing the trappings of traditional Hellenistic royalty, Nero intended to redefine the principate along much more monarchical lines. At the most extreme, the octagonal hall was linked to the throne rooms of Parthian kings, one element of a wider appropriation of Eastern solar imagery.[72] A different approach examined the building's roots in a purely Roman villa tradition (although luxury villas in themselves were Greek-influenced in architectural and cultural terms) (Figs 183 and 184). The Domus Aurea thus became a vast tract of *rus in urbe*, or countryside transplanted right into the city, and a preserve of *otium*, the leisured pursuit of Greek culture. In this interpretation, the palace and its parklands served as an escape from the routine of government, a venue for Nero's artistic pursuits.[73] None of this seems particularly convincing.

The Esquiline building, but even more so the colonnaded squares on the Velia and in the valley, may indeed have recalled the vast terraced villas that could be found in the countryside and by the sea (Figs 185 and 186). In the capital, however, this kind of architecture had long taken on a different meaning. It was associated with amenities for the general population, first in the Campus Martius, and then the imperial *fora* in the old centre. These marble porticoes

Fig. 183 (top)
Architectural landscapes
AD 40–5
Pompeii, Italy
Plaster and paint
H. 28 cm, W. 78 cm, D. 9 cm
Museo Archeologico Nazionale
di Napoli
9406

Fig. 184 (bottom)
**Fragment of a fresco
decorated with buildings
and boats**
AD 1–37
Pompeii, Italy
Plaster and paint
H. 59 cm, W. 69 cm, D. 7 cm
Museo Archeologico Nazionale
di Napoli
9482

Fig. 185 (top)
Maritime landscape
AD 45–79
Pompeii, Italy
Plaster and paint
H. 28 cm, W. 39 cm, D. 7 cm
Museo Archeologico Nazionale
di Napoli
9463

Fig. 186 (bottom)
Maritime landscape
AD 45–79
Pompeii, Italy
Plaster and paint
H. 22 cm, W. 46 cm, D. 8 cm
Museo Archeologico Nazionale
di Napoli
9484

Frescos from Pompeii and other Vesuvian cities evoke the lavish architecture of coastal villas and resort towns around the Bay of Naples. These rich houses often sprawled over terraced landscapes, linked by extensive porticoes with large garden peristyles. From a distance, they could appear like small cities or sanctuaries, echoing Suetonius' description of the Domus Aurea.

Fig. 187

Fig. 187
Reconstruction of the centre of Rome, seen from the east, around AD 68 with the Domus Aurea and other Neronian buildings

In the right foreground is the Esquiline building (compare to Fig. 169b, p. 225), followed by the baths and Nero's new *stagnum*. To the left is the Temple of Claudius, with the nymphaeum façade visible just below its massive podium. On higher ground behind the *stagnum* is the colonnaded square (*vestibulum*) on the Velia, from which new porticoes lead along the Via Sacra to the Forum. The Palatine building is above it to the left, with the Circus Maximus and the River Tiber beyond.

This reconstruction captures the vast Domus Aurea evoked by the poet Martial and other highly critical authors. There is no evidence that the extensive parklands in the central foreground ever existed. Instead, there were probably further structures on the higher ground behind the Esquiline building. The colossus (seen inside the columned *vestibulum*) was only finished eight years after Nero's death.

provided pleasant, sheltered surroundings that offered the *plebs* respite from the city's overcrowded living quarters.[74] There is now a growing consensus that the Velia and most of the valley between the Esquiline and the Caelian must have been accessible to ordinary Romans throughout.[75] In fact, other than Martial's and Suetonius' words, there is no evidence that they were considered part of the Domus Aurea at all (Fig. 187).[76]

Nero's *stagnum* instead could have been intended for mass entertainments like the *stagna* of Agrippa in the Campus Martius and of Augustus in the Transtiberim district. Suetonius' brief remark that Augustus had already considered building an amphitheatre in this location, 'in the middle of the city', hints at long-standing plans to develop the area. The Great Fire may have provided Nero with the opportunity to take up these ideas.[77] Even if the Velia square was indeed intended to serve as the vestibule of Nero's new palace, as Suetonius' text might suggest, this is not as clear cut as it may seem.[78] By tradition, *vestibula* were areas outside the mansions of leading men, defined architecturally through the façade behind, but still part of the public streetscape. Nero's *vestibulum*, on the saddle between the Palatine and Esquiline Hills, therefore allowed it to serve both palace areas but also created a large public square in between.[79]

However, the Esquiline wing and many of the surrounding structures (for example, the colonnades along the Via Sacra) were clearly unfinished at the time of Nero's death, and there would have been little time for the *princeps* to make even momentary use of them in his final months.[80] It may have been this short life-span and undefined nature of the Neronian Domus Aurea that allowed the first generation of writers in the Flavian period such wide leeway in defining Nero's project in negative terms. The poet Martial, who came to Rome from Spain just after the Great Fire, was influential in promoting a particular notion of the Golden House. He enshrined the Domus Aurea in collective memory as the vast abode of a tyrant who deprived the people of what was rightfully theirs.[81] Nero's intentions may have been the exact opposite.

The colossus

At some point after AD 64 Nero commissioned a monumental bronze statue of the god Sol-Helius from the Greek artist Zenodorus. He was an experienced specialist who had spent ten years creating a bronze colossus of Mercury for the central sanctuary of the Arverni tribal community in Gaul.[82] Statues of this type required artistic vision, but even more so expert engineering skills and great technical proficiency in bronze casting. As a result, they were extremely costly and time-consuming to produce. The new monument, 120 ft tall according to Suetonius (about 35 m), was destined to stand in the new square that Nero's engineers built on the Velia, or possibly by its entrance, facing the Via Sacra.[83]

The iconography of the colossus defined it as an emphatically Roman version of Sol, with clear imperial overtones: the statue's right hand held a ship's rudder, which in turn rested on a globe, signifying rule over land and sea (Fig. 188). This may have suggested a specific identification of the statue as Sol Augusti, protector of *princeps* and empire. The monument's intended location on the Via Sacra marked the approximate halfway point of the *pompa circensis* procession that led from the Capitoline to the Circus Maximus, where Sol's main temple was located, while its proximity to the imperial palace stressed the link to the ruler.

Pliny the Elder claims that he saw a clay model of the statue in Zenodorus' workshop, and that it was destined to show Nero. He adds that the colossus was later dedicated to Sol, 'in condemnation of the crimes committed by this princeps' – implying that it was not executed as originally planned.[84] Suetonius merely asserts that the statue portrayed Nero, without any mention of Sol. This interpretation has come to dominate modern discussions of the colossus, even if other ancient writers are far less explicit.[85] It is clear from the sources that the colossus was unfinished at the time of Nero's death and only completed under Vespasian seven years later, in AD 75.[86] There are good reasons to doubt that it was ever meant to represent Nero in the first place.[87] Suetonius' insistence that some of Nero's coins showed the princeps as Apollo provides a good parallel for such a misinterpretation, wilful or not. A close personal link between Nero and Sol may have been suggested in many viewers' minds through public imagery and specific performances, not least Nero's own appearances as a charioteer, but these were usually allusive rather than explicit (Fig. 189).[88] Ceremonies that accompanied the 'Golden Day' of AD 66 or Nero's triumphant return from Greece in AD 67 or 68 may have reinforced this connection (see below, p. 246 and p. 266).[89]

Pliny mentions a second colossus that is rarely discussed. This was an immense painting on canvas, of the same dimensions as the bronze giant, but it perished, reportedly struck by lightning, soon after its completion. Perhaps it was created to gauge the effect of the statue's design and test its location. It was the closest anyone would have come to seeing the colossus in Nero's lifetime.[90] The sheer scale and artistry of Zenodorus' statue instantly turned it into one of the marvels of Rome when it was finally complete. Together with the enduring popularity of Sol's cult, this ensured that the statue Nero had commissioned survived into late antiquity.[91]

Luxury

Tacitus soberly opined that Celer and Severus merely 'frittered away the resources of a Caesar'. This was one of many expressions of indignant senatorial censure that criticised the Domus Aurea, and Nero's supposedly extravagant way of life more generally.[92] But it is clear from statements by the same writers that Nero's lifestyle was not unusual for the time, even if the princeps' wealth far exceeded that of any other individual (Figs 190 and 191).[93]

According to Suetonius, for example, Nero 'always travelled with at least a thousand carriages, the mules shod with silver and mule-drivers clothed in Canusian wool, and with a train of Mauretanian horsemen and couriers, decked out with bracelets and breastplates' (a passage that recalls Pliny's description of Poppaea's mule-trains, see p. 189).[94] However, referring to the wealthy in one of his letters, Seneca remarks with some rhetorical exaggeration that 'everyone now travels with Numidian [of north-west African origin] outriders preceding him, with a troop of slave-runners to clear the way [...]. Everyone now possesses mules that are laden with crystal and myrrhine cups carved by skilled artists of great renown.'[95] Myrrhine cups in particular became potent symbols of the excesses of the age (Fig. 192).

Fig. 188
Finger ring with an amethyst gem carved with a depiction of the colossus of Sol
After AD 64
Uncertain provenance
Amethyst set in metal
Diam. 1.1cm
Antikensammlung, Staatliche Museen zu Berlin
FG 2665

The amethyst set into this ring has been carved with an image of the bronze colossus of Sol. Large rays encircle the god's head. He leans on a column and holds a large rudder in his right hand. There is no evidence that the colossus was ever intended to represent Nero, as later tradition told. It was, in fact, only completed under Vespasian in AD 75.

Fig. 189
Obverse of a dupondius
AD 64
Minted in Rome, Italy
Copper alloy
Weight 14.5 g
British Museum
R.9989

Nero's later coin portraits
frequently showed the *princeps*
with a radiate crown, an attribute
originally associated with the
deified Augustus. It simultaneously
stood for a symbol of the sun and
an imperial honorific emblem,
which was now extended to the
living emperor.

Seneca, himself a target thanks to the extreme wealth he had accumulated, describes how prosperity enabled luxury to spread from men's personal appearance to furniture, their houses and dinner tables. Some of this has been read as veiled criticism of Nero and his palaces, but this need not be the case, particularly when compared to similar, clearly more generic passages in Pliny. Sprawling mansions that resembled country houses, walls glittering with imported marbles, a 'roof adorned with gold, so that it may match the brightness of the inlaid floors', had become commonplace status markers among the wealthy elite.[96]

Raging with old-fashioned disdain against extravagant imports, Pliny claims that 'at the very lowest computation, India, the Seres [China], and the Arabian Peninsula, withdraw from our Empire one hundred million sesterces every year – so dearly do we pay for our luxury and our women' (Fig. 193).[97] The *Natural History* is full of references to costly innovations fuelled by competitive excess, from marbles inlaid with artificial veins in contrasting colours to furniture with tortoiseshell inlays perversely painted to look like wood. All this led to an inflationary rise in prices for the most sought-after items.[98]

Excessive dining luxury, from expensive tableware to exotic foods, became another standard topic of moralising discourse, though not entirely without justification. Seneca claims to have seen 'embossed work in silver and gold equalling the wealth of a whole city' at a particularly elaborate entertainment, along with 'colours and tapestry devised to match objects which surpassed the value of gold or of silver – brought not only from beyond our own borders, but from beyond the borders of our enemies'.[99]

As customary expressions of senatorial status and prestige became more limited under the principate, such luxuries offered one of the few remaining alternatives for social distinction.[100] However, under these conditions any notion that leading men could continue to treat the *princeps* as their aristocratic peer could soon prove ruinously costly. Suetonius relates the enormous expense

Fig. 190
Portrait of Nero (Type IV)
AD 64–8
Rome, Italy
Marble
H. 43 cm, W. 32 cm, D. 32 cm
State Collection of Antiquities and
Glyptothek, Munich
321

Fig. 191
Cuirassed statue
AD 66–8
Roman theatre at Caere
(Cerveteri), Italy
Marble
H. 190 cm, W. 90 cm, D. 60 cm
Musei Vaticani, Vatican City
9948

While Nero may occasionally have
performed on stage, most Romans
would have seen statues like this
of the *princeps*, displayed as part
of dynastic Julio-Claudian portrait
galleries in theatres all over the
Empire. Ever since the reign of
Augustus, the symbolic presence
of the emperor in such venues
reinforced the notion of an ordered
and hierarchical Roman society.

incurred by Nero's friends for dinners he attended as their guest, one of whom was reported to have spent more than 4 million sesterces for a banquet.[101] The nobility's tradition of mutual visits and reciprocal gift exchange, an important element of maintaining the façade of the 'Restored Republic', thus came under impossible strain.[102] Lack of money to maintain this lifestyle and its associated prestige motivated a number of anti-Neronian conspirators.

The increasing importance of wealth and the conspicuous consumption of costly goods in maintaining and displaying social status opened the field to the newly rich, who could just purchase such items without regard to tradition and inheritance. The author Petronius (in all likelihood the suffect consul of AD 62, Titus Petronius Niger, who served as a high-ranking 'arbiter of taste' at Nero's court and had a privileged insight into these phenomena) made this the central theme of his satirical *Cena Trimalchionis*. It describes a hilarious banquet, hosted by the fictitious newly rich freedman Gaius Pompeius Trimalchio Maecenatianus, full of hollow social pretension conveyed through expensive status symbols.[103] It is not hard to detect behind Petronius' mocking and disdainful humour the fundamental threat that emanated from social climbers of Trimalchio's ilk. Much of the professed contempt for vulgar opulence expressed by Pliny and other authors came from the perception that it diminished the value of pedigree, service and tradition and replaced it with something that could simply be acquired for money. The *princeps*' pursuit of luxuries in this sense set entirely the wrong example. For the elite, education and philosophy therefore became an alternative status marker, as these required not only money, but also years of devotion and study in which freedmen, focused on their business

Fig. 192
The Barber Cup
AD 50–100
Ancient Cilicia, Turkey
Fluorite
H. 15 cm, W. 9.5 cm
British Museum
2003,1202.1
Purchased with contributions from
the British Museum Friends, Art
Fund (as NACF), Caryatid Fund
and Mr Frank A. Ladd

Myrrhine vessels, made from fluorspar imported mostly from Parthia (ancient Iran), were the ultimate status symbol in the Julio-Claudian period. Pliny claimed that Nero paid 1 million sesterces for a single cup, and that the consular Petronius purposefully broke a myrrhine basin worth 300,000 sesterces to deprive the *princeps* of it. The rarity and fine colouration of the material meant that it was highly prized. The resin that was used to coat the fluorspar during the manufacture of these cups was even thought to improve the flavour of wine – a senator is said to have gnawed the edge of his favourite vessel (Pliny, *Natural History*). This is one of only two complete myrrhine cups known to have survived from antiquity. The carved scroll around its mid-section conjures the convivial pleasures of a banquet.

interests, could or would not invest.[104] An alternative was service in the military, which remained a bastion of more conservative values.[105]

Less controversially, the Vesuvian cities provide plentiful evidence for the way fashions from the capital and the affluent resorts around the Bay of Naples were keenly adapted on a more modest domestic level, from the architecture of houses to the entertainments offered by their inhabitants (Fig. 194).[106] The use of silver tableware is testimony to the economic prosperity and more widely spread aspiration that became such defining hallmarks of the Julio-Claudian period (Figs 195, 196a and b).[107]

The Golden Day

The high point of Nero's reign, nicknamed the 'Golden Day', came in AD 66 with the arrival of a large Parthian royal delegation on a long-planned state visit to Rome. It was of a significance and splendour never before witnessed in the capital, and Suetonius judges that it should fairly be counted among Nero's public spectacles.[108]

The Parthians were led by Tiridates, whom Nero was to crown publicly as king of Armenia, as had been agreed during the peace negotiations that followed the battle of Rhandeia two years earlier (see p. 123). Tiridates travelled with his wife and sons, as well as the sons of his brothers Vologases and Pacorus, the Parthian great king and the ruler of Media Atropatene. They were joined by the sons of king Monobazus of Adiabene.[109] The members of the royal family were accompanied by a vast retinue of servants, along with three thousand Parthian horsemen and a Roman military escort led by Domitius Corbulo's son-in-law, Annius Vinicianus.[110]

From the border on the Euphrates River, the Parthian delegation travelled for nine months over land through the eastern and Balkan provinces.[111] Along their route, they were met by local provincial governors and passed through cities thronging with cheering crowds. All this had been planned well in advance; the considerable cost was borne by the hosts.[112]

Fig. 194
Wall painting showing birds and a *velarium* (awning) from which dried fruit, flowers and bread tumble to the ground
AD 50–79
House of M. Fabius Rufus,
Pompeii, Italy
Plaster and paint
H. 64 cm, W. 64 cm
Museo Archeologico Nazionale
di Napoli
9624

This fresco from a Pompeian dining room shows a suspended fabric drape or awning (*velarium*), from which flowers and various delicacies tumble down after it has been unfastened. Generous hosts could surprise and delight their dinner guests in this way – a more improvised version of the hidden ceiling compartments of grand mansions that served a similar purpose. Suetonius also recorded such devices for the ivory ceilings of Nero's Domus Aurea. The House of Marcus Fabius Rufus combined several buildings into the largest domestic dwelling discovered at Pompeii so far. Built on four levels over the old walls of the city, it was richly decorated with coloured marble floors and enjoyed fine views onto the sea.

Fig. 195 (top)
Moregine Treasure
50 BC–AD 79
Moregine (Pompeii), Italy
Silver
Dish (back, centre): diam. 29.2 cm;
spoon (front, centre): L. 14.6 cm
Parco Archeologico di Pompei
86757–86776

Figs 196a and b (bottom)
Cantharus (both sides)
40 BC
Moregine (Pompeii), Italy
Silver
H. 12.5 cm
Parco Archeologico di Pompei
86775

The 'Moregine Treasure' is a twenty-piece silver dining set. It includes items for holding, serving and receiving food, as well as vessels for mixing, pouring and drinking wine, and its combined weight is almost 4 kg. The two elaborate *canthari* (drinking cups), dating to the mid-first century BC, may have been highly prized antiques. The silver was discovered in 2000, just outside Pompeii in a building associated with the Sulpicii, a family of freedmen bankers from Puteoli, who seem to have used it as part of their business interests.

Fig. 197

**Honorific inscription of
Cassius Cerealis with erasure
of Nero's name**

AD 54–68
Forum, Puteoli (Pozzuoli), Italy
Marble
H. 58 cm, W. 119 cm, D. 13.8 cm
Museo Archeologico dei Campi
Flegrei nel Castello di Baia

This inscription from Puteoli
honours Lucius Cassius Cerealis.
After a list of Cerealis' offices,
including overseer of public works
and curator of the Aqua Augusta
aqueduct, it states that 'the entire
plebs acclaimed him when he held
games for Nero Claudius Caesar
Augustus in the amphitheatre'
(Nero's name was later erased).
Some scholars now believe that
Nero (not the Flavians, as
previously thought) initiated the
construction of Puteoli's new arena
to complement a much smaller
Augustan predecessor. With
capacity for 40,000 spectators, it
was the third largest amphitheatre
in Italy and would have formed a
spectacular venue for Tiridates'
visit in AD 66.

In Italy, Tiridates switched from horseback to a two-horse carriage sent by Nero as a further gesture of honour and respect. He was then conveyed south to Naples via the Adriatic coastal region of Picenum, bypassing Rome. This gave more time for final preparations in the still heavily fire-damaged city.[113] At Naples Nero finally met Tiridates in person. The protocol had been arranged in every detail: Tiridates knelt before Nero with crossed arms, called him his master and paid obeisance, but crucially he was allowed to keep his dagger.[114] Nero in turn put on a number of entertainments, the most spectacular being a gladiatorial show at nearby Puteoli, organised by his freedman Patrobius (Fig. 197).[115] The event lasted several days and was remembered because on one of the days all the performers without exception were Ethiopians, a demonstration of the Empire's powerful reach far beyond its borders.[116] According to Cassius Dio, Tiridates shot at wild beasts from his elevated seat and transfixed and killed two bulls with a single arrow.[117]

From Campania, Nero and Tiridates finally proceeded to Rome, where 'the whole city streamed out to welcome the *princeps* and see the king'.[118] On the day of the coronation, the streets had been decorated with lights and garlands, and dense crowds gathered everywhere, particularly in and around the Forum, where spectators packed the roofs for a better view. In the square, the people had been positioned in distinct groups to form a highly symbolic living tableau of ordered Roman society. The centre was occupied by civilians, 'arranged according to rank, clad in white and carrying laurel branches; everywhere else were the soldiers, arrayed in shining armour, their weapons and standards flashing like the lightning', as Dio says.[119]

At daybreak (the ceremony had been moved to ensure bright skies), Nero entered the Forum, dressed like a triumphal general. He was accompanied by the senators and Praetorian Guard, and proceeded to the *rostra*, where he sat on

a magistrate's chair, surrounded by military standards. Tiridates approached and knelt before Nero, who raised and kissed him. Both gave short prepared speeches; Tiridates' words were translated and proclaimed to the crowd by a high-ranking senator. Nero then crowned Tiridates by placing the diadem on his head, affirming that he had 'power to take away kingdoms and to bestow them'. However, here, too, the protocol fundamentally reflected Parthian status as an equal power: in both cultures, the kiss was a gesture among aristocratic peers, and Tiridates had arrived wearing his *tiara*, a traditional Parthian headdress, rather than bare-headed.

There followed a special celebration in the Theatre of Pompeius, where Tiridates again paid obeisance in a repeat of the earlier ceremony, before taking his seat at the emperor's right side. The entire theatre had been gilded for the day and all the items brought in were decorated with gold (Fig. 198).[120] The awnings above were purple, and in the centre was an 'embroidered figure of Nero driving a chariot, with golden stars gleaming all about him'.[121] A splendid state banquet concluded the ceremonies. Nero presented Tiridates with numerous gifts, according to Dio worth a staggering 200 million sesterces. He furthermore granted Tiridates permission to rebuild the Armenian capital of Artaxata, destroyed at the beginning of the Armenian war in AD 58, and provided the king with skilled craftspeople for the purpose.[122]

In celebration of Tiridates' investiture, Nero accepted an imperial acclamation and dedicated a laurel wreath in the Capitol. As a sign that universal peace had been restored, he ordered the closure of the doors of the Temple of Janus (see p. 30). This was an act of great symbolism, a direct reference to Divus Augustus, which was propagated throughout the Empire with special coin issues (Fig. 199). Nero also added the title 'imperator' to his personal names: from now on, he was Imperator Nero Claudius Caesar Augustus Germanicus.

For Nero, the ceremonies enacted in front of mass audiences in Campania and Rome were a staggering success that greatly heightened his standing with the Roman people, but also the Greek-speaking provinces. Since this had been the main objective of the Armenian war in the first place, it vindicated his change of policy after Rhandeia, and put relations with Parthia on a much sounder footing (see p. 123).

The 'Golden Day' thus took its place alongside the 'Golden House' and the rearising post-fire city as another expression of a new Neronian golden age that, long foretold, now finally seemed to begin in earnest. Informal images attest the emperor's continuing popularity among broad swathes of the population in those years (Fig. 200).[123]

Greece and the East

With the crisis in Armenia officially settled and hostilities with the Parthians brought to an end, Nero could finally embark on his long-postponed tour of the East. Over the previous years, various domestic threats had repeatedly prevented his departure, and even now he had to deal with a further conspiracy before his final embarkation (see pp. 259–63). Unrest in Judaea flared up in the middle of AD 66, but it was hoped at first that the local governor could control the situation.

Fig. 198
Stele of Alcimus
AD 54–68
Necropolis Santa Rosa, Vatican City
Limestone
H. 90 cm, W. 50 cm, D. 17 cm
Musei Vaticani
52426

This gravestone commemorates 'Alcimus, servant of Nero Caesar Augustus'. Alcimus was buried in a cemetery along the Via Triumphalis, close to Nero's Circus and gardens. Other tomb monuments for members of Nero's household were found nearby. The relief depicts him in a short tunic with the tools of his trade as 'custodian of the stage of the Theatre of Pompeius'. It is not quite clear what this entailed, but perhaps he was in charge of set works. The entire theatre had been gilded in AD 66 for Nero's coronation of the Parthian prince Tiridates as king of Armenia.

Fig. 199
Sestertius
AD 66
Minted in Lugdunum (Lyon), Gaul
(modern France)
Copper alloy
Weight 27.1 g
British Museum
1847,0309.32

Nero celebrated a new era of
universal peace in a series of coins
that showed the Temple of Janus
with its doors closed and
garlanded. The doors of the
temple had not been closed
since the reign of Augustus.

Fig. 200
**Copy of a graffito found
on the Palatine**
AD 1st century

This image, from a tavern or
common room on the Palatine
covered in graffiti, was probably
intended to depict Nero. Together
with other graffiti and painted
inscriptions from places like
Pompeii, it gives a sense of how
the *princeps* was perceived and
memorialised by the people.

The ultimate objective of Nero's Eastern expedition was a major military campaign, led by the *princeps* in person. Preparations had been made for many years, including extensive troop movements to the East and the levy of a new legion (see p. 116).[124] To begin with, however, there was a goodwill tour of the Greek-speaking provinces, starting with the Greek heartland of Achaea.[125] Tacitus' account for this period is lost. Only Suetonius and Dio, always more blunt and selective in their reporting, remain as principal sources.[126] By the middle of AD 66, Nero's relationship with the senate had broken down irretrievably, and this clearly heavily clouded their respective accounts. Dio's opening statement on this journey sets the tone:

> [Nero] crossed over into Greece, not as Flamininus or Mummius [famous Roman conquerors] or his ancestors Agrippa and Augustus had done, but for the purpose of driving chariots, playing the lyre, making proclamations, and acting in tragedies. Rome, it seems, was not enough for him […], but he desired a foreign tour, in order to become, as he said, victor in the [festival] circuit.[127]

There is no doubt that Nero had planned to take part in the six festivals that formed the *periodos* of Greek athletic and musical contests in the first century AD (the dates of several had to be brought forward so they would all conveniently fall within a single year).[128] Yet his reasons for doing so may have been far more complex than Dio suggests. Nero's presence at these gatherings ensured that he would be seen by tens of thousands from all over the Greek world. This included a broad spectrum of Greek elites, perhaps also allies and friendly rulers from neighbouring states, as he was the first reigning emperor since Augustus to travel to the region in person. The wider symbolism and diplomatic import of the visit were therefore obvious. The Greek city of Alexandria in Egypt, where preparations for Nero's visit had long been underway, issued in advance a series of coins that celebrated Nero's attendance at the six *periodos* festivals, a clear sign that it was considered highly significant and expected to win him sympathies.[129]

Nero's tour was also the first time a *princeps* had left Rome since Claudius' short expedition to Britain twenty-three years earlier (see p. 98). The entire enterprise was a calculated risk; as a precaution, Nero left two of his trusted freedmen, Helius and Polyclitus, in charge of his affairs in Italy. He travelled with a large contingent of Praetorians, led by Ofonius Tigellinus, presumably alongside his Germanic bodyguard, units that undoubtedly would have joined the campaign. There were also his *Augustiani*, at this stage probably a particularly loyal paramilitary force rather than merely a claque (Dio calls them 'soldiers'). In addition, Nero was accompanied by his new wife Statilia Messalina, and various official companions or *comites* that included the loyal general Vespasian and the consular Cluvius Rufus. The presence of the imperial secretariat ensured the full functioning of court and administration; throughout his stay, Nero made important appointments and received embassies.[130] In many ways, his visit foreshadowed the extensive journeys of second-century emperors like Hadrian.

Nero's main base was Corinth, the provincial capital of Achaea. Major construction seems to have taken place there in advance, in preparation for the city becoming the de facto capital of the entire Empire for more than a year.[131] Nero also embarked on an immense engineering project nearby: a canal through the isthmus that was designed to facilitate maritime traffic. The opening ceremony reflected the magnitude of the enterprise: according to Suetonius, Nero 'called together the Praetorians and urged them to begin the work, then at a signal given on a trumpet he was first to break ground with a pickaxe and to carry off a basketful of earth upon his shoulders' (Fig. 201).[132] Six thousand Jewish prisoners, sent by Vespasian (who had in the meantime been given command of the escalating war in Judaea), were put to work afterwards.[133] At Olympia, too, the foremost sanctuary of the Greek world, there is evidence for heavy Neronian investment into a new water supply and other buildings that could accommodate high-ranking visitors.[134]

The propagandistic high point of the visit came at the Isthmian Games, when Nero declared in front of the assembled crowds that he would restore Greece's ancient freedom. In practice, this encompassed an exemption from tribute, which beyond its symbolism was perhaps intended to stimulate the local economy that had been in long decline.[135] Expectations of the emperor were

Fig. 201
Straight pickaxe head (*dolabra*)
AD 1–100
Iron
L. 31.5 cm, W. 5 cm, D. 6 cm
British Museum
1975,1107.4

Nero's planned canal through the isthmus at Corinth (the narrow stretch of land near the city that connected the Peloponnese to the rest of mainland Greece) took up an idea contemplated by Caligula and Caesar before him. Work progressed considerably, but it was brought to a halt after Nero's death (the modern Corinth canal was only completed in 1893). Iron pickaxes of this type were used by the military and civilians throughout the Empire.

NERO

Fig. 202
Fresco of Apollo or possibly a Muse, previously identified as Nero, with a cithara (lyre)
AD 50–79
Moregine (Pompeii), Italy
Plaster and paint
Parco Archeologico di Pompei

great. In Athens the famous Theatre of Dionysus had been furnished with a new stage, and an inscription honouring Nero had been added to the Parthenon in large bronze letters, but Nero left Greece before he could visit.

Suetonius and Dio focus almost exclusively on Nero's keen desire to emerge as *periodonikes* ('winner of circuit') and go into great detail about his performance activities, with fairly obvious elements of distortion and bias. In fact, most of the information about his repertoire, his relationship with competitors and judges, and his other stage habits (see p. 170) relates to this trip. Yet it is not difficult to see in Nero's actions a successful attempt to engage with his Greek subjects through a cultural language that resonated in the East, rather than the disgraceful eccentricity presented by the sources. The renowned Greek citharodes Terpnus, Diodorus and Pammenes, with whom Nero appeared in various contests (favourites of the crowds in Italy just as much as in the Greek world), were part of his carefully selected entourage (Fig. 202). At Olympia he raced a ten-horse chariot team, a demonstration of extreme skill and bravery in the tradition of Hellenistic kings.[136]

Many members of the senate must have come to Greece as well. Dio, short on detail, states that Nero kept them at a distance and treated them with contempt. There followed purges among leading military men, all senior senators, that must have caused widespread alarm in Rome and the provinces. Meanwhile, ever more insistent reports arrived from Helius, urging Nero to return to the capital. With great reluctance the *princeps* relented, making his way back to Italy in late AD 67 or early AD 68.[137]

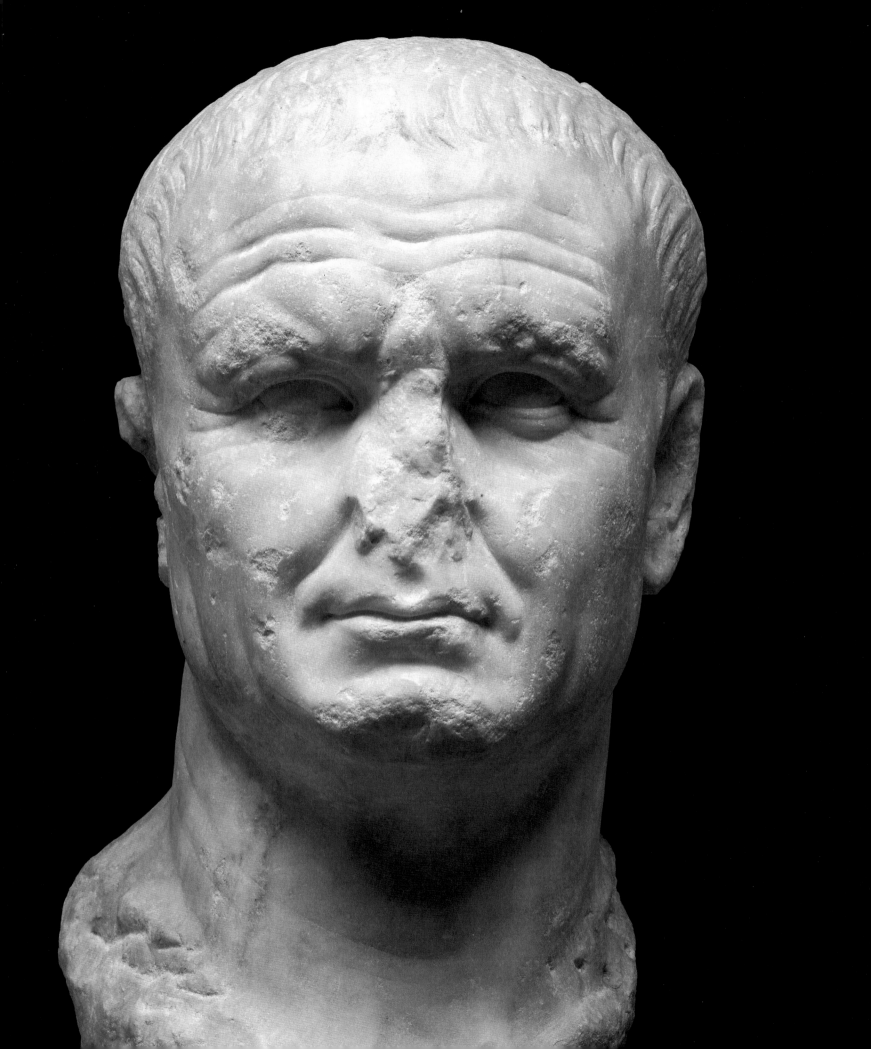

VIII

CRISIS
AND DEATH

Senatorial factions and family alliances

Despite the assurances of a new beginning at the outset of Nero's reign, there were many among the senatorial elite who had actively opposed Caligula and Claudius and continued to command great influence and powerful family networks. Tacitus is very sparing in the information he divulges about these men, their political alliances and private deliberations, as it would have distracted from – even contradicted – his chosen theme of justified senatorial resistance to tyrannical rule. However, it has long been recognised that there was a history of opposition among some important families, and that this opposition resulted from rival claims to supreme power rather than an adherence to the old ideals of Republican government.[1]

To Nero, this posed a constant and dangerous challenge. Many of his early appointments and policies seem to have been designed to conciliate these factions, echoing similar (but ultimately futile) efforts by Claudius decades earlier (see p. 55). Undoubtedly, the Silani formed one of the most dominant of these family clans. They espoused conservative policies in line with the most authoritarian leaders of the old Republic and had sponsored much of the legislation relating to the rights of the enslaved population and freedmen, and various performers, that caused such controversy in the early part of Nero's principate. The prominent, even intimidating, role Gaius Cassius Longinus was allowed to play in the senate, and the supreme command awarded to Domitius Corbulo in the East, may have been an effort, in the absence of any alternative, to appease this faction. Nero's popularity with the *pleb*s and his early successes, particularly in the Armenian war (see p. 94), made his position relatively secure. This changed after the enforced death of Agrippina, and even more so with the severe setbacks in Britain and the East between AD 60 and 62. Nero's lack of an heir also began to make him look vulnerable. The question remains whether senatorial opposition to Nero was indeed a reaction to his actions, as the sources suggest, or, conversely, if some of Nero's behaviour (including elements of his later performance practices) reflected his increasing alienation from a disloyal senate.

There may have been attempts to move against Nero long before the crisis years of the early 60s. In the febrile atmosphere after the end of Claudius' reign, rumours of conspiracies swirled up regularly, focusing on prominent nobles who might serve as figureheads of regime change.[2] Two names, mentioned several times already, appear regularly in the sources: Faustus Cornelius Sulla Felix (see p. 178) and Rubellius Plautus.

Faustus Sulla, a patrician descended through his father from the famous first-century BC Roman leader Lucius Cornelius Sulla, had married Claudius' elder daughter Claudia Antonia in AD 47.[3] Nero's senior by about a decade and a half, Faustus Sulla continued to enjoy Claudius' favour even after Nero's adoption. He served as *consul ordinarius* for all of AD 52, a rare honour.[4] Yet in AD 55, he was accused of conspiring against Nero together with Claudius' former freedman secretary Pallas and the Praetorian Guard commander Sextus Afranius Burrus. The timing, shortly after the sudden death of Britannicus, indicates that there was at least an outside perception of tensions at court, something that undermined Nero's position.[5] Tacitus next reports an incident in AD 58, dismissed as 'juvenile frolics' but perhaps a genuine attempt on Nero's life, when his attendants were set upon by anonymous attackers. An imperial freedman named Graptus blamed

Sulla, against whom Nero 'harboured deep suspicions', for being behind the attack.[6] Tacitus' arguments for Sulla's innocence seem decidedly peculiar. He claims that Sulla's nature, 'most despicable and incapable of any daring', made him shrink back from committing any crime; earlier he mentions that Nero misinterpreted Sulla's 'slothful character' as hiding the opposite qualities of cunning and dissimulation. It seems mysterious that Claudius should have chosen a man with such qualities as his son-in-law, and odder still that Tacitus describes several other potential conspirators in almost identical terms. As a precaution, Nero relegated Sulla to Massilia in southern Gaul.

Also in AD 55, Rubellius Plautus (Tiberius' grandson) was first caught up in reports of a conspiracy, this time involving Agrippina and quickly dismissed (see p. 178).[7] In AD 58, however, there were further rumours about Plautus, so serious that Nero felt compelled to remove him from Rome by advising him to retire to his family estates in the province of Asia. Allegedly a comet had hinted at a change of ruler and the people had considered Plautus the likely successor. Yet this interpretation was by no means the prevailing one at the time (Seneca gives a very different reading of the comet) and feels like a story embellished in hindsight; the turbulent events of the year, including the unrest in Puteoli (see p. 132), seem a much more likely explanation for mooted plots.[8] Nero's reaction appears measured, given the circumstances.[9]

The purges of AD 62

Four years later, there was a serious crisis. The source narratives link this to the waning influence of Nero's senior advisors who had hitherto kept his baser instincts in check. Burrus' death and Seneca's withdrawal in AD 62 brought the rise of Ofonius Tigellinus as Nero's new Guard prefect and the beginning of Nero's relationship with Poppaea Sabina. Tigellinus accused Faustus Sulla and Rubellius Plautus of harbouring aspirations for power and pointed out the danger of their proximity to the legions stationed in Germany and in the East.[10] Plautus in particular was suspected of secret contacts with Corbulo, and rumours to this effect circulated widely. This time, Nero did not hesitate. Men were sent to execute Sulla in Massilia and Plautus in Asia.[11] He now also divorced Claudia Octavia. The aftermath of the Boudica disaster in Britain, the ongoing impeachment trials and other tensions in Rome provide a far more likely context for senatorial discontent and the emergence of potential challengers than the sources admit, with their purposefully distracting focus on Nero's personal life.

The year AD 62 also saw the first *maiestas* trials of Nero's reign (see pp. 137–9), a significant change for a *princeps* who had so far shown a remarkable tolerance even for public taunts and criticism.

The great conspiracy and its lead-up

A much more extensive plot against Nero – its reality now wholly undisputed – unfolded in April AD 65. It came to be known as *coniuratio Pisoniana*, or the Pisonian conspiracy, after its main figurehead, the former consul Gaius Calpurnius Piso.[12] There seems to have been a complex network of parallel schemes, loosely connected because some of the main conspirators knew each other and eventually vaguely coordinated their plans, even if they had different motives and aims.[13] It was a situation with striking similarities to the AD 41 conspiracy against Caligula (see p. 59). The history of Piso's doomed enterprise was mostly written by authors sympathetic to the conspirators (in some cases their friends or relatives). Accordingly, they describe the main protagonists and their actions in an overwhelmingly positive, even heroic light. Many of the men involved professed to be followers of Stoicism, and are therefore sometimes referred to as 'Stoic opposition' – united in a noble attempt to rid the Empire of an unworthy ruler, by now notorious for his shocking transgressions. But there is little reason to assume that their supposed philosophical creed (in many cases probably no more than a distinguishing marker of upper-class education) influenced their actions.[14]

From the outset, this was an elite scheme, with narrow appeal even among the nobility, and no discernible popular support base or plan to secure a broader following. Tacitus ascribes its beginnings to AD 62, which saw the *maiestas* trials and the executions of Sulla and Rubellius Plautus, as well as Nero's alienation from Seneca. A man by the name of Romanus had accused Seneca at the time of being involved in a conspiracy, but the charges were dismissed. Romanus also implicated Piso, who was sufficiently alarmed to advance his plot.[15] It was claimed by some that the Great Fire of Rome and construction of the Domus Aurea spurred the conspirators into action, but these events long predated both so that assertion can surely be dismissed.

The core group was made up of senators (including several former consuls and possibly one of that year's serving consuls), supported by a substantial number of knights. Much more serious was the spread of the conspiracy among the Praetorian Guard, where it involved many of its most senior officers, led by the joint commander, Faenius Rufus. With him were at least three of the Guard's tribunes, as well as some centurions.[16] Tacitus suggests that the conspiracy, once conceived, instantly gathered numerous supporters. Yet the beginnings may have been slow, starting with guarded, disparaging remarks about Nero at banquets and other social meetings in private houses, in a manner similar to the libellous verses shared at a dinner in AD 62 that had led to *maiestas* charges.[17] Tacitus no doubt imagined something comparable, for he writes that the inner core began to reach out gradually by 'spreading remarks, among themselves or their friends, about the *princeps*' crimes, the approaching end of the Empire, and the need for choosing someone to stop things from falling apart'.[18] The plotters considered various schemes, including an assassination at Piso's villa at Baiae, which Nero frequently visited as a guest, and where he trustingly went without his bodyguard. Nothing was put into motion, and only the involvement of the Praetorian officers eventually gave real impetus. The final plan was to kill Nero in the Circus Maximus, during the April *ludi Cereales*. The *princeps* had been aware that a conspiracy was in the making, but none of the names of the plotters were known.[19] This changed when the freedman of one of the conspirators alerted Nero through his secretary Epaphroditus, and decisive action was taken immediately. The conspirators were rounded up; most revealed more names under torture. There was a heavy military presence in Rome and the nearby towns and loyal troops mixed with Nero's trusted Germanic bodyguards. A great many plotters were executed or forced to commit suicide (including Seneca, who

Fig. 203
Aureus
AD 65–6
Minted in Rome, Italy
Gold
Weight 7.4 g
British Museum
1964,1203.96
Bequeathed by Sir Allen
George Clark

Nero's salvation from the Pisonian conspiracy was celebrated throughout the Empire. Among the honours decreed by the senate was a new temple to the goddess Salus ('Salvation'). Her image was circulated through a new coin issue that depicted her seated on a throne, an offering bowl in her right hand. Other issues showed Iupiter Custos, 'Jupiter the Guardian'. Nero dedicated one of the conspirators' daggers in Jupiter's temple on the Capitoline.

had again been implicated); others were relegated.[20] Piso had been an unlikely head of the conspiracy.[21] Tacitus speculates that he had been afraid he would be eclipsed by Lucius Silanus, a prominent noble of the famous family, when it came to choosing the next *princeps*.[22] Piso allegedly enlisted Claudius' surviving daughter Antonia (the late Faustus Sulla's widow) to provide the conspirators with dynastic legitimacy. She was to stand by him in the Circus and then accompany him to the Praetorian camp. Nero was later said to have asked her to become his wife (presumably to prevent her from becoming involved with another potential conspirator), but had her executed when she refused.[23]

The senate decreed thanksgivings and public sacrifices. Special honours were devoted to the god Sol, who had an old temple in the Circus and was given credit for revealing the conspiracy through divine intervention, and additional horse races were added to the *ludi Cereales*. A new temple was erected to the goddess Salus ('Salvation'), whose image was widely circulated on coins, and the name of the month of April was changed to Neroneus (Fig. 203). Public and private monuments to celebrate Nero's salvation were erected throughout the Empire (Figs 204a and b, 205).[24] Nero's devotion to Sol, and his subsequent public racing in the Circus Maximus, must be related to these events, as was presumably his commissioning of the bronze colossus (see p. 241). He provided a donative of 2,000 sesterces to the soldiers. The men who had led the suppression of the conspiracy were given triumphal insignia, an honour normally reserved for military victories over external enemies (Fig. 206).[25]

Prosecutions of men involved with the great conspiracy continued into the following year. Among the last to be executed were the prominent senators Barea Soranus (accused of having plotted with Rubellius Plautus while he served as proconsul of Asia in AD 61/2) and Thrasea Paetus, who had defied Nero publicly for many years in the senate.[26]

The long aftermath of the Pisonian conspiracy involved a second serious plot, the *coniuratio Viniciana* ('conspiracy of Vinicius'). Suetonius, the only extant source, provides almost no detail beyond its name: it followed Piso's failed endeavour and was 'hatched by Vinicius at Beneventum and detected there'.[27]

Fig. 204a
**Inscription from the base of
the Mainz Jupiter column**
Late 1st century AD
Mainz, Germany
Marble
H. 914 cm (column only)
Landesmuseum, Mainz
Inv. Nr. S 137

The inscription reads: 'I(OVI)
O(PTIMO) M(AXIMO) PRO
[SA]L(UTE) [NERONIS] CLAU[D]I
CAESARIS AU[G](USTI)
IMP(ERATORIS) CANABA[RII]
PUBLICE P(UBLIO) SULPICIO
SCRIBONIO PROCULO
LEG(ATI) AUG(USTI) P[R](O)
[P](RAETORE) CURA ET
IMPENSA Q(UINTI) IULI PRISCI
ET Q(UINTI) IULI AUCTI' –
'Dedicated to Iupiter Optimus
Maximus for the salvation of
Imperator Nero Caesar Claudius
Augustus, the inhabitants of the
cannabae by public decree,
under the governorship of
Publius Sulpicius Scribonius
Proculus. Executed and paid for
by Quintus Iulius Priscus and
Quintus Iulius Auctus.'

The inhabitants of the civilian
settlement (*cannabae*) outside
the large legionary fortress of
Mogontiacum (Mainz) in Upper
Germany dedicated a column in
gratitude for Nero's salvation. It
was crowned by a gilded bronze
statue of the god Jupiter, which
would have added another 2 m in
height, and decorated with images
of twenty-eight different deities.
The governor Publius Scribonius
Proculus mentioned in the
inscription was purged in AD 67.
After Nero's death, his own names
and titles were erased from
monuments such as this.

Fig. 204b
**Reconstruction of the
complete Jupiter column
in Mainz, Germany**

Fig. 205
Three mirror cases
AD 64–8
Coddenham, England (open);
near Paris, France
Copper alloy (open); bronze
Diam. 5.1 cm (open); Diam. 3.1 cm
British Museum
1838,0331.1 (open), 1850,0517.2,
1850,0517
Donated by Sir William Middleton
(1838,0331.1)

Small mirrors that incorporated
coins with Nero's portraits allowed
people to show their loyalty to the
princeps. They may also have been
distributed as gifts.

Fig. 206
Cast of a tomb inscription to Tiberius Claudius Epaphroditus
AD 69–96 (original)
Rome, Italy
Plaster
H. 80 cm, L. 278 cm, D. 18 cm
Terme di Diocleziano, Museo
Nazionale Romano, Rome
ILS 9505

Inscribed in Latin: [A]UG(USTI)
L(IBERTO) EPAPHRODIT[O] […]
[APPARITORI CAE]SARUM
VIATORI TRIBUNIC[IO] […]
[HASTIS P]URIS CORONIS
AUREIS DONA[TO], 'to the
freedman of the Emperor,
Epaphroditus, […] clerk of the
Caesars, tribunician messenger
[…] rewarded with honorific spears
and golden crowns'.

Tiberius Claudius Epaphroditus,
one of Nero's trusted freedmen,
served in the imperial administration
as a *libellis* or secretary in charge
of petitions. In AD 65, he helped to
uncover the Pisonian conspiracy
and was richly rewarded for his
service. This tomb inscription
proudly mentions some of his
offices and the unusual military
honours he received. Epaphroditus
was also present at Nero's death.

The complete inscription, unusual
with its large-scale lettering, would
have been some 5 metres long,
hinting at the tomb's monumental
size. Epaphroditus' great wealth and
influence contrasted with his social
position as a freedman. His tomb
was located not far from that of the
noble Licinii Crassi family, on the
Esquiline in Rome.

The main perpetrator was almost certainly Annius Vinicianus, Corbulo's son-in-law who had escorted Tiridates and his retinue to Italy. The context and exact chronology are uncertain, but most scholars assume that Vinicianus' attempt followed Tiridates' coronation in AD 66.[28] Beneventum was located on the Via Appia, which connected Rome to Brindisum (modern Brindisi), so events may have unfolded during Tiridates' return journey (he crossed the Adriatic at Brindisum). Whether Nero was present is unknown; if so, perhaps the conspiracy was an attempt to assassinate him there. Vinicianus disappears from the record thereafter and was in all likelihood executed.

Nothing is noted about Vinicianus' motives, but Nero's imminent departure on his eastern expedition, the banishment of the prominent senatorial leader Cassius Longinus and the executions of Paetus and Soranus may have spurred him into action. Soranus' daughter Servilia, who also committed suicide, was his sister-in-law, wife of his brother Annius Pollio.[29] Vinicianus and Pollio came from a family that had been involved in previous conspiracies.[30] Nero had shown Vinicianus particular favour in allowing him to serve as commander of a legion under Corbulo at an unusually young age. The betrayal at Beneventum must have embittered him greatly. There were again public sacrifices for his salvation, but with the conspiracies of AD 65 and 66 Nero's relationship with the senate at large was deeply affected, as certain gestures made very clear. Suetonius states that 'neither on beginning a journey nor on returning did [Nero] kiss any member [of the senate] or even return his greeting', a stark contrast to the scrupulous politeness and respect that had characterised his relationship with the senate for most of his reign. He further claims that Nero now 'threw out unmistakable hints that he would not spare even those of the senate who survived, but would one day blot out the whole order from the State' and that he would 'hand over the rule of the provinces and the command of the armies to the Roman knights and to his freedmen'. Whether truthful or not, it seems a reasonable summary of senatorial fears towards the end of Nero's reign, heightened by his actions in Greece where Nero withheld the traditional symbolic and formal expressions of *civilitas* that determined the relationship between emperor and senate under the principate. At the opening ceremony of the isthmus project (see p. 252), Nero's prayer, 'which he uttered in a loud voice before a great crowd, was that it might turn out well for himself and the people of Rome, without any mention of the senate'.[31] Far more consequential were his oustings among the military leadership. The Scribonii brothers, Publius Sulpicius Scribonius Proculus and Publius Sulpicius Scribonius Rufus, governors of Upper and Lower Germany respectively, were summoned for consultations and driven to suicide. The fact that two members of the same family had been allowed to hold office in two adjoining, key military provinces over such a long period was a public sign of Nero's trust and respect. That they were now caught up in the purges demonstrates the *princeps*' dramatic shift in attitude. The same fate finally befell Corbulo. After years of rumours that linked him to various plots (justly or not, though it is highly likely that he was at least approached by various conspirators), the failed conspiracy by his son-in-law Vinicianus, together with his inability to control the worsening situation in Judaea, made his position untenable. Nero summoned him to Corinth with expressions of great respect, but as soon as Corbulo landed, he was forced to take his own life.[32]

Military rebellion

Helius, the freedman Nero had instructed to monitor the situation in Italy, finally came to Greece in person to urge the *princeps*' return; clearly, he had picked up signs of a further plot.[33] Nero arrived back on Italian soil in late AD 67 or early AD 68, at first making his way to Naples where he remained for several months. It was here that news reached him in March AD 68 of a revolt by Gaius Julius Vindex, the governor of Gallia Lugdunensis (allegedly on the anniversary of Agrippina's death).

The sources describe Nero's reaction, and his general behaviour over the following weeks, as largely aloof, a failure to engage with reality in a fatal continuation of the artistic obsessions that had dominated his stay in Greece (see p. 251). He reputedly received the report on Vindex while watching athletic contests at Naples, and did not send instructions to the senate for a full eight days thereafter. However, Nero's actions and delay in returning to Rome may in part have been prompted by the advantages offered by Campania, in particular the proximity of the fleet at nearby Misenum and Puteoli's extensive port facilities. He now hastily raised a new legion from the loyal non-citizen sailors of the fleet (Fig. 207).[34]

The motives for Vindex' rebellion are not quite clear; the Gallic provinces had been heavily taxed, leading to a mood of discontent that Vindex shared or thought he could exploit for his own purposes. He now sought to organise a wide uprising of tribes. Cassius Dio describes him as a man with 'a passionate love of freedom and a vast ambition'.[35] He was descended from south-western Gaulish royalty in Aquitania and had inherited the status of a Roman senator from his father. Vindex' provincial roots ruled him out as a contender for the throne; he therefore wrote to his fellow governors to incite rebellion and seek a member of the nobility to replace Nero. He found him in Servius Sulpicius Galba, governor of Hispania Tarraconensis.[36]

Nero's initial reaction was calm, not without justification. Several governors had dutifully forwarded Vindex' letters, providing intelligence; Vindex commanded no Roman troops, only Gaulish tribesmen. The provincial capital Lugdunum, always loyal to Nero, remained faithful and was besieged by the rebels. Vindex eventually had to lift his siege and move north, only to encounter Roman troops led against him by the new governor of Upper Germany, Verginius Rufus, whom Nero had appointed in Greece.[37] The two armies met at Vesontio (modern Besançon). Vindex' tribal contingents proved no match for the legions and were cut down with heavy losses. Vindex himself committed suicide. With this victory, Nero seemed safe.[38]

Galba, meanwhile, a patrician of the old Republican nobility, was of a very different stature. Now in his early seventies, he commanded the authority and respect of a senior consular. In his youth he had been a protégé of Livia, and while he was not related to Augustus, he fulfilled all the other criteria that marked out a potential *princeps* (see p. 56). Nero had appointed Galba to govern his Spanish province in AD 60 and kept him in post for an unusually long period: a mark of honour, but also perhaps a precautionary measure to ensure he was safely distant from Rome.[39] At the time of Vindex' rebellion, Nero clearly suspected Galba of disloyalty and arranged to have him killed, but the attempt failed. When news of Galba's open rebellion reached him, he became

Fig. 207
Helmet linked to the civil war
AD 60–70
River Po, near Cremona, Italy
Brass
H. 35 cm
Römisch-Germanisches Museum
der Stadt Köln
RGM 2003,7

This legionary helmet was discovered near the River Po, west of Cremona. It shows signs of hasty manufacture that link it to three other helmets with similar characteristics. They may have been produced in Campania to equip Nero's new legion (Legio I Adiutrix), which was raised from sailors of the Misenum fleet in AD 68. After Nero's death, the legion fought with Otho in the first battle of Bedriacum on 14 April AD 69, where it suffered heavy losses against Vitellian forces. Three deep impact marks on the skullcap are likely the result of blows suffered during the fighting.

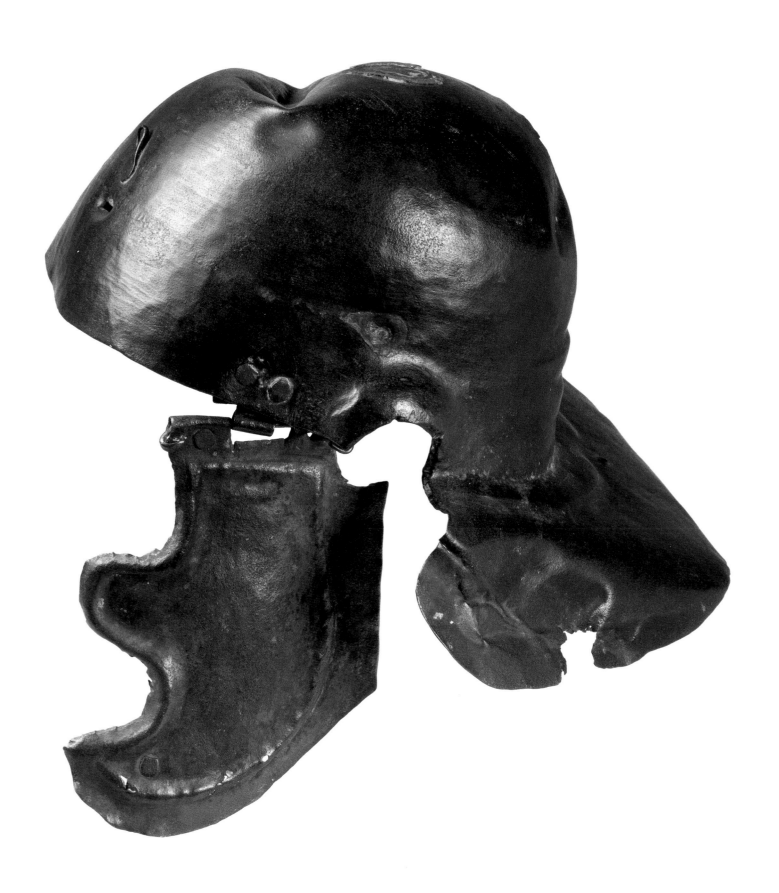

for the first time seriously concerned.[40] Galba's local troops comprised one legion with additional auxiliary units, a relatively modest force. He now enlisted further troops in his province, along with a personal bodyguard of knights. He declared his break from Nero in a carefully prepared public ceremony, surrounded by portraits of those recently condemned or killed and accompanied by a young noble whom Nero had exiled, voicing his deep concern about the state of affairs. When the crowd acclaimed him emperor, he declared himself merely an emissary of the senate and people of Rome. From the leading Roman citizens of the province he formed a senate-like council and issued various edicts exhorting others to join the cause.[41] The governor of neighbouring Lusitania, Nero's old companion Marcus Salvius Otho, heeded his call along with other local officials. The news of Vindex' defeat, while these preparations were ongoing, came as a great shock to Galba.

The source reports about Nero's last *adventus* or formal entry into Rome, when he finally heeded Helius' calls to return, are extraordinary. If taken literally, they imply that he combined elements of a traditional triumphal procession with the Greek custom of receiving victors in the sacred games in their home cities in a final, highly innovative spectacle. He had entered Naples through a breach in the city walls in a carriage drawn by white horses, and later made similar entries into Antium and Albanum near Rome, followed by the capital itself. In Rome he made use of Augustus' own triumphal chariot, dressed in 'a purple robe and a Greek cloak adorned with stars of gold, bearing on his head the Olympic crown and in his right hand the Pythian', according to Suetonius. 'His other victory crowns were carried before him, with inscriptions telling where he had won them and against what competitors, and giving the titles of the songs or of the subject of the plays' – victorious generals traditionally presented their booty and names of their battle victories in this manner. He was followed by his chanting *Augustiani*. The procession then wound its way through the Circus Maximus (an arch had symbolically been demolished at its eastern end), across the Velabrum and Forum to the Palatine and the Temple of Apollo. Along the way, animals were sacrificed and the streets sprinkled with saffron water, while birds, ribbons and sweetmeats were showered upon Nero, in scenes reminiscent of the *ludi*.[42] Dio's account, though clearly based on the same source, differs in some details. According to him, Nero ascended the Capitoline (rather than the Palatine), like a traditional triumphator, while the senators formed part of the procession and joined in with the *Augustiani*'s chants.[43]

Most scholars have accepted the veracity of these accounts and tried to interpret Nero's behaviour, but there is little reason not to assume they were as distorted as most other Nero stories.[44] In the extant source narratives, Nero appeared a failure to the end, not even behaving like a true emperor when his throne and life were threatened. Suetonius claims that he refused to address his troops, in order to preserve his singing voice; when he finally prepared to lead an expedition against Vindex in person, he was busy planning the transport of stage machinery and had prostitutes fitted out as Amazons to accompany him. Similarly, when he assembled members of the senate for an emergency meeting, he supposedly talked about the latest types of water organ rather than urgent military matters.[45] Perhaps these were calculated gestures of calm and contempt for his adversaries, wilfully given an all too literal interpretation by

Fig. 208
Funerary inscription for Claudia Ecloge ('the most faithful'), Nero's wet nurse
AD 70–100
Rome, Italy
Marble
H. 33 cm, W. 45 cm, D. 19 cm
Antiquarium Comunale del Celio, Rome
NCE 4424

Claudia Ecloge, together with Nero's second wet nurse, Alexandria, and his former lover, Claudia Acte, buried Nero's ashes in the Domitii Ahenobarbi family tomb on the Pincian Hill.

his detractors – Vindex allegedly taunted Nero by calling him Ahenobarbus and a poor lyre-player.[46]

Nero's actual military and administrative measures contrasted strongly with the picture of deluded incompetence and escapist denial painted by the main sources. In April AD 68 he dismissed the two serving consuls and assumed the office himself, for the fifth and last time, *sine collega* (without a fellow consul). He summoned the people of Rome to arms (citizens from Italy were normally exempt from service in the legions). When the response was underwhelming, Nero enlisted enslaved men instead. He recalled numerous military units that had been moved to the East and instructed Publius Petronius Turpilianus, who had been awarded triumphal insignia for his loyalty during the Pisonian conspiracy, to establish a defensive cordon in the Po Valley, in the north of Italy. Additional finances were raised through a special income tax and all tenants had to pay one year's rent directly to the imperial treasury.[47]

Following his victory over Vindex, Verginius Rufus now failed to take further action on Nero's behalf. His troops, an elite force perhaps keen not to be upstaged and sidelined by Galba's single legion, repeatedly offered to acclaim Verginius emperor, but he refused, putting himself instead at the service of senate and people.[48]

In addition, the governor of the province of Africa, Clodius Macer, rebelled. Africa was vital for Rome's grain supply, so Macer was now in a position to exert serious pressure on the capital. Rumours quickly spread and, for a moment, the mood in Rome was one of concern, verging on hostility, for the people were always afraid of famine. For Nero, this temporary loss of the support of the *plebs urbana* was both unprecedented and unnerving. It seems to have seriously weakened his resolve.[49]

Further defections threatened the position of the Neronian forces in northern Italy. There were reports of rumours that Petronius Turpilianus had changed sides.[50] The Batavian auxiliaries attached to one of Nero's loyal legions joined the rebellion, effectively neutralising its strength – the Batavians later claimed to have won Italy from Nero.[51] With his other trustworthy troops still too far away, the *princeps* decided to abandon the capital and join the fleet.[52] He sent his most reliable freedmen ahead to Ostia to make preparations. Yet when he tried to convince the officers of the Praetorian Guard to go with him, they were evasive or refused outright. Much of this was due to the underhand actions of Nymphidius Sabinus, the joint commander with Tigellinus, who had decided to support Galba out of personal ambition and promised the Praetorians a huge donative if they changed sides.[53] From this moment, Nero's hold on power unravelled very quickly. Suetonius recounts the emperor's last hours with novelistic drama, fully intent on sketching a final character portrait that confirmed Nero's moral deficiencies and unsuitability for the principate. During the night, Nero discovered that his guard detail had been withdrawn and that all his friends had left the palace, effectively abandoning him to his fate. Only some servants and a small group of his most trusted freedmen remained: Phaon, Epaphroditus, Neophytus and Sporus (this in itself was a metaphorical indictment of Nero's rule). With the road to Ostia blocked, the party made for Phaon's suburban villa at the northern outskirts of the city. Along the way, they learnt that the Guard had declared for Galba. Emboldened by the Guard's action, the senate finally followed suit and officially declared Nero a *hostis*, an enemy of the state. On learning of this and with soldiers approaching to arrest him, Nero committed suicide, plunging a dagger into his throat with the aid of the loyal Epaphroditus.[54] It was 9 June AD 68; Nero had lived for thirty years and six months and reigned for thirteen and a half years.[55] With his death, the Julio-Claudian line came to an end. Among his last words, he was said to have uttered *qualis artifex pereo* – 'what an artist dies with me'.[56]

It is a gripping story, full of pathos and supposedly based on eyewitness accounts. Yet in reality, this, too, is mostly a literary construct, depriving Nero of dignity even in his final hours, an end styled to contrast with the noble deaths of his senatorial victims, whose descriptions became such a powerful genre of biography in the following years.[57] Even within Suetonius' more limited narrative Nero's petulant end strongly contrasts with his mother Agrippina's 'manly' demeanour in her last moments.

Nero's body was spared mutilation; he was cremated in white robes embroidered with gold and buried by his nurses, Ecloge and Alexandria, and his first love Claudia Acte, in the ancestral tomb of the Domitii Ahenobarbi (Fig. 208; see also Fig. 163, p. 216).[58] His final resting place was a porphyry sarcophagus, crowned by an altar of white marble, within an enclosure of Thasian stone.[59] What may seem a touching account to modern readers was probably not intended that way. For Suetonius Nero reverted to being a Domitius, mixing with *liberti* rather than noblewomen, as if his adoption by Claudius – of which he had proven unworthy – had never happened.

Under pressure from his rival
Vitellius, the childless Galba
adopted the young noble Lucius
Calpurnius Piso as his heir. Piso's
parents and eldest brother had
been executed under Claudius,
while two other brothers were
exiled under Nero. The family's
long-held ambitions for imperial
power finally seemed close to
fulfilment, but then Otho's
supporters killed Piso along
with Galba. Some seventy years
later, another member of the
family was executed for plotting
against Hadrian.

Aftermath

Suetonius and Dio report joy and celebrations as the news of Nero's death
spread through Rome, with people donning liberty caps and toppling his
statues.[60] Some of Nero's prominent supporters were lynched, among them
the commander of Nero's bodyguard, Spiculus, and several of his freedmen.[61]
Tacitus is much more circumspect, claiming that senators and leading knights
rejoiced (with the new emperor Galba still away from Rome), as did the
'respectable' part of the people – those connected to the households of the
leading families and the dependants and freedmen of those Nero had killed and
banished. Yet the 'vulgar crowd' (*plebs sordida*), 'used to the circus and theatre',
along with the 'poorest slaves' and those who had 'squandered their property',
were dejected and alert to every rumour about Nero's fate.[62] Tacitus' deep-seated
contempt exemplified the prejudices of the senatorial class: the people he so
disdained formed the vast majority of the capital's population. Soon, they
decorated Nero's tomb with fresh flowers and defiantly put up his images
(most of which had been removed).

Fig. 210
Aureus of Galba
AD 68–9
Minted in Rome, Italy
Gold
Weight 7.4 g
British Museum
R.6577

Fig. 211
Reverse of as of Galba
AD 68
Minted in Rome, Italy
Copper alloy
Weight 10.5 g
British Museum
BNK,R.790
Donated by Bank of England

Fig. 212
Aureus of Otho
AD 69
Minted in Rome, Italy
Gold
Weight 7.3 g
British Museum
R.6333

Fig. 213
Obverse of aureus of Vitellius
AD 69
Minted in Lugdunum (Lyon), Gaul
(modern France)
Gold
Weight 7.3 g
British Museum
R.6661
Donated by Marmaduke Trattle

Fig. 214
Aureus of Vitellius
AD 69
Minted in Lugdunum (Lyon), Gaul
(modern France)
Gold
Weight 5.9 g
British Museum
1867,0101.636

Fig. 215
Aureus of Vespasian
AD 69–70
Minted in Ephesus, modern Turkey
Gold
Weight 7.6 g
British Museum
1936,0604.1

Fig. 216
**Reverse of aureus
of Vespasian**
AD 69–71
Minted in Gaul (modern France)
Gold
Weight 7.3 g
British Museum
1923,1015.5

Nero's successors aimed to assert their legitimacy through new coin issues. Servius Sulpicius Galba honoured Livia ('DIVA AUGUSTA'), to whom he had been close as a young man, but he also stressed, through military motifs and the formula 'S(ENATUS) C(ONSULTUM)', that the senate and army were behind him (Fig. 211). He reigned for seven months. Marcus Salvius Otho had been a close friend of Nero. His coin portrait resembled that of the late *princeps* in its youthfulness and coiffure, while the reverse showed the goddess of victory (Fig. 212). Otho ruled for only three months. Aulus Vitellius enjoyed the support of the legions in Germany, Gaul and Britain. His coins pointed to the loyalty of the armies ('FIDES EXERCITUM') (Figs 213 and 214). He was killed after an eight-month reign. Titus Flavius Vespasianus, the ultimate victor, celebrated imperial concord ('CONCORDIA AUG(USTA)') and military backing ('CONSEN(SUS) EXERCI(TUM)') (Figs 215 and 216). His accession signalled the beginning of the Flavian dynasty.

Otho and Vitellius honoured Nero's memory and continued work on the Domus Aurea. This changed under Vespasian, when a strong anti-Neronian tradition began to take hold, even though Vespasian had remained loyal to Nero until the end.

The Year of the Four Emperors

When Galba, scion of the old nobility, finally made his entry into Rome, he quickly proved out of touch.[63] Well into his seventies, he was more than twice the age of Nero at his death. A reputation for severity, even cruelty, preceded him (Figs 210 and 211). His failure to pay out the expected donatives alienated the army, and the Praetorians, to whom he ultimately owed his throne. During the games, the people publicly ridiculed him in a powerful display of *theatralis licentia*.[64] Increasingly isolated, he relied on a small coterie of ambitious advisors. At the beginning of AD 69, the German army, having seen no reward for their defeat of Vindex, refused to take its customary annual oath of loyalty to the new *princeps*. Galba, still childless, needed to adopt an heir. He chose the noble Lucius Calpurnius Piso Frugi, younger brother of the Pompeius Magnus who had perished under Claudius (two middle brothers were exiled under Nero, one eventually executed). This enraged Otho, who had only joined Galba in the hope of being nominated as his successor, and he immediately set in motion a plot with the Praetorians. Soon after, Galba and Piso were cut down in the Forum (Fig. 209). In the meantime, and unbeknown to Otho, who was now recognised as *princeps* by the senate, the German legions had acclaimed the governor of Lower Germany, Aulus Vitellius, as their emperor in a rival insurrection. Despite attempts to come to a negotiated settlement, Otho eventually had to march against Vitellius' army.[65] In order to win support in Rome, he aligned himself with the late Nero, allowing his statues and images to be restored and reinstating Nero's procurators and freedmen to their former offices (Fig. 212). According to Suetonius, Otho not only permitted the crowds to hail him as a 'new Nero', but even added this name to his own in official correspondence and contemplated marrying Nero's widow, Statilia Messalina.[66] Vitellius' and Otho's armies clashed in northern Italy, citizen fighting citizen in scenes not seen since the bloody civil wars of the first century BC.[67] In April the Vitellian forces prevailed in a major battle at Bedriacum, near the city of Cremona in the Po Valley (Figs 217–19).[68] Otho took his own life, bringing to an end a reign of only three months. Soon after, Vitellius made his triumphant entry into Rome (Figs 213 and 214). He, too, felt obliged to honour Nero's memory, making public funeral offerings to him in the Campus Martius with the assistance of state priests and urging a citharode to play some of Nero's popular songs ('from the Master's book') at a major banquet.[69]

Yet in July AD 69, the eastern legions hailed Vespasian, who still pursued the war in Judaea, as emperor (see p. 252). These events ushered in the Flavian dynasty that would rule the Roman Empire for a further twenty-seven years. His allies now led forces into Italy. A second battle took place at Bedriacum, even bloodier than the first. The Vitellians suffered a catastrophic defeat. Their camp outside the city of Cremona was stormed, followed by the city itself, one of the most prosperous in northern Italy (Fig. 220).[70] Its destruction and the suffering of its civilian population came to symbolise the horrors of the post-Neronian civil war (Figs 221–2).[71] Rome, too, now saw major fighting, when the supporters of Vitellius clashed with the Flavian faction in the city.[72] During the conflict, the Temple of Iupiter Capitolinus, Rome's main sanctuary and symbol of city and Empire, burned down; soon after, Vespasian's legions stormed the city, with much bloodshed. Vitellius was killed after an eight-month reign. On 20 December the senate formally recognised Vespasian as *princeps* (Figs 215–16).

These pieces of military equipment from the Bedriacum battlefield include a caltrop (a weapon made of multiple sharp spines arranged so that one spike always points upwards – highly effective against cavalry), a spearhead, ballista bolt and an arrowhead. The Greek author Plutarch later visited Bedriacum when researching his *Lives of the Caesars*, which concluded with the civil wars following Nero's death.

Fig. 217
Caltrop
AD 69–71
Calvatone, Italy
Iron
H. 4.5 cm, W. 4.5 cm
Museo Archeologico di Cremona
MC293

Fig. 218
Spearhead and arrowhead
AD 69–71
Calvatone, Italy
Bronze
L. 9.5 cm; L. 12 cm
Museo Archeologico di Cremona
MC292, MC1000

Fig. 219
Ballista bolt
AD 69–71
Calvatone, Italy
Bronze
L. 7.1 cm
Museo Archeologico di Cremona
MC1003

Fig. 220
Metal plate from a catapult
AD 56–69
Cremona, Italy
Bronze
H. 4.2 cm, W. 7. 3 cm
Museo Archeologico di Cremona
MC20

Inscribed: '[P(UBLIO) CORNELIO SCIPIONE Q(UINTO) VOLU]SIO SATUR[NINO CO(N)S(ULIBUS) POMP]EIO PAUL[INO LEG(ATO)]', 'under the consulship of Publius Cornelius Scipio and Quintus Volusius Saturninus, and Pompeius Paulinus as governor'.

This fragment of a metal plate originally belonged to a catapult of one of the Vitellian legions from Lower Germany. According to the inscription, it was made in AD 56. It was lost thirteen years later when the Flavian forces captured the Vitellian camp outside Cremona.

Fig. 221
Mosaic fragment
AD 1–100
House of the Nymphaeum,
Piazza Marconi, Cremona, Italy
Mosaic
W. 21 cm, L. 30 cm
Museo Archeologico San Lorenzo,
Cremona
ST. 161749

Fig. 222
Fresco fragment
20–1 BC
Room of Ariadne, House of the
Nymphaeum, Piazza Marconi,
Cremona, Italy
Plaster and paint
H. 33 cm, W. 37 cm
Museo Archeologico San Lorenzo,
Cremona
ST. 161709

Cremona, situated along important
communication links in the fertile
Po valley, was one of the most
prosperous cities in northern Italy.
Its destruction by victorious Flavian
forces after the second battle of
Bedriacum in October AD 69
became a byword for the horrors
of the civil war. These fragments
(Figs 221 and 222) from recent
excavations come from a grand
mansion in the ancient city and
attest Cremona's wealth at the time.

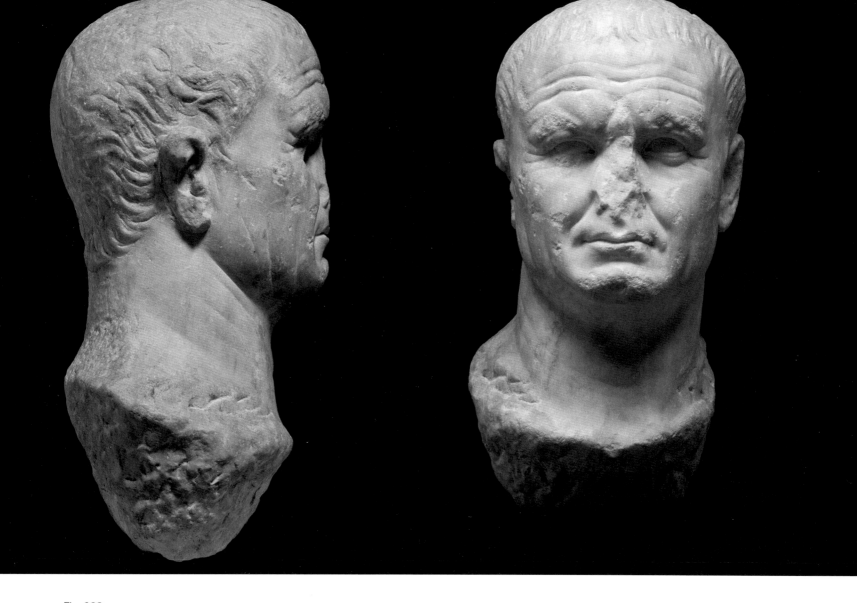

Fig. 223
Portrait head of Vespasian
AD 64–8
Carthage (Tunis), Tunisia
Marble
H. 45.7 cm, W. 26 cm, D. 23.5 cm
British Museum
1850,0304.35

Following Nero's death his public
images were destroyed or removed
and warehoused in gestures of
damnatio memoriae. Many were
subsequently re-carved into
portraits of his successors. Clear
marks in the back of the neck of
this portrait of Vespasian show
where Nero's long hair was cut
back; other alterations are evident
in the coiffure. The small, deep-set
eyes are characteristic of Nero's
portraits (see Fig. 190, p. 244).

The year and a half of chaos and bloodshed that followed Nero's death in
June AD 68 led to widespread popular nostalgia for his reign.[73] For Vespasian,
who had remained loyal to Nero until the end, this required a delicate balance
between the people and the remnants of the senatorial elite that had opposed
the late *princeps*. He therefore broke with Otho's and Vitellius' gestures aimed
towards a rehabilitation of Nero's memory, but embraced his popular policies,
much aided by the immense booty of the unrest in Judaea (Jerusalem fell in
AD 70). The inauguration of the Colosseum under his son Titus in place of
Nero's former *stagnum* in AD 80 exemplified this approach. The conflict over
Nero's images came to a quiet end after the half-hearted *damnatio memoriae* (which
also included the erasure of his name from official inscriptions) that had been
vigorously contested by his remaining supporters. Nero's portraits were removed
and warehoused, to be re-carved into images of the new *princeps* and his sons
(Fig. 223).[74] The first generation of emphatically anti-Neronian writers now
produced their plays, poems and histories, legitimising the new dynasty that was
no longer linked to the bloodline of Augustus, providing vital source material
for Tacitus, Suetonius and Cassius Dio later.

EPILOGUE

For many of his contemporaries, Nero's sudden and lonely end in June AD 68 was shrouded in mystery. Alert to every rumour, they refused to accept that Nero had really died. Writing decades later, the Greek author Dio of Prusa states: 'So far as the rest of his subjects were concerned, there was nothing to prevent his continuing to be Emperor for all time, seeing that even now everybody wishes he were still alive. And the great majority do believe that he is.' Dio continues, 'in a certain sense [Nero] has died not once but often, along with those who had been firmly convinced that he was still alive'.[1] This was a reference to at least three Nero lookalikes ('False Neros'), who had appeared in the three decades after the *princeps'* death and attracted followers among the soldiery and the population of the eastern provinces.[2] In Rome, the *plebs urbana* continued to honour Nero's memory, as did the Parthians beyond the Empire's borders. It was a tradition strong enough to be acknowledged even by sources otherwise overwhelmingly hostile, evidence of a lingering regard for a ruler who seemed to have cared for the people.[3]

Nonetheless, highly partisan narratives soon exerted a dominant hold that has lasted for nearly two millennia. It is easy for modern readers to dismiss as pure fiction the many portents that allegedly accompanied Nero's 'troubled' reign: mountains that shifted, rivers that flowed backwards, earth that spilt blood, tombs that called out for him, to name but a few.[4] Harder perhaps to disbelieve are the tales of murder, incest and other sexual transgressions of a deluded artist who wilfully burned down the city and built a palace that surrounded all of Rome. All these claims, even the lesser and seemingly more straightforward anecdotes, should best be read as metaphors, a history arranged in hindsight to justify the bloody end of Rome's first dynasty and the violent civil war that followed.[5]

From beyond the grave, Seneca inspired the first formative anti-Neronian accounts in what might be termed posthumous vengeance: the historian Fabius Rusticus and the anonymous author of *Octavia* were members of his circle.[6] Trajan, the emperor in power when Tacitus wrote his *Annals* and *Histories*, was a great-nephew of one of the men embroiled in the Pisonian conspiracy, Barea Soranus. Different motives, from the personal to the politically opportune, therefore quickly led to a cumulative bias in accounts of Nero's reign. The Christian Church Fathers eagerly embraced this hostile Nero tradition, and perhaps they did most to shape and preserve the *princeps'* image as tyrannical monster over the centuries. Yet in one of the many twists in Nero's complex legacy, Rome's late antique pagan senatorial aristocracy for the very same reason rehabilitated Nero as a model of traditional *Romanitas* (Fig. 224).[7]

Fig. 224
Contorniate, or medallion, with a laureate bust of Nero on the obverse and a race in the Circus Maximus on the reverse
Late 4th century–5th century AD
Minted in Rome, Italy
Copper alloy
Weight 37 g
British Museum
R.5026

Contorniates of this type were produced from *c.* AD 355–410 and may have been distributed as New Year's gifts. Nero was the most frequently portrayed former emperor after Trajan.

Beyond his youth and the fact he espoused cultural values more in tune with his own generation than with some influential senatorial elders, there was little that predicated Nero's eventual fall. Ultimately, he was the victim of a political system structurally ill-suited to survive the death of its founder, Augustus. Nero was brought down by rival members of the nobility who aspired to lead the principate themselves; a consistent argument can be made that these men used his behaviour as a justification for their actions, often retrospectively, but were not necessarily motivated by them.

History seemed to repeat itself when another young ruler, Domitian, was assassinated in AD 96, thus ending the Flavian dynasty.[8] For a brief period thereafter, it seemed that a successful compromise had finally been achieved,

Fig. 225
Louis XIV of France as Apollo, the Sun God, in a costume sketch for the court ballet *Ballet de la Nuit*
1653
Pen, wash and gouache enhanced with gold
H. 27.2 cm, W. 17.8 cm
Collection Michel Hennin, Bibliothèque nationale de France
RESERVE FOL-QB-201 (41)

Between 1651 and 1659 Louis XIV performed in nine court ballets (*ballets de cour*). Among his principal roles was that of Apollo, who killed the Python in Greek mythology. The slaying of the serpent became a metaphor for Louis' victory in the Fronde, a series of rebellions in which the nobility and aristocracy combined in opposition to the king.

when the principate was informally redefined as an elective rather than hereditary monarchy and every senator could hope to become emperor through adoption by his predecessor. This spirit of senatorial power and optimism pervaded the writings of Tacitus and the Younger Pliny.

In the end, Nero was perhaps simply unlucky. A radical change of perspective helps to put his reign into a much wider context: Louis XIV of France (1638–1715) was another youthful, Apolline 'Sun King' who took to the stage (Fig. 225). Yet Louis permanently defeated a rebellious nobility and went on to a long and glorious reign.[9] Discarding the familiar tales about Nero's life comes at a loss, but it frees the mind to engage anew with a society that had a profound and inspiring impact on European art and history. A more rational Nero, victim as much as perpetrator, remains just as fascinating at the monster of old.

Notes

Note on Classical texts: the ancient sources quoted in this publication, including those by Tacitus, Cassius Dio and Suetonius, are freely available in various translations on the internet and in print. Reliable editions include those published in the Loeb Classical Library series, Harvard University Press.

Introduction

1   Rogers (1953); Flaig a (2003).
2   Fittschen and Zanker (1994), 34, no. 31, pls 32, 33.
3   Malitz (2005).
4   Manuwald (2013).
5   Scholl (2016), 28–9, no. 19.
6   Schulz (2019), with extensive bibliography.
7   Quintilian, *Institutio Oratorio* 10.1.107; Cicero, *De Oratore* 2.236.
8   Griffin (1984); Champlin (2003); Buckley and Dinter (2013); Bartsch, Freudenburg and Littlewood (2017); Elsner and Masters (1994); now also Drinkwater (2019).
9   Tomei and Rea (2011); Merten (2016).

Chapter I

1   For the date and names, see Kienast (1996), 96.
2   Rose (1997); Boschung (2002).
3   Suetonius, *Nero* 51.1.
4   Winterling (1999).
5   For Augustus and the principate, see Zanker (1988); Eck (2003); Galinsky (2005).
6   Suetonius, *Augustus* 28.2.
7   On senators see Talbert (1987) with bibliography.
8   Similarly, members of the senior orders wore different types of boots (*calcei*), with patricians yet further distinguished among senators and knights. On Roman dress and status in general, see Edmondson and Keith (2008).
9   Duncan-Jones (2016).
10   The average property requirement for *decuriones* was about 100,000 sesterces, but much depended on the size and wealth of the town, so it could be considerably above or below that mark.
11   The philosopher Epictetus, born during Nero's reign and himself a *liberti*, recounts how the wealthy Epaphroditus, one of Nero's powerful freedmen, suddenly treated his own *liberti* Felicio, whom he had sold as a good-for-nothing, with exquisite courtesy and respect once Felicio had been acquired for the imperial household (Epictetus, *Dialogues* 19).
12   Seneca, *On Benefits* 6.34.3. See also Juvenal, *Satires* 1.102–13 about a wealthy freedman given precedence over a praetor and tribune. For the wider context, see Winterling (1999), 117–44, and Goldbeck (2010).
13   Augustus was born as Gaius Octavius in 63 BC; he lost his father aged four. For adoption in the Roman world, see Lindsay (2009) with bibliography.
14   First-century AD literature abounds in tales of men driven to despair or fortune-hunting.
15   Given the prevailing conditions in antiquity, this often meant that they were not yet physically mature enough to bear children, or they developed pregnancies that posed a very high risk to themselves and their foetuses.

Few children survived beyond the age of five. For details, see Scheidel (2007) with further bibliography.
16   A consequence of these practices for modern audiences is the near impossibility of providing clearly legible family trees: individuals frequently change position, and the generations are out of alignment, as wives can often be around the same age as their stepchildren, husbands the age of their wives' parents.
17   Varus' defeat in AD 9, the notorious *clades Variana*, haunted Augustus' last years and he never quite accepted its consequences.
18   Tiberius' policy was strategically sensible, but it riled ambitious Roman generals eager for glory. This is probably reflected in later sources that claimed Tiberius acted out of envy for Germanicus' achievements.
19   The boys were Nero Julius Caesar (b. AD 6), Drusus Julius Caesar (b. AD 7 or 8) and Gaius Julius Caesar ('Caligula', b. AD 12), the girls Julia Agrippina ('Agrippina the Younger', b. AD 15), Julia Drusilla (b. AD 16) and Julia Livilla (b. AD 18).
20   Tacitus, *Annals*, 3.1–2.
21   Attempts had been made to reduce rivalries through the usual marriage of cousins: Germanicus' first-born son Nero Julius Caesar wed Tiberius' granddaughter Julia in AD 20.
22   Tacitus relates examples of such interactions in the senate, including a senator's request that Tiberius should make his opinion known before the senators began debating an issue, so that they would not inadvertently find themselves arguing against him. Tiberius, less patient and respectful in this regard than Augustus, occasionally goaded them on and hid his intentions, perhaps at times genuinely interested in a real debate.
23   Agrippina the Elder died in exile in AD 33, having starved herself to death. Her first son passed away in AD 31, also while banished; his widow Julia (Tiberius' granddaughter) remarried, but her new husband Rubellius Blandus came from outside the imperial family.
24   Caligula convinced the senate to set aside Tiberius' last will.
25   The bust was long believed to have been excavated in Colchester (see, for example, Von den Hoff (2009), 250–1), but it is more likely to be a Grand Tour acquisition from Italy. This will be argued by Peter Berridge in his forthcoming article 'Henry Vint and the Bust of Caligula', which he kindly shared in advance of publication.
26   Caligula also had the ashes of his exiled mother and brother transferred to Rome and placed in the Mausoleum of Augustus. The senate awarded his grandmother Antonia the Younger the title *Augusta* and all other honours Livia had enjoyed.
27   Senators spoke in order of the offices they had held (for example former consuls before former praetors and so on), and within these groups ranked by age.
28   Tiberius had continued to keep Claudius away from meaningful political offices, although he awarded him *ornamenta conularia*, honours equivalent to a consul.
29   Winterling (2011).
30   In addition, Caligula put his sisters' entire household possessions up for auction, including enslaved servants and freedmen.
31   Caligula remained at the Rhine frontier in AD 39 and appointed new commanders to prepare the troops. The sources are extremely hostile with regard to the *princeps*, but a number of Germanic incursions do seem to have been repelled. He briefly turned his attention to Britain, but was recalled urgently to Rome.
32   See Winterling (2011).
33   Suetonius' account of Nero's life begins with a discussion of his most important paternal ancestors. This could have made interesting reading, but was merely meant to demonstrate how 'Nero lapsed from the virtues of his ancestors yet reproduced each one's legacy of vice' (a standard method of invective that could come straight out of a rhetorical manual). With the outcome thus predetermined, Suetonius' judgement of their character and individual actions is of little factual value, but it has tarnished their reputation for posterity, along with Nero's. The extreme bias of Roman authors is evident when descriptions of earlier Ahenobarbi written before and during Nero's lifetime (for example, by Caesar, Velleius Paterculus or Lucan) are contrasted with later ones.
34   This is the current consensus view. Alternatively, the temple has been dated to the second half of the first century BC and linked to the Ahenobarbus who minted the coins, himself a successful fleet commander, see Coarelli (2007).
35   Rossini (2007); Zanker (1988).
36   He commanded the senatorial left wing.
37   Rossini (2007) with bibliography.
38   Tacitus, *Annals* 5.75.1.
39   Tacitus, *Annals* 6.47–8 hints at a wider conspiracy against Tiberius, in which Gnaeus Ahenobarbus was involved.
40   Suetonius, *Nero* 6.3. The implication must be that Nero was exposed to lower-class people from early on, and that exposure to a dancer may have set him on the course to his later stage performances.
41   See for example Griffin (1984), 30. Two of Nero's nurses helped to prepare his body for the funeral in AD 68, so are likely to have been close to him and remained in his household, see p. 268.
42   Suetonius, *Claudius* 27.2.
43   See Varner (2001) for a discussion of the impact of *damnatio memoriae* on the identification of imperial women.
44   Men married to women of the imperial family generally seem to have regarded these unions merely as an acknowledgement of their status that raised their own aspirations to the principate even further, as numerous examples from the Julio-Claudian period demonstrate.
45   Cf. Cassius Dio, *Roman History* 60.5.9 and Winterling (2011), 143–5.
46   This is the Licinian tomb near the Porta Pia in Rome. The structure was discovered during construction work in the 1880s and insufficiently documented before the finds were dispersed. It is not entirely clear if it was a secondary location for the sculptures and funerary altars discovered (they may have been transferred from a more prominent tomb location, the sculptures from a family mansion), see Kragelund, Moltesen and Østergaard (2003); Van Keuren *et al.* (2003) and this volume, Chapter VII.
47   Appius Silanus had been governor of Spain before he was called back to Rome. The marriage to Domitia Lepida brought honour, but also meant he no longer had command of the legion stationed there, in light of later events possibly another motive for Claudius' choice.
48   Comparable to Augustus' line-up of Agrippa, Tiberius and Drusus as stand-ins for his adopted sons Gaius and Lucius.
49   Tacitus, *Annals* 12.64.1; Suetonius, *Nero* 6. Passienus Crispus was a descendant by adoption of the famous author Sallustius Crispus.
50   Suetonius, *Galba* 5.1.
51   Galba was governor of upper Germany at the time and in command of a strong army. The news of Caligula's assassination and offers of the principate may have reached him too late to take action before Claudius was confirmed as *princeps*.
52   Pliny the Elder, *Natural History* 16.91.242.
53   For the conspiracies, see McAlindon (1956).
54   Allegedly, Seneca had only been spared on account of his ill health and was not expected to live.
55   Suetonius, *Claudius* 37; Cassius Dio, *Roman History* 60.14.3; see McAlindon (1956), 117–18.
56   Suetonius, *Claudius* 13.
57   McAlindon (1956).
58   The newly raised legions were Legio XV Primigenia and Legio XXII Primigenia. As they were as yet untested, they were used to replace crack units moved up for the invasion, Legio IX Hispana from Dalmatia and Legio II Augusta from Upper Germany.
59   Inscriptions from Ephesus, the provincial capital, attest Passienus Crispus' presence; see 'Inschriften von Ephesus', 7.1.3025 and 3026, in Wankel (1979–84).
60   Beryllus became his secretary for Greek correspondence, Anicetus commander of the Misenum fleet, cf. Josephus, *Jewish Antiquities* 20.182–3; Tacitus, *Annals* 14.3.3; Suetonius, *Nero* 35.2.
61   Seneca, *Apocolocyntosis* 11; see McAlindon (1956), 126–7.
62   Large *horti* in Rome seem to have been a crucial status symbol for men who aspired to the principate.
63   *Ludi seculares* had been celebrated with great pomp under Augustus and were not due to be repeated for several decades, but Claudius laboured various antiquarian points to argue that his date was the correct one.
64   Suetonius, *Nero* 7.1 calls his performance 'constantissime' and 'favorabiliter'.
65   The detailed description of the wedding ceremony sounds suspiciously like certain Bacchic rites, so whether there really was a 'wedding' is not certain, see Colin (1956).
66   Tacitus, *Annals* 11.28–9; see also Levick (1990), 67.
67   Tacitus, *Annals* 12.1–2.
68   Tacitus, *Annals* 12.1.1 and 12.3.1.
69   Agrippina is said to have insisted that Nero's tuition should concentrate on rhetoric, rather than philosophy, see Suetonius, *Nero* 52.
70   Tacitus, *Annals* 12.4.
71   Augustus had asked the senate in his will to confer the title on Livia after his own death.
72   Cassius Dio, *Roman History* 60.33.7.
73   The normal minimum age was forty-two, but there were some exceptions for patricians, see Talbert (1987).
74   Tacitus, *Annals*, 12.41.
75   Tacitus, *Annals* 12.41.
76   Dio even refers to Nero as 'Domitia', to add effeminacy to his insult.
77   Tacitus, *Annals* 12.43.
78   These included a new harbour at Ostia, new aqueducts to bring fresh water to Rome, the draining of the Fucine Lake near Rome (to prevent flooding and gain fertile agricultural land), and innovations in performances and gladiatorial shows, see also this volume, Chapter IV.
79   Tacitus, *Annals* 12.42.

80 McAlindon (1956).
81 Suetonius, *Nero* 7.2. He adds that Claudius had explicitly discouraged this.
82 Cassius Dio, *Roman History* 60.33.9.
83 Cassius Dio, *Roman History* 60.33.10, where Claudius' proclamation and letter are linked to a bread riot. This (unless there were several) happened during the previous year. Claudius' announcement would, however, make more sense in connection with his illness, hence the chronological sequence proposed here.
84 Lucius Iunius Silanus chose the day to commit suicide; Tacitus, *Annals* 12.
85 Cassius Dio, *Roman History* 60.33.10. Suetonius, *Nero* 7.2. Suetonius explicitly says the games were given for Claudius' recovery, so presumably both authors refer to the same event. Dio puts it before the wedding, Suetonius after.
86 Tacitus, *Annals* 12.58.1.
87 Tacitus, *Annals* 12.64.1.
88 Tacitus (*Annals* 12.65.1) cites two grounds for prosecution, one of which seems potentially more serious. Apparently, Domitia Lepida was accused of tolerating (or even inciting) a disturbance of the peace of Italy by bands of enslaved individuals from her vast Calabrian estates. Calabria and Puglia were very underdeveloped at the time; wealthy landowners used armed and mounted pastoralists to look after their herds. These could easily be mobilised as paramilitary forces, as did happen on occasion. In addition, he states that Domitia was charged with the use of black magic against Agrippina.
89 Tacitus, *Annals* 12.64.1.
90 Suetonius, *Nero* 7.1.
91 Tacitus, *Annals* 12.66–7; Suetonius, *Claudius* 44.1.
92 The first record is an irreverent insinuation by the actor Datus during a public theatre performance attended by Nero, sometime after AD 59 (Suetonius, *Nero* 39.2), see p. 283. The tragic play *Octavia* has Claudius 'perish by his wife's crime' (*Octavia* 9 or 10).
93 Tacitus, *Annals* 12.66–7.
94 Suetonius, *Claudius* 44, lists some of the theories: Halotus applied the poison when Claudius attended a dinner with some priest on the Capitol or Agrippina mixed it in with some mushrooms during a family dinner at the palace. Some claimed that Claudius immediately lost his speech, passed the night convulsed with pain and died just before dawn. Others stated that he immediately lost consciousness, then vomited up the contents of his stomach and was poisoned again. This was mixed in with some porridge or, alternatively, applied by syringe. Suetonius does not mention the physician Xenophon, nor that a different type of poison was used for the second attempt.
95 Cassius Dio, *Roman History* 60.34.2–3. In Dio's version, Agrippina sourced the poison from Locusta and applied it to a particularly fine mushroom reserved for Claudius during a joint meal. Claudius was carried to his bed as if heavily intoxicated from strong drink, as happened frequently. During the night, he died of the poison without having regained his senses.
96 Pliny, *Natural History* 23.47.96 refers to whole families and all the guests at a particular banquet being killed by accidentally eating poisonous mushrooms.
97 They also make no secret of Claudius' insalubrious heavy drinking, which may have imperilled his health even further.
98 Tacitus, *Annals* 12.64.1.
99 Tacitus, *Annals* 12.66.1; Suetonius *Claudius* 43.1; Cassius Dio, *Roman History* 60.34.1–2.
100 Pliny, *Natural History* 22.46.92. Pliny's 'History from the End of Aufidius Bassus' (an important source text for Tacitus and Suetonius) is lost, but echoes of it can be found in his later work on natural history.

Chapter II

1 Tacitus, *Annals* 12.68.1.
2 For courtly transition rituals including fictive bulletins and enacted periods of recovery and agony when death had already occurred, see Zanker (2004).
3 Some of the atmosphere is captured in the *Apocolocyntosis* (see p. 73): the funeral is a great concourse of men, a gorgeous spectacle for which no expense has been spared, there are masses of trumpeters, horn and other brass instrument players, concordant acclamations of the people (*Apocolocyntosis* 12.1) and laments chanted by large choirs (*Apocolocyntosis* 12.3).
4 Tacitus, *Annals* 13.3.1, states that the eulogy had been drafted by Seneca.
5 Tacitus, *Annals* 13.4.1.
6 Cassius Dio, *Roman History* 61.3.1, records that the senators voted to have the speech inscribed on a silver tablet and read out whenever new consuls entered office – an honour presumably designed to hold Nero to his word in future.
7 Suetonius, *Nero* 10.1. Similar speeches had been given by Nero's predecessors, a sign that the senate's recurring grievances were caused by structural failings of the principate system, rather than those of individual *principes*.
8 Tacitus, *Annals* 13.5.1.
9 Tacitus, *Annals* 13.10.1; Suetonius, *Nero* 8.1. Tacitus also mentions that the senate offered to let the official year begin with Nero's birth month of December, instead of January.
10 Griffin (1984), 58–9; Wolters and Ziegert (2014), 48–9.
11 Suetonius seems to suggest that Nero also had an *ustrinum*-type structure (he uses the term *bustum*) for Claudius built on the Campus Martius, a ritual precinct that marked the actual cremation site, see Suetonius, *Nero* 33.1, where he criticises its modest appearance.
12 At the end of the year, Nero also asked for the senate's permission to set up a statue of his natural father, Gnaeus Domitius Ahenobarbus. In addition, the Arval Brethren from then on performed an annual sacrifice in memory of Nero's father outside the Domus Domitiana: Tacitus, *Annals* 13.10.1; Suetonius, *Nero* 9.1.
13 For a recent discussion with ample bibliography see Whitton (2013).
14 *Apocolocyntosis* 4.3.
15 For Seneca's *De clementia* see Griffin (2013); S. Braund (2009).
16 Suetonius, *Nero* 10.2.
17 Suetonius, *Nero* 10.2 and *Augustus* 53.1.
18 Seneca, *Apocolocyntosis* 4.28.
19 Calpurnius Siculus, *Eclogue* 1 and 4. For the dating controversy see Bönisch-Meyer *et al.* (2014), with bibliography.
20 Calpurnius Siculus, *Eclogue* 7.
21 Anonymus Einsiedlensis, *Eclogue* 2.
22 For the message and impact of Nero's portraits, see Schneider (2003).
23 The images of Caligula, the only other young *princeps* to rule before Nero, could have been an obvious model. However, these had all been removed from public view after Caligula's short reign, and therefore would have left much less of a lasting visual impact.
24 Smith (1987).
25 Tacitus, *Annals* 13.2.1; Suetonius, *Nero* 9.1.
26 For Agrippina, see Barrett (1996) and Moltesen and Nielsen (2007).
27 Cassius Dio, *Roman History* 61.3.2. Dio's claim (ibid.) that Agrippina managed all Nero's business for him, received embassies and sent official diplomatic letters to foreign peoples, governors and kings is clearly exaggerated.
28 Tacitus, *Annals* 13.5.1.
29 Cassius Dio, *Roman History* 60.31.1, mentions that Agrippina 'greeted in public all who desired it, a fact that was noted in the records'.
30 Cassius Dio, *Roman History* 61.3.3–4. Tacitus, *Annals* 13.5.1.
31 Tacitus, *Annals* 13.13.1.
32 Tacitus, *Annals*, 13.13.1; Suetonius, *Nero* 28.2. In Suetonius' version, it was Nero who desired incestuous relations with his mother. Lurid male fantasies imagined illicit sex during their joint litter rides: Suetonius cites stains on Nero's clothing after he and Agrippina shared a litter as evidence that Nero's desires had been consummated. Cassius Dio, *Roman History* 61.8.5 refers to the atmosphere of rumour and gossip that pervaded the city at the time, in which even the most sensational tales were believed.
33 Tacitus, *Annals* 14.2 cites the histories of Cluvius Rufus and Fabius Rusticus as his primary sources. Perhaps not surprisingly, they give slightly different versions of what happened, thereby not encouraging trust in their veracity.
34 Tacitus, *Annals* 13.13.1; Cassius Dio, *Roman History* 61.7.1 says that she had originally been sold into slavery in Asia. Claudia Acte owned properties at Velitrae and Puteoli, as well as substantial landholdings on the island of Sardinia, see Mastino and Ruggeri (1995) with further bibliography.
35 Tacitus, *Annals* 13.12.1 calls Acte *muliercula*, 'common little woman'.
36 Tacitus, *Annals* 13.12–13. Suetonius, *Nero* 28.1 states that Nero even attempted to make Acte his lawful wife.
37 Tacitus, *Annals* 13.18.1.
38 Tacitus, *Annals* 13.19.1; Cassius Dio, *Roman History* 61.3.4–6.
39 Epileptic seizure as official cause of death: Suetonius, *Nero* 33.
40 Tacitus, *Annals* 13.15 also states that Britannicus at a palace banquet sang of his unjust fate; Suetonius, *Nero* 33 adds Nero's jealousy of Britannicus' beautiful singing voice.
41 Tacitus, *Annals* 13.7.1.
42 Tacitus, *Annals* 13.14–17 and Suetonius, *Nero* 33. Nero supposedly contracted Locusta, the same woman implied in the alleged poisoning of Claudius, through an officer of the guard. The poison was administered to Britannicus by his tutors, but his first attempt was unsuccessful. Stronger doses were prepared and tested on two different animals over the course of several hours. The most potent version was then mixed with cold water and added undetected to a hot drink that had already been checked for Britannicus by a food taster during a banquet.
43 Suetonius, *Nero* 35.4 claims that Nero similarly forcibly sexually abused another young aristocrat, Aulus Plautius, before he had him executed. Since sex with freeborn males was considered morally repugnant, the purpose is simply to heighten the moral outrage about Nero in connection with the alleged murders. At about the same time, the governor of Cilicia, Marcus Iunius Silanius, died and it was alleged that he had been poisoned on Agrippina's orders. He, too, was a great-great-grandson of Augustus from a different branch of the family; his younger brother and sister had already been executed under Claudius. Contemporary observers may have seen these deaths as signs of a purge intended to remove anyone in a position to endanger Nero's claim to the throne; Tacitus, *Annals* 13.1.1.
44 In addition, this constituted the purge of a powerful faction at court that had initially championed Messalina and then Britannicus.
45 See, for example, Tacitus, *Annals* 13.2 with a positive assessment of Seneca's and Burrus' role.

Chapter III

1 Tacitus, *Annals* 13.6.1–9.3. Tacitus' account extends over several paragraphs to include events of the following year, AD 55.
2 This was when Agrippina attempted to join the reception on the dais (Tacitus, *Annals* 13.5.1; Cassius Dio, *Roman History* 61.3.3–4; see this volume, p. 82).
3 See most recently Schlude (2020), with bibliography.
4 For a recent overview with further bibliography, see Curtis and Magub (2020).
5 Heil (1997), 11–26 (Chapter 2).
6 A number of archaeologists have attempted to link further monuments to Nero's wars and their public reception (for example Meyer (2000) and Strocka (2010)).
7 D. Braund (1984).
8 *Imperium sine fine*; Virgil, *Aeneid* 1.279.
9 Roman policy in this regard could alter repeatedly; the status of the prosperous Eastern border principality of Commagene on the Euphrates, for example, changed several times between the reigns of Caligula and the Flavians.
10 The presence of client rulers and foreign emissaries in Nero's Rome is often reported only in passing, frequently in connection with Nero's entertainments.
11 For Rome and Armenia, see Heil (1997) with bibliography; for ancient Armenia, see Chahin (2001).
12 Zanker (1988), 183–8.
13 Claudius may have expected the neighbouring client kings to intervene on his behalf, as they had in the past.
14 Tacitus, *Annals* 12.44.1–51.4.
15 Tacitus' account is spread over several chapters, although he occasionally summarises the events of several years: *Annals*, 13.6.1–9.3, 13.34.1–41.4, 14.23.1–26.2, 15.1.1–17.3, 15.24.1–31. Dio (or his epitomiser) only provides a summary: *Roman History* 69.19.1–23.3. See also Heil (1997), 28–57.
16 Tacitus, *Annals* 13.6.1.
17 See Heil (1997).
18 Augustus had come to entrust his armies to close relatives, an option not open to Caligula, Claudius or Nero.
19 On the nature of Corbulo's command, see Heil (1997), 201–12.
20 For Corbulo's life and general background, see Syme (1970).
21 *Retinendae Armeniae*; Tacitus, *Annals* 13.8.1.
22 See Heil (1997) for Corbulo's disputed role as governor of Cappadocia and Galatia. He now had legions III Gallica, VI Ferrata and X Fretensis under his command; IV Scythica and X Fretensis remained in Syria.
23 Tacitus, *Annals* 13.8.1.
24 Tacitus, *Annals* 13.9.1. Tacitus suggests that sending hostages from among the Parthian Arsacid royal family allowed Vologases to rid himself of potential rivals. Roman reports of events over the following years focused much on the various commanders involved and conflicts between Corbulo and his temporary successor Lucius Caesennius Paetus. Corbulo himself seems to have composed an account of his actions, as did officers on his staff. Tacitus hints at the existence of conflicting assessments, either more favourable to Corbulo or critical of him; see Heil (1997), 30–57.
25 Tacitus, *Annals* 13.9.1.

26   See Kleiner (1985) and La Rocca (1992). The arch was dedicated in AD 62, after an unusually short construction period.

27   For the date, see Heil (1997), 216. The timing of the Parthian attack may have been pure coincidence, but it is perfectly possible that the Parthians had some intelligence about events in Rome and other parts of the Empire. Apart from the Parthian hostages, there was for example a large Palmyran merchant community in Rome and Naples that may have relayed information.

28   Tacitus firmly places the Boudican rebellion in the year AD 61, but most scholars agree that it probably started to unfold towards the end of AD 60, see Mattingly (2006), 107; Webster (1978).

29   See Birley (2005). While the governors may have received instructions from the *princeps* in Rome, much was left to their individual judgement. The clear policy change after AD 60/61, however, is likely to have been ordered by Nero directly.

30   For a concise overview of the run-up to the Roman invasion and its aftermath, see Mattingly (2006), 47–113 with further bibliography.

31   For Aulus Plautius, linked to Claudius by marriage, see Birley (2005), 17–25 with references.

32   Camulodunon was the settlement's original Celtic name, which later lived on in the Latinised Camulodunum. Its strategic location near the estuary of the River Colne furthered Catuvellauni expansion. For general background and further references, see Crummy (1997) and Radford and Gascoyne (2013).

33   The kings' surrender was explicitly mentioned in the inscriptions of Claudius' triumphal arches in Rome (*Corpus Inscriptionum Latinarum* (*CIL*) VI 920 + add = *Inscriptiones Latinae Selectae* (*ILS*) 216 = *CIL* VI 40416) and Cyzicus.

34   Legion XX Valeria Victrix remained at Camulodunon, IX Hispana took on the Corieltavi, XIV Gemina headed west and II Augusta entered the territory of the Durotriges.

35   This operation was led by Vespasian, who later became one of Nero's leading generals.

36   The expansion of the eastern Catuvellauni–Trinovantes coalition towards the south-west had provided a pretext for Roman intervention in support of its allies. In connection with Togidubnus, Tacitus gives a brutally frank assessment of the reality of Roman rule: 'It is an ancient and long-established practice of the Roman people to use even kings as instruments of enslavement' (Tacitus, *Agricola* 14.1). The establishment of Togidubnus as client king is not precisely dated and may not have happened until relatively late, around AD 52 (see Birley (2005), 29; alternatively, he may have been granted additional territories at that point. None of the client kings in place before the AD 43 invasion seem to have been allowed to hold on to their fiefs, see Mattingly (2006), 90.

37   Tacitus, *Agricola* 12.6: *Fert Britannia aurum et argentum et alia metalla, pretium victoriae* – 'Britain contains gold and silver and other metals, as the prize of conquest'. For Ostorius Scapula, see Birley (2005), 25–31. Tacitus, *Annals* 12.31.1–40.1 is the main narrative account for these years.

38   The legion, Legion XX, moved to a new base at Kingsholm near Gloucester. The old fort's ramparts and defensive ditches were levelled; see Radford and Gascoyne (2013). For Facilis' tombstone, see Phillips (1975); Hayward (2006).

39   The Brigantes had not been part of the pre-conquest Roman client network, see Mattingly (2006), 90. Cartimandua was richly rewarded for her loyalty: Tacitus, *Histories* 3.45.

40   Nero was honoured on the arch as *princeps iuventutis* (see p. 71); he would have been well aware of events in Britain.

41   For the Roman lead mining industry and the individual ingots, see Tylecote (1964); Elkington (1968).

42   Tacitus, *Annals* 12.39.2 says Scapula threatened the Silures with the same fate as the Germanic (or Celtic) Sugambri earlier, mostly killed and the few survivors resettled elsewhere.

43   Tacitus, *Annals* 12.39.3 speaks of *avaritia praefectorum*, the avarice of their equestrian commanders.

44   For Aulus Didius Gallus, see Birley (2005), 31–7. According to Tacitus (*Annals* 12.40.1) another Roman legion under Manlius Valens suffered a defeat before Didius Gallus reached his new province.

45   Tacitus' veiled criticism of Didius Gallus as someone who merely held on to the territories under Roman control when he took up his post, reveals much about the mindset of the senatorial class (Tacitus, *Agricola* 14.2; *Annals* 14.29.1). It would become a major criticism of Nero also.

46   See Birley (2005), 37–43 with references.

47   Tacitus, *Annals* 14.29.

48   Tacitus, *Annals* 14.29 refers to Veranius' *suprema ambitio* – supreme ambition.

49   For Paulinus, see Birley (2005), 17–25 with further references. Nero's biographer Gaius Suetonius Tranquillus was not a relation or otherwise connected to the governor or his family.

50   Pliny the Elder (*Natural History* 5.1.11) states that it became a boast at the time among men of consular rank and senatorial commanders to have penetrated as far as 'Mount Atlas', and this was repeated by equestrian procurators of the provinces afterwards – a clear hint at the competitive atmosphere that prevailed among these circles. Paulinus, who had reached even further, gave a description of the local flora and fauna in his campaign report, which served Pliny as a source of information (ibid. 5.1.14–15).

51   Tacitus, *Annals* 14.29.1 explicitly says that with regard to Corbulo, Paulinus was *decus aquare cupiens* – keen to equal his glory.

52   Birley (2005), 43–50 with sources and bibliography.

53   Tacitus, *Annals* 14.30.1.

54   Tacitus, *Annals* 14.31.1. Cassius Dio, *Roman History* 62.2, claims that Seneca had extended loans worth 40 million sesterces, which he demanded back in one payment and retrieved through harsh measures. Whether this was true or not, the scenario must have appeared believable to Dio's readers. As references to Britain in the *Apocolocyntosis* indicate, Seneca was very well informed about the situation in Britain from at least AD 54.

55   According to Tacitus' dramatic account (*Annals* 14.31.1), the Romans subjected Boudica to the lash and raped her daughters.

56   Webster (1978), 15; Millett (1990), 38.

57   Tacitus, *Annals* 14.31.

58   Cassius Dio, *Roman History* 62.7.1–3. The remains of human bones illustrated here were excavated in 2014 at the Williams & Griffith store on Colchester's High Street (where the 'Fenwick Hoard' also came to light). The information provided in the caption is based on a preliminary report by Philip Crummy of Colchester Archaeology Trust: www.thecolchesterarchaeologist.co.uk/?p=13560. A clear Boudican destruction layer can be observed throughout the city. Cassius Dio (*Roman History* 62.7.1–2) describes atrocities including the mutilation and impalement of Roman women.

59   Tacitus, *Annals* 14.32, however, refers to the entire legion (Legion IX). For the Witcham Gravel helmet, see Kaminski and Sim (2014). It comes from a Fenland area that preserves plentiful evidence of deliberate deposits in watery contexts. In the vicinity were several Roman military installations, dating to the period of the Boudican rebellion and after. The fort at Longthorpe, sometimes linked to Petilius Cerealis, was 34 km away.

60   Tomlin (2016), WT 44. The translation and interpretation given in the caption are Tomlin's.

61   Paulinus' assembled troops were drawn from Legion XIV, Legion XX and nearby auxiliary units.

62   Tacitus, *Annals* 14.34–37. He adds that a high-ranking officer of Legion II committed suicide because he had failed to come to Paulinus' aid with his troops – a sign of the panic among the Roman ranks. Cassius Dio (*Roman History* 62.8.2) gives the size of Boudica's army as 230,000 men, generally considered a gross exaggeration of British strength.

63   *Gravis clades*, Tacitus, *Annals* 14.29.1; Paulinus' 'admirable steadfastness' and his decision to 'sacrifice Londinium in order to save the rest' of the province, ibid. 14.33.1. Paulinus a 'diligent and moderate commander', *Agricola*, 5.1.

64   Accounts of Roman civilian casualties in Asia Minor range from 80,000 (Memnon, *History of Heracleia* 22.9) to 150,000 (Plutarch, *Life of Sulla* 24.4). For Roman and allied casualty numbers in Britain, see Tacitus, *Annals* 14.33.1 and Cassius Dio, *Roman History* 62.1. Many modern commentators have doubted their figures, but there may have been large numbers of itinerant traders and other opportunity seekers, especially from Gaul and the Rhenish region, who perished alongside Roman citizens.

65   Tacitus identified with the senatorial governor not least because his own father-in-law Gnaeus Iulius Agricola later served in the same position; Agricola nearly succeeded in conquering the entire island of Britain, but was recalled by the emperor Domitian, according to Tacitus out of envy (Tacitus, *Agricola* 39–40). Agricola had spent his entire military career in Britain and Tacitus probably drew on his knowledge of the province.

66   Tomlin (2016), WT 33; WT 48. The translations and interpretation given in the captions are Tomlin's.

67   Tacitus, *Annals* 14.38. The Roman forces are estimated at 20,000 legionaries and the same number of auxiliaries, see Millett (1990), 58.

68   Tacitus, *Annals* 14.38.1.

69   Suetonius, *Nero* 18.1. This seems by far the most likely context for such considerations. If so, it is Suetonius' only, and highly oblique, reference to the turmoil in Britain, which he otherwise does not mention at all. Some scholars have doubted that Nero seriously considered withdrawing from Britain or would have preferred a different moment in time for such deliberations, see for example Mattingly (2006), 104.

70   This argument had already been made by the writer Strabo in the time of Augustus (who had contemplated invasion on at least three occasions). Strabo estimated that the customs duty on trade between Britain and Roman-occupied Gaul brought in more revenue than a tribute would have realised, once the cost of maintaining a garrison was deducted: Strabo, *Geography* 2.5.8. For an estimate of the military's staggering financial needs post-conquest, see Millett (1990), 57–60.

71   For Turpilianus, see Birley (2005), 50–2 with references.

72   This is now clear from some of the recently discovered Bloomberg tablets, especially the Neronian examples dating to the immediate post-Boudican layers, see Tomlin (2016). The new finds modify previous assumptions of a very slow recovery; see Fulford (2008), 6 with references.

73   One of the structure's oak beams is dendrochronologically dated to AD 63, an associated beam was branded by a *cohort* or *ala Thraecorum Augusta*, see Fulford (2008), 10, with further references.

74   For the recent excavations that brought the fort to light, see Dunwoodie, Harward and Pitt (2015).

75   See Grasby and Tomlin (2002) with bibliography.

76   Turpilianus and Polyclitus paid a high price for their association with Nero; both were executed by Galba.

77   It is thought that his son became consul in AD 66.

78   Birley (2005), 52–3.

79   Fulford (2008), 6–9.

80   *Roman Inscriptions of Britain* (RIB) 92: 'For Nero Claudius Caesar Augustus, son of the deified Claudius, grandson of Germanicus Caesar, great-grandson of Tiberius Caesar Augustus, great-great-grandson of the deified Augustus, in his fourth year of tribunician power, four times acclaimed Imperator, consul for the fourth time, by decree of the Senate the vow was deservedly fulfilled.' The inscription, recorded in the eighteenth century, is now lost; it dates to after the middle of AD 60.

81   Fulford (2008), 8, with further references.

82   This was XIV Gemina, which had been active at Camulodunum under Claudius.

83   Claudius' brother Germanicus had already recovered the other two in AD 15.

84   Italicus, the Romanised son of Arminius' Rome-friendly brother Flavius, was assigned to the Cherusci, but ultimately could not overcome their factional strife; Tacitus, *Annals* 12.16–17. Charismatic individuals could attract armed followers and form inter-tribal war bands eager for glory and booty, even against the will of other tribal elites. Rome-friendly leaders were often unable to impose their authority, rendering the 'client-ruler' system much less effective in this region than elsewhere. In AD 50, the Suebi expelled their overlord Vannius, who had been installed by Claudius' father Drusus as client king some thirty years earlier; Tacitus, *Annals*, 12.49. He and his followers were taken in by Claudius and settled in Pannonia. His nephews Vangio and Sido who had been responsible for Vannius' ousting took over, but remained loyal to Rome. The situation there is reminiscent of events in and around Armenia at the same time.

85   Tacitus, *Annals* 11.8.1.

86   Tacitus, *Annals* 11.19.

87   Tacitus, *Annals* 11.20.1; Cassius Dio, *Roman History* 60.30.5. Corbulo subsequently kept his troops busy by digging a canal, the *fossa Corbulonis*, that was 23 Roman miles long to connect the Rhine and Meuse rivers, which facilitated Roman naval operations and stayed in use for more than two centuries. Tacitus hints that Claudius feared Corbulo's successes might make him too powerful. Meanwhile, Claudius awarded the new governor of Upper Germany, Curtius Rufus, triumphal ornaments for opening up silver mines in friendly tribal territory across the Rhine, among the Mattiaci; Tacitus, *Annals* 11.20.1. In Britain, the Mendips mines were beginning to operate soon after, also under army control.

88   For Pliny's career, see Syme (1969).

89   As Pliny recorded in the introduction to his *Natural History*, which he dedicated to Titus (Praefatio 3).

90 Tacitus, *Annals* 13.54.
91 See Griffin (1984), 231; 300 note 55.
92 Tacitus *Annals*, 13.55–6. The Ampsivarii were led by a Rome-friendly chief, Boiocalcus, but to no avail; they were later destroyed by other hostile tribes. Soon after, a war between the Chatti and Hermunduri tribes eased pressure on the Roman border; ibid. 13.56.
93 Tacitus reports that in AD 58 the governor of Upper Germany, Lucius Vetus, planned to use his idle troops to dig a canal between the rivers Moselle and Saone (which would then have allowed navigation between the Rhone and Rhine rivers and therefore between the Mediterranean and North Sea), but his envious senatorial colleague in Gallia Belgica prevented him from going ahead; *Annals* 13.53.1. This is reminiscent of Nero's own canal-building projects, see p. 252.
94 Pliny the Elder, *Natural History* 33.50.143 on Pompeius Paulinus, whom the author criticises for this excessive luxury; ibid. 34.18.47 on Duvius Avitus. Avitus commissioned the contemporary Greek artist Zenodoros to produce two facsimile copies of his Kalamis cups (perhaps intended as a high-status gift); Zenodoros worked on a bronze colossus of Mercury for the Arverni while Duvius Avitus was governor of the province of Gallia Aquitania. Avitus may have had a hand in recommending Zenodoros to Nero, who subsequently employed him to create the colossal Sol-Helius for the vestibule of the Domus Aurea (see p. 241). Patronage by Nero's chief ministers might also be in evidence in the promotion of both men: Pompeius Paulinus was Seneca's brother-in-law; Duvius Avitus came from Gallia Narbonnensis, like Nero's Praetorian prefect Burrus.
95 Castra Vetera is where Pliny was based as cavalry commander. The new fort was destroyed during the civil war following Nero's death.
96 Erdrich (2000), esp. 195–6 (clusters of Neronian and early Flavian coinage that may reflect targeted diplomatic gifts rather than general trade contacts).
97 See *ILS* 986, from the family tomb of the Plautii near Tibur (modern Tivoli), outside Rome.
98 For Silvanus' career, see Conole and Milns (1983). He was a relative of Britain's first governor, Aulus Plautius, and may have taken part in the British campaign.
99 D. Braund (2013), 89 with further bibliography.
100 Plautius sent Legion V Macedonica to support Paetus' men in Armenia.
101 The governor of Pannonia, Lucius Tampius Flavianus, similarly received *ornamenta triumphalia* from Vespasian for successful measures along middle Danube in Pannonia, including the settlement of populations from across the river, maybe perhaps still under Nero; see Griffin (1984), 118, 266 note 112 and *ILS* 985.
102 He continued to rule a coastal area of Cilicia on the Mediterranean coast that had been part of his realm or was now made over to him.
103 Heil (1997), 144–58; D. Braund (2013).
104 Heil (1997) argues convincingly that a later Corbulo-friendly tradition, which claimed that the final outcome of the Armenian question had already been proposed, is a manipulation of events.
105 These were legions IV Macedonica and XII Fulminata; in addition, Paetus had been assigned V Alaudae, which was still in Pontus en route from Moesia, and auxiliary units from Cappadocia, Galatia and Pontus. Corbulo retained III Cyrenaica, VI Ferrata and X Fretensis, along with the local Syrian contingents.
106 Tacitus, *Annals* 15.8.1.
107 See Heil (1997); others interpret Tacitus' account differently and place all these events in a single year.
108 Paetus' supporters accused Corbulo of deliberately slow progress during his relief operation, while Corbulo's side intimated that Paetus had enough supplies to hold out for much longer and avoid surrender.
109 In all probability, Paetus had already pledged Rome's recognition of Tiridates as king of Armenia (Heil (1997), 113–16), which Nero was now meant to confirm. The following negotiations were about the methods and face-saving ways of presenting this to the Roman public.
110 Cassius Dio, *Roman History* 62.22.4 may contain a hint. He reports that Nero fell during a sacrifice and abandoned his plans due to this ill omen; however, he may really have intended to join the troops, but changed his mind perhaps due to other political considerations – or the plans were merely designed to boost morale through a show of determination.
111 The scale in Roman lives of Paetus' battlefield losses is not clear, but may have been considerable. Corbulo sent Paetus' two legions back to Syria, their fighting power much diminished, and instead took III Cyrenaica and VI Ferrata from there with him. Legion XV Apollinaris was sent from Pannonia. In total, Corbulo now commanded seven legions, almost a quarter of Rome's entire military strength.
112 Suetonius, *Nero* 39.1. He adds, almost certainly incorrectly, that Paetus' legions had to pass under the yoke – in Roman terms, a grave dishonour – and that Syria was barely retained.

Chapter IV

1 Tacitus, *Annals* 13.48.1: *vis multitudinis* and *avaritia magistratuum et primi cuiusque*, in reference to events at Puteoli in AD 58; he uses almost the same words to describe scenes of unrest there and in Rome in AD 62 (see ibid. 14.45.1), and in both cases the people are armed with stones and firebrands.
2 Tacitus (*Annals* 13.11.1) describes how the senate intended to use honours as a means to influence Nero's behaviour.
3 Tacitus, *Annals* 13.5.1. In the Roman legal system anyone could be a *delator*, or prosecutor. Successful prosecutors were paid a fee taken from the convicted individual's fortune. Financial greed and attempts to win political favour compromised the system, so that the term could take on the overwhelmingly negative meaning of 'informer', see Rutledge (2001).
4 Tacitus, *Annals* 13.10.1. The senator was Carinas Celer, not otherwise recorded.
5 Tacitus, *Annals* 13.23.1. The *delator* was a certain Paetus, who had accused the Guard prefect Burrus and the freedman Pallas of a conspiracy against Nero, but seems mostly to have targeted Pallas' wealth.
6 See Rathbone (2008), 255.
7 Nero only held the highest office for two months, his colleague for four, thus allowing seven others the honour of a consulship as *suffecti* (among them Seneca).
8 Tacitus, *Annals* 13.11.1. This was Plautius Lateranus, a nephew of the general commanding the Claudian conquest of Britain, Aulus Plautius. Lateranus had been involved in an alleged conspiracy with Messalina in AD 48. Due to his uncle's reputation, he was spared the death penalty at the time, but removed from the senate.
9 Tacitus, *Annals* 13.24.1.
10 Tacitus, *Annals* 13.24.1. Ibid. 1.77.1 about the earlier riots of AD 15, when numerous members of the *plebs* as well as many soldiers and a centurion of the guard were killed; a tribune was also wounded. The Praetorians had been sent in to stop insults against the leading magistrates; for general context, see Slater (1994).
11 Tacitus (*Annals* 13.28.1) mentions the attempt by a tribune to force the release of supporters who had been incarcerated on the orders of a praetor. The senate endorsed the praetor's decision and then moved against the rights of the tribunes.
12 Tacitus, *Annals* 13.28.1. Rathbone (2008), 258–9, argues that the 'poor' (*inopes*) were the knights rather than the *plebs*. Probably in response to the tribune's failed initiative, Nero transferred the charge of these accounts from the quaestors of the aerarium to prefects. This is often described as a mere administrative detail (see, for example, Griffin (1984), 56–7), but the prefects served for three years and were appointed by the *princeps* rather than the senate. Presumably this allowed Nero more direct control, whereas the previous system had led to abuses.
13 Tacitus, *Annals* 13.26.1–27.1.
14 Suetonius, *Nero* 15.1; 10.1. Subsidies for some impoverished senators reached 500,000 sesterces, or half the full census requirement.
15 Tacitus, *Annals* 13.28.1.
16 Tacitus claims (with some hyperbole) that gangs roamed the streets and Rome at night felt like a captured city; *Annals* 13.25.1.
17 Tacitus, *Annals* 13.25.1. A good example from later in Nero's reign is the fun poked at Nero and the senators by the actor Datus; Suetonius, *Nero* 39.3. It is unclear whether the decision to reinstate the guards and expel the actors was Nero's or the senate's, although the military was under imperial command (Tacitus uses the generic term 'soldier'; the Praetorians took their orders from the *princeps*, the urban cohorts theoretically from the *praetor urbanus*, a senator).
18 Tacitus, *Annals* 13.25.1; Suetonius, *Nero* 26.1; Cassius Dio, *Roman History* 61.8.1–4; 9.24; see also Pliny the Elder, *Natural History* 13.43.126 (perhaps his lost history was the common source). The interpretation offered here differs sharply from most Nero studies, which tend to accept the source version with few modifications; see, for example, Champlin (2003), 150–3: 'Here was a young emperor, a tough brawler who actually joined and encouraged his people in their unrestrained pleasures' (ibid. 152). The obvious contradictions and its different versions further mitigate against taking it literally, although there is evidence of raucous behaviour by *iuvenes* in Roman cities that may have been used as inspiration.
19 The *lex Iulia de repetundis* passed during Caesar's consulship in 59 BC tightened existing regulations regarding senatorial office holders; it did not cover equestrians, who only became important under the principate. Senators were thereby generally forbidden to accept gifts in cash or kind while in their provinces and could not levy unauthorised taxes or requisitions. Clearly, this had been common practice by officials aiming to enrich themselves. See also Brunt (1961).
20 Tacitus, *Annals* 13.31–3. The *princeps* now forbade magistrates from holding gladiatorial *munera* in their provinces, a measure aimed at limiting bribery and extortion.
21 Brunt (1961).
22 Tacitus, *Annals* 13.32.1.
23 Both measures may have been connected to the inauguration of his new amphitheatre. Among other fiscal interventions, Nero also remitted the sales tax on enslaved individuals; for the context, see Rathbone (2008), 258.
24 Tacitus, *Annals* 13.48.1. This was clearly a *concordia ordinum* to the liking of the senate, enforced from above. Many modern scholars have adopted Tacitus' language and point of view without questioning; see, for example, Griffin (1984), 56.
25 Cassius Longinus was finally exiled in AD 66 in the aftermath of the Pisonian conspiracy. His son-in-law Domitius Corbulo was forced to commit suicide in AD 67.
26 Tacitus, *Annals* 13.50.1. On *publicani* in general, see Cottier et al. (2008) with bibliography; Badian (1972).
27 Various interest groups could try to steer these interactions through organised claques, including certain senators and knights, but on occasion also the *princeps*. Big performances in the theatres provided the main opportunities for this basic form of 'dialogue' between all the different orders. For a discussion of the events surrounding this particular tax reform and the way it was implemented, see Rathbone (2008), 260–1.
28 Tacitus, *Annals* 13.51.1. See also Rathbone (2008), 262–4.
29 The list in Brunt (1961), 227 shows that the overwhelming majority of known cases was brought by Greek-speaking provinces.
30 Tacitus, *Annals* 13.51.1.
31 Tacitus, *Annals* 13.52.1. In the impeachment trials, Nero acquitted two former proconsuls of the province of Africa, Sulpicius Camerinus and Pompeius Silvanus. However, the Bythinians successfully prosecuted Marcus Tarquitius Priscus for extortion while in office, apparently to the delight of the senate; he had previously been restored to the senate by Nero, after an earlier expulsion. Nero also assigned stipends to three senators who had fallen on hard times, so that they could meet their census requirements and maintain their rank.
32 Tacitus, *Annals* 13.42.1–43.1. See also Brunt (1961).
33 Tacitus, *Annals* 14.17.1. See also Moeller (1970). The consuls introduced a ten-year ban on gladiatorial shows in Pompeii and dissolved some of the local clubs; the organiser of the spectacle, a former senator named Livineius Regulus, was exiled.
34 Tacitus (*Annals* 14.42.1) cites that the reason was that Secundus had denied the enslaved man his manumission, for which the latter had already made payments. Yet he immediately undermines what might be considered a just grievance by claiming that the motive for the murder may also have been homosexual rivalry between master and enslaved individual over a third man (an interesting notion in itself in terms of its social implications).
35 Tacitus, *Annals* 14.40.3.
36 Watson (1987), chapter 2. Seneca (*On Mercy* 1.24.1) advised Nero that, for this very reason, a proposal once introduced in the senate that suggested the enslaved population should wear distinctive clothing was later withdrawn – it would have been too dangerous if they had realised their vast number compared to the free. See Bradley (1988).
37 Tacitus uses very similar expressions to describe the revolts in Rome and Puteoli; both are called sedition, and both involved 'stones and firebrands' (*Annals* 14.42.1/45.1; 13.48.1).
38 Tacitus, *Annals* 15.18.1.
39 Tacitus, *Annals* 15.18.1. The former consuls were Lucius Piso, Ducenius Geminus and Pompeius Paulinus.
40 See Cottier et al. (2008).
41 See Rathbone (2008).

42 This measure was long misunderstood as devaluation aimed at covering increasing budget deficits caused by Nero's overspending. The academic consensus has shifted the other way; the utility of Nero's reforms meant that the new standard was kept in place by later *principes*, except for a symbolic and short-lived reversion to the old gold-standard under Domitian. See Griffin (1984), 197–8; Rathbone (2008), 266 with note 44; Butcher and Ponting (2014), 201–38.
43 Elsner (1994); Hesberg (2016).
44 Suetonius, *Claudius* 18.2.
45 Griffin (1984), 119–25; 238–9; see also Leoni (2011).
46 Weiss (2013).
47 Suetonius, *Nero* 9.
48 Cassius Dio, *Roman History*, 61.18.3.
49 Rainbird, Sear and Sampson (1971).
50 *CIL* VI 9183 = *ILS* 7501. See Marzano (2013), 285–8 with the interesting suggestion that on occasion the market may also have sold surplus fish from Nero's *vivaria*, or marine fishponds.
51 Ghini (1988), 121–77.
52 Martial 7.34.4.
53 See Filippi (2010).
54 Although dedicated by T. Statilius Taurus, the amphitheatre was an important part of the wider Augustan building programme in Rome. It appears to have influenced the typology of such structures throughout Augustan Italy, not least through the likely use of the Tuscan order for its façade, see Welch (2007), 108–27. For the arguments concerning a largely wooden interior, see ibid. 116.
55 See Edmondson (1996), 78 with note 34.
56 Suetonius, *Caligula* 21.1.
57 The original location of Nero's amphitheatre has not been identified. Perhaps it was constructed in the same spot as Caligula's aborted project, which would place it *iuxta Saepta*, 'near the Saepta'.
58 Pliny the Elder, *Natural History* 16.76.200. He gives the length as about 36 m.
59 Flaig b (2003), 232–42 also points out that the theatres and other entertainment venues provided the main opportunity for the *plebs* to interact with the senate as a body.
60 The sequence of the main *ludi* over the course of the calendar year was this: *ludi Megalenses* (4–10 April); *ludi Ceriales* (12–19 April: *Cerealia* 12 April); *ludi Florales* (28 April – 3 May: *Floralia* 1 May); *ludi Apollinares* (6–13 July); *ludi Victoriae Caesaris* (20–30 July); *ludi Romani* (4–19 September); *ludi Augustales* (3–12 October: *Augustalia* 12 October); *ludi Plebeii* (4–17 November: Ides of Jupiter 13 November).
61 Tacitus, *Dialogus de Oratoribus* 29.
62 Suetonius, *Claudius* 21.
63 Suetonius, *Claudius* 34.1.
64 Champlin (2003), 68–77 provides a broad chronological overview. Some of the details are open to discussion. Suetonius, for example, explicitly states that Nero gave only one gladiatorial show, but Champlin attributes a whole sequence to him.
65 Calpurnius Siculus, *Eclogues* 7.23–84.
66 Pliny the Elder, *Natural History* 37.11.45. The largest piece of amber brought back from this expedition weighed an astonishing 13 Roman pounds, more than 4.2 kg. According to Pliny, the journey involved traversing just under 900 km of Germanic tribal territory each way.
67 Pliny the Elder, *Natural History* 19.6.23–5. These awnings may have been the model for those of the Flavian Colosseum later, which were operated by sailors from the Misenum fleet.
68 Seneca, *Naturales Questiones* 2.9.2.
69 Tacitus, *Annals* 13.31.1.
70 The evidence for the moment remains somewhat inconclusive; see Campbell (2019), 250–1 with a summary of the argument and bibliography in note 26.
71 Campbell (2019), 251 note 28.
72 Tacitus, *Annals* 15.46.1.
73 Seneca, *Letters to Lucilius* 70.22–3; 70.20–1.
74 See Cagniart (2000) with references and bibliography. A particularly striking letter is 7.2–5, where Seneca refers to the executions as 'pure murder'.
75 Wealthy Romans often supported friends who organised spectacles as part of their political career with gifts of cash or the provision of animals and gladiators; see Seneca, *De Beneficiis* 1.12.3; 2.21.5–6.
76 Pliny the Elder, *Natural History* 35.33.52.
77 Tacitus, *Annals* 15.34.1–35.1.
78 Bellen (1981), 44–6; Speidel (1994), 29.
79 Suetonius, *Nero* 30.1.
80 Cassius Dio, *Roman History* 61.9.1; see Champlin (2003), 68. Claudius similarly had a squadron of mounted Praetorians led by their prefects and tribunes hunt panthers in the circus; see Suetonius, *Claudius* 21.3.
81 For the Circus Maximus in general, see Humphrey (1986); Nelis-Clément and Roddaz (2008); Marcattili (2009); Letzner (2009). Its capacity was steadily increased. Pliny claims that it later could accommodate 250,000 spectators.
82 The Murcia stream ran through the valley towards the Tiber. The valley itself was about 300 m across at its widest point and some 700 m long; soil accretion has much altered its shape since antiquity. The Roman arena floor is now 7 to 9 m below the modern ground level.
83 The Temple of Sol was integrated into the seating at the south-western end of the circus; the shrines of Consus and Murcia were located on the central reservation. Elsewhere on the Aventine were temples to Ceres, Liber, Flora and Venus. The Ara Maxima, with its own important cults, lay beyond the starting gates.
84 Favro (1999).
85 In Nero's time these were the theatres of Pompeius, Marcellus and Balbus, all located in the Campus Martius, with a combined capacity estimated at about 60,000 people.
86 Caesar added the first tiers of stone seating and a broad ditch, the *euripus*, that provided a protective barrier between the arena and the spectators.
87 This obelisk was rediscovered during excavations in 1587 under Pope Sixtus V and set up on the modern Piazza del Populo two years later.
88 In Latin they were called *russati* (Reds), *albati* (Whites), *veneti* (Blues) and *prasini* (Greens). The Blues and Greens were by far the dominant factions, the other two subsidiary. Charioteers and riders were normally employed by a particular faction, but could change.
89 Suetonius, *Nero* 22.2; see Horsmann (1998), 93–4 with note 8. Cassius Dio reports that the praetor Fabricius Veiento during the first part of Nero's reign refused to bow to the financial demands of the faction managers and prepared to replace horses with dogs; the smaller Red and White factions gave in, but the Greens and Blues stuck to their claims. In the end, Nero provided the prize money out of his personal funds, so that the horse races could go ahead (Cassius Dio, *Roman History* 61.6.2).
90 Suetonius, *Nero* 22.
91 Horsmann (1998), 31 with references.
92 The headquarters of the Greens were located under the Palazzo della Cancelleria, the Blues not far away in the area of Palazzo Farnese and the others presumably nearby. See Richardson (1992), 366 s.v. 'Stabula IIII Factionum' and *LTUR*, vol. 4, 339–40 s.v. 'Stabula IIII Factionum' (Coarelli (2007)).
93 Suetonius, *Caligula* 55.2–3.
94 Horsmann (1998) remains the most thorough study.
95 In addition to regular prize money, there could be lavish gifts. Caius gave the Green charioteer Eutychus 2 million sesterces, twice the minimum census requirement of a senator (Suetonius, *Caligula* 55.2).
96 Apart from social stigma, *infamia* brought exclusion from public offices and many restrictions in a legal context (*infames* could not serve as jurors or act as prosecutors, for instance); *infames* might also be subject to corporal punishment. See Leppin (1992) with source references and bibliography. The focus of the study is on actors, but it discusses *infamia* more widely. See also Edwards (1993), 98–136.
97 Suetonius, *Nero* 16.2.
98 Suetonius, *Nero* 22.1. Dio claims that Nero later provided fanciful apparel for famous racehorses that had been retired and gave money towards their food (Cassius Dio, *Roman History* 61.6.1). According to Suetonius, he was particularly fond of a Spanish steed (Suetonius, *Nero* 46.1).
99 Suetonius, *Nero* 22.1. Suetonius, however, mentions the *princeps*' eager attendance in order to slur Nero's character, adding that Nero at first attended secretly, but then let go of any pretence.
100 Suetonius, *Nero* 22.1.
101 Pliny the Elder, *Natural History* 33.90. See also Cameron (1976), 62.
102 Cameron (1976) focuses on the Byzantine period, but discusses earlier developments in passing. The transformation of the factions into quasi-political organisations was a much later phenomenon. During the first century, organised theatre claques seem to have been more important in this respect.
103 Suetonius, *Nero* 11.1. Another innovation of the time of Claudius and Nero were fights between elephants and individual gladiators; see Pliny the Elder, *Natural History* 8.7.22.
104 See Humphrey (1986), 101. Claudius had already reinstated dedicated seating for the senators, which Caius previously seems to have temporarily revoked in order to humiliate them. This had led to several deaths when senators and knights were crushed among the crowds when the gates to the circus were opened.
105 For an overview, see Coleman (1993).
106 Cassius Dio, *Roman History* 69.9.5. The most famous of these battles was fought at Salamis in 480 BC, but there were a number of other notable engagements between Athenian and Persian fleets during the fifth and fourth centuries BC.
107 Coleman (1993); Dunkle (2013), 197.
108 Seneca, *Letters to Lucilius* 70.26.
109 Suetonius, *Nero* 12.1 (however, his reference to 'salt water' poses a problem in connection with the *naumachia*, which was supplied by sweet water from an aqueduct and drained into the Tiber); Cassius Dio, *Roman History* 61.9.5.
110 Alternatively, Augustus' basin could be described as *stagnum*, for example by Tacitus; see Van Buren and Stevens (1927) with source references.
111 Suetonius, *Nero* 11.2: *ludi 'pro aeternitate imperii'*. For the link, see Champlin (2003), 69. Cassius Dio (*Roman History* 61.21.1) records a similar motto for the *Neronia* in AD 60 ('for his salvation and the continuance of his power'). Heinemann (2014), 226 links this to Nero's *quinquennalia* only.
112 Cassius Dio, *Roman History* 61.17.2.
113 Suetonius, *Nero* 11.2; Cassius Dio (*Roman History* 61.18.1–2) gives a similar account, but specifies that Nero threw the crowd small inscribed balls that served as tokens for the various gifts.
114 Tacitus, *Annals* 14.15; Suetonius, *Nero* 12.4; Cassius Dio, *Roman History* 61.19.1–20.1. Nero collected the hair in a golden box (Suetonius mentions a golden box adorned with priceless pearls, Dio a golden globe) and dedicated it in the Temple of Iupiter Capitolinus. The ritual was accompanied by a 'splendid sacrifice of bullocks'.
115 Schneider (2003) with earlier bibliography.
116 Big hair was the mark of young gods; Alexander the Great became the model for ruler portraits in this style.
117 See Cain (1993) for the portraits of the Neronian and Flavian eras.
118 Suetonius, *Nero* 27.2. For Nero's banquets, see also Vössing (2004), esp. 439–45. He posits that Nero and his fellow banqueters dined by themselves, with the populace watching from a distance.
119 Tacitus, *Annals* 15.37.1. He locates the festivities at the 'Stagnum of Agrippa', an ornate pool near the Baths of Agrippa in the Campus Martius. Cassius Dio (*Roman History* 62.15.1–6, a Xiphilinus epitome) seems to describe the same feast (partly conflated with events at the *Iuvenalia*) but places it in Augustus' *naumachia* (which was sometimes also called *stagnum*). The narrative is very similar and possibly derived from a common source, although some of the descriptions differ slightly; here, the booths are erected on wooden planking fastened to floating wine barrels. Nero's and Tigellinus' debauchery is elaborated in more (invented) detail, including that they engaged in sexual acts with high-born women – topical elements of vituperation that need not be taken literally.
120 Tacitus, *Annals* 15.37.1.
121 See Allen *et al.* (1962). Many elements of Tacitus' account match Ovid's description of genuine *Floralia* in every detail, for example prostitutes dancing in the nude.
122 Tacitus links Nero to unspecified sexual transgressions during the banquet and claims that he married a male prostitute (a man named Pythagoras) in an official ceremony a few days later. There is no need to believe any of this. Allen *et al.* (1962) proposes that Tacitus here wilfully took out of context a formal ceremony linked to one of the oriental cults fashionable in Rome at the time, in which new initiates ritually married the deity. This idea has not found wide acceptance, but it is of considerable merit nonetheless. Tacitus follows this alleged incident with an account of the infamous fire of Rome in AD 64, which he could thus implicitly blame on Nero's utter depravity.
123 Lebek (1990); Lebek (1991); Levick (1983); Slater (1994).
124 Tacitus, *Annals* 1.77.1, see Slater (1994), 125.
125 It soon became clear that a minor misdemeanour might lose them their seat in the 'fourteen rows' (see p. 160). This loss of knightly status freed them to go on stage without risking banishment. See Lebek (1991), 41–6; Slater (1994), 140–3.
126 Suetonius, *Divus Julius* 39. Cassius Dio, *Roman History* 43.23.5; 51.22.4; 53.31.3. These references collected in Slater (1994), 131.
127 Suetonius, *Nero* 4.1.
128 The age specifications of the AD 19 *senatus consultum* are particularly revealing in this context, see Slater (1994), 139–40.
129 Peacetime prosperity, however, brought ever more conspicuous consumption and therefore also made it harder to maintain a senatorial (or equestrian) lifestyle for some.
130 See Lebek (1990), 52–3. Nerva, loyal to Nero until the end, became emperor in AD 96 through election by the senate.

131 Slater (1994), 125 and 129.
132 See Lebek (1990), 45–6; Slater (1994), 129–31.
133 See, for example, the exaggerated reference in Juvenal (*Satires* 6.63–5): 'When sinuous Bathyllus dances his pantomime Leda, Tucia loses control of her bladder, and Apula yelps, as if she were making love, with sharp tedious cries.'
134 Harrison (2000); Zanobi (2014).
135 See Champlin (2003).
136 Suetonius, *Nero* 12.1.
137 For the staging of such executions, see Coleman (1990).
138 This may, of course, have included an element of peer pressure on individuals less comfortable with performing in public because they adhered to more traditional social norms.
139 Cassius Dio, *Roman History* 61.9.1.
140 Tacitus, *Annals* 15.32.1. The reference to women is particularly interesting.
141 Champlin (2003), 73 and 76 conversely identifies Nero as patron of these shows. However, Suetonius states that Nero sponsored only a single *munus* (*Nero* 11.1).
142 Suetonius, *Nero* 11.2. Dio omits the mention of a knight, but has a little more detail on the act: 'It was on this occasion that an elephant was led up to the highest gallery of the theatre and walked down from that point on ropes, carrying a rider' (*Roman History* 61.17.2).
143 Cassius Dio, *Roman History* 61.17.1–4.
144 The lack of coercion is also stressed by Champlin (2003), 68–77.
145 Tacitus, in his outrage moving into a rare first-person narrative, states about those who took part: 'They have passed away, and I regard it as a debt due to their ancestors not to record them by name' (*Annals* 14.14.1). Dio, by contrast, goes on to name and shame (although his list seems to be made up to suit his narrative): 'So the men of that day beheld the great families – the Furii, the Horatii, the Fabii, the Porcii, the Valerii, and all the rest whose trophies and whose temples were to be seen – standing down there below them and doing things some of which they formerly would not even watch when performed by others' (*Roman History* 61.17.4). He then imagines people from the provinces conquered by the scions of these families pointing out their descendants in the arena and on stage.
146 Suetonius, *Nero* 11.1. Much here hinges on a correct contextual translation of the Latin. Suetonius uses the verb *recipere*, literally 'to receive' – there is no hint whatsoever of compulsion, rather the opposite ('to accept'). Older English versions can be subtly misleading.
147 Cassius Dio (*Roman History* 61.19.1–4) makes much of the shame felt by those who had to perform, and claims that Nero forced them to take their masks off, in order to humiliate them in front of the common crowd. This element seems entirely made up; Tacitus, ever critical, does not mention it at all.
148 Tacitus, *Annals* 14.15.1.
149 Tacitus, *Annals* 14.15.1; Suetonius, *Nero* 20.3; Cassius Dio, *Roman History* 61.19.3–4. Dio quotes some of their chants: 'Glorious Caesar! Our Apollo, our Augustus, another Pythian! By yourself we swear, O Caesar, no one surpasses you.' According to Suetonius, the different rhythmic cadences of applause had specific names, like 'the bees', 'the roof tiles' and 'the bricks'.
150 Suetonius, *Nero* 20.3.
151 Suetonius, *Nero* 12.3.
152 Tacitus, *Annals* 14.21.4. For the popularity of *certamina Graeca*, see Weeber (1994), 73–9; Newby (2005), esp. chapter 2; Heinemann (2014), 219.
153 See Weeber (1994), 75–6.
154 Tactius, *Annals* 15.74.1.
155 See Slater (1994), 138. After AD 59, Nero had also constructed a new gymnasium in Ravenna, on grounds inherited from his aunt Domitia; see Cassius Dio (*Roman History* 61.17.2), who tellingly calls them 'magnificent' and 'very popular still' in his own day.
156 See Slater (1994), 139–40.
157 Nero also assigned seats of honour to the Vestals, highly respected priestesses, during the athletic contests, citing the attendance of the priestess of Demeter at the contests in Olympia as examples.
158 Suetonius, *Nero* 12.3.
159 Tacitus, *Annals* 16.2.1; 4.1–5.1; Suetonius, *Nero* 21.1–2. See Heinemann (2014), 224–7 on the date.
160 Suetonius, *Vitellius* 4.1.
161 For Titus, see Suetonius, *Titus* 3.2. For Nero and Britannicus, see Tacitus, *Annals* 13.15.1.; Suetonius, *Nero* 33.2. Tacitus focuses on the song's critical theme (which may have been his invention), while Suetonius claims that Nero killed Britannicus in part because he was jealous of his brother's more agreeable singing voice. All one might reasonably take from this assertion is that princes and their peers routinely sang or performed music on certain intimate palace occasions.
162 Suetonius, *Nero* 20.1. Suetonius mentions various exercises related to strengthening and preserving the voice in particular. They include Nero lying on his back with lead plates on his chest (to build breathing muscles), purging his stomach (presumably before performances) and excluding foods that might have an ill effect on his voice.
163 See Champlin (2003), 57–8.
164 Quintilian, *Institutio Oratoria* 11.3.170–1, with reference to orators. See also Power (2010), 7–8 with note 8.
165 Cassius Dio, *Roman History* 61.20.2. According to Suetonius (*Nero* 20.1), Nero often quoted the Greek proverb 'Hidden music counts for nothing'. Evidently, this sentiment was shared by many other amateur performers at the time.
166 Naples: Suetonius, *Nero* 20.2. Nero also dined in the theatre with the crowds all around him, similar to the lavish public banquets he had given in Rome. 'Niobe': ibid. 21.2.
167 Tacitus, *Annals* 16.21.1. The occasion was the ancient Patavian festival of the *ludi cetasti*, perhaps in AD 56 or 57. It may be that Publius Pomponius Secundus, a celebrated author of tragedies and recent governor of Upper Germany, wrote the play in which Paetus performed; see Linderski (1992); Champlin (2003), 66.
168 Tacitus, *Annals* 15.65.1. For Piso as citharode, see *Laus Pisonis*, 166–8 (Apollo himself may have tutored Piso).
169 Champlin (2003), 42–4.
170 Suetonius, *Nero* 25.2.
171 Suetonius (*Nero* 21.3) records Nero taking on the following tragic roles: 'Canace in childbirth', 'Orestes the matricide', 'Oedipus blinded', 'Hercules insane'. Cassius Dio (*Roman History* 63.9.4–5; 10.2; 22.6), presumably with recourse to a common source (perhaps Cluvius Rufus), lists Oedipus, Thyestes, Hercules, Alcmaeon, Orestes and Canace. See also Champlin (2003), 77.
172 See Champlin (2003), 96–111 for an attempt to decode the motivations behind Nero's adoption of specific roles.
173 See Champlin (2003), 110: 'For Nero, it was not a matter of art for art's sake. He used the stage […] as a platform for his views, presented in mythological dress.'
174 Cassius Dio, *Roman History* 63.9.4. The role of 'Canace in childbirth' is a prime example. For a male actor to convey the agonised moans of a woman in labour posed the ultimate artistic challenge, but, more importantly, Canace was a mythological figure who gave birth to a child conceived through incest, and, in the end, she committed suicide. Nero would thus both publicly confirm the prevailing rumours to the senatorial readers for whom the source texts were originally intended, and prefigure his own end. Similarly, modern readers might be amused by anecdotes about desperate audiences locked into theatres during Nero's performances. Allegedly, women were forced to give birth in their seats and men pretended to be dead, so they could be carried out for burial (Suetonius, *Nero* 23.2); on one occasion, Nero supposedly continued his performance through an earthquake (ibid. 20.2).
175 Tacitus, *Annals* 13.3.1.
176 Tacitus, *Annals* 14.16.1; Suetonius, *Nero* 52.1.
177 Suetonius, *Nero* 10.1.
178 Martial, *Epigrams* 8.70; Suetonius, *Vitellius* 11.
179 Suetonius, *Nero* 4.1; 5.1; 22.1–2; 24.2; Suetonius, *Vitellius* 4.1. It is possible that Nero's family owned stud farms and had links to the racing industry; they almost certainly kept horses on their estates. Many private villas of the period had their own tracks for racing.
180 According to Pliny, Nero even adopted the curious habit of professional charioteers who drank the ashes of dried boar's dung dissolved in water, before triga races; wild boar's dung, dried or fresh (or dissolved in vinegar), apparently was routinely used to treat contusions from accidents suffered on the racetrack; Pliny the Elder, *Natural History* 28.72.237–8.
181 Suetonius, *Nero* 22.2; Tacitus, *Annals* 14.14.1. Tacitus claims that Nero's advisors Seneca and Burrus had tried to channel and contain Nero's energies by steering him towards racing rather than performing as a citharode, and restricting his activities to his private gardens.
182 Suetonius, *Nero* 20.3.

Chapter V

1 For their portraits, see for example Wood (2001) with ample bibliography. Rose (1997) and Boschung (2002) give a sense of the high proportion of female images in Julio-Claudian statue galleries. For the deliberate destruction of their images, see Varner (2001).
2 Edwards (1993), 34–62.
3 See Joshel (1995) with examples and further bibliography. The contrast between Joshel and Syme (1981) shows the sea change in scholarship on this issue.
4 Cassius Dio, *Roman History* 61.11.4 with particular reference to Fabius Rusticus and Cluvius Rufus.
5 Tacitus, *Annals* 13.1.1. For literary effect, Tacitus echoes here his opening passage of Tiberius' reign, which began with the killing of Agrippa Postumus (ibid. 1.6.1).
6 Tacitus, *Annals* 13.1.1.
7 Tacitus, *Annals* 13.1.1: *vulgi fama* – the 'rumour of the crowd'.
8 Tacitus, *Annals* 13.20.3.
9 Pliny the Elder, *Natural History* 7.13.58: Silanus 'was poisoned by Nero, on his accession to the throne'.
10 Tacitus, *Annals* 13.19.1. Rubellius Plautus was Tiberius' great-grandson, and therefore, by virtue of Tiberius' adoption by Augustus, the first *princeps*' great-great-grandson, like Nero (Tacitus stresses that they ranked equally in terms of descent).
11 Tacitus, *Annals* 13.18.1: 'quasi quaereret ducem et partes'.
12 Tacitus, *Annals* 13.19.1.
13 Tacitus, *Annals* 4.53.1.
14 Tacitus, *Annals* 13.20.1: 'inimica domo' in reference to Iunia Silana.
15 Tacitus, *Annals* 13.21.1–22.1.
16 Tacitus, *Annals* 13.23.1.
17 *Delatores* like Paetus, prosecutors and informers, were a normal part of the Roman legal system; prosecutions were encouraged by granting the *delator* a financial share in the accused's property in the case of a successful conviction.
18 See Tacitus, *Annals* 13.12–14; 14.1–3.
19 Tacitus, *Annals* 4.53.2.
20 Pliny the Elder, *Natural History* 7.8.46. Tacitus adds an ambiguous passage (*Annals* 13.14.3) that has sometimes been linked to the contents of Agrippina's memoirs, but this may not be warranted. He writes that Agrippina claimed she would expose the 'ills' of her unfortunate house, from her own marriage to her poisonings.
21 Tacitus, *Annals* 14.3.1.
22 Tacitus had earlier alluded to her contacts with guards' tribunes and centurions (*Annals* 13.18.1).
23 Suetonius' claims (*Nero* 34.1) that Nero stripped Agrippina of all powers and honours therefore are plainly exaggerated. His remarks that Nero continued to harass her and encouraged others to do the same lack any detail.
24 This is very much the way Tacitus and Cassius Dio characterised Boudica and Cartimandua, with slight variations in the imaginary speeches they composed for them (in the tradition of Roman historiography as a literary genre, authors were allowed considerable freedom here; what mattered was to capture character and intent). Cassius Dio writes that Boudica claimed Rome was ruled by Messalina, followed by Agrippina and then Nero, who 'though in name a man, is in fact a woman' (*Roman History* 62.6.3).
25 Tacitus, *Annals* 14.2.1 again enumerates Agrippina's alleged affairs and sexual advances in the pursuit of power.
26 See Drinkwater (2019), 179 and 190. See also Cassius Dio, *Roman History* 62.13.1.
27 Cassius Dio, *Roman History* 61.12.1 refers to the statements of 'many trustworthy men'. Dio mentions Poppaea as the other driving force. In connection with the Boudica rebellion, he similarly preferred sources that held Seneca chiefly culpable.
28 Tacitus, *Annals* 14.1.1, where these statements are attributed to Poppaea Sabina, most likely a purposeful transference to exculpate the senate from subsequent events.
29 Suetonius, *Nero* 34.2, contradicted by Tacitus (*Annals* 14.3.1) and Cassius Dio (*Roman History* 62.12.1) who claim that poisoning Agrippina was explicitly ruled out.
30 Dawson (1969); Barrett (1996), 181–95; Ginsburg (2006), 46–53; Drinkwater (2019), esp. 179–87 with the most recent bibliography.
31 Apparently, there were fears that Agrippina had too many supporters among the Praetorians, so the operation was entrusted to the marines instead, with whom she enjoyed no particular rapport.
32 Tacitus, *Annals* 14.10.1.
33 Scheid (1998), 71 nos 28a–c; 25–30. See also Champlin (2003), 220–1.
34 Tacitus, *Annals* 14.10.1–11.1. Apparently, Nero stated that Agrippina had opposed his donatives to the troops: a clear indication that there was a fear of residual loyalty to the war hero Germanicus' daughter among the army that had to be countered.
35 Anonymous ('Pseudo-Seneca'), *Octavia* 368–74 is the complete passage.
36 Cassius Dio, *Roman History* 61.13.5.

37 Tacitus, *Annals* 14.8.1. Tacitus adds that Agrippina's fate had been predicted by astrologers, whereupon she supposedly exclaimed '*occidat, dum imperet*', 'let him kill, so that he may rule!': a dramatic sentence to imply that both mother and son were monstrous, made for performance on stage – and beautifully invented by the historian.

38 Seneca, *Oedipus* 1038–9.

39 Tacitus, *Annals* 14.12.1. No sacrifices for Agrippina by the Arval Brethren are recorded after AD 59, see Scheid (1998).

40 For Poppaea, see Holztrattner (1995) with bibliography.

41 AD 9 was the year of Varus' catastrophic defeat in Germany. Poppaeus' brother, Quintus Poppaeus Secundus, served as suffect consul in the same year and later rose to become proconsul of Asia. Poppaeus co-sponsored the *lex Papia Poppaea*, an important piece of Augustan legislation concerning marriage, with strict provisions against adultery and celibacy.

42 Tacitus, *Annals* 13.45.2.

43 His new wife almost certainly accompanied him (their newborn son received the cognomen Asiaticus, perhaps because he was born in the province), in which case it is likely that Poppaea was there as well. Hypothetically, the first meeting between Poppaea and a five-year-old Nero might have happened there, too, for Nero's stepfather Passienus Crispus took over the proconsulship from Poppaea's stepfather Scipio. For the dates, see Syme (1983).

44 The preserved part of book 11 of Tacitus' *Annals* begins in the middle of Valerius Asiaticus' alleged conspiracy against Claudius; the elder Poppaea supposedly was linked to him in an adulterous affair; see *Annals*, 11.1.1–4.1. Poppaea's husband, in other words, had a part in the downfall of her mother.

45 Tacitus, *Annals* 12.42.1.

46 Tacitus, *Annals* 13.45.1.

47 It is often assumed that ill feeling between Poppaea and Agrippina began with Agrippina's dismissal of Poppaea's husband, and Tacitus vaguely links Poppaea's separation from Rufrius Crispinus to Nero's emerging interest in her. However, if the divorce was instead connected to the forced suicide of Poppaea's mother, or Crispinus' dismissal in AD 51, the opposite might be the case.

48 Tacitus, *Annals* 13.2.1 on Annaeus Serenus and Acte. Other versions mention Nero falling for Poppaea when she was already Otho's wife (with whom she supposedly had an affair while still married to Rufrius Crispinus); there are varied descriptions of a relationship that involved Nero, Otho and Poppaea all together, ending with a jealous Nero sending Otho away as governor of distant Lusitania (modern Portugal and part of western Spain).

49 Tacitus, *Annals* 13.45.1 introduces Poppaea in characteristic fashion: *maritos nec adulteros non distinguens*, 'not distinguishing between husbands and (adulterous) lovers'.

50 Tacitus, *Annals* 14.1.1 states that Poppaea incited Nero to take action. Ibid. 14.60.1 describes Poppaea as a 'woman who had long been Nero's concubine and first ruled him as his adulterous lover, then as his wife'.

51 Wilson (2003); Kragelund (2016).

52 For this portrait, see Tacitus, *Annals* 14.60.1.

53 Tacitus, *Annals* 14.60.1 on the divorce.

54 Tacitus, *Annals* 14.60.1; 62–3 on two different adultery charges.

55 Tacitus, *Annals* 14.61.1 states that Octavia claimed the unrest was organised by her political supporters.

56 Some evidence for ongoing loyalty to Octavia may come from the Vesuvian cities, see Capaldi

and Gasparri (2017) on images of Octavia in private houses at the time of their destruction in AD 79.

57 Caligula had similarly divorced several wives who did not give him children, and only married Milonia Caesonia after she had given birth to his daughter; see Winterling (2011), 105.

58 Tacitus, *Annals* 15.23.1.

59 Notably, Nero's main antagonist in the senate, Thrasea Paetus, had alone been forbidden to attend the senatorial reception at Antium. Apart from Octavia's death, the birth came not long after the military setbacks in Armenia and the deaths of Faustus Cornelius Sulla and Rubellius Plautus.

60 Tacitus, *Annals* 15.23.1 rather unsympathetically states that Nero was 'as incontinent in sorrow as in joy'; earlier, he had referred to Nero's 'more than human joy' at the birth of his daughter.

61 Miniero and Zevi (2008), 161 with bibliography.

62 The villa is now largely below sea level, due to the ongoing effects of bradyseism caused by the area's volcanic activity.

63 This would also rule out an identification as Claudia Octavia, who was nineteen or twenty when Nero's portraits began to show this hairstyle, far older than the girl depicted in the Baiae statue.

64 Apart from the coin evidence, Tacitus (*Annals* 15.23.1) mentions that her statues were added to the pulvinar, that is, the ritual feasting of the gods when their images were placed on special seats or dining couches to receive food offerings.

65 Smallwood (1959). Some years before, Poppaea had already supported the priests of the temple in Jerusalem against the Roman client king.

66 For the wider context and full bibliography, see Gazda, Clarke and McAlpine (2016).

67 Mules shod in gold, Pliny the Elder, *Natural History* 33.49; Poppaea bathing in asses' milk, ibid. 11.96; 28.50.

68 See Vout (2007), 160 with references.

69 Pliny the Elder, *Natural History* 37.12.

70 Tacitus, *Annals* 16.6.1; Suetonius, *Nero* 35.3; Cassius Dio, *Roman History* 62.27.4. Earlier, Nero had supposedly killed the son from Poppaea's first marriage, Rufrius Crispinus.

71 See, for example, Mayer (1982).

72 Tacitus, *Annals* 16.6.1–7.1.

73 Cassius Dio, *Roman History* 62.28.1.

74 Cassius Dio, *Roman History* 63.26.3.

75 Pliny the Elder, *Natural History* 12.41.

76 See Schubert (2011); Gillespie (2014) with bibliography.

77 Alleged sexual transgressions were an important element of vituperation, see Edwards (1993), 34–62. For a detailed discussion of Nero's sexuality, or rather its construction by various source authors, see Vout (2007), 136–66.

Chapter VI

1 The key accounts are Tacitus, *Annals* 15.38–45; Suetonius, *Nero* 38 and Cassius Dio, *Roman History* 62.16–18.

2 Panella b (2011) and Panella (2016) provide the most accessible summaries; for more detail and references, see also Panella (1996).

3 Tacitus, *Annals* 15.43.1.

4 The literature on the Neronian fire is vast; for an overview, see most recently Barrett (2020) with bibliography. Few scholars now believe that Nero caused the fire, but many still maintain he was responsible for the blemish it left on his reputation through his supposed mismanagement of the disaster.

5 See Priester (2002) for a collection of relevant sources.

6 Seneca the Elder, *Controversiae* 2.11. Similarly, his

son, some decades later: 'Think of the fires, the collapses' (Seneca, *Dialogues* 6.22.1).

7 Juvenal, *Satires* 3.5–9, 3.196–7.

8 Cicero (*De Lege Agraria Orationes Tres* 2.35.96) worries that Rome's poor streets and narrow lanes, with tall housing squeezed into tight valleys and up the mountain slopes, might compare unfavourably to the large cities in the Greek East.

9 Pliny the Elder, *Natural History* 3.5 (9).67.

10 Vitruvius, *De Architectura* 2.8.17.

11 Strabo, *Geography* 5.3.7.

12 Vitruvius, *De Architectura* 2.8.20. Pliny the Elder points out other instances of poor construction, with insufficient foundations and cracking walls, all in order to spend as little money as possible and maximise profits (*Natural History* 36.22 (51).172; 23 (55).176).

13 See Vitruvius, *De Architectura* 2.9.16.

14 For lists of major fires, see for example Werner (1906), Canter (1932) and Sablayrolles (1996) with sources and further bibliography.

15 Suetonius (*Tiberius* 50.3) reports in passing that Tiberius angrily demanded that Livia should not interfere after she had personally rushed to a fire near the Temple of Vesta and 'urged the people and soldiers to greater efforts, as had been her way while her husband [Augustus] was alive.'

16 Seneca, *Quaestiones Naturales* 1.15.5–6. It was a false alarm, caused by a natural phenomenon.

17 Suetonius, *Tiberius* 48.1. He claims that Tiberius spoilt this impression of selfless liberality by changing the name of the Caelian Hill to the Augustan Hill (*Mons Augustus*).

18 Tacitus, *Annals* 4.64.1.

19 Tacitus, *Annals* 6.51.1. The only major public building projects Tiberius sponsored in Rome were a temple for the deified Augustus and a new stage façade in the Theatre of Pompeius.

20 The other members were Cassius Longinus, Marcus Vinicius and Rubellius Blandus. The consuls added Publius Petronius as a fifth commissioner (Tacitus, *Annals* 6.51.1).

21 Suetonius, *Claudius* 6.2.

22 Cassius Dio, *Roman History* 59.9.4. The same incident may be Suetonius, *Caligula* 16.3: '[Caligula] made good to many their losses from fires'. A fire involving the Horrea Aemiliana in AD 38 is recorded in the Fasti Ostienses, see Sablayrolles (1996), 785–6, no. 49, who links all these references to one specific incident.

23 Pliny the Elder, *Natural History* 35.19.

24 Suetonius, *Claudius* 18.1.

25 See Cassius Dio, *Roman History* 61.33.12: 'once, when a great conflagration was consuming the city, she [Agrippina] accompanied him [Claudius] as he lent his assistance'.

26 Pliny the Elder, *Natural History* 34.19.69.

27 Juvenal (*Satires* 3.198–202) describes how those high up below the roof ('where the gentle doves lay their eggs') were doomed if a fire broke out on the ground floor. The upper floors housed the poorest tenants.

28 During the late Republic, Marcus Licinius Crassus established a private fire brigade of 500 enslaved men, as well as architects and engineers. Whenever a building was ablaze, he acquired it cheaply from the distressed owner, together with any neighbouring properties threatened by the flames. Only then did his men try to contain the fire; see Plutarch, *Crassus* 2.4.

29 Cassius Dio, *Roman History* 53.24.4–6.

30 Cassius Dio, *Roman History* 54.2.4.

31 See Rainbird (1976) and Rainbird (1986). Much of the *vigiles*' basic organisational structure must have been in place from early on, even if most of the detailed evidence is from later centuries.

32 Scholion to Juvenal, *Satires* 14.305 and Tertullian, *Apology* 39; see Sablayrolles (1996), 356 with note 98.

33 This entitled them to the corn dole. Numbers of the *plebs frumentaria* were capped at around 200,000, so vacancies normally arose only through deaths and entrance was strictly regulated.

34 Petronius (*Satyricon* 78) jokingly alludes to the night patrols of the *vigiles* when he has the drunken host Trimalchio order his musicians to sound their horns, whereupon the *sparteoli*, mistaking it for an alarm signal, burst in and break up his dinner party.

35 Tacitus, *Annals* 15.38–41.

36 Tacitus, *Annals* 15.38.1–40.1.

37 The prevailing wind at the time of the fire may have been the Sirocco.

38 The scale of the fire clearly overwhelmed the *vigiles*, who must have been repeatedly outrun by it in their efforts to create firebreaks. Daugherty (1992), 239–40 suggests there may have been an unfortunate lack of experienced officers and senior NCOs that had an impact on the initial response, due to a recent freak event when the prefect of the *vigiles* and many of his senior staff had died of food poisoning after a banquet (caused by poisonous mushrooms; see Pliny the Elder, *Natural History* 22.47.96 and Seneca, *Epistles* 63.14–15). The prefect was Annaeus Serenus, a friend and relative of Seneca's. However, the date of this fateful banquet and the exact number and identity of fatalities are unknown.

39 Tacitus, *Annals* 15.38.1.

40 Suetonius, *Nero* 38.1.

41 Cassius Dio, *Roman History* 62.17.1.

42 Tacitus, *Annals* 39.1.

43 Tacitus, *Annals* 12.58.1; Suetonius, *Nero* 7.2.

44 Tacitus (*Annals* 15.22.2) claims that a bronze statue of Nero was melted down in the blaze, which together with the lightning strike was an ominous sign of divine displeasure. Some scholars think the Pompeii earthquake may have caused a tsunami that overwhelmed the ships in the port of Ostia; see Tuck (2019) with references.

45 Nero's and Poppaea's visit(s) to Pompeii must date to between AD 62 and 65.

46 Tacitus, *Annals* 15.39.1.

47 Tacitus, *Annals* 15.40.1

48 See Tacitus, *Annals* 15.1.1 with examples.

49 Tacitus, *Annals* 44.1.

50 *CIL* VI.826 = 30837, from the Quirinal Hill. The altars were only set up decades later, under Domitian. One precinct is preserved on the Quirinal; three sets of inscriptions (all lost) were recorded before the seventeenth century; see Closs (2016). The inscriptions clarify Tacitus' account about the duration of the fire; Suetonius and Cassius Dio wrongly believed that it lasted only six days.

51 See Johnstone (1992) with further examples of collective blame and punishment following suspected arson.

52 Tacitus (*Annals* 15.44.1) speaks of an 'immense multitude'; St. Jerome, in his letters, refers to 971 Christian martyrs.

53 *Digest* 47.9.9 (Gaius).

54 *Digest* 47.9.12.1 (Ulpian).

55 See Coleman (1990).

56 Tacitus, *Annals* 15.44.1.

57 Tacitus goes on to provide more detail on the Christians in general, but this may reflect the concern of Roman officials of his own rather than Nero's day; see Shaw (2015).

58 Paul may have been arrested in Jerusalem around AD 58 as a suspected rebel leader and executed in Rome in AD 60 or 61. However, the later Christian tradition sought to link the martyrdoms of St Paul and St Peter to the Great Fire; see Shaw (2015). Shaw interprets their martyrdoms as 'typological replays of the

executions of John the Baptist (beheading) and Jesus of Nazareth (crucifixion)', ibid. 75. For a range of different opinions, see also Keresztes (1984); Gray-Fow (1998); Fiedrowicz (2016) with further references and bibliography.

59 However, if Christian predictions of an impending apocalypse were more widely known, they may have provided a reasonable cause for suspicion; see Luke 12:49 ('I have come to bring fire on the earth, and how I wish it were already kindled!') and the Book of Revelations (8:8).

60 Tacitus, *Annals* 15.44.1.

61 Newbold (1974), the only study concerned with the economic consequences of the Great Fire for the urban *plebs*, does not consider this aspect. However, Brunt (1980) makes the case that the *plebs* had to earn a living and could be employed in this way.

62 Tacitus, *Annals* 15.43.1. See also Suetonius, *Nero* 16.1. The porticoes may also have been intended to protect people from falling debris when they took to the streets in a conflagration; see Hermansen (1982), 223.

63 See MacDonald (1982), 29.

64 Tacitus, *Annals* 15.43.1.

65 Gaius, *Institutes* 1.33; see Newbold (1974), 862.

66 Tacitus, *Annals* 16.13.3.

67 Seneca, *Letters* 91.14. The date of Seneca's letter is disputed: it ought to have been written after the Great Fire of Rome, but oddly makes no direct reference to it (perhaps in order not to distract from the Lugdunum disaster and the letter's consolatory intent); see Griffin (2013), 93, 97–8 with bibliography.

68 Tacitus, *Annals* 15.43.1.

69 Statius, *Silvae* 2.7.60–1.

70 Cassius Dio, *Roman History* 62.16.1–2.

71 Suetonius, *Nero* 38.1–2 (the quote may be a line from Euripides' lost play *Bellerophon*); Anonymous ('Pseudo-Seneca'), *Octavia* 831–3; Tacitus, *Annals*, 15.40.1.

72 Tacitus, *Annals* 15.39.1. It would have taken considerable time for a messenger to travel to Antium in the middle of the night and inform the emperor, and then for Nero to make his way back to Rome.

73 Tacitus, *Annals* 15.39.1.

74 Suetonius, *Nero* 38.2; Cassius Dio, *Roman History* 62.18.1. The different locations (stage/tower/palace roof) reflect the casual use these authors made of their likely source(s), which did not depend on facts to begin with.

75 As crown prince, Nero had given a well-received speech in Greek on behalf of the city of Ilium (Troy), much of which featured the city's mythological past and links to Rome; see Tacitus, *Annals* 12.58.1; Suetonius, *Nero* 7.2. The topic continued to resonate with him.

76 *Carmina Einsiedlensia* 1.40–1. This is the attractive interpretation advanced by Scheda (1967). However, the chronology of the poem and the identity of its author are much disputed, making this one reading of many. See also Schulz (2019), 212–13.

77 Suetonius, *Nero* 11.2.

78 Tacitus, *Annals* 15.38.1; Cassius Dio, *Roman History* 62.17.1.

79 Quintilian, *Institutio Oratoria* 8.3.67–9.

80 Tacitus, *Annals* 15.41.1. The Gaulish sack of 390 BC was discussed at length by the Roman historian Livy (*Ab Urbe Condida* 5.34–49) and others, who transformed this distant disaster into a Roman foundational myth.

81 Suetonius, *Nero* 38.1.

82 Tacitus, *Annals* 15.45.1 (who added that even temples were 'despoiled' and deprived of their precious offerings); Suetonius, *Nero* 38.1; Cassius Dio, *Roman History* 62.18.4 (he also falsely alleged that Nero deprived the Roman people of their corn dole).

83 Rathbone (2008), 252.

84 Suetonius, *Nero* 38.1.

85 Seneca (*Controversiae* 5.5.1–2) provides an often-quoted example of a rich man burning down a poor man's house to protect his own. Roman law stipulated that a property owner was entitled to this course of action. The legislation itself is a clear indication of the frequency of such conflicts. Normally, it involved a wealthy person securing his property at the expense of a poorer neighbour. In this case, however, the neighbours were men from Rome's oldest families.

Chapter VII

1 Winterling (1999).

2 Neronian court poetry may have praised the new palace, but nothing has survived. Some descriptions in Seneca's writings have been interpreted as coded references to the excessive luxury of Nero's buildings, but they may equally refer more generally to the top end of elite villa culture of the time.

3 This aspect was stressed by Cicero, who owned a substantial property on the Hill in the mid-first century BC, along with many other grandees and political leaders. These mansions were 'in sight of practically the whole city' and therefore ideal for important public figures, see Cicero, *De domo sua* 39.100, 38.101.

4 A well-located and furnished house could launch a career or document its owner's political success and status, see Cicero, *De officiis* 1.39; Cicero, *De domo sua* 103, 132. In the late Republic, such houses were fiercely fought over among political rivals. They changed hands for enormous sums of money (and sometimes through force or coercion) and were often expanded and remodelled at great cost, in order to outshine neighbouring properties. The local topography strictly limited the number of prime properties available, see *Lexicon Topographicum Urbis Romae* (*LTUR*) II, s.v. Cermalus.

5 See Tacitus, *Annals* 3.9.3. The *urbs quadrata* was the early settlement laid out to a square grid system.

6 Before Augustus, the most notable of these mansions had belonged to Quintus Hortensius and Quintus Lutatius Catulus. Augustus originally hailed from the more humble 'Ox Street' (*ad capita Bubuli*).

7 The 'House of Augustus' that can be visited on the Palatine today predates the construction of the Apollo Temple. Buried in the temple's foundations, it was replaced by a new residence that left few traces.

8 At the same time, Augustus had some of the most conspicuous senatorial mansions demolished, namely the houses of Marcus Aemilius Scaurus on the Palatine and of Vedius Pollio on the Esquiline, see Edwards (1993), 164 note 72 with literature.

9 See Wiseman (1987).

10 In reverence to the first emperor, his widow Livia later dedicated a shrine, or *sacrarium*, in Augustus' house along with memorial games, the *ludi Palatini*. His successors seem to have kept this area largely intact, although at some point, at the latest after AD 64, it was remodelled and turned into a sanctuary, the Templum Divorum or Aedes Caesarum.

11 The so-called Villa Iovis, or Villa Ionis as Suetonius calls it. Tiberius is said to have taken over twelve existing villas on the island, perhaps crowding out other senatorial owners, as would happen on the Palatine later (see Suetonius, *Tiberius* 43–4; Tacitus, *Annals* 4.67).

12 Caligula had been brought up in the Palatine houses of various female relatives and later took over his father Germanicus' mansion.

13 Suetonius, *Caligula* 22.2.

14 For the portraits, see Von den Hoff (2009). Caligula used his palace to assert his dominance over the senators in other ways, too. He turned *convivia*, formal dinner parties hosted to maintain bonds of friendship between aristocrats, into frightening displays of power. Later, he seems to have forced senatorial wives and children to lodge in part of the residence, in order to exert his control over individual senators, see Winterling (2011), chapters 3–5.

15 See Flavius Josephus, *Jewish Antiquities* 19.14, whose account of the events relating to Caligula's assassination includes reference to a temporary wooden theatre connected to the palace compound further east on the Palatine Hill and linked by an underground passage.

16 Suetonius, *Claudius* 17.3; Suetonius, *Nero* 8.1. It is, of course, entirely possible that Suetonius and Tacitus wrongly projected elements of the palace's physical appearance in their own day backwards into the Claudian period.

17 Recent archaeological research on this sector of the Palatine has not confirmed previous assumptions about the appearance of the palace under Caligula and Claudius, which therefore remains unknown. Instead, all visible remains seem to date firmly to the Neronian period. For a concise overview, see Krause (2004) with further literature. See also Krause (1998). The area in question is still covered by the vestiges of the Renaissance-era Horti Farnesiani (Farnese Gardens), and therefore not fully excavated.

18 In modern archaeological literature this palace building is known as Domus Tiberiana, but in the ancient sources this name is first attested after the end of Nero's reign.

19 See Krause (2004), 49–50. The Neronian walls and cryptoportici kept the orientation of the area's original grid layout. The podium measured 450 × 500 Roman feet. Its north, west and south walls followed the outer walls of the old residential quarter, while the cryptoportici ran parallel to its former streets. With their strict axial symmetry, they corresponded to the still buried structures on top of the platform above.

20 As a modern convention, these have been attributed to the Domus Transitoria, although this application of the name may be incorrect.

21 See Hesberg (2004), 65. Only the floor and column bases survive; the walls were later razed to make way for new buildings.

22 See Tomei (2011) and Borghini, D'Alessio and Scoccianti (2019) with references and bibliography.

23 In plan, the apartment forms a long rectangle of 32 × 11.5 m. Its walls align with the temple terrace of Apollo Palatinus. The rooms were symmetrically arranged in two not fully identical suites that flanked a central courtyard measuring 14 × 11.5 m. One of the anterooms seems to have connected to a still unexcavated corridor or further rooms to the north-east. The first excavations took place in the 1720s and were widely reported throughout Europe, as the area was known to be closely associated with the imperial palaces (excavations in Herculaneum and Pompeii did not commence until the following decades); see Miranda (2000). Further fragments of the original wall and floor decoration were discovered in the early twentieth century.

24 The platform was long mistaken for a water basin. Its depth increases from 60 cm on either side to at least 1.75 m in the centre, perhaps enough for a single performer or a small group in a fairly static set-up, such as a reading or instrumental performance; see Manderscheid (2004), 79, 85.

25 Some scholars have seen here specific allusions to Nero and his reign, but the fragmentary preservation and relative ubiquity of these themes in the late Julio-Claudian period perhaps preclude such detailed interpretation; see de Vos (1990).

26 The most detailed study of the hydraulics is Manderscheid (2004). The water displays could be regulated and provided a pleasant soundscape in addition to lively visual interest.

27 Philo of Alexandria, *On the Embassy to Gaius* 351.

28 Tacitus, *Annals* 15.39 ('the house by which he had connected the Palatine with the Gardens of Maecenas'), see Tamm (1963), 72–3. Modern naming conventions for these palace buildings are largely arbitrary and applied inconsistently.

29 See Seneca the Elder, *LTUR*, s.v. Domus Domitiana.

30 The sacrifices were mentioned in the partially preserved records of the Arval Brethren. Nero's father's birthday was marked on 11 December every year; on 11 September AD 59 Nero sacrificed a cow in front of the house, perhaps evidence that the Domus Transitoria project had not yet begun; see Smallwood (1967), 16, 19, 21–2; and Scheid (1998).

31 On this structure, see MacDonald (1982), 21–5 (note 6 with earlier literature and interpretations); Carandini and Carafa (2017); Yegül and Favro (2019); more cautious as to the date and reconstruction of the remains is Hesberg (2004), 63 with note 16.

32 See Beste a (2011). Previous attempts to locate any additional remains of the Domus Transitoria within the later Esquiline building now seem superseded.

33 Pliny the Elder, *Natural History* 17.1.5. He relates that Nero's ancestor Gnaeus Domitius Ahenobarbus had offered Crassus the princely sum of 10 million sesterces for the property, mainly on account of these trees.

34 See Eck (1997), 177 (esp. note 80 with further literature), 180. Nero later appointed Mucianus as governor of Syria, where he became a crucial supporter of Vespasian's rise to imperial power. Opinions are divided on whether his Palatine *domus* pre- or post-dated the AD 64 fire.

35 The 600 members of the senate were required by law to reside in Rome. Their mansions must have been a major feature of the city; see Eck (1997); Eck (2010).

36 Nero seems to have spent much time in the Horti Serviliani; see Tacitus, *Annals* 15.55.1; Griffin (1984), 140–1 (the exact location of the Horti Serviliani is unknown). Nero's villas were located at Anzio and Albano close to Rome and Subiaco a little further inland, as well as at Baiae in the south.

Tacitus' account for the year AD 65 is inconsistent and hard to interpret, for he says that Nero 'rarely left home', but also that he 'delighted in frequent excursions by sea' and often visited a villa at Baiae belonging to Calpurnius Piso to 'indulge in a bath or banquet' (*Annals* 15.53.1, 15.51.1, 15.52.1). The conspirators around Piso finally decided to assassinate him in 'that hated palace reared from the spoils of his countrymen', a reference to the Domus Aurea, but when captured were brought to Nero in the Horti Serviliani (*Annals* 15.52.1, 15.58.1).

37 Perrin (2003) suggested that the Praetorian prefects may have had their main offices here; see also Perrin (2009). References to the building as *arx imperii* ('fortress of the empire') in the months after Nero's death highlight its practical and symbolic significance.

38 This is the prevailing view. Carandini and Carafa (2017), 239 are alone in dating these structures to after the fire, citing an unpublished brick-stamp of AD 67 (*CIL* XV 1449, ibid. note 322).

39 Tacitus, *Annals* 15.42.1.

40 Panella (1996).

41 Recent excavations give a sense of the scale of the destruction. In the valley floor, debris from Republican-era and early imperial buildings destroyed in the disaster created a rubble layer up to 4 m deep.

42 See Panella a (2011). Caesar decided to construct his Forum in 54 BC. The acquisition of the necessary building ground from private owners in the densely settled Argiletum cost 60 million sesterces alone. Extensive demolition and earth works were necessary to create level ground for the square, which measured approximately 160 × 70 m, or 1.16 hectares. The final cost of the Forum, still not finished when it was dedicated nine years later in 46 BC, came to 100 million sesterces (see Cicero, *Ad Atticum* 4.16.12; Pliny the Elder, *Natural History* 36.103; Suetonius, *Julius Caesar* 26.2). For the Augustan Forum, see Panella (1996), 172–80.

43 Van Deman (1923) and Van Deman (1925) first discussed these porticoes at length, but her results have been much modified since; see Panella (1996), esp. 168–72 and Perrin (2009).

44 This terrace, with the eastern end cut slightly back, was later used by Hadrian for his Temple of Venus and Rome. The general terrain looks quite different today, because the saddle between the Velia and the Oppian was deeply cut by Mussolini's Via del'Impero, the current Via dei Fori Imperiali.

45 The pool of Nero's *stagnum* measured approximately 175 × 195 m, the entire square including the surrounding colonnades about 195 × 205 m. The bottom of the basin consisted of the compacted debris of demolished houses that had perished in the fire; the surrounding area in turn was raised by 4–6 m, making use of much of the accumulated rubble; see Panella (1996), 180–8.

46 Suetonius, *Nero* 31.1–2.

47 Tacitus, *Annals* 15.42.1.

48 Pliny the Elder, *Natural History* 33.16.54, 36.24.111; Martial, *Liber de Spectaculis* 2.1.

49 Suetonius, *Nero* 39.2.

50 Ovid (*Fasti* 6.639–42) had already claimed that Vedius Pollio's 'immense *domus*' (later torn down by Augustus) occupied a space larger than many towns. See Edwards (1993), 137–72. Champlin (2003), 208–9 also links this to accusations that Nero, by giving huge feasts in public places, treated the whole city as his own house.

51 The most detailed attempt (based on archaeological remains and an acceptance of the various source accounts) to define the limits and estimate the extent of the Domus Aurea is Van Essen (1954). See also Boëthius (1960). By comparison, Vatican City comprises 49 hectares.

52 Whereas Suetonius and Tacitus vaguely describe the Domus Aurea as a palace that linked the Palatine and Esquiline Hills, modern definitions tend to include the entire Palatine area. Accordingly, *LTUR*, for example, divides its entry for the Domus Aurea into Palatine, Esquiline and other subsections (similarly for the Domus Transitoria).

53 The terrace varied between 30 m and 60 m in depth. The façade can currently be traced over 240 m. Only the west wing has been explored, along with the first rooms of its likely eastern twin. If the 'Baths of Titus' to the west of the Esquiline building originally formed part of the Neronian complex, the two buildings together would have extended over 500 m; see Hemsoll (1990), 16; Segala and Sciortino (1999), 19. Exterior polychrome stuccoes at the eastern end of the west court hint at the existence of protective cover. This may have been provided by a protruding gallery that was supported by travertine consoles set 10 m above ground level (see Beste and Filippi (2016), 196 and 197, fig. 8). Nothing is presently known about the central façade; proposals include a light, pavilion-like circular lantern supported by slender columns, which may have resembled the rock-cut tombs at Petra; see Hemsoll (1990), 24–6 with fig. 2.13. Others assume the oculus was left open to the sky; see Ball (2003), 11, fig. 5. Carandini and Carafa (2017) vol. 2, fig. 111 assume a turret above the oculus and otherwise a uniform two-storey colonnade along the entire façade.

54 See Hemsoll (1990), 13–15. Carandini and Carafa (2017), vol. 2, fig. 112, followed by Yegül and Favro (2019), 230, suggest porticoes, a xystus and multistorey service facilities on two terraces immediately in front of and below the southern façade of the Esquiline building, but presently the evidence for all this is scant.

55 *LTUR*, s.v. 'Domus Aurea', p. 60 (L. Fabbrini).

56 The upper floor is only partially known through small-scale excavations in the 1980s in the area above the octagonal room; see Fabbrini (1982) with further literature, and, for the upper floor, *LTUR*, p. 60, fig. 25 (L. Fabbrini); Hesberg (2004), 65–6; See also Beste b (2011). Corresponding sets of rooms may have existed on the far side of the upper peristyle. There are also some ruins to the north-west of the Esquiline building that follow its axial alignment and may have been linked to it.

57 What has been discovered of the eastern court so far hints at a similar arrangement there.

58 In sculpture, it is known from Tiberius' villa at Sperlonga and a villa at Baiae traditionally ascribed to Claudius. Later on, the villas of Domitian at Castel Gandolfo and Hadrian at Tivoli contained similar Homeric groups.

59 This extended southward beyond the main façade, where it may have formed a corner risalit that projected beyond the rest of the building.

60 On each side, a central hall was flanked by a sequence of three lateral rooms, in themselves arranged symmetrically around the respective middle chamber. These rooms had beautiful *opus sectile* decorations in marble – only the imprints in the floor and clamp holes in the walls remain. The original ceiling frescos, now much deteriorated, were documented in eighteenth-century drawings and watercolours.

61 These ceilings combined a wide range of different mythological themes that invited the viewer's prolonged immersion and stimulated rich responses to the complexity of their visual allusions; see Haug (2014). For the fragments in the British Museum see Payne and Booms (2014).

62 Hemsoll (1990), 20–4.

63 Nero's fabulous tent was lost in a shipwreck; see Plutarch, *Moralia* 13.

64 Pliny the Elder, *Natural History* 35.37.120. Famulus' most famous work depicted a Minerva whose gaze always seemed to follow the spectator. Pliny claims that Nero requisitioned many sculptures in Greece for display in the Domus Aurea's reception rooms, presumably during his tour of the region (ibid., 34.19.84). Empty plinths that may have served as statue bases were found in front of the north wall of the west wing peristyle and at the bottom of the octagonal hall's nymphaeum cascade. The only piece of sculpture found inside the Esquiline building was a marble statue of a Muse discovered in the 1950s, presumably already damaged in antiquity and therefore left behind; see Segala and Sciortino (1999), 59, fig. 48.91.

65 Domitian's *coenatio Iovis* would allow similarly lavish, carefully choreographed mass dinners in the Flavian palace on the Palatine. The ambience was described in panegyric literature, for example Martial's *Epigram* 8.39.

66 Previously, it was thought that the earlier remains had belonged to the Domus Transitoria; see the detailed study by Ball (2003). Ball interpreted some of the remains of the Domus Aurea west wing as remnants of pre-fire shops and perhaps the assembly rooms of a *collegium*, or guild, but this now seems unlikely. For new research, see Beste (2016), Filippi (2016), and Beste and Filippi (2016). The entire Esquiline building is the result of a single, post-fire planning phase, although some of the room layouts were altered subsequently. In connection with the fire, Suetonius (*Nero* 38.1) mentions warehouses near the Domus Aurea, much coveted by Nero. The story of their destruction by military siege engines during the conflagration seems fanciful, but may reflect the full or partial demolition of commercial buildings in the area to make way for the new building.

67 See Meyboom and Moormann (2013) with full bibliography, and the short summary in Meyboom and Moormann (2012).

68 There were no permanent kitchens, and no latrines or integrated heating system. Most rooms had multiple doorways, but there are no traces of hinges for fixed doors, suggesting curtains instead; see Segala and Sciortino (1999), 28–9. Only two flights of stairs connected the service areas in the back to the upper floor; others may have existed north of the west wing peristyle; see MacDonald (1982), 34. By contrast, Yegül and Favro (2019), 229–38 repeatedly refer to the Esquiline building as the Domus Aurea's 'residential wing'; they also follow Ball (2003) and others in assuming that the west wing may have been part of the original Domus Transitoria and provided the main residential function, with entertainment concentrated in the central pavilion.

69 The concrete barrel vaults and domed halls transferred new elements of public construction (for example, the slightly earlier bath buildings at Baiae) into domestic contexts. Domitian's palace on the Palatine and Hadrian's villa at Tivoli built on these Neronian precedents.

70 The octagonal room's domed vault has a raw concrete surface. A number of different proposals have been put forward for its original appearance, from a mosaic decoration to a complex mechanical apparatus, operated from above to create a rotating ceiling. The recent discovery of other round structures on the Palatine has now led some scholars to locate the famous *coenatio* there instead, but these proposals remain equally hypothetical.

71 An important early exception was Morford (1968), followed by Edwards (1993), Elsner (1994) and Champlin (2003).

72 L'Orange (1942); L'Orange (1953).

73 See Bergmann (1993); Bergmann (1998).

74 See Zanker (2010). Administrative, commercial and all kinds of leisure activities were conducted in these halls. Champlin (2003), 206–9 argues that Nero wanted to extend the kind of lifestyle the rich enjoyed in the villas around Baiae and the Gulf of Naples to the urban *plebs*, thus turning the lower grounds of the Domus Aurea into a 'people's villa'.

75 Several scholars have long pointed out that for reasons of access alone, the lower grounds of the Domus Aurea ought to have been open to the public, as important transport corridors like the Via Labicana could not simply be closed off; see Griffin (1984), 139–40; Champlin (2003), 206.

76 Martial was also the only author to claim that the Domus Aurea extended all the way to Claudius' temple, a problematic statement.

77 Suetonius, *Vespasian* 9.1. While it is well known that the Flavian amphitheatre rose in place of Nero's *stagnum*, it is not normally considered that both structures could have served a similar function and that Flavian activity in the area may have been an extension of Nero's. Vespasian's Templum Pacis was also built on fire-damaged land in the Argiletum, perhaps already earmarked by Nero for further development. A pre-existing urbanistic vision might also explain why Nero and Agrippina had chosen the north-western slope of the Caelian as the site for the Temple of the Deified Claudius a decade earlier, and why Nero's market, the Macellum Magnum, had been constructed nearby.

78 For the *vestibulum*, see Panella (1996), 172–80.

79 The basic study on *vestibula* and atria remains Tamm (1963). *Vestibula* provided an outdoor gathering space for clients, friends and followers of the master of the house, who came to pay their tribute during the ritual morning salutation; see Goldbeck (2010). Nero's provision of a large, well-appointed *vestibulum* for the imperial palace therefore was part of a wider trend, but it also sent a double message: the *princeps* would make himself available to his people, but no senator could possibly compete with the size of his clientele.

80 It seems that the Via Sacra colonnades had been completed as simple column screens rather than the deep halls originally projected; see Panella (1996).

81 See Coleman (2006).

82 Pliny the Elder, *Natural History* 34.18.45–7.

83 Suetonius, *Nero* 31.1 Pliny other sources provide a slightly lower figure, see Albertson (2001), 103–06. The discrepancy may stem from the inclusion or omission of the statue's solar rays. By comparison, the Statue of Liberty in New York is 46 metres tall without its base.

84 Pliny the Elder, *Natural History* 34.18.45–6. He may have elaborated this in his book on Roman history.

85 Pliny, perhaps purposefully, chose the ambiguous term *simulacrum* to describe the statue's features. Suetonius instead used the term *effigies*, a word more suggestive of a portrait likeness. He also mentioned that Vespasian handsomely rewarded a *refector* (restorer) of the statue (*Vespasian* 18.1), implying that the statue was altered from an image of Nero to one of Sol. Tacitus was silent on the matter, while Cassius Dio was only generally aware of the portrait features (*Roman History* 65.5.1). Perhaps most telling, Martial, otherwise so critical of Nero and the Domus Aurea, spoke of the 'heavenly colossus' (*Liber de Spectaculis* 2.1). For a detailed discussion, see Bergmann (1993); Bergmann (1998); Smith (2000); Albertson (2001).

86 Cassius Dio, *Roman History* 65.5.1; see Albertson (2001), 96–103. The complex in-situ casting process probably meant that the statue had not progressed beyond the early stages by AD 68.

87 See Smith (2000), 536–8.

88 Sol was celebrated for his role in protecting Nero during the foiled Pisonian conspiracy of AD 65, so his opponents may have considered the colossus an offensive taunt, see p. 259.

89 Court poetry and private commissions could be far more open in stressing the association between *princeps* and god.

90 Pliny the Elder, *Natural History*, 35.33.51.

It might be that the portrait features of the painted colossus were transferred onto the statue in later memory, but even here the identification as Nero is doubtful; see Albertson (2001), 109 with further references (and a different interpretation).

91 Under Hadrian, the colossus was moved by twenty-four elephants to a new position next to the Flavian amphitheatre, which then became known as 'colosseum' (from *amphitheatrum ad colossum*).

92 Tacitus, *Annals* 15.42.1; see Edwards (1993); Cordes (2017), chapter 2.

93 For the wider context, see Mratschek-Halfmann (1993).

94 Suetonius, *Nero* 30.1. Canusium, a town in Apulia, was famous for the quality of its wool.

95 Seneca, *Letters* 123.

96 Seneca, *Letters* 114.9. See also Edwards (1993), chapters 4–5.

97 Pliny the Elder, *Natural History* 12.41.84.

98 Pliny the Elder, *Natural History* 35.1.3 (marble), 16.84.232 (painted tortoiseshell). According to Pliny, the prices for particular ('Babylonian') fabric covers for dining couches rose from 800,000 sesterces during the Republic to 4 million under Nero (ibid. 8.74.196).

99 Seneca, *Letters* 110.13; see Cordes (2017), chapter 2.

100 See Eck (2010) on the ever more limited opportunities for the expression of senatorial status in the capital's public realm through dedications of major buildings, and so on.

101 Suetonius, *Nero* 27.3. He claims that Nero forced himself on his friends, but surely this is entirely misleading.

102 For the wider cultural context of imperial *convivia*, see Vössing (2004).

103 Petronius Arbiter, *Satyricon* 26–78. For Petronius see Prag and Repath (2009) with further references and bibliography. For freedmen more generally, see Petersen (2006).

104 Trimalchio's Greek and Latin libraries remained mere props. Many authors mocked freedmen who employed trained and enslaved servants to provide educated table conversation. For *larvae conviviales* (models of skeletons) and similar objects, see Barraco (2020).

105 Only freeborn citizens were allowed to join the legions.

106 For the social aspirations expressed in Pompeian houses, see Zanker (1998). Another phenomenon of the period was the 'affordable luxury' offered through technical innovations, such as glass pastes that credibly imitated the appearance of expensive cameos made of precious stones.

107 For the social context of the possible owners of the Moregine Treasure, see Jones (2006). They may have been freedmen clients of the *gens* Sulpicia, including the two brothers who served as high officials under Nero.

108 The main sources are Cassius Dio, *Roman History* 63.1.1–7 (including 'Golden Day' reference), 63.2.1–3; Suetonius, *Nero* 13.1, 30.2; Pliny the Elder, *Natural History* 30.6.16–17, 33.16.54; Tacitus, *Annals* 16.23.1–24.1 (Tacitus' main account of the visit must have followed in the lost section of book 16). See also Heil (1997), 130–5; Champlin (2003), 221–9. The Egyptian queen Cleopatra's visits to Rome in 46 and 44 BC must have been similarly remarkable, but they were far less consequential geopolitically.

109 Cassius Dio, *Roman History* 63.1.2. Media Atropatene bordered Armenia and the Caspian Sea; Adiabene was just to the south.

110 For Vinicianus, see Cassius Dio, *Roman History* 62.23.5.

111 The journey led through Cappadocia, Bithynia and Pontus, Thrace, Moesia, Pannonia and/or Dalmatia. Pliny (*Natural History* 30.6.16–17) claims that the Parthians opted for the land route because their Zoroastrian faith imposed restrictions on sea crossings.

112 See Tacitus, *Annals* 15.31.1. Pliny (*Natural History* 30.6.26) mentions the financial burden this imposed on the affected provinces (and, presumably, the local elites). Dio, by contrast, states that the costs (which he put at an extraordinary 800,000 sesterces per day) were met by the public treasury (*Roman History* 63.2.2).

113 Alternatively, the Hellenised setting of Campania may have been culturally more familiar to the Parthians and better suited for a first meeting and final discussions.

114 The dagger, however, had been fixed to the scabbard with nails.

115 Cassius Dio, *Roman History* 63.3.1.

116 This may be related to an expedition Nero had sent out to trace the sources of the Nile and explore the potential for a military campaign in the region; see Pliny the Elder, *Natural History* 6.35.181–6.

117 See Cassius Dio, *Roman History* 63.3.2.

118 Tacitus, *Annals* 16.24.1.

119 Dio's and Suetonius' accounts, perhaps reflecting a common source, convey a good sense of the profound impression the ceremony left on the Roman public (Cassius Dio, *Roman History* 63.4.1–6.1, and Suetonius, *Nero* 13.1–2).

120 *CIL* XIV 2832 = *ILS* 1760; see Liverani and Spinola (2010), 235–40.

121 For the Vatican statue and further references, see Cadario (2011), esp. 176–7, fig. 1; Wolsfeld (2014), esp. 193–5, fig. 5.

122 On his return journey, Tiridates crossed the Adriatic from Brundisium to Dyrrachium and then proceeded through the provinces of Macedonia and Asia (with its rich cities) back to Armenia, possibly via Thrace and Bithynia, then Galatia and Cappadocia.

123 The likely Nero doodle is from a taberna on the south-west slope of the Palatine, see Langner (2001) 41, 126–7, cat. no. 317.

124 The sources mention Ethiopia and the Caucasus as potential objectives.

125 In a way, this could also be seen as a tour to outshine Tiridates' prior progress through the eastern Empire, which certainly would have left an impression.

126 The core narratives are Suetonius, *Nero* 22.3–24.1; Cassius Dio, *Roman History* 63.8.1–19.2. Both seem to reflect a common source. Various Greek authors, including Pausanias, provide snippets of more specific additional information; there are also relevant sections in Flavius Josephus' *Jewish War*. See Bradley (1979); Kennell (1988); Champlin (2003), 54–61; and Heil (1997), 159–82 for the military context.

127 Cassius Dio, *Roman History* 63.8.2.

128 They comprised the Aktia at Nikopolis (founded by Augustus), the Pythia at Delphi, the Isthmia at Corinth, the Nemeia and Heraia, both held at Argos, and finally the Olympics at Olympia.

129 Suetonius, *Nero* 35.5 and Cassius Dio, *Roman History* 63.18.1 mention new baths had been built in the city for Nero's use.

130 Flavius Josephus, *Jewish War* 2.556 mentions a Jewish delegation.

131 Strocka (2010).

132 Suetonius, *Nero* 19.1. Dio, by contrast, reports: 'when the first workers touched the earth, blood spouted from it, groans and bellowings were heard, and many phantoms appeared' (*Roman History* 63.16.1). See also Pettegrew (2016).

133 See Flavius Josephus, *Jewish War* 3.532.

134 See Sinn (2004), 200–2. According to Pausanias, Nero had various statues sent to Rome (presumably to make up for losses of Greek works in the capital caused by the Great Fire).

135 A transcript of Nero's speech was inscribed in stone in the town of Akraphia. To compensate the public treasury, Nero assigned it the revenue of Sardinia instead, which until then had been designated for the privy purse.

136 Suetonius, *Nero* 24.2 (who only claims that Nero was thrown off and did not finish the course, but was awarded the prize anyway); Cassius Dio (*Roman History* 63.14.1), however, states that Nero was nearly crushed to death. This was a show of prowess to match Tiridates' marksmanship in Puteoli.

137 Cassius Dio, *Roman History* 63.15.1–3, 17.1–19.2.

Chapter VIII

1 Rogers (1955); McAlindon (1956); McAlindon (1957); Vogel-Weidemann (1979); Vogel-Weidemann (1982). Rudich (1993) often takes a different view.

2 In addition to great wealth and distinguished ancestry, such men needed to have a family link to Augustus, as Tacitus makes very clear (*Annals* 13.1.2).

3 Sulla's mother, Domitia Lepida, was Nero's paternal aunt (making him Nero's cousin). Through her, Sulla was descended through the Ahenobarbi line from Augustus' sister Octavia, like Nero (who was, however, related to Augustus on both his father's and mother's side).

4 Sulla was Messalina's half-brother. This made him the uncle of Britannicus and Claudia Octavia, as well as Claudius' son-in-law through his marriage to Antonia (their child, Claudius' only grandson, died in infancy).

5 Tacitus suggests that the poor reputation of the accuser, Paetus, led to a quick dismissal of the charges and his banishment.

6 Tacitus, *Annals* 13.47. Nero's *ministri* were set upon at night when returning from the Milvian Bridge just outside Rome to the city centre along the Via Flaminia. Nero himself had taken an alternative route to the Horti Sallustiani and escaped unharmed. Tacitus argues that Graptus' accusations were spurious as no enslaved individuals or clients of Sulla's had been identified, and that the incident was instead a harmless example of juvenile *licentia* so common at the time. He uses the event to attack Nero's morals, claiming that he 'tried to hide his shameful vices and crimes' by engaging in debauched activities outside the city, including the notorious area around the Milvian Bridge.

7 Tacitus, *Annals* 13.19.1.

8 Tacitus, *Annals* 14.22.1.

9 Tacitus quotes Nero's letter to Plautus as advising him 'to consider the peace of the capital and extricate himself from the scandal-mongers' (*Annals* 14.22.1).

10 Given the way local governors revolted with their armies in precisely this way in AD 68, Tigellinus' warning may have had some merit.

11 Tacitus, *Annals* 14.57–9. The reports that Nero mocked both men when their severed heads were presented to him, smack of typical anti-tyrant rhetoric.

12 The main extant source is Tacitus' long account in the *Annals* (15.48.1–74.1), complemented by Suetonius (*Nero* 36.1) and Dio (*Roman History* 62.24.1–4).

13 Tacitus (*Annals* 14.65.1) characterises the plot as *moles magna et improspera insidiarum*, a 'huge and unfortunate web of plots'.

14 See Griffin (1984), 171–7.

15 Tacitus, *Annals* 14.65.1. There clearly was a more extensive source tradition that implicated Seneca and others (still known to Dio, for example), but this was later largely ignored.

16 See Drinkwater (2019), 212–14 for a helpful list of names and further references.

17 Tacitus, *Annals* 14.48.1.

18 Tacitus, *Annals* 15.50.1. 'Crimes' may have alluded to Nero's recent executions of various nobles (as well as Claudia Octavia), the 'end of empire' perhaps to the defeat at Rhandeia in the Armenian war.

19 A freedwoman named Epicharis, frustrated by Piso's slow progress, had tried to win fellow conspirators among the fleet, but she was reported; see Tacitus, *Annals* 15.51. However, even under torture she did not give up any names. The fleet's loyalty as opposed to the Praetorians' treachery is significant, perhaps in part a reflection of the different social background of sailors and soldiers.

20 Other prominent victims were Seneca's nephew Lucan and Petronius.

21 For Piso, see Champlin (1989).

22 He was the son of Marcus Iunius Silanus, who had been executed many years before, brought up by his aunt Iunia Lepida and her husband Cassius Longinus; see Tacitus, *Annals* 15.52.

23 Tacitus, *Annals* 15.53; Suetonius, *Nero* 35.

24 For examples, see Bönisch-Meyer (2014), 93–5.

25 Tacitus, *Annals* 15.71.1. These included the consular Petronius Turpilianus, the praetor designate Cocceius Nerva (the future emperor), and the Guard prefect Tigellinus. Nymphidius Sabinus, Faenius Rufus' successor as second Guard commander, received consular insignia. For Epaphroditus, see Eck (1976); and D'Andrea (2018).

26 See Ronning (2006). Thrasea Paetus very effectively exploited Nero's strict adherence to the formal rituals of the 'Restored Republic', and Nero for a long time only responded with significant gestures rather than violence or coercion. Another member of the Silani, Decimus Iunius Silanus Torquatus, committed suicide before he could be put on trial. He had given official court titles to members of his own household, surely a sign of seditious ambition, see Tacitus, *Annals* 15.35.1.

27 Suetonius, *Nero* 36.1. More information may have been provided in the lost section of Tacitus' *Annals*; there is no reference to Vinicianus' plot in the summary excerpts of Cassius Dio' *Roman History*.

28 However, Drinkwater (2019), 222–4 argues that the plot unfolded in Campania, before Nero and Tiridates reached Rome.

29 Alternatively, these may have been a consequence of Vinicianus' failed plot.

30 Rogers (1955); Rudich (1993).

31 Suetonius, *Nero* 37.3.

32 See Vervaet (2002) with references and bibliography.

33 Cassius Dio, *Roman History* 63.19.1.

34 This was Legio I Adiutrix ('The Helpers').

35 Cassius Dio, *Roman History* 63.22.1. Vindex' speech that vilified Nero as actor and lyre-player is Dio's invention (in line with the rules of the genre in antiquity).

36 Galba had been governor of Aquitania in AD 33, so there may have been established links between him and Vindex' family.

37 Verginius Rufus brought with him Legions XXII Primigenia and IIII Macedonica from Mogontiacum and additional detachments from the Lower German legions.

38 Vindex had boasted to Galba that he could mobilise 100,000 armed men; 20,000 allegedly fell at Vesontio, see Plutarch, *Galba* 4.

39 Galba had spent the first half of Nero's reign in 'retirement', although he was a member of various prestigious priestly colleges. According

to Suetonius, he always travelled with the equivalent of a million sesterces in gold, presumably to be ready for any eventuality should Nero take action against him; see Suetonius, *Galba* 8.1. Plutarch, *Galba* 4.

40 Galba supposedly intercepted letters Nero had sent to his procurators in the province; an assassination attempt by various enslaved men led by one of Nero's freedmen failed; see Suetonius, *Galba* 9.2, 10.4. On Nero's reaction, see Suetonius, *Nero*, 42.1.

41 Suetonius, *Galba* 10.1–3.

42 Suetonius, *Nero* 25.1–2.

43 Cassius Dio, *Roman History* 63.20.1–6. According to Suetonius, Nero displayed the crowns in the chambers of his palace, along with statues of himself as lyre-player, whereas Dio states that he displayed them on the *spina* of the Circus around the obelisk – as an offering to Sol.

44 See Champlin (2003), 229–34 (with references) for a sensitive interpretation based on a general acceptance of the source narratives.

45 Suetonius, *Nero* 44.1.

46 Suetonius, *Nero* 41.1.

47 All this was recounted by Suetonius, in an odd contrast to the remainder of his narrative (*Nero* 44).

48 A friend of the Elder and Younger Pliny, he survived into Nerva's reign. Tacitus, then serving as consul, gave the eulogy at his funeral. Verginius himself had composed the lines to be inscribed on his tomb: 'Here lies Rufus, who after defeating Vindex, did not take power, but gave it to the fatherland', see Pliny the Younger, *Letters* 9.19.

49 Suetonius (*Nero* 45.1) claims that a ship arrived from Alexandria when people had already begun to go hungry, but it was laden with sand for the arena instead of corn, leading to an eruption of popular discontent (this may, of course, have been a rumour spread by Nero's enemies); see also Flaig a (2003) and Bradley (1979).

50 Presented as a fact by Dio (*Roman History* 63.27.1). There is some debate over whether Nero gave up hope prematurely – Tacitus holds that 'Nero had been driven from his throne by messages and rumours rather than by arms' (*Histories* 1.89) – but much of it is speculative.

51 See Tacitus, *Histories* 2.27. On Legion XIV's special relationship with Nero (due to its valour during the Boudica rebellion), see ibid. 2.11. There was also Nero's newly recruited elite Legio I Italica, along with detachments from the Illyrian army. The consular Rubrius Gallus seems to have been sent north to support Turpilianus; see Syme (1982), 467.

52 Suetonius and Dio claim that Nero intended to move as a private citizen to Alexandria and live off his art as a professional citharode, a statement (along with his alleged intention to appeal to the rebels for mercy and perform before them) that should perhaps be treated with more scepticism than hitherto common.

53 See Plutarch, *Galba* 2.1–2. Nymphidius, the son of a freedwoman, aspired to the throne himself and claimed to be Caligula's illegitimate son. He was killed under Galba.

54 In Dio's version, Nero was so inept that Epaphroditus had to finish him off with a final blow; Cassius Dio, *Roman History* 63.29.2.

55 This date is the most accepted; an alternative is 11 June.

56 The line invites (unfavourable) comparison with Augustus' alleged last words ('if I have played my role well, clap your hands'); see Suetonius, *Augustus* 99.1; Cassius Dio, *Roman History* 63.29.2. Suetonius' and Dio's common source may have been Cluvius Rufus; see also Champlin (2003), 49–51 with additional bibliography.

57 Among these were Gaius Fannius' *History of Those Executed or Exiled by Nero* and Titinius Capito's *Deaths of Illustrious Men*. Both authors were friends of Pliny the Younger (see Pliny, *Epistulae* 5.5, 8.12, see also 5.8).

58 This had been granted by Icelus, one of Galba's freedmen who looked after his affairs in Rome and clandestinely coordinated the Galban faction in the capital. The respect for Nero's body might be a sign that Icelus could not afford to antagonise Nero's supporters among the people.

59 Suetonius, *Nero* 50.1 (the funeral cost 200,000 sesterces, still a substantial sum given the circumstances).

60 Suetonius, *Nero* 57.1. Similarly, Cassius Dio, *Roman History* 63.29.1.

61 See Plutarch, *Galba* 8.5.

62 Tacitus, *Histories* 1.4.

63 'The Year of the Four Emperors' is a modern term. Tacitus (*Dialogus de Oratoribus*, 17.2) calls it a 'single and long year' in which four emperors ruled. For an overview, see Wellesley (1989) with references and bibliography.

64 Suetonius, *Galba* 13.

65 Suetonius, *Otho* 8.1.

66 Suetonius, *Otho* 7.1, 10.2.

67 Among Otho's generals was Gaius Suetonius Paulinus, who had suppressed (or, according to some, caused) the Boudica rebellion in Britain under Nero. Suetonius Laetus, father of the imperial biographer, served as tribune in one of Otho's legions; see Suetonius, *Otho* 10.1.

68 For the helmet, see Fischer (2004).

69 Suetonius, *Vitellius* 11.2. A collection of Nero's poetry was apparently known as *Dominico liber*.

70 See Baatz (1980).

71 Vera (2003); Pitcher (2017).

72 They were led by Vespasian's brother Flavius Sabinus, who had continued to serve as *praetor urbanus*, and Vespasian's younger son Domitian, the future emperor.

73 Mouritsen and Gradel (1991).

74 See Varner (2004) with further bibliography; Flower (2006).

Epilogue

1 Dio of Prusa (Dio Chrysostom), *Oration* 21 [On Beauty], 9–10. See also Tacitus, *Histories* 2.8.

2 For the False Neros, see Tuplin (1989). Lion Feuchtwanger's sensitive and well-researched 1936 novel captures some of the popular appeal of these figures, see Feuchtwanger (1936).

3 See, for example, Suetonius, *Nero* 57. A mention of Nero's continuing support by the *plebs* and 'barbarian' foreigners may of course have been intended as a negative comment, as these were the 'wrong' kind of people.

4 See Pliny the Elder, *Natural History* 2.85.199 and 17.38.245 (mountain); 2.106.232 (river); Cassius Dio, *Roman History* 63.16.1 (blood); Suetonius, *Nero* 46 (tomb, and other omens).

5 The main source texts are full of coded allusions. Suetonius' reference to Nero's 'blotchy skin' (*Nero* 51), for example, may have been likening him to a panther, a deceitful creature in the ancient imagination; see Gladhill (2012); Curry (2014).

6 For Fabius Rusticus' friendship with Seneca and possible bias, see Tacitus, *Annals* 13.20.2.

7 See Mittag (1999) with further bibliography and some reservations about the anti-Christian symbolism of the *contorniates* (medallions).

8 Bönisch-Meyer *et al.* (2014).

9 Burke (1992).

Bibliography

Fred C. Albertson, 'Zenodorus's "Colossus of Nero"', *Memoirs of the American Academy in Rome* 46 (2001), 95–118

Walter Allen *et al.*, 'Nero's eccentricities before the fire (Tac. *Ann.* 15.37), *Numen* 9 (1962), 99–109

Dietwulf Baatz, 'Ein Katapult der Legio IV Macedonica aus Cremona', *Mitteilungen des deutschen archäologischen Instituts. Römische Abteilung* 87 (1980), 283–99

Ernst Badian, *Publicans and Sinners: Private Enterprise in the Service of the Roman Republic*, Ithaca, NY 1972

Larry F. Ball, *The Domus Aurea and the Roman Architectural Revolution*, Cambridge 2003

Maria Elisa Garcia Barraco, *Larvae Conviviales: Gli scheletri da banchetto nell' antica Roma* [= Antichità Romane 35], Rome 2020

Anthony A. Barrett, *Agrippina: Sex, Power, and Politics in the Early Empire*, London 1996

Anthony A. Barrett, *Rome Is Burning: Nero and the Fire that Ended a Dynasty*, Princeton 2020

Shadi Bartsch, Kirk Freudenburg and Cedric Littlewood, *The Cambridge Companion to the Age of Nero*, Cambridge 2017

Heinz Bellen, *Die germanische Leibwache der römischen Kaiser des julisch-claudischen Hauses*, Mainz and Wiesbaden 1981

Marianne Bergmann, *Der Koloss Neros, die Domus Aurea und der Mentalitätswandel im Rom der frühen Kaiserzeit* [= Trierer Winckelmann Programm 13], Mainz 1993

Marianne Bergmann, *Die Strahlen der Herrscher: Theomorphes Herrscherbild und politische Symbolik im Hellenismus und in der römischen Kaiserzeit*, Mainz 1998

Heinz-Jürgen Beste a, 'La Domus Transitoria, un' ipotesi di collocazione' in Tomei and Rea (2011), 152–5

Heinz-Jürgen Beste b, 'Domus Aurea, il padiglione dell' Oppio' in Tomei and Rea (2011), 170–5

Heinz-Jürgen Beste, 'Neue Einblicke in die Errichtung der Domus Aurea des Nero', *Archäologischer Anzeiger*, 2 (2016), 295–308

Heinz-Jürgen Beste and Fedora Filippi, 'Die Domus Aurea – das neue Konzept eines Herrschersitzes' in Merten (2016), 189–99

Anthony R. Birley, *The Roman Government of Britain*, Oxford 2005

Axel Boëthius, *The Golden House of Nero*, Ann Arbor 1960

Sophia Bönisch-Meyer, Lisa Cordes, Verena Schulz, Anne Wolsfeld and Martin Ziegert (eds), *Nero und Domitian: Mediale Diskurse der Herrscherrepräsentation im Vergleich*, Tübingen 2014

Stefano Borghini, Alessandro D'Alessio and Maria Maddalena Scoccianti (eds), *Aureo Filo – la prima reggia di Nerone sul Palatino*, Milan 2019

Dietrich Boschung, *Gens Augusta: Untersuchungen zu Aufstellung, Wirkung und Bedeutung der Statuengruppen des julisch-claudischen Kaiserhauses* [= Monumenta Artis Romanae 32], Mainz 2002

Keith R. Bradley, 'Nero's retinue in Greece, A.D. 66/67', *Illinois Classical Studies* 4 (1979), 152–7

Keith R. Bradley, 'Roman slavery and Roman law', *Historical Reflections / Réflexions Historiques* 15(3) (1988), 477–95

David C. Braund, 'Apollo in arms: Nero at the frontier' in Buckley and Dinter (eds) (2013), 83–101

David C. Braund, *Rome and the Friendly King: The Character of Client Kingship*, London 1984 (new edn 2014)

Susanna Braund, *Seneca, De Clementia*, Oxford 2009

Peter A. Brunt, 'Charges of provincial maladministration under the early principate', *Historia: Zeitschrift für Alte Geschichte* 10(2) (1961), 189–227

Peter A. Brunt, 'Free labour and public works at Rome', *The Journal of Roman Studies* 70 (1980), 81–100

Emma Buckley and Martin T. Dinter (eds), *A Companion to the Neronian Age*, Oxford 2013

Peter Burke, *The Fabrication of Louis XIV*, New Haven and London 1992

Kevin Butcher and Matthew Ponting (eds), *The Metallurgy of Roman Silver Coinage: From the Reform of Nero to the Reform of Trajan*, Cambridge 2014

Matteo Cadario, 'Nerone e il "potere delle immagini"' in Tomei and Rea (2011), 176–89

Pierre F. Cagniart, 'The philosopher and the gladiator', *Classical World* 93 (2000), 607–18

Petra Cain, *Männerbildnisse neronisch-flavischer Zeit*, Munich 1993

Alan Cameron, *Circus Factions: Blues and Greens at Rome and Byzantium*, Oxford 1976

Virginia Campbell, 'Casting a wide net: searching for networks of gladiators and gamer-givers in Campania' in Carlos F. Noreña and Nikolaos Papazarkadas (eds), *From Document to History: Epigraphic Insights into the Greco-Roman World*, Leiden 2019, 250–1

Howard V. Canter, 'Conflagrations in ancient Rome', *The Classical Journal* 27(4) (January 1932), 270–88

Carmela Capaldi and Carlo Gasparri (eds), *Complessi monumentali e arredo scultoreo nella 'Regio I Latium et Campania'*, Pozzuoli 2017

Andrea Carandini and Paolo Carafa, *The Atlas of Ancient Rome: Biography and Portraits of the City*, Princeton 2017

Mack Chahin, *The Kingdom of Armenia: A History*, Richmond 2001

Edward Champlin, 'The life and times of Calpurnius Piso', *Museum Helveticum* 46 (1989), 101–24

Edward Champlin, *Nero*, Cambridge, MA 2003

Virginia Closs, '*Neronianis temporibus*: the so-called "Arae Incendii Neroniani" and the fire of A.D. 64 in Rome's monumental landscape', *The Journal of Roman Studies* 106 (2016), 102–23

Filippo Coarelli, *Rome and Environs: An Archaeological Guide*, Berkeley 2007

Kathleen M. Coleman, 'Fatal charades: Roman executions staged as mythological enactments', *The Journal of Roman Studies* 80 (1990), 44–73

Kathleen M. Coleman, 'Launching into history: aquatic displays in the early Empire', *The Journal of Roman Studies* 83 (1993), 48–74

Kathleen M. Coleman (ed.), *M. Valerii Martialis Liber Spectaculorum*, Oxford 2006

Jean Colin, 'Les vendanges dionysiaques et la légende de Messaline', *Les Etudes Classiques*, 24 (1956), 25–39

P. Conole and Robert David Milns, 'Neronian frontier policy in the Balkans: the career of Ti. Plautius Silvanus', *Historia: Zeitschrift für Alte Geschichte* 32(2) (1983), 183–200

Lisa Cordes, *Kaiser und Tyrann: Die Kodierung und Umkodierung der Herrscherrepräsentation Neros und Domitians* [= Philologus Supplement 8], Berlin 2017

Corpus Inscriptionum Latinarum (*CIL*), 17 vols, Berlin 1893–

Michel Cottier *et al.*, *The Customs Law of Asia*, Oxford 2008

Philip Crummy, *City of Victory: The Story of Colchester – Britain's First Roman Town*, Colchester 1997

Susan A. Curry, 'Nero *quadripes*: animalizing the emperor in Suetonius' *Nero*', *Arethusa* 47(2) (Spring 2014), 197–230

Vesta Sarkhosh Curtis and Alexandra Magub, *Rivalling Rome: Parthian Coins and Culture*, London 2020

Francesca D'Andrea, 'Il sepolcro del liberto *Epaphroditus*: una proposta di identificazione e nuovi spunti di riflessione sugli *horti* dell'Esquilino sud-orientale', *Mélanges de l'École Française de Rome – Antiquité* (2018), 130–1, https://journals.openedition.org/mefra/4782 (accessed 6 May 2021)

Gregory N. Daugherty, 'The *cohortes vigilum* and the Great Fire of 64 AD', *The Classical Journal* 87(3) (February–March 1992), 229–40

Alexis Dawson, 'Whatever happened to Lady Agrippina?', *The Classical Journal* 64(6) (1969), 253–67

Esther Boise van Deman, 'The Neronian Via Sacra', *American Journal of Archaeology* 27(4) (October–December 1923), 383–424

Esther Boise van Deman, 'The Sacra Via of Nero', *Memoirs of the American Academy in Rome* 5 (1925), 115–26

Hermann Dessau (ed.), *Inscriptiones Latinae Selectae* (*ILS*), 3 vols, Berlin 1892–1916

John F. Drinkwater, *Nero: Emperor and Court*, Cambridge 2019

Richard Duncan-Jones, *Power and Privilege in Roman Society*, Cambridge 2016

Roger Dunkle, *Gladiators: Violence and Spectacle in Ancient Rome*, London 2013

Lesley Dunwoodie, Chiz Harward and Ken Pitt, *An Early Roman Fort and Urban Development on Londinium's Eastern Hill: Excavations at Plantation Place, City of London, 1997–2003* [MOLA Monograph Series 65], London 2015

Werner Eck, 'Nero's Freigelassener Epaphroditus und die Aufdeckung der pisonischen Verschwörung', *Historia: Zeitschrift für Alte Geschichte* 25(3) (1976), 381–4

Werner Eck, '*Cum dignitate otium*: senatorial *domus* in imperial Rome', *Scripta Classica Israelica* 16 (1997), 162–90

Werner Eck, *The Age of Augustus*, Oxford 2003

Werner Eck, 'Emperor and senatorial aristocracy in competition for public space' in Ewald and Noreña (2010), 90–110

Jonathan C. Edmondson, 'Dynamic arenas: gladiatorial presentations in the city of Rome and the construction of Roman society during the early Empire' in William J. Slater (ed.), *Roman Theater and Society*, Ann Arbor 1996, 69–112

Jonathan Edmondson and Alison Keith, *Roman Dress and the Fabrics of Roman Culture*, Toronto 2008

Catharine Edwards, *The Politics of Immorality in Ancient Rome*, Cambridge 1993

H.D.H. Elkington, *The Development of the Mining of Lead in the Iberian, Peninsula and Britain under the Roman Empire until the End of the Second Century A.D.*, PhD thesis, Durham University 1968

Jaś Elsner, 'Constructing decadence: the representation of Nero as imperial builder' in Elsner and Masters (1994), 112–27

Jaś Elsner and Jamie Masters, *Reflections of Nero: Culture, History, & Representation*, London 1994

Michael Erdrich, 'Römische Germanienpolitik im 1. Jahrhundert n. Chr.' in Ludwig Wamser (ed.), *Die Römer zwischen Alpen und Nordmeer: Zivilisatorisches Erbe einer europäischen Militärmacht*, Mainz 2000, 193–6

Carel C. van Essen, 'La topographie de la Domus Aurea Neronis', *Mededelingen der Koninklijke Nederlandse Akademie van Wetenschappen, Nieuwe Reeks, Deel 17, Afdeling letterkunde 1–12*, (1954), 371–401

Bjorn Ewald and Carlos F. Noreña (eds), *The Emperor and Rome: Space, Representation, and Ritual* [= Yale Classical Studies 35], Cambridge 2010

Laura Fabbrini, 'Domus Aurea. Il piano superiore del quartiere orientale', *Memorie della Pontificia Accademia Romana dell'Archeologia* 14 (1982), 5–24

Diane Favro, 'The city is a living thing: the performative role of an urban site in ancient Rome, the Vallis Murcia', *Studies in the History of Art* 56 (1999), 204–19

Lion Feuchtwanger, *Der Falsche Nero*, Amsterdam 1936 (English edn: Lion Feuchtwanger, *The False Nero*, trans. Willa and Edwin Muir, New York 1937)

Michael Fiedrowicz, 'Die römische Christenverfolgung nach dem Brand Roms im Jahr 64' in Merten (2016), 250–5

Fedora Filippi, 'Le indagini in Campo Marzio occidentale. Nuovi dati sulla topografia antica. Il ginnasio di Nerone (?) e l'"Euripus"', *Bollettino d'Arte* (2010), 82–92

Fedora Filippi, '"Progetto Domus Aurea" – die Sicherung des Denkmals zwischen Erhalt und Erforschung', *Archäologischer Anzeiger* 2 (2016), 309–34

Thomas Fischer, 'Ein römischer Legionärshelm des ersten Jahrhunderts n. Chr. aus dem Po bei Cremona im Römisch-Germanischen Museum zu Köln', *Kölner Jahrbuch* 37 (2004), 61–76

Klaus Fittschen and Paul Zanker, *Katalog der römischen Porträts in den Capitolinischen Museen und den anderen kommunalen Sammlungen der Stadt Rom. Kaiser und Prinzenbildnisse*, Vol. 1, Mainz 1994

Egon Flaig a, 'Wie Kaiser Nero die Akzeptanz bei der Plebs urbana verlor. Eine Fallstudie zum politischen Gerücht im Prinzipat', *Historia: Zeitschrift für Alte Geschichte* 552(3) (2003), 351–72

Egon Flaig b, *Ritualisierte Politik: Zeichen, Gesten und Herrschaft im Alten Rom. Historische Semantik*, Vol. 1, Göttingen 2003

Harriet I. Flower, *The Art of Forgetting: Disgrace & Oblivion in Roman Political Culture*, Chapel Hill, NC 2006

Michael Fulford, 'Nero and Britain: the palace of the client king at Calleva and imperial policy towards the province after Boudicca', *Britannia* 39 (2008), 1–14

Karl Galinsky (ed.), *The Cambridge Companion to the Age of Augustus*, Cambridge 2005

Elaine K. Gazda, John Clarke and Lynley J. McAlpine (eds), *Leisure & Luxury in the Age of Nero: The Villas of Oplontis Near Pompeii*, Ann Arbor 2016

Giuseppina Ghini, *Le terme alessandrine nel Campo Marzio*, Rome 1988

Caitlin Gillespie, 'Poppaea Venus and the Ptolemaic Queens', *Histos* 8 (2014), 122–45

Judith Ginsburg, *Representing Agrippina: Representations of Female Power in the Early Roman Empire*, New York 2006

Bill Gladhill, 'The emperor's no clothes: Suetonius and the dynamics of corporeal ecphrasis', *Classical Antiquity* 31(2) (October 2012), 315–48

Fabian Goldbeck, *Salutationes. Die Morgenbegrüßungen in Rom in der Republik und der frühen Kaiserzeit* [= Klio: Beiträge zur Alten Geschichte. Beihefte, New Series 16], Berlin 2010

Richard D. Grasby and Roger S.O. Tomlin, 'The sepulchral monument of the procurator C. Julius Classicianus', *Britannia* 33 (2002), 43–75

Michael J.G. Gray-Fow, 'Why the Christians? Nero and the Great Fire', *Latomus* 57(3) (July–September 1998), 595–616

Miriam T. Griffin, *Nero: The End of a Dynasty*, London 1984

Miriam T. Griffin, *Seneca on Society*, Oxford 2013

Annette Haug, 'Das Ornamentale und die Produktion von Atmosphäre: das Beispiel der Domus Aurea' in Johannes Lipps and Dominik Maschek (eds), *Antike Bauornamentik: Grenzen und Möglichkeiten ihrer Erforschung* [= Paul Zanker (ed.), *Studien zur antiken Stadt* 12], Wiesbaden 2014, 219–46

G.W.M. Harrison (ed.), *Seneca in Performance*, Swansea 2000

Kevin M.J. Hayward, 'A geological link between the Facilis Monument at Colchester and first-century army tombstones from the Rhineland frontier', *Britannia* 37 (2006), 359–63

Matthäus Heil, *Die orientalische Aussenpolitik des Kaisers Nero* [Quellen und Forschungen zur Antiken Welt 26], Munich 1997

Alexander Heinemann, 'Sportsfreunde: Nero und Domitian als Begründer griechischer Agone in Rom' in Bönisch-Meyer *et al.* (2014), 217–64

David Hemsoll, 'The architecture of Nero's Golden House' in Martin Henig (ed.), *Architecture and Architectural Sculpture in the Roman Empire* [= Oxford University Committee for Archaeology Monograph 29], Oxford 1990, 10–34

Gustav Hermansen, *Ostia: Aspects of Roman City Life*, Edmonton 1982

Henner von Hesberg, 'Die Domus Imoeratoris der neronischen Zeit auf dem Palatin' in Hoffmann and Wulf (2004), 59–74

Henner von Hesberg, 'Neros Bautätigkeit in Rom' in Merten (2016), 180–8

Ralf von den Hoff, *Caligula: Zur visuellen Repräsentation eines römischen Kaisers*, Munich 2009

Adolf Hoffmann and Ulrike Wulf (eds), *Die Kaiserpaläste auf dem Palatin in Rom: Das Zentrum der römischen Welt und seine Bauten*, Mainz 2004

Franz Holztrattner, *Poppaea Neronis potens: Studien zu Poppaea Sabina* [= Grazer Beiträge, Supplement 6], Horn 1995

Gerhard Horsmann, *Die Wagenlenker der römischen Kaiserzeit: Untersuchungen zu ihrer sozialen Stellung*, Stuttgart 1998

John H. Humphrey, *Roman Circuses: Arenas for Chariot Racing*, Berkeley and Los Angeles 1986

Stephen Johnstone, 'On the uses of arson in classical Rome' in Carl Deroux (ed.), *Studies in Latin Literature and Roman History* 6 [= Collection Latomus 217], Brussels 1992, 41–69

David Francis Jones, *The Bankers of Puteoli: Finance, Trade and Industry in the Roman World*, Stroud 2006

Sandra R. Joshel, 'Female desire and the discourse of Empire: Tacitus's Messalina', *Signs* 21(1) (1995), 50–82

Jaime Kaminski and David Sim, 'The production and deposition of the Witcham Gravel Helmet', *Proceedings of the Cambridge Antiquarian Society* 103 (2014), 69–82

N.M. Kennell, 'Nerwn Periodonikhs', *American Journal of Philology* 109 (1988), 239–51

Paul Keresztes, 'Nero, the Christians and the Jews in Tacitus and Clement of Rome', *Latomus* 43(2) (April–June 1984), 404–13

Frances Van Keuren *et al.*, 'Unpublished documents shed new light on the Licinian Tomb, discovered in 1884–1885, Rome', *Memoirs of the American Academy in Rome* 48 (2003), 53–139

Dietmar Kienast, *Römische Kaisertabelle: Grundzüge einer römischen Kaiserchronologie*, Darmstadt 1996

Fred S. Kleiner, *The Arch of Nero in Rome: A Study of the Roman Honorary Arch before and under Nero*, Rome 1985

Patrick Kragelund, *Roman Historical Drama: The Octavia in Antiquity and Beyond*, Oxford 2016

Patrick Kragelund, Mette Moltesen and Jan Stubbe Ostergaard, *The Licinian Tomb: Fact or Fiction?*, Copenhagen 2003

Clemens Krause, *Domus Tiberiana I: Gli scavi*, Rome 1998

Clemens Krause, 'Die Domus Tiberiana – Vom Wohnquartier zum Kaiserpalast' in Hoffmann and Wulf (2004), 32–58

Martin Langner, *Antike Graffitizeichnungen: Motive, Gestaltung und Bedeutung* [= Palilia 11], Wiesbaden 2001

Eugenio La Rocca, 'Disiecta membra Neroniana: l'arco partico di Nerone sul Campidoglio' in Heide Froning, Tonio Hölscher and Harald Mielsch (eds), *Kotinos: Festschrift für Erika Simon*, Mainz 1992, 400–14

Wolfgang Dieter Lebek, 'Standeswürde und Berufsverbot unter Tiberius: das SC der Tabula Larinas', *Zeitschrift für Papyrologie und Epigraphik* 81 (1990), 37–96

Wolfgang Dieter Lebek, 'Das SC der Tabula Larinas: Rittermusterung und andere Probleme', *Zeitschrift für Papyrologie und Epigraphik* 85 (1991), 41–70

Daniele Leoni, *The Coins of Rome: Nero*, Verona 2011

Hartmut Leppin, *Histrionen: Untersuchungen zur sozialen Stellung von Bühnenkünstlern im Westen des römischen Reiches zur Zeit der Republik under des Prinzipates*, Bonn 1992

Wolfram Letzner, *Der römische Circus: Massenunterhaltung im römischen Reich*, Mainz 2009

Barbara Levick, 'The *senatus consultum* from Larinum', *The Journal of Roman Studies* 73 (1983), 97–115

Barbara Levick, *Claudius*, London 1990

Jerzy Linderski, 'Games in Patavium', *Ktema* 17 (1992), 55–76

Hugh Lindsay, *Adoption in the Roman World*, Cambridge 2009

Paolo Liverani and Giandomenico Spinola, *The Vatican Necropoles: Rome's City of the Dead*, Vatican City 2010

Hans Peter L'Orange, 'Domus Aurea: der Sonnenpalast', *Symbolae Osloenses* (1942), 68–100

Hans Peter L'Orange, *Studies on the Iconography of Cosmic Kingship in the Ancient World*, Oslo 1953

D. McAlindon, 'Senatorial opposition to Claudius and Nero', *The American Journal of Philology* 77(2) (1956), 113–20

D. McAlindon, 'Claudius and the senators', *The American Journal of Philology* 78(3) (1957), 279–86

William L. MacDonald, *The Architecture of the Roman Empire*, New Haven and London 1982

Jürgen Malitz, *Nero*, Oxford 2005

Hubertus Manderscheid, 'Was nach den "ruchlosen Räubereien" übrigblieb – zu Gestalt und Funktion der sogenannten Bagni di Livia in der Domus Transitoria' in Hoffmann and Wulf (2004), 75–85

Gesine Manuwald, *Nero in Opera: Librettos as Transformations of Ancient Sources*, Berlin and Boston 2013

Francesco Marcattili, *Circo Massimo, architetture, funzioni, culti, ideologia*, Rome 2009

Annalisa Marzano, *Harvesting the Sea: The Exploitation of Marine Resources in the Roman Mediterranean*, Oxford 2013

Attilio Mastino and Paola Ruggeri, 'Claudia Augusti liberta Acte. La liberta amata da Nerone ad Olbia', *Latomus* 54 (1995), 513–44

David Mattingly, *An Imperial Possession: Britain in the Roman Empire*, London 2006

Roland Mayer, 'What caused Poppaea's death?', *Historia* 31 (1982), 248–9

Jürgen Merten (ed.), *Nero: Kaiser, Künstler und Tyrann*, Darmstadt 2016

Paul G.P. Meyboom and Eric M. Moormann, 'Decoration and ideology in Nero's Domus Aurea in Rome' in Corrie Bakels and Hans Kamermans, *The End of Our Fifth Decade* [= Analecta Praehistorica Leidensia 43/44], Leiden 2012, 131–43

Paul G.P. Meyboom and Eric M. Moormann, *Le decorazioni dipinte e marmoree della domus aurea di Nerone a Roma*, 2 vols, Leuven, Paris and Walpole, MA 2013

Hugo Meyer, *Prunkkameen und Staatsdenkmäler römischer Kaiser: Neue Perspektiven zur Kunst der frühen Prinzipatszeit*, Munich 2000

Martin Millett, *The Romanization of Britain: An Essay in Archaeological Interpretation*, Cambridge 1990

Paola Miniero and Fausto Zevi (eds), *Museo archeologico dei Campi Flegrei. Catalogo generale (Liternum, Baia, Miseno)*, Vol. 3, Naples 2008

Silvana Miranda, *Francesco Bianchini e lo scavo Farnesiano del Palatino (1720–1729)*, Milan 2000

Peter Franz Mittag, *Alte Köpfe in neuen Händen. Urheber und Funktion der Kontorniaten*, Bonn 1999

Walter O. Moeller, 'The riot of AD 59 at Pompeii', *Historia: Zeitschrift für Alte Geschichte* 19(1) (1970), 84–95

Mette Moltesen and Anne Marie Nielsen (eds), *Agrippina Minor: Life and Afterlife*, Copenhagen 2007

Mark P.O. Morford, 'The distortion of the Domus Aurea tradition', *Eranos* 66 (1968), 158–79

Henrik Mouritsen and Ittai Gradel, 'Nero in Pompeian politics. *Edicta munerum* and imperial *flaminates* in late Pompeii', *Zeitschrift für Papyrologie und Epigraphik* 87 (1991), 145–55

Sigrid Mratschek-Halfmann, *Divites et praepotentes: Reichtum und soziale Stellung in der Literatur der Prinzipatszeit* [= Historia Einzelschriften 70], Stuttgart 1993

Jocelyne Nelis-Clément and Jean-Michel Roddaz (eds), *Le cirque romain et son image*, Bordeaux, 2008

R.F. Newbold, 'Some social and economic consequences of the A.D. 64 fire at Rome', *Latomus* 33(4) (October–December 1974), 858–69

Zahra Newby, *Greek Athletics in the Roman World: Victory and Virtue*, Oxford 2005, 21–44

Clementina Panella (ed.), *Meta Sudans I. Un' area sacra in Palatino e la valle del Colosseo prima e dopo Nerone*, Rome 1996

Clementina Panella a, 'La Domus Aurea nella valle del Colosseo e sulle pendici della Velia e del Palatino' in Tomei and Rea (2011), 160–9

Clementina Panella b, 'Nerone e il grande incendio del 64 d.c.' in Tomei and Rea (2011), 76–91

Clementina Panella, 'Nero und der große Brand von Rom im Jahr 64' in Merten (2016), 241–9

Emma Payne and Dirk Booms, 'Analysis of gold pigment palettes as evidence for room status in Nero's Golden House', *British Museum Technical Research Bulletin* 8 (2014), 117–26

Yves Perrin, '*Imperii arx*: métaphore ou réalité? Les fonctions de la *domus tiberiana* néronienne' in Pol Defosse (ed.), *Hommages à Carl Deroux III: Histoire et épigraphie, Droit*, Brussels 2003, 35–54

Yves Perrin, 'Le forum romain sous Néron (54–68 ap. J.-C.). La resémantisation monarchique de la place républicaine' in Yves Perrin (ed.), *S'approprier les lieux: Histoire et pouvoirs*, Saint-Etienne 2009, 340–55

Lauren Hackworth Petersen, *The Freedman in Roman Art and Art History*, Cambridge 2006

David Pettegrew, *The Isthmus of Corinth: Crossroads of the Mediterranean World*, Ann Arbor 2016

E.J. Phillips, 'The gravestone of M. Favonius Facilis at Colchester', *Britannia* 6 (1975), 102–5

Lynn Arslan Pitcher, 'La distruzione della citta' in Lynn Arslan Pitcher, Ermanno A. Arslan, Paul Blockley and Marina Volonte (eds), *Amoenissimus … Aedificiis: Gli scavi di Piazza Marconi à Cremona* [= Studi e Ricerche di Archeologia 4, Vol. 1 – Lo Scavo], Mantua 2017, 73–8

Timothy Power, *The Culture of Kitharoidia*, Cambridge, MA and London 2010

Jonathan Prag and Ian Repath, *Petronius: A Handbook*, Oxford 2009

Sascha Priester, *Ad Summas Tegulas: Untersuchungen zu vielgeschossigen Gebäudeblöcken mit Wohneinheiten und Insulae im kaiserzeitlichen Rom* [= Bullettino della Commissione Archeologica Comunale di Roma 11], Rome 2002

David Radford and Adrian Gascoyne, *Colchester, Fortress of the War God: An Archaeological Assessment*, Oxford 2013

John S. Rainbird, *The Vigiles of Rome*, PhD thesis, Durham University 1976

John S. Rainbird, 'The fire stations of imperial Rome', *Papers of the British School at Rome* 54 (1986), 147–69

John S. Rainbird, Frank B. Sear and Jean Sampson, 'A possible description of the Macellum Magnum of Nero', *Papers of the British School at Rome* 39 (1971), 40–6

Dominic Rathbone, 'Nero's reforms of Vectigalia and the inscription of the Lex Portorii Asiae' in Cottier *et al.* (2008), 251–78

Lawrence Richardson, *A New Topographical Dictionary of Ancient Rome*, Baltimore 1992

Robert Samuel Rogers, 'The Neronian comets', *Transactions and Proceedings of the American Philological Association* 84 (1953), 237–49

Robert Samuel Rogers, 'Heirs and rivals to Nero', *Transactions and Proceedings of the American Philological Association* 86 (1955), 190–212

Christian Ronning, 'Der Konflikt zwischen Kaiser Nero und P. Clodius Thrasea Paetus: rituelle Strategien in der frühen römischen Kaiserzeit', *Chiron* 36 (2006), 329–55

Charles Brian Rose, *Dynastic Commemoration and Imperial Portraiture in the Julio-Claudian Period*, Cambridge 1997

Orietta Rossini, *Ara Pacis*, Milan 2007

Vasily Rudich, *Political Dissidence under Nero: The Price of Dissimulation*, London 1993

Steven H. Rutledge, *Imperial Inquisitions: Prosecutors and Informants from Tiberius to Domitian*, London 2001

Robert Sablayrolles, *Libertinus Miles: Les cohortes de vigiles* [= Collection de l'École Française de Rome 224], Rome 1996

Gunther Scheda, 'Nero und der Brand Roms', *Historia: Zeitschrift für Alte Geschichte* 16(1) (March 1967), 111–15

John Scheid, *Commentarii Fratrum Arvalium qui supersunt*, Rome 1998

Walter Scheidel, 'Demography' in Walter Scheidel, Ian Morris and Richard P. Saller (eds), *The Cambridge Economic History of the Greco-Roman World*, Cambridge 2007, 38–86

Jason M. Schlude, *Rome, Parthia, and the Politics of Peace: The Origins of War in the Ancient Middle East*, London 2020

Rolf Michael Schneider, 'Gegenbilder im römischen Kaiserporträt: die neuen Gesichter Neros und Vespasians' in Martin Büchsel and Peter Schmidt (eds), *Das Porträt vor der Erfindung des Porträts*, Mainz 2003, 59–76

Andreas Scholl (ed.), *Katalog der Skulpturen in der Antikensammlung der Staatlichen Museen zu Berlin*, Vol. 1, Berlin 2016

Paul Schubert, 'P. Oxy. LXXVII. 5105: apotheosis in hexameters', *The Oxyrhynchus Papyri* 77 (2011), 59–80

Verena Schulz, *Deconstructing Imperial Representation: Tacitus, Cassius Dio, and Suetonius on Nero and Domitian*, Leiden 2019

Elisabetta Segala and Ida Sciortino, *Domus Aurea*, Milan 1999

Brent D. Shaw, 'The myth of the Neronian persecution', *The Journal of Roman Studies* 105 (2015), 73–100

Ulrich Sinn, *Das antike Olympia: Götter, Spiel und Kunst*, Munich 2004

William J. Slater, 'Pantomime riots', *Classical Antiquity* 13(1) (1994), 120–44

E. Mary Smallwood, 'The alleged Jewish tendencies of Poppaea Sabina', *The Journal of Theological Studies*, New Series, 10(2) (1959), 329–35

E. Mary Smallwood, *Documents Illustrating the Principates of Gaius, Claudius and Nero*, Cambridge 1967

R.R.R. Smith, 'The imperial reliefs from the Sebasteion at Aphrodisias', *Journal of Roman Studies* 77 (1987), 88–138

R.R.R. Smith, 'Nero and the sun-god: divine accessories and political symbols in Roman imperial images', *Journal of Roman Archaeology* 13 (2000), 532–42

Michael P. Speidel, *Riding for Caesar: The Roman Emperors' Horse Guards*, Cambridge 1994

Eva M. Steinby (ed.), *Lexicon Topographicum Urbis Romae* [*LTUR*], 4 vols, Rome 1993–2000

Volker Michael Strocka, *Die Gefangenenfassade an der Agora von Korinth: Ihr Ort in der Römischen Kunstgeschichte* [= Eikonika. Kunstwissenschaftliche Beiträge 2], Regensburg 2010

Ronald Syme, 'Pliny the procurator', *Harvard Studies in Classical Philology* 73 (1969), 201–36

Ronald Syme, 'Domitius Corbulo', *Journal of Roman Studies* 60 (1970), 27–39

Ronald Syme, 'Princesses and others in Tacitus', *Greece & Rome* 28(1) (1981), 40–52

Ronald Syme, 'Partisans of Galba', *Historia: Zeitschrift für Alte Geschichte* 31(4) (1982), 460–83

Ronald Syme, 'Problems about proconsuls of Asia', *Zeitschrift für Papyrologie und Epigraphik* 53 (1983), 191–208

Richard J.A. Talbert, *The Senate of Imperial Rome*, Princeton 1987

Birgitta Tamm, *Auditorium and Palatium: A Study on Assembly-Rooms in Roman Palaces during the 1st Century B.C. and the 1st Century A.D.* [= Stockholm Studies in Archaeology 2], Stockholm 1963

Maria Antonietta Tomei, 'Nerone sul Palatino' in Tomei and Rea (2011), 118–35

Maria Antonietta Tomei and E. Rossella Rea (eds), *Nerone*, Milan 2011

Roger S.O. Tomlin, *Roman London's First Voices: Writing Tablets from the Bloomberg Excavations, 2010–14* [MOLA Monograph Series 72], London 2016

Steven L. Tuck, 'Was the *tempestas* of AD 62 at Ostia actually a tsunami?', *The Classical Journal* 114(4) (April–May 2019), 439–62

Christopher Tuplin, 'The false Neros of the first century AD' in Carl Deroux (ed.), *Studies in Latin Literature and History* 5 [= Collection Latomus 206], Brussels 1989, 364–404

R.F. Tylecote, 'Roman lead working in Britain', *The British Journal for the History of Science* 2(1) (1964), 25–43

Albert William Van Buren and Gorham Phillips Stevens, 'The Aqua Alsietina on the Janiculum', *Memoirs of the American Academy in Rome* 6 (1927), 137–46

Eric R. Varner, 'Portraits, plots, and politics: "damnatio memoriae" and the images of imperial women', *Memoirs of the American Academy in Rome* 46 (2001), 41–93

Eric R. Varner, *Mutilation and Transformation: Damnatio Memoriae and Roman Imperial Portraiture*, Leiden and Boston 2004

Domenico Vera, 'Cremona nell'età imperiale: da Augusto alla tarda antichità' in Pierluigi Tozzi (ed.), *Storia di Cremona. L'età antica*, Cremona 2003, 274–307

Frederik Juliaan Vervaet, 'Domitius Corbulo and the senatorial opposition to the reign of Nero', *Ancient Society* 32 (2002), 135–93

Ursula Vogel-Weidemann, 'The opposition under the early Caesars: some remarks on its nature and aims', *Acta Classica* 22 (1979), 91–107

Ursula Vogel-Weidemann, *Die Statthalter von Africa und Asia in den Jahren 14–68 n. Chr.: Eine Untersuchung zum Verhältnis Princeps und Senat*, Bonn 1982

Mariette de Vos, 'Nerone, Seneca, Fabullo e la Domus Transitoria al Palatino', in *Gli Orti Farnesiani sul Palatino*, Rome 1990, 167–86

Konrad Vössing, *Mensa Regia. Das Bankett beim hellenistischen König und beim römischen Kaiser*, Munich and Leipzig 2004

Caroline Vout, *Power and Eroticism in Imperial Rome*, Cambridge 2007

Hermann Wankel, *Die Inschriften von Ephesos*, 8 vols, Bonn 1979–84

Alan Watson, *Roman Slave Law*, Baltimore and London 1987

Graham Webster, *Boudica: The British Revolt against Rome AD 60*, London 1978

Karl-Wilhelm Weeber, *Panem et circenses. Massenunterhaltung als Politik im antiken Rom*, Mainz 1994

Naomi A. Weiss, 'The visual language of Nero's harbor of Sestertii', *Memoirs of the American Academy in Rome* 58 (2013), 65–81

Katherine E. Welch, *The Roman Amphitheatre: From Its Origins to the Colosseum*, Cambridge 2007

Kenneth Wellesley, *The Long Year AD 69*, Bristol 1989

Paul O. Werner, *De Incendiis Urbis Romae Aetate Imperatorum*, Leipzig 1906

Christopher L. Whitton, 'Seneca, *Apocolocyntosis*' in Buckley and Dinter (2013), 149–69

Marcus Wilson, *The Tragedy of Nero's Wife: Studies on the Octavia Praetexta*, Auckland, 2003

Aloys Winterling, *Aula Caesaris: Studien zur Institutionalisierung des römischen Kaiserhofes in der Zeit von Augustus bis Commodus (32 v. Chr. – 192 n. Chr.)*, Munich 1999

Aloys Winterling, *Caligula: A Biography*, Berkeley 2011

T.P. Wiseman, '*Conspicui postes tectaque digna deo*: the public image of aristocratic and imperial houses in the late republic and early principate' in *L'urbs: Espace urbain et histoire* [= Collection de l'École Française de Rome 98], Rome 1987, 393–413

Anne Wolsfeld, 'Der Kaiser im Panzer. Die bildliche Darstellung Neros und Domitians im Vergleich' in Bönisch-Meyer *et al.* (2014), 181–216

Reinhard Wolters and Martin Ziegert, 'Umbrüche: die Reichsprägung Neros und Domitians in Vergleich' in Bönisch-Meyer *et al.* (2014), 43–80

Susan E. Wood, *Imperial Women: A Study in Public Images 40 BC – AD 68*, Leiden 2001

Fikret Yegül and Diane Favro, *Roman Architecture and Urbanism: From the Origins to Late Antiquity*, Cambridge 2019

Paul Zanker, *The Power of Images in the Age of Augustus*, Ann Arbor 1988

Paul Zanker, *Pompeii: Public and Private Life*, Cambridge, MA 1998

Paul Zanker, *Die Apotheose der römischen Kaiser: Ritual und städtische Bühne*, Munich 2004

Paul Zanker, 'By the emperor, for the people: "popular" architecture in Rome' in Ewald and Noreña (2010), 45–87

Alessandra Zanobi, *Seneca's Tragedies and the Aesthetics of Pantomime*, London 2014

Acknowledgements

This book was written over a relatively short period during the height of the Covid-19 pandemic. That it could at all appear in print is mostly due to the brilliant effort of Kathleen Bloomfield, whose dedication and kindness as editor went far beyond the ordinary. I owe a great debt of gratitude to my colleague Francesca Bologna for many stimulating discussions about Nero. Neither the book nor the exhibition would have been possible in the present form without her skill and good-spirited tenacity in liaising with partner institutions throughout Europe during repeated lockdowns. It is also a pleasure to thank my colleagues Natalie Buy, who made working on the exhibition text such a rewarding experience, and Kate Morton, who as ever produced excellent maps and plans. I will greatly miss my late colleague Ian Jenkins, a good friend in the department over 19 years, who took a keen interest in the project but sadly did not live to see it come to final fruition.

Among other British Museum colleagues, I would like to thank: Richard Abdy, David Agar, Iain Birkett, Joseph Borges, Clark Henry Brown, Duygu Camurcuolgu, Jessica Clarke, Vesta Sarkhosh Curtis, Stephen Dodd, Amy Drago, Julia Farley, Joanna Fernandes, Mark Finch, Hartwig Fischer, Georgia Goldsmith, Richard Hobbs, Deklan Kilfeather, Kevin Lovelock, Susan Kent, Jill Maggs, Jamie Moore, Sam Moorhead, Michael Neilson, Saul Peckham, Helen Richardson, Michael Row, Hannah Scully, Neal Spencer, Christopher Stewart, Bradley Timms, Ross Thomas, Stephanie Vasiliou, Sam Waizeneker, Keeley Wilson and John Williams. Further afield I am grateful to Rune Frederiksen, Sophie Descamps and Françoise Gaultier.

Thanks also go to the many UK and international institutions that agreed to lend objects to the exhibition: Amgueddfa Cymru – National Museum Wales, Cardiff; Bloomberg LP, London; Colchester Archaeological Trust; Colchester Museums; Egypt Exploration Society, London; Musée du Louvre, Paris; Musei Capitolini, Rome; Musei Vaticani; Museo Archeologico e d'Arte della Maremma, Grosseto; Museo Archeologico dei Campi Flegrei nel Castello di Baia – Parco Archeologico dei Campi Flegrei; Museo Archeologico di Cremona; Museo Archeologico Nazionale di Cagliari; Museo Archeologico Nazionale di Firenze; Museo Archeologico Nazionale di Napoli; Museo Archeologico Nazionale di Venezia; Museo Nazionale Romano, Rome; Ny Carlsberg Glyptotek, Copenhagen; Parco Archeologico del Colosseo, Rome; Parco Archeologico di Pompei; PAS Cymru, National Museum Wales and Wrexham County Borough Museum and Archive; Petit Palais, musée des Beaux-Arts de la Ville de Paris; Römisch-Germanisches Museum der Stadt Köln; Soprintendenza Archeologia, Belle Arti e Paesaggio per le province di Cremona, Lodi e Mantova; State Collections of Antiquities and Glyptothek Munich and Stiftsbibliothek St. Gallen.

For the design of the exhibition this book accompanies, thanks are due to Angela Drinkall and Merle Emberson at Drinkall Dean. David Robertson at DHA designs worked on lighting, and Lisa O'Neil and Joel Hepworth at Centre Screen contributed digital media expertise. I am grateful too for the support of our exhibition sponsor bp.

Will Webb designed this publication, Julia Bettinson at Altaimage, London, worked on colour reproductions, and Sarah Vernon-Hunt, Linda Schofield and Marianne Fisher provided editorial support. In the British Museum's Publishing Department thanks also go to Toni Allum, Claudia Bloch and Beata Kibil.

T.O.

Picture credits

The publisher would like to thank the copyright holders for granting permission to reproduce the images illustrated. Every attempt has been made to trace accurate ownership of copyrighted images in this book. Any errors or omissions will be corrected in subsequent editions provided notification is sent to the publisher. Registration numbers for British Museum objects are included in the image captions. Further information about the museum and its collection can be found at britishmuseum.org. Unless otherwise stated below, copyright in photographs belongs to the institution mentioned in the caption. British Museum objects are © 2021 The Trustees of the British Museum, courtesy of the Department of Photography and Imaging.

Fig. 1 (and p. 10) Archivio Fotografico dei Musei Capitolini © Roma, Sovrintendenza Capitolina ai Beni Culturali

Fig. 2 Salva Ruano Martín, cesaresderoma.com

Fig. 3 Adam Eastland/Alamy Stock Photo

Fig. 4 bpk/Alfredo Dagli Orti

Fig. 5 bpk/Antikensammlung, SMB

Map, p. 23 © studio Lombaert

Fig. 6 (and frontispiece) Photo © RMN-Grand Palais (musée du Louvre)/Hervé Lewandowski

Fig. 7 Reproduction with authorisation of the Italian Ministry of Cultural Heritage, Activities and Tourism – Complesso Monumentale della Pilotta

Fig. 8 With permission of the Ministero della Cultura – Museo Nazionale Romano

Fig. 9 Leemage/Corbis Historical via Getty Images

Figs 10a and b With permission of the Ministero della Cultura – Museo Nazionale Romano

Fig. 15 Photo: Ny Carlsberg Glyptotek

Fig. 16 Reproduction authorised by the Soprintendenza Archeologia Belle Arti e Paesaggio per le province di Siena Grosseto e Arezzo. Photo by Carlo Bonazza

Fig. 18 Photo: Ny Carlsberg Glyptotek

Fig. 19 ©Colchester Museums. Image: Douglas Atfield

Fig. 21 Photo © RMN-Grand Palais (musée du Louvre)/Hervé Lewandowski

Fig. 22 Photo © RMN-Grand Palais (musée du Louvre)/Hervé Lewandowski

Fig. 23 Staatliche Antikensammlungen und Glyptothek München, photograph by Renate Kühling

Fig. 26 Museum of the Ara Pacis, Rome, Italy/Bridgeman Images

Fig. 27 Photo © RMN-Grand Palais (musée du Louvre)/Patrick Leroy

Fig. 28 Source: Bibliothèque nationale de France, département Monnaies, médailles et antiques

Fig. 32 Photograph courtesy I. Shurygin

Fig. 33 Photo: Ny Carlsberg Glyptotek

Fig. 34 Archäologisches Museum Frankfurt

Fig. 36 B. Seifert/Lübke+Wiedemann, Germany

Fig. 41 Photo © RMN-Grand Palais (musée du Louvre)/Hervé Lewandowski

Fig. 45 Su autorizzazione del S. 39 – Parco archeologico e paesaggistico di Siracusa, Eloro, Villa del Tellaro e Akrai

Fig. 46 St. Gallen, Stiftsbibliothek, Cod. Sang. 569 (www.e-codices.ch)

Fig. 47 bpk/Antikensammlung, SMB/CoDArchLab

Fig. 48 Photo by Francesco Piras. With permission of the Ministero della Cultura – Museo Archeologico Nazionale di Cagliari

Fig. 49 With permission of the Ministero della Cultura – Museo Nazionale Romano

Fig. 50 (and pp. 68–9) New York University Excavations at Aphrodisias (G. Petruccioli), reproduced courtesy of the Republic of Turkey Ministry of Culture and Tourism

Fig. 52 DEA / C. SAPPA/ De Agostini via Getty Images

Figs 53–5 New York University Excavations at Aphrodisias (G. Petruccioli), reproduced courtesy of the Republic of Turkey Ministry of Culture and Tourism

Fig. 60 Su concessione del Museo Archeologico Nazionale di Firenze (Direzione regionale Musei della Toscana)

Map, p. 89 © studio Lombaert

Fig. 65 Erin Babnik/Alamy Stock Photo

Fig. 70 Courtesy of Fred S. Kleiner, originally published in *The Arch of Nero in Rome*, Rome 1985

Fig. 71 Archivio fotografico dei Musei Capitolini; © Roma, Sovrintendenza Capitolina ai Beni Culturali

Figs 73–5 New York University Excavations at Aphrodisias (G. Petruccioli), reproduced courtesy of the Republic of Turkey Ministry of Culture and Tourism

Map, p. 99 © studio Lombaert

Fig. 79 © Colchester Museums. Image: Douglas Atfield

Fig. 82 © National Museum of Wales

Fig. 83 PAS Cymru, National Museum Wales and Wrexham County Borough Museum and Archive

Fig. 84 © National Museum of Wales

Fig. 85 © Colchester Museums Image: Douglas Atfield

Fig. 86 Colchester Archaeological Trust ©Colchester Museums. Image: Douglas Atfield

Fig. 89b R.D. Grasby and R.S.O. Tomlin, 'The Sepulchral Monument of the Procurator C. Julius Classicianus', *Britannia*, 33 (2002), pp. 43–75, Fig. 21. Reproduced with permission. Image courtesy Centre for the Study of Ancient Documents, University of Oxford

Figs 90–2 Photographs ©Andy Chopping. Illustration © Roger Tomlin, from the Bloomberg Collection

Fig. 95 https://edh-www.adw.uni-heidelberg.de/edh/foto/F004558 (Conc. Min.BB.AA.CC.Div.riprod.|© G. Alföldy))

Fig. 96 Photo © RMN-Grand Palais (musée du Louvre)/Hervé Lewandowski

Fig. 97 With permission of the Ministero della Cultura – Museo Archeologico Nazionale di Venezia – Direzione regionale Musei Veneto

Figs 99–100 bpk/Museum für Islamische Kunst, SMB/Johannes Kramer

Fig. 102 Gertrude Bell Archive, Newcastle University

Fig. 107 Photo © Raffaello Bencini/Bridgeman Images

Fig. 108 With permission of the Ministero della Cultura – Museo Nazionale Romano

Fig. 112 © 2021. Photo Scala, Florence

Fig. 113 Map by Kate Morton, based on Champlin (2003) and Merten (2016)

Fig. 114 With permission of the Ministero della Cultura – Museo Nazionale Romano

Fig. 117 With permission of the Ministero della Cultura – Museo Archeologico Nazionale di Napoli

Fig. 118 Photo © RMN-Grand Palais (musée du Louvre)/Hervé Lewandowski

Fig. 119 Photo © RMN-Grand Palais (musée du Louvre)/Hervé Lewandowski

Fig. 121 Raffaele Garrucci, *Graffiti de Pompei: Inscriptions et gravures tracées au stylet, recueillies et interprétées*, vol 2, Paris 1856, pl. XIII

Fig. 123 KHM-Museumsverband

Fig. 124 Heritage Image Partnership Ltd/Alamy Stock Photo

Figs 128–9 With permission of the Ministero della Cultura – Museo Nazionale Romano

Fig. 131 Su concessione del Ministero della Cultura – Parco Archeologico del Colosseo

Fig. 132 Photo by Luigi Grandillo, su concessione del Ministero della Cultura – Direzione Regionale Musei Molise

Fig. 133 With permission of the Ministero della Cultura – Museo Archeologico Nazionale di Napoli

Figs 134–5 With permission of the Ministero della Cultura – Museo Archeologico Nazionale di Napoli. © Foto Giorgio Albano

Fig. 136 Alinari Archives, Florence

Figs 137–8 With permission of the Ministero della Cultura – Museo Archeologico Nazionale di Napoli

Fig. 139 Paris Musées/Petit Palais, musée des Beaux-arts de la Ville de Paris, ADUT192

Fig. 142 With permission of the Ministero della Cultura – Museo Archeologico Nazionale di Napoli

Fig. 144 Archivio Fotografico dei Musei Capitolini © Roma, Sovrintendenza Capitolina ai Beni Culturali

Fig. 145 Image courtesy Classical Numismatic Group, LLC. www.cngcoins.com

Fig. 146 With permission of the Ministero della Cultura – Museo Nazionale Romano

Fig. 147 With permission of the Ministero della Cultura – Museo Archeologico Nazionale di Napoli

Fig. 148 (and p. 174) Museo Archeologico dei Campi Flegrei nel Castello di Baia – Parco Archeologico dei Campi Flegrei – MiC (photo Luigi Spina)

Fig. 149 Ministero della Cultura – Parco Archeologico di Pompei

Fig. 152 Courtesy of the Egypt Exploration Society and the University of Oxford Imaging Papyri Project

Fig.153 Image courtesy Classical Numismatic Group, LLC. www.cngcoins.com

Fig. 154 Archivio Fotografico dei Musei Capitolini © Roma, Sovrintendenza Capitolina ai Beni Culturali

p. 196 Photo: Department of Photography and Imaging, The British Museum. With permission of the Ministero della Cultura – Museo Nazionale Romano

Figs 155–6 Map by Kate Morton, based on Panella b (2011) and Panella (2016)

Fig. 157 C. Panella, *Scavare nel centro di Roma: storie uomini paesaggi*, Rome 2013, 85, Fig. 7. Courtesy of Prof. Clementina Panella

Fig. 158 C. Panella, 'Nero und der große Brand von Rom im Jahr 64' in Jürgen Merten (ed.), *Nero: Kaiser, Künstler und Tyrann*, Darmstadt 2016, 246, Fig. 5(b). Courtesy of Prof. Clementina Panella

Fig. 159 C. Panella, Scavare nel centro di Roma: storie uomini paesaggi, Rome 2013, 79, Fig. 86. Courtesy of Prof. Clementina Panella

Fig. 160 Ministero della Cultura – Parco Archeologico di Pompei

Fig. 161 American Academy in Rome, Photographic Archive

Figs 163–4 Map by Kate Morton, based on Champlin (2003) and Merten (2016)

Fig. 165 Drawing by Kate Morton, based on Manderscheid (2004)

Figs 166–7 Su concessione del Ministero della Cultura – Parco Archeologico del Colosseo

Fig. 168 Drawing by Kate Morton, based on MacDonald (1982)

Figs 169a and b Maps by Kate Morton, based on Borghini (2019)

Figs 170–1 Su concessione del Ministero della Cultura – Parco Archeologico del Colosseo

Fig. 172 Archivio fotografico dei Musei Capitolini © Roma, Sovrintendenza Capitolina ai Beni Culturali

Figs 173a and b Axonometry by Kate Morton, based on Ball (2003); Section and floor plan by Kate Morton, based on Carandini and Carafa (2017)

Fig. 174 Steve Heap/Shutterstock.com

Fig. 177 Backyard Productions/Alamy Stock Photo. Altered with permission.

Fig. 178 REUTERS/Alamy Stock Photo

Fig. 182 With permission of Museo Archeologico Nazionale di Firenze (Direzione regionale Musei della Toscana)

Fig. 183 With permission of the Ministero della Cultura – Museo Archeologico Nazionale di Napoli.

Fig. 184 With permission of the Ministero della Cultura – Museo Archeologico Nazionale di Napoli. © Foto Giorgio Albano

Figs 185–6 With permission of the Ministero della Cultura – Museo Archeologico Nazionale di Napoli

Fig. 187 Su concessione del Ministero della Cultura – Parco Archeologico del Colosseo

Fig. 188 bpk/Antikensammlung, SMB/Johannes Laurentius

Fig. 190 (and p. 214) Staatliche Antikensammlungen und Glyptothek München, photograph by Renate Kühling

Fig. 191 © Governorate of the Vatican City-State Directorate of the Vatican Museums

Fig. 194 With permission of the Ministero della Cultura – Museo Archeologico Nazionale di Napoli

Fig. 195 Ministero della Cultura – Parco Archeologico di Pompei

Figs 196a and b Ministero della Cultura – Parco Archeologico di Pompei

Fig. 197 Photo: Department of Photography and Imaging, The British Museum. Reproduced by permission of Museo Archeologico dei Campi Flegrei nel Castello di Baia – Parco Archeologico dei Campi Flegrei – MiC

Fig. 198 © Governorate of the Vatican City-State Directorate of the Vatican Museums

Fig. 200 Langner (2001), original by Paavo Castren, *Graffiti del Palatino. II. Domus Tiberiana*, Helsinki 1970

Fig. 202 ArchaiOptix/Wikimedia Commons/CC BY-SA 4.0. Reproduced by permission of the Parco Archeologico di Pompei

Fig. 204a GDKE, Landesmuseum Mainz, Foto: Steyer

Fig. 204b Martin Bahmann/Wikimedia Commons/CC BY-SA 3.0

Fig. 206 With permission of the Ministero della Cultura – Museo Nazionale Romano

Fig. 207 Römisch-Germanisches Museum/Rheinisches Bildarchiv Köln (Anja Wegner)

Fig. 208 Archivio Fotografico dei Musei Capitolini © Roma, Sovrintendenza Capitolina ai Beni Culturali

Fig. 209 With permission of the Ministero della Cultura – Museo Nazionale Romano

Figs 217–20 With permission of Comune di Cremona – Museo Archeologico di Cremona

Figs 221–2 With permission of Soprintendenza Archeologia, Belle Arti e Paesaggio per le province di Cremona, Lodi e Mantova

Fig. 225 Source: Bibliothèque nationale de France, département Estampes et photographie

List of lenders

Amgueddfa Cymru – National Museum Wales, Cardiff

Bloomberg LP, London

Colchester Archaeological Trust

Colchester Museums

Egypt Exploration Society, London

Musée du Louvre, Paris

Musei Capitolini, Rome

Museo Archeologico e d'Arte della Maremma, Grosseto

Museo Archeologico dei Campi Flegrei nel Castello di Baia

Museo Archeologico Nazionale di Cagliari

Museo Archeologico Nazionale di Firenze

Museo Archeologico Nazionale di Napoli

Museo Archeologico Nazionale di Venezia

Museo Civico Archeologico, Comune di Cremona

Museo Nazionale Romano, Rome

Museum of London Archaeology

Ny Carlsberg Glyptotek, Copenhagen

Parco Archeologico del Colosseo, Rome

Parco Archeologico di Pompei

Petit Palais, Musée des Beaux-Arts de la Ville de Paris

Römisch-Germanisches Museum der Stadt Köln

Soprintendenza Archeologia, Belle Arti e Paesaggio per le Province di Cremona, Lodi e Mantova

Staatliche Antikensammlungen und Glyptothek, Munich

Stiftsbibliothek St.Gallen

Vatican Museums

Wrexham County Borough Museum and Archive

Index